Joseph Roth

Report from a Parisian Paradise: Essays from France, 1925–1939

What I Saw: Reports from Berlin, 1920–1933

The Collected Stories of Joseph Roth

The Wandering Jews

Rebellion

The Tale of the 1002nd Night

Right and Left and *The Legend of the Holy Drinker*

Job: The Story of a Simple Man

The Emperor's Tomb

Confession of a Murderer

The Radetzky March

Flight Without End

The Silent Prophet

Hotel Savoy

Tarabas

The Antichrist

Weights and Measures

Zipper and His Father

The Spider's Web

The Leviathan

Joseph Roth

A LIFE IN LETTERS

Translated and Edited by

Michael Hofmann

W. W. NORTON & COMPANY

NEW YORK · LONDON

Frontispiece: Joseph Roth on a railway platform, somewhere in France, in 1925.

Stefan Zweig letters copyright © Williams Verlag AG, Zurich, 1976

Grateful acknowledgment is made for permission granted
by PEN American Center to quote the letter from Dorothy Thompson
to Joseph Roth, dated January 21, 1929. © PEN American Center, 2011.

Joseph Roth Briefe copyright © 1970 by Verlag Kiepenheuer
& Witsch Köln and Verlag Allert de Lange Amsterdam

Copyright © 2012 by Michael Hofmann

For information about permission to reproduce selections from this book,
write to Permissions, W. W. Norton & Company, Inc.,
500 Fifth Avenue, New York, NY 10110

For information about special discounts for bulk purchases, please contact
W. W. Norton Special Sales at specialsales@wwnorton.com or 800-233-4830

Manufacturing by RR Donnelley, Harrisonburg
Book design by Chris Welch Design
Production manager: Julia Druskin

Library of Congress Cataloging-in-Publication Data

Roth, Joseph, 1894–1939.
Joseph Roth : a life in letters / translated and edited
by Michael Hofmann. — 1st ed.
p. cm.
Includes bibliographical references and index.
ISBN 978-0-393-06064-5 (hardcover)
1. Roth, Joseph, 1894–1939—Correspondence.
2. Authors, Austrian—20th century—Biography.
I. Hofmann, Michael, 1957 Aug. 25– II. Title.
PT2635.O84Z48 2012
833'.912—dc23
[B]
2011032677

W. W. Norton & Company, Inc.
500 Fifth Avenue, New York, N.Y. 10110
www.wwnorton.com

W. W. Norton & Company Ltd.
Castle House, 75/76 Wells Street, London W1T 3QT

1 2 3 4 5 6 7 8 9 0

For my friend Rosanna Warren

Contents

PART IV

1933–1939

After Hitler: Work, Despair, Diminishing Circles,
Work, and Death

227

Introduction

Nothing to parents (but Joseph Roth never saw his father, Nahum, who went mad before he knew he had a son, and reacted to his overproud and overprotective mother, Miriam, or Maria, to the extent that he sometimes claimed to have her pickled womb somewhere). Nothing to his wife (poor, bewitching Friedl Reichler, who after six years of a restless, oppressive, and pampered marriage disappeared into schizophrenia, and left him to make arrangements for her, and pay for them, and wallow in the guilt and panic that remained). Nothing to the lovers and companions of his last years—the Jewish actress Sibyl Rares, the exotic half-Cuban beauty Andrea Manga Bell, the novelist Irmgard Keun, his rival in cleverness and dipsomania—nothing to perhaps his very best friends (with such a protean, or polygonal character as Roth's, who contrived to present a different aspect of himself to everyone he knew, it's hard to tell for sure)—Stefan Fingal, Soma Morgenstern, Joseph Gottfarstein. Except to family, very few—initially, I had the sense, none at all—in the intimate *Du* form, and most of those there are, ironically, to near-strangers, because they had served, as he had, briefly, in the Austrian army, where it was form to address a brother officer, even if one didn't know him from Adam, as *Du*. Very few early—barely a dozen before 1925, when Roth, thirty, a married professional, a published novelist, and an experienced vagrant already on to his third country and maybe his fourth newspaper, gets his big break as a journalist, in Paris,

for the liberal *Frankfurter Zeitung*. Very little explicitly or frontally about
aesthetics, ambition, writing, shop (references to the novels, when he does
talk about them, are so grudgingly or airily unspecific, it's often impossible to be sure which one of them he's talking about). Little in the way of
chat, description, narrative, confession, or scandal—this was a man with
books to write, and columns to fill.

So why read them? If they have little bearing on his literary output,
and are not even addressed to the people who mattered most in his life?
Well, to get a sense, first of all, and in the absence of a biography in
English, of the stations of the man's life, his classic westward trajec-
tory (like that of *Flight Without End* or *The Wandering Jews*) from the
Habsburg crown land of Galicia just back of the Russian border, on the
edge of Europe if not of the civilized world, in quick, brief stages to
Vienna, to Berlin and Frankfurt, and then to Paris—a sort of schizoid
Paris, first (in 1925) the paradisal place of the fulfillment of hopes and
dreams, and then, after 1933, the locus of exile, disappointment, trepida-
tion, punishment. It was like day and night. And, within the context of
that broad, simple, westward movement, the endless, frenetic stitching
back and forth among Frankfurt, Berlin, Paris, Vienna, Amsterdam to
wherever he had temporarily pitched his tents; the long, journalistic visits
to the south of France in 1925, to the Soviet Union in 1926, Albania and
the Balkans in 1927, and Italy and Poland in 1928; the many tours the
length and breadth of the German regions throughout the 1920s, for
what became a sort of dreaded and dispiriting enemy terrain to which
his newspaper bosses were quite deliberately dispatching their acutest,
most high-strung war correspondent (the atmosphere in one particular
town, Roth noted, was like that "five minutes before a pogrom"); the
number of places (eleven, by my count) where he stopped to compose his
masterpiece, *The Radetzky March*, between 1930 and 1932, on the face of
it, his most comfortable circumstances ever, with a monthly retainer, less
journalism, and Friedl cared for; and then the places of exile, where one
has to picture him practically as a mendicant, borrowing or scroung-

ing train fare, leaving Paris for Amsterdam to haggle over a new—and newly ruinous—publishing contract, or for Marseille because there was the prospect of free accommodation, albeit of a sort detested by this self-described "hotel patriot," or Ostend, so that he might have daily access to his, alas, always pedagogically minded patron, Stefan Zweig. This swarming movement is one of the points of these letters.

Then to get something where the writer's own character and predicaments are front and center, neither adapted nor softened nor broken up among his stories and novels. To understand something of the circumstances in which these stories and novels were written; first, up to around 1930, competing for breath with hundreds upon hundreds of iridescent-colored soap bubbles (his metaphor) of articles for daily newspapers (most of his life, Roth was much better known as a columnist and feuilletonist than as a novelist); then against the clock, both his personal clock and the unignorably ticking collective clock of the 1930s, bringing (as Roth in particular very well foresaw) war and genocidal murder to millions. Writing novels no one realistically wanted; for publishers as hard up as he was, who wrote him (the Dutch ones) flinty, respectful letters in broken German; a diminishing number of readers; in return for desperately small advances already received, spent, and borrowed against. At one stage, he had the haunting sense of being able to read the begging letters through the surface of the narrative prose. To see him correctly, as a sort of lemming among lemmings, an unusually farsighted and fearless and bloody-minded lemming, quick to sink his teeth into the flanks of René Schickele or Stefan Zweig or Klaus Mann when they stepped out of line. Some of their wounded, plaintively reasonable, or plain defensive replies are included. To understand that this grievously disappointed and multiply broken man somehow continued to align himself toward the true and the beautiful in his articles, and the beautiful and the true in his books; that, long past having anything himself, he went on helping others—a tailor, a charwoman, a doctor, a fellow veteran stuck in Switzerland; that even as he seemed to lapse into unreality—a scheme on the very eve of the Anschluss, in February 1938, to meet the then Austrian chancellor Schuschnigg, to talk him into backing the restoration of the Habsburg monarchy—in other parts of his mind he was as mordant and accurate and graceful as ever.

Roth is both contradictory and changeable, and always, always vehement with it. Something in him can't abide and doesn't understand hierarchies; that's why he was never able to find a niche and defend it at the *FZ*—that newspaper that was all niche and pecking order. He doesn't pace himself or moderate himself or disguise himself. "I am wriggling in a hundred nets," he brilliantly puts it. There is turbulence, emergency, thrashing around, panic wherever he is. He doesn't deal in anything less than an ultimatum. The letters are anxiously registered, or they demand instant acknowledgment, or they go by expensive wire or *pneumatique*. They are what the diplomats call démarches. (He is no sort of diplomat, though he does love his Old World courtesies.) All he seeks, on the face of it, is fair recompense, and calm in which to work. The work itself is contradictory and changeable. He is *Neue Sachlichkeit*, and he is a poet and a fabulist, you can find him on both sides of both arguments—though "romantic" is always a dirty word for him. I described him once as mysteriously managing "to combine a novelist's oeuvre with a journalist's calling and habits." He drinks to dull his nerves, and writes to understand the world. He is industrious from despair, assiduous and ineffectual, a tireless, incorruptible, terrifying, and quixotic moralist:

> I am not in a tizzy about the letter from [. . .] In view of the approaching end of the world, it's no big deal. But even then, in the trenches, staring death in the face 10 minutes before going over the top, I was capable of beating up a son of a bitch for claiming he was out of cigarettes when he wasn't, for instance. The end of the world is one thing, the son of a bitch is another. You can't put the son of a bitch down to the general condition of things. He's separate.

He works to bring about practical remedies, on refugees' committees, and so forth, and he is the most impractical man who ever lived. He has no money, no books, no bank account, no clothes. What doesn't falter is tone and imagination in his importunings: "Kesten got the 10 pounds. He gave me none of it. I am torn, so to speak, between shirts and a suit." And then: "I'm thinking a shroud would be a useful acquisition." He lives out of two suitcases (by some accounts, three, but I prefer to think of him with two), a large one and a small one. He collects penknives, watches, and canes. Every relationship with every correspondent is tested to its destruction; it's hard to think of one who comes through (all right, the Bertaux, father and son, do; all the others are put through usually terminal crises). Not the personally disappointing Brentano, or the over-optimistic and compromising Reifenberg; not the loyal and persistent Mme Gidon, whom he begins by trying to fire as his translator, or the ever devoted, ever inadequate Stefan Zweig; not Kesten or Schickele; not Landauer or Landshoff. He mocks his publishers—it doesn't matter which ones—appealing with mounting irony, "not only to your publisher's conscience, but to your human feelings." Roth's existence feels syncopated throughout; he is a Jew in Austria, an Austrian in Germany, and a German in France. He is "red Roth" and a royal and imperial loyalist; he is an Eastern Jew and an Austrian; he is gallant and passionate—both a kisser of hands and a kisser of feet; he is generous and unforgiving; he demands hope, and sees despair as a badge of reason. He drills through the newspaper world in the 1920s and in the 1930s tunnels through the world of books; by the end, he stands there without anything and beyond everything, illusionless as Rimbaud. In 1938 again, it is unclear whether he will enter a monastery, pack his ancestral bundle and take to the road like his Jewish forefathers, or rejoin the Austrian army—all three are mooted. Or failing that, Mexico, or Rio, or Shanghai, or Baudelaire's favorite destination, "anywhere out of the world."

We read for knowledge and atmospheres, but also for the chance to develop and exercise empathy, to extend the weft and warp of our emotions and nerves over the situations of others. In these letters—these IOUs and SOSes—we have something like the protocol of a man going over the edge of the world in a barrel. How can we not be amazed, harrowed, quickened, awed?

THE BASIS OF the present selection is the volume *Joseph Roth Briefe, 1911–1939* (1970), edited by his friend, housemate, fellow writer, and sometime editor, Hermann Kesten. It is a little strange that there has been no subsequent, fuller, or more authoritative edition in the forty years since—the Rothian Heinz Lunzer has spoken to me of Kesten's occasional grave errors of transcription—and reading, say, David Bronsen's biography, one is made aware that many interesting letters are unfortunately not included. Kesten, though, was not a scholar—and nor am I. For my book, I chose as many of the letters as I thought might be comprehensible and of interest to an English readership, erring always on the side of generosity; it's my sense that I have included upwards of 90 percent of them, 457 in all—I through-numbered them, for ease of reference. Two individual volumes of correspondences have been brought out since 1970 in German, containing Roth's exchanges with his Dutch exile publishers: one with Querido and Allert de Lange, the other with De Gemeenschap. These, in my view, were too specialized and—as perhaps may be imagined—too repetitive, and too arduous to warrant inclusion.

A letter—perhaps especially in our time, when letters are no longer written much, and when Hey Mike! is presumed to be a proper form of address from a complete stranger—is situated somewhere between speech and script. (Perhaps especially these letters, remote from book-lined studies and desks, written or dictated in public places, in cafés or bars, at all hours, and in the midst of friends and hangers-on and conversation.) This was a novel and a lovely challenge to the translator, who values voice in all writing: "Nothing but men is like a desert full of sand," "It's shocking, I have no copies of any of my books," "Haven't you got that yet? The word has died, men bark like dogs," "Even a letter is a colossal effort. Don't be cross if I don't write. Frankly, even a stamp is a significant item for me." As I mentioned earlier, Roth does not go in for the *Du* form much, but that doesn't mean that he is a hidebound or kid-gloved letter writer. Most of the people he wrote to were known to him, some of them very well, and most of the subjects or occasions of the letters were of intense importance to him. This is perhaps the single most striking quality of Roth's letters: their fervor, their temperature. Even if they are set out in little numbered and lettered sections—perhaps especially then—they burn off the page with their indignation, their desperation, their indifference to excuses, their terminal wretchedness, and combusted dignity. Roth was, moreover, a great and passionate hater (it's yet another one of the many, many, unbridgeable differences between him and Zweig, who wasn't, and who wasn't easy in the presence of hatred either). Even so, I was surprised by the occasionally cloacal forthrightness of his language, especially in the later letters; in his fiction and feuilletons there is no suggestion of such language (he is not Joyce, not even Hemingway), but then we are talking here about his most intense private and personal communications. German—and Roth when wrought up—is liberal with *Scheisse* and also with animals; *Hund, Schwein, Sau,* but also *Tier, Biest, Bestie* are all strong terms. English, evidently, a little less so. Anyway, this is by way of saying that "my" Roth in English says "fuck" as he doesn't in German; it's a perfectly natural and reasonable vehicle—one might even claim a sine qua non—for the way strong feelings are expressed in English, since Tynan and Hitchens and too many others to mention. It's a necessary cultural adjustment in the translation and, in its way, perfectly faithful.

As I read and translated, and reread and retranslated, I was repeatedly reminded of a couple of lines of Goethe's *Faust*—Malcolm Lowry used them as one of the epigraphs for *Under the Volcano*—"wer immer strebend sich bemüht, den können wir erlösen," roughly, whoever strenuously endeavors, him can we rescue. No more strenuous trier before the Lord than Joseph Roth.

Michael Hofmann
Gainesville, Florida
January 2011

PART I

1894–1920

Youth, War, Brody, and Vienna

JOSEPH ROTH, AGE THREE

[M]oses] Joseph Roth was born in Brody in Galicia, then part of the Austro-Hungarian Empire, on 2 September 1894, "under the sign of the Virgin," as he writes drily in no. 98, "to whom my given name of Joseph stands in some vague relation." He was Joseph, Mary in this instance was his mother, but there was no immaculate conception, no baby Jesus, and no man in the house. While "Mu" remained an only child, his mother was one of seven, and he had many Grübel or Grubel uncles and aunts and cousins, with some of whom he remained in touch all his life. (After his death, his favorite cousin, Paula Grübel, traveled to Paris, to give her stock of his early manuscripts and offprints to Blanche Gidon, his translator into French, who kept them safe during the occupation and the war.) They were not exactly poor (there were visits to the photographer, smart clothes, violin lessons, even a maid, at least some of the time), but Roth's lifelong aversion to the idea of home will have dated from then (a lodger, his mother's brave face and forbidding bosom, and pride and shame and continual anxiety); the town—whose very name he was often careful to suppress later, in favor of the more German-sounding "Schwaby," or even "Schwabendorf," so redolent was Brody (anti-Semitically evoked in a 1900 English *Baedeker*: "They differ in their dress and the mode of wearing their hair from the other inhabitants, who despise them")[1] of Galicia and the poor, dirty, and, above all, Jewish east; while dealings with his uncles will have left him neuralgically sensitive to any subsequent combination of money and advice (when forthcoming from Stefan Zweig, say).

The young Moses went to gymnasium in Brody. He was gifted, precocious, and studious, took his exams with distinction, enrolled at the University of Lemberg in 1913, and went on to complete six semesters

1. Quoted in David Bronsen, *Joseph Roth: Eine Biographie* (Cologne, 1974), p. 47.

of German at the University of Vienna. As his first poems and articles
started to appear, he took the "Moses" off his name (it's there for his
Viennese Jewish in-laws, though, and during one crisis in 1926, in letters
to Reifenberg, it makes a short and moody reappearance). It's curious
that he started to publish and learned to dissemble at the same time. In
1917 in a typical volte-face—he was a pacifist just three years before—he
volunteered for the army; saw his native Galicia, only now under Mars;
made his way back to Vienna; found himself (as the British say) cushy
billets as a censor and on an army newspaper. It is good to read those
sensibly less than valiant lines to his cousin Paula on the advantages of
being out of range of the Russians; before Roth launched the myth of his
officer's career—a corrective myth his life seemed to require, something
like a pair of spectacles, as David Bronsen sweetly puts it. Similarly, those
epically haphazard and chaotically adventurous returns from the front
described in *Flight Without End* or *The Emperor's Tomb* or *Hotel Savoy*
were not his lot. He was back in Vienna pretty promptly in December
1918, in the same awkwardly dyed ex-army gear as everyone else, got
his start on a new progressive newspaper, *Der Neue Tag*, in April 1919,
published a hundred pieces in the year before it folded, and in June 1920,
a refugee from unemployment and inflation in Austria, he moved to
Berlin.

The early letters are all personal and familial, to his Grübel cousins
in Lemberg. They are joshing and showing off, affectionate and conde-
scending. One can see in Roth a desire for independence (he needs license
not to write to his uncle), and, at the same time, rather movingly, a wish
to support, educate, encourage, cultivate these younger or female cousins.
(One might think of the regular pattern, later in his life, where, hard up
and managing to obtain a little money for himself, he straightaway trans-
fers half of it to others; their need seems as great, or greater.) Unfledged
himself, he shelters others under his wings. One might note, finally, that
these are the only letters in which Roth sounds *young*, in fact like a young
shuttlecock: frisky and agile, youthfully pompous or lightheartedly pug-

nacious, boasting of his publications, his undergraduate "red sofa with yellow trim," amusing himself with Venice and Vienna, observing his Flemish neighbors and their Christian dogs, and entertaining the prospect of Albania. It is a tone worth cherishing, because once he's twenty-five and in Germany, you won't hear it again.

Dear Resia,

I want to answer your letter as promptly as you wrote it—if not more so, seeing as it's Sunday, and there's little to do. When I wrote in my last letter to ask if I might come, that wasn't a serious inquiry: you shouldn't take everything seriously. I am a sworn enemy to etiquette.[2] Now I'm not sure if I will be able to come, because I've been set some reading to do. It's all because I'm an "A" student, and more is required of us. Anyway, I know I won't be able to talk Mama into going, she never wants to leave the house. She seeks various pretexts for this, and since the help was discreetly "let go" yesterday, and there's little chance of finding a suitable replacement, the prospect of my visit has rather receded. Well, the sky won't fall down on top of us. And if we should be able to come after all, then we can do all the nice things you suggest.

I gave Christiampoller[3] your best; he would have leapt straight into an eighth heaven, had it existed. But as there are only seven, he contented himself with the seventh of them, and thousands of little lights sparkled before his eyes, and he heard choirs of seraphim and cherubim, just like in Goethe's *Faust*, which, alas and alack, you haven't read. He— i.e., Christiampoller, not Faust—will probably come to Lemberg. It'll be good. He's been brushing his hair and pressing his pants for three weeks now. All for Lemberg. Of course, he's not as industrious as he used to be, and his studies suffer as a consequence.

I don't understand why you're so worried about the war. It seems to preoccupy you all day.

Why do I not hear from Paula?[4] Perhaps she's waiting for me to turn up on the doorstep? If we do come, I'll give you notice. For the moment, be well, and write back! Pronto!

Kisses   Your cousin M.[5]

With much love to everyone.

1. Resia Grübel was Roth's cousin, daughter of his mother's brother Siegmund Grübel. The family lived in Lemberg/Lvov/Lviv, not far from Brody.

2. sworn enemy to etiquette: either never true or subsequently abandoned. JR was Old World in his courtliness. The phrase itself has, one might note, an element of etiquette within it.

3. Christiampoller: a local character, in Brody (two names presumably run together as one, for comic effect).

4. Paula: Resia's younger sister. See note in following letter.

5. M. short for Muniu, Roth's nickname as a child, the Polish diminutive form of Moses, his given name.

2. To Resia and Paula Grübel   *[Brody, 2 September 1912]*

Dear Resia,

you're quite right, time hurries on and the years go around quickly, and already I've completed seventeen of them. I was very pleased to get your birthday congratulations; that's not just a manner of speaking either, I mean I felt real, deep, inner, genuine-in-every-fiber pleasure. I know how devoted you are to me, and that you really are concerned for my welfare. It's not so hard to tell real feelings from false. I see you take delight in the way my writing is coming on, and I want to thank you for that especially. Thank you too for your wishes regarding my studies. This last year will soon be over, and after my final exams all the trials and tribulations of school will be behind me, and I will go on to the great school of life. Let's hope I earn equally good grades at that institution. [. . .]

Thanks again, and kisses from your

Cousin Muniu

Dear Paula,[1] I want to thank you as well for writing. I'm delighted that my dear younger cousin is thinking of me as well

Kisses,

Muniu

1. Paula: Paula Grübel (1897–1941?). Lifelong friendship with Roth. She was murdered in the Holocaust.

3. To Heini Grübel   [Brody, no date]

Dear Heini,[1]

your sweet little note pleased me every bit as much as a long letter would have done! You are still so young, and frankness and straight-forwardness are the plants native to the childish soul. That's why good wishes from you made me so happy, because from whom other than a child, symbol of the life to come, should one desire wishes? I in turn wish you success at school. It's not so long ago that I started wearing the school uniform myself, and quite soon now I will set it aside. I hope you get through gymnasium cheerfully and in good health. What makes me especially happy is the thought that we're now both scholars together.

Servus,[2] my dear chap,

Kisses from your Muniu

1. Heini: Heinrich Grübel, younger brother of Paula and Resia.
2. Servus: familiar Austrian greeting, classically used between intimates and equals, i.e., classmates at school, or fellow officers in the army.

4. To Paula Grübel   Vienna, 14 August 1916

Dear Paula,

it really was coincidence. Who ever would have guessed it: all of nine-teen! But then, nineteen years are like a piece of fluff on the scales of eternity. And it's in eternity that we live. From eternity, in eternity, for eternity. Yes, *for* eternity as well.

What do I have to give you? I don't have any money. But I get paid 6 hellers a line. Count the number of lines in this letter,[1] and you'll have a tidy sum.

What can I wish for you? Three kingly things: a crown, a scarlet cloak, a scepter. The golden crown of imagination, the scarlet cloak of solitude, and the scepter of irony. It's hard to come by these things at nineteen. They're not much in evidence.

But there's one thing I wish you above all: that you don't forget your laugh. Laughter is a tinkling silver bell that some good angel gave us on our life's road. But because it's so light and loose, it's easily lost. Somewhere by the wayside. And big fate goes by with squeaking boots, and grinds it underfoot, the laughter.[2] Some people are lucky and find another. Or someone else finds it, and picks it up, and returns it to its rightful owner. Not often, though! So look after it!

I'm going to be in Baden later this week. At any rate, before I join the army.

Bye! Till soon!   Mu[3]

1. Roth numbers the lines of this letter.
2. laughter: a passage like this has absolutely the same rhythms and diction as some of JR's very late writing; cf. "Rest While Watching the Demolition," from 1938.
3. Mu: Muniu.

5. *To Paula Grübel*   *Vienna, a Wednesday [1915 or 1916]*

Dear Paula,

I have a pretty next-door neighbor. She spends all day in front of her embroidery frame, doing petit point. A thoroughly Dutch figure, in spite of the fact that she's a brunette. In the afternoon, when the sun shines, a sunbeam falls plumply and lingeringly on her embroidery. And then when her blond little boy stands beside her, the whole scene is utter Holland. Unfortunately, Mme Sun has had a toothache these past few days. She's wrapped her face in black cloths. From time to time a bit of white cotton wool peeps out.

And now it's gone and started raining. M. Wind, my friend, has married Mme Cloud. I attended their wedding, a jolly affair. Now Mme Cloud is giving birth to their children on a daily basis: small and great Showers. What a to-do. I must ask the wind to desist, because his sons will insist on spoiling my creases. And you know how sacrosanct *they* are.

We have cake. It's resting quietly in a corner just now, giving off a splendid aroma. It's almost like Brody, on a Friday. Or do you know of two phenomena more indissolubly connected than home and baking smells?

A couple of days ago, I went out. It was gorgeous. The fields look just like my cheeks when I haven't been to the barber's for a couple of days. The song of the last scythe hangs unseen in the air. In the clouds there's still a last verse of lark song. The dandelions have a patriotic shimmer. Somewhere in the distance, smoke rises vertically into the sky. The ground is decked out in all the cast-off glory of the trees. And in the air there's the bitter whiff of steaming earth and wet foliage . . .

Ever since 1 October, the library has been open all day. Soon lectures will begin. This year, Brecht[1] is giving a course on classical drama (less interesting, unfortunately). Then the girl students will show up, with their earnest expressions and tousled hair. Anxious faces, like a three-day rain. How I hate those women! Though students are no more women than streetwalkers are.

Do you remember Csallner? The fellow who used to borrow lecture notes from me in German? We've become friends. He has some admirable qualities. Including an attractive fiancée. I would back him to achieve, oh, half a dozen children, a small pot belly, and a professorship in Budapest—and still to remain a Philistine.

I have poems due to appear in *Österreichs Illustrierte Zeitung*, if they haven't come out already. I haven't the cash or the inclination to go to a café or to invest in a copy. Either would set me back 60 hellers. If you wouldn't mind, perhaps you can see if they've run something of mine. No royalty, alas. But a few short stories I sent in, I should be paid quite well for. Then I'll be in Baden. I'm looking forward to All Souls' and Christmas. Two poems in the supplement will earn me 12 crowns.

What do you think about money? I don't think it's worth bothering about. If I had it, I would chuck it out the window. Money's the opposite of women. You think highly of a woman until you've got her, then when you get her, you feel like chucking her out (or at least you ought). Whereas money you despise as long as you don't have it, and then you think very highly of it.

I was pleased that you came around yesterday. Even more pleased, admittedly, that I was out. Even so, I'd like to see you. You'll be needing to find me in any case, so that I can read you this letter . . .

It's too bad you live so far away. I have thin soles, and shoemakers are expensive. A shoemaker's heart is tougher than his soles. [. . .]

Things are all right. I myself am better than all right. My heart is heavy and my pockets are light. Mind you, if my pockets were as heavy as my heart, then my heart would be as light as my pockets.

When are we going to see each other?

Greetings   Muniu Faktisch[2]

1. Brecht: Walter Brecht, professor of German literature at the University of Vienna.

2. The full version of Roth's nickname; *faktisch*—actually, or in point of fact—was something he was much given to saying when he was still a young pedant and "A" student.

6. *To Paula Grübel*   *Vienna, a Thursday [1916]*

Dear Paula,

it's summer outside, and a holiday, and a scent of lime blossom has snuck in from somewhere, and perched on my windowsill. Alas, my neighbor is a Jewess, and scares away my lime blossom with her appalling squawks. Her voice is shrill, and smells of onions. There is little sign of the holiday in my courtyard. At best, its denizens have rest days. They can only rest, not be holy. Outside, meanwhile, girls dressed in white sell badges. I was approached by a score of them, and I didn't buy. Then one came—and I bought. For I am an individualist, and despise the mass. And the girl from whom I bought was an aristocrat. She walked alone, and offered her wares to no one. She was like a priestess among temple prostitutes.

There is something of Venice[1] in the air today, as there sometimes is on summer days, and I am in a mood as if after lunch I were going by gondola to some wharf. Open before me is a book: Vischer's *Aesthetics*,[2] I was reading it yesterday and the day before yesterday, but I am too uncultivated to understand it. It's so terribly learned, and only when Professor V. condescends to climb down from the dizzy heights of his lectern—which is rarely enough—do I understand him. The things I do understand in the book give me little pleasure, because I knew them all anyway. I will give it back to my colleague, who won't understand it either, but even so we will discuss it endlessly between ourselves, and one day I will give my colleague a fearful slap, for being such a liar.

I am going to have my lunch soon, and am looking forward to it. Today we are having something cheesy and prosy, but the Venetian element in the air today will ennoble and Italianize it, and I will eat nothing cheesy or prosy, but macaroni. And then I really will go out on a gondola, past the Ring and the Volksgarten, and I will encounter a pretty Venetian girl, and will accost her thus: May I bore you, Signorina? And the pretty Venetian girl will reply in purest Viennese: See if I care. And for all that, I am in Venice today. Today, today only, I am the doge of Venice and an Italian tramp rolled in one, but tomorrow, tomorrow I will go back to being the dreamy German poet, art enthusiast, and 3rd year German student studying under Professor Brecht. Tomorrow *Faust* is being performed at the Burgtheater—the play, not the horrible opera!—with Ludwig Wüllner in the title role. And I will stand up in the gods, dog-tired or god-tired, and will imagine I shall have seen *Faust*.

Lunch wasn't good, because firstly, my neighbor beat his wife with a broomstick. Secondly, the macaroni weren't proper macaroni at all. And thirdly, Auntie Rieke ate cheese off the point of her knife. Just as well Aunt Mina confiscated my revolver in Lemberg, otherwise I might have committed tanticide.

A Christian is a rarity in my courtyard. But even so, there is one living here. The window across the courtyard from me is very pretty. A fair-haired boy is doing his homework. His dog is beside him. Does a Jew keep a dog? The fair-haired boy, the dog, and I—we are the only decent people in the whole building.

Last week, I went to hear Professor Brecht every day, and watched Miss Lumia write everything down with her awful industry. She looks so comically serious when she does that, and she's so serious, I can feel it against my back—because she sits behind me. There are women who are moving in their beauty. Lumia is moving, too—but in her dimness.

I have a pretty red sofa with yellow trim, which I am about to go and lie down on. It's 3 o'clock now, and I'll remain horizontal till 5. Then I'll wash and go for a walk. No, take a gondola. Because it's still Venice.

Maybe I'll come to Baden next week. If I have any money, I'll bring Wittlin[3] along, so you can see there are other young men than Baden lawyers.

Now write and tell me about the three pines.

Byebye!   Muniu

And in this space you can draw me something pretty:[4]

1. Venice: this refers to a contemporary feature in the big Viennese funfair, the Prater, an installation called Venice in Vienna.

2. Vischer: Friedrich Theodor Vischer (1807–1887). Author of *On the Sublime and the Comic* (1837) and *Aesthethics, or the Science of Beauty* (1846–1857).

3. Wittlin: Jozef Wittlin (1896–1976), friend of JR's. A Polish author and essayist, Wittlin studied in Vienna with Roth, and served in the same regiment in World War I. Lived in exile in Paris after 1939, after 1941 in New York. Wrote *Salt of the Earth* (1935), and translated several of Roth's novels into Polish. Paula, JR's favorite cousin, never married.

4. The page was left blank aside from this injunction.

7. To Paula Grübel   *Field Post 632 on 24 August 1917*

Dear Paula,

among the accumulated mail of four weeks I found your letter, which I was all the more pleased to see because of the quite astonishing maturity of its language, and its thought. Have you really become so old?

I am currently in some Augean shtetl in East Galicia. Gray filth, harboring one or two Jewish businesses. Everything's awash when it rains, and when the sun comes out it starts to stink. But the location has one great advantage: it's about 6 miles behind the lines. Reserve encampment.

Materially, I'm not so well off as I used to be. Our newspaper is failing, and once the aura of reporter has faded away, there'll be nothing left of me but a one-year volunteer. And I'll be treated accordingly.

But for the likes of me that doesn't really matter. The main thing is experience, intensity of feeling, tunneling into events. I have experienced frightful moments of grim beauty. Little opportunity for active creation, aside from a couple of lyric poems, which were more out of passive sensation anyway.

What you have to say about reading with Frau Szajnocha[1] makes me very happy—by the way, said reading is clearly manifested in the stylistic quality of your letter. Please salute the lady for me, and give her my best.

I enclose a poem at your request, kindly read it carefully. Its beauty lies in the originality of its imagery. I consider it one of the few of mine that have completely succeeded.

On August 5 I had a poem in the *Prager Tagblatt*.[2] Please, order up a copy. I should like to have it for reference for some possible future collection.

I hope to be in Lemberg sometime in the next few days. I view your decision to go there as a little premature. I'll have more to say on the matter in a letter to Uncle.

I think I'll be gone from here in 2 to 3 weeks. I may be transferred to Lemberg, to the Record Office, or possibly Sternberg. It's also possible that our office will be moved to Albania, to start a paper there, in which case it's Albania here I come.

Best wishes   Your M.

1. Szajnocha: Helena von Szajnocha, née Baroness von Schenk (ca. 1863–1945), lived in the same house as the Grübel family in Lemberg/Lvov, Hofmana 7. The divorced wife of a university professor in Cracow, she was a French tutor. A personal and literary influence on Roth and Wittlin. Chronically infirm, she made her rooms a sort of literary and musical salon.

2. The *Prager Tagblatt* was a leading German-language newspaper in Prague.

8. To Paula Grübel   *Vienna, 24 February 1918*

Dear Paula,

when I came here, it was freezing cold and clouded over, you could stare at the sun with your naked eye, it was small and round and red like a Christmas blood orange. On Friday, it suddenly warmed up, a hot wind, the foehn. It was very pleasant on our street, among other things I saw on the streetcar a man in a stiff hat, and a wreath around it, presumably of paper, attaching it to his chin, like two bonnet strings. A young lady ran into my arms on the Ring. She presumably took me for a lamppost. Another lady's skirts flew up in the wind, you could see her stocking was ripped, and she had a provisional red garter. Nice.

At home, I found I had an invitation from the "Scholle,"[1] and I duly went along on Saturday. A couple of dilettantes read their contemptible poems. A young lady condescended to participate. Her mother, a Jewess from Leopoldstadt, stood up and said: That's my little girl. Those four words made her—the mother—immortal. More than the daughter will ever be by her writing. The mother will take up residence in the "Scholle," and, please God, in a book of mine.

On Monday I went to the Burgtheater to buy tickets. I looked for my friend, Roth the actor, but didn't find him. He wasn't at home, maybe he's left town. Nothing to be had at the box office. I went to the Deutsches Volkstheater. A lady cashier with a mustache. The mustache of an actor, who had had it taken off. She was frowning and hard as if she had food to sell. She looked as though she wanted me not to go near her theater. Purely to annoy her, I bought a ticket for the matinee show of Molnar's *Herrenmode*, a piece of filth. On Tuesday I went to listen to Hubermann.[2] He played a Bach etude with skill, *froideur*, and physical exertion. Then some Italian music with warmth and fervor. Finally, as I'd wished, "Ave Maria." He played it in such a way that I can't possibly torture you with it any more. Divine.

I felt a little rush of sympathy when he bowed stiffly afterwards. While playing, his expression was austere; the instant he puts down his bow, he loses all his majesty, he's a poor wretch, almost shy. I thought of my story about the violinist.

I smoke Turkish cigarettes, a delicious aroma, and play with Helene's little son. He's blond and blue-eyed, wears a velvet jacket with two big pockets where he stores pencils, pens, pocket knives, chains, crumbs, gingerbread, and chocolate. He gets very dirty at times, and takes particular delight in making me dirty.

I took out a subscription at Last's, and borrowed Otto Flake's *Logbuch*. Flake[3] is from Luxembourg, an Alemanne by birth, a cheery, healthy, and sensual type. Occasionally, in his descriptive passages he combines naïveté and inspiration, childish and serious touches so brusquely that you have the sense you're reading Heine. But then he doesn't have Heine's Jewish sentiment, or French elegance. Sometimes he's clear and objective, like Gottfried Keller, and as bitter and bracing as that. Keller was Alemannic too. You should borrow something of Flake's, you won't regret it. Resia[4] should read him.

I was ill for three days, with the flu. I had myself looked after, drank chamomile tea, took quinine and aspirin. Today I'm feeling better.

Please tell your father—I'm writing to him under a separate cover—not to go off the deep end if I didn't send him a card. Does he need a postcard from me with a couple of lines of writing on it to prove my gratitude and devotion? Where would that take us! It's absurd to be so fixated on externals. I got sick, otherwise I would have written long ago.

If you have any mail for me, would you kindly forward it to me. I'm leaving next Sunday or Monday. Keep me posted.

Greetings to Aunt Resia, and Heini   Your Mun.

Best wishes to Frau v. Szajnocha!

1. *Scholle*: "soil" or "sod" in German. Almost always—as here—with an unpleasantly patriotic taint.

2. Hubermann: Bronislav Hubermann (1882–1947), a renowned violinist. There is a childhood photograph of Roth in 1905 with a violin.

3. Flake: Otto Flake (1880–1962), writer and essayist. *Das Logbuch* had just come out with S. Fischer in 1917.

4. Roth's aunt Resia, wife of Siegmund Grübel.

PART II

1920–1925

Berlin, Newspapers, Early Novels, and Marriage

JOSEPH ROTH WITH FRIEDL IN BERLIN, IN 1922

"No Eastern Jew goes to Berlin voluntarily," Roth says in *The Wandering Jews.* "Who in all the world goes to Berlin voluntarily?" Not himself, for sure. But there was in the twenties in the German-speaking world no way around that often invoked "Moloch." It had the appeal, within a relatively new federation, of an even newer center, with its score of daily newspapers putting out editions around the clock, its myriad openings in film and theater and book publishing, its evidently insatiable appetite for fresh provincial talent. Even if its streets weren't paved with gold but with particularly unyielding paving stones, it still played the role of London in the story of Dick Whittington. (It was one of the jokes about Berlin that no one actually *came* from there; it understood all about outsourcing long before the word existed.)

Joseph Roth fetched up there in the summer of 1920, ready if need be, as he stylized it with his typical brio, to sleep on park benches and live on cherries. He had nothing organized, and went there on spec, and perhaps in a hurry. He had met Friedl Reichler in Vienna in the autumn of 1919, and successfully wooed her away from her fiancé (a fellow journalist, as it happens). But being—already—under no illusion about the unsteadiness of his life and prospects, and his besetting need for freedom (Brecht's line in "Vom armen BB" might have been written for Roth: "In me you have someone on whom you *can't* rely"), some honest and old-fashioned part of him (substantial, by the way: he wasn't a principled cad like Brecht) would have conceded that he couldn't offer stability, home, and a living to the young woman. Perhaps it was Friedl—only moderately disguised, by Roth's standards—who was the "married woman" who threatened him (in no. 98) with losing his freedom, and for whose sake, so to speak, he upped sticks and went to Berlin (thereby breaking the engagement). Berlin, originally, was perhaps as much about personal liberty (Roth uses the phrase in no. 244, about his move to France, "La liberté PERSON-NELLE") as about professional advancement.

The professional advancement side of things went well. A writer as diligent, as versatile, as spirited, and as inspired as Roth did not want for work. By 1921, he had a regular engagement at one of the twenty dailies, the *Berliner Börsen Courier*, and made occasional appearances in a number of the others. (He made his debut in the *Frankfurter Zeitung* in January 1923.) This having "made good" elsewhere permitted him to return to Vienna in triumph (as one can imagine a man with his pride would have insisted on doing, not as a suppliant or a lucky winner) and swoop up Friedl after all. They were married in Vienna in March 1922. Roth, I think, loved Friedl and was proud of her—her sweetness, her appearance, stylish enough to pass for French—but never knew what to do with her. He kept her with him in hotels, or, on the frequent occasions when he was on the road somewhere, whether tours of provincial Germany or abroad to Russia, Albania, and Italy, he parked her somewhere alone, with just his money and his jealousy for company. No. 9 seems, touchingly and ominously, to cover many of the bases of the new existence, from the enigmatic ailment (what's the matter with her arm?) and her curious misdating of the letter (they weren't married in December 1921; is it that she hankers for that still to be the case?), to her anxiously trying to fit into *his* life, which could be no other way than the way it was, and half the time meant being alone and waiting up for him. With the benefit of hindsight, Roth almost always sounds regretful, as for instance in no. 79, a sadly ruminative but still relatively discreet letter to Stefan Zweig, whom at that stage he had yet to meet: "In a fit of mindlessness, I took on the responsibility for a young woman. I need to keep her somewhere, she is frail, and physically not up to a life at my side." But even before Friedl began behaving erratically in 1928, Roth could sound resentful of his marriage: if you are synesthetically minded, you can surely hear the sailor's tattoos in no. 21, from Marseilles, in the tough bit of worldly wisdom: "It's only in a port that you know you're married." It's there in his approval of a man going to Shanghai, of meeting the (ex-Austrian) Mexican chief of police, it's there everywhere in his fiction where being stuck somewhere with someone is doom, and the final movement of so many stories and novels is an impetuous sudden departure: in *Right and Left;* in the magnificent, useless last scene of *Flight Without End* (whose title is often used to emblematize Roth's life) where Tunda seems briefly to have outrun all his pursuers (one pictures his life, panting in the distance with its hands on its hips); of *Hotel Savoy;* of "April" and "Stationmaster Fallmerayer" and "Rare and ever rarer in this world of empirical facts . . ." in which the narrator congratulates himself on not having to describe a man "duped into love by a shallow affect," but instead one "prompted by a profound instinct to flee bourgeois existence."

But of the (very few) letters from this time, few are personal, and really none are consciously clouded. Instead, we get an early taste of Roth with his elbows out, taking the fight to the enemy. The enemy, it has to be said, is almost invariably head office. It is a little surprising that, coming from the periphery of things as he did, nothing should have been further from Roth than awe or respect for the personalities and institutions of the center (at this stage of his life, he certainly wasn't making a good imperial subject; the "frontiersman" in him showed itself differently). His letters are quite fearless in their bluntness, and worse in the jaunty disrespect they imply. Whether he's putting up two fingers to the *BBC*, or selling himself on the sly—a contracted author—to another publisher, he seems always in a hurry, and to have little regard for the sensitivities of the persons or institutions he's dealing with, neither the ones he's trying to charm ("I am told you are sometimes to be found in Berlin") nor the ones from whom he's—perhaps not so discreetly—pursuing a disseverance: "Nor do I think the Schmiede will be overjoyed to learn of my new terms." In a way, it's as though he's playing a game, or taking on a dare: to Ihering (no.10) it would be: maintain a cordial personal relationship with your boss, in case you need his support at some future time, while giving in your passionate resignation because the paper he edits is insufficiently left wing for you (make sure he feels bad about this), and also launching a noble gripe that he wasn't paying you enough, financial and ideological reasons to receive equal weight. You have twenty minutes. Begin. And lo and behold, Roth invented the perfumed kipper.

9. *Friederike Reichler*[1] *to Paula Grübel*   *Berlin, 28 December 1921*[2]
                                                      half past 11 at night

Servus Paulinchen,

don't be annoyed by the long silence. My arm got very bad, and hurt a lot. The swelling's only just starting to go down.

Today I was unwell again—I had a terrible cough. I followed your advice, hot bath, aspirin, sweating; now I'm feeling better. Muh is at the theater, and I'm so worried about him I couldn't stay in bed any more, and got up to write to you.

He's terribly busy. He's working very hard on his novel, which Frau Szajnocha will have told you about. It makes him moody, so he can't write letters.

Please apologize for him to your father, and put in a good word for him.

How is Frau Szajnocha?

Beierle[3] is still staying with us, and says hello.

Your father mentioned a jeweler by the name of Pume Torczyner. Please tell him that that's my grandmother, my mother's maiden name was Torczyner.

All roads lead to Brody!

Please give my best regards to your father and mother, and many kisses,

Friedl.

I can't get hold of Galsen.

12 o'clock already, and Muh's still not back, what do you say to that?! Shocking!!!!

1. Friederike Reichler (born 12 May 1900 in Vienna) married Roth on 5 March 1922 in Vienna. Always physically delicate, she became schizophrenic in 1929, and was put in asylums in Austria; in 1940 she was euthanized, in accordance with the prevailing practices of the Nazis. Her sweet, rather nervous tone here is ominous.

2. 1921: *recte* 1922, according to Bronsen.

3. Beierle: Alfred Beierle, friend of Roth's, an actor and reciter.

10. To Herbert Ihering   *Berlin, 17 September 1922*

Dear Mr. Ihering,[1]

please don't see this letter as a formal goodbye, nor as a polite substitute for a meeting with you, but purely as the expression of a necessity. I regret the all too short period of our collaboration, and freely admit that, while I came to the *BBC*[2] with certain prejudices against you, I am now pleased to entertain high opinions of both your humanity and your literary effectiveness.

I am writing a farewell letter by the same post to Dr. Faktor,[3] informing him that his letter occasioned, but did not cause, my resignation. I am no longer able to share the outlook of a bourgeois readership and remain their Sunday chatterbox if I am not to deny my socialism on a daily basis. It's possible that, out of weakness, I might have repressed my convictions in return for a higher salary or more frequent recognition of my work. Only Dr. Faktor, already sapped by hard work, constant negotiations with the editorial board, and the difficulties of his own position, treated me with a smiling condescension, often doubted the truth of my protestations, smiled at this and that, and, while I am certainly aware of my own sensitivities, I am forced to conclude that I was treated in a way that was dangerously close to that extended to Herr Schönfeld and other employees of bygone days. As far as my salary was concerned, after the latest raise, it was 9,000 marks. I was allowed to write for other papers, but not to write with all my power for the *BBC*. The one I was permitted to do on grounds of economy, the other was frowned upon to suppress my ambitions.

I write you this, because I wouldn't like you to form a false picture of what happened. I would be very glad to meet you in some neutral place, but am not proposing such a thing, but am content to wait for chance to bring it about, if it will.

I remain, with best wishes, your humble servant

Joseph Roth

1. Herbert Ihering (1888–1977), theater critic with the *Berliner Börsen Courier*, and famously an early supporter of the plays of Bertolt Brecht; later on worked at the Burg-theater in Vienna during the Third Reich, and was a theater critic again in the German Democratic Republic (East Germany) after 1945. This letter is an early instance of Roth's rhetorical power—which sometimes becomes ferocity—and his fearlessness when confronting others in authority.

2. Not the British Broadcasting Corporation, but the *Berliner Börsen Courier*.

3. Faktor: Dr. Emil Faktor (born in 1876 in Prague, gassed after 1941 in Lodz), feuilleton editor of the *Berliner Börsen Courier*, deposed under Hitler, left for Czecho-slovakia in 1933.

11. Friederike Roth to Paula Grübel   Berlin, 14 July 1924

in the next few days, we are going to go to Prague and then on to Kra-kow. Please, will you tell me what the prices are like in Poland now, and how well we can live on rentenmarks.[1]

Perhaps it would even be possible for you to make a side trip to Kra-kow yourself? Certainly, we would like that.

Please write straightaway, because we're only waiting for an address from you before leaving.

Then we may all go to France together in August.

Please give Frau Szajnocha our best regards, from both of us—I'll send off a copy of *Hotel Savoy*[2] this week.

Fräulein Idelsohn has been here. How are your parents doing?

Please congratulate Wittlin[3] from us both.

Kisses from   Friedl and Muh.

1. The rentenmark was introduced in November 1923 in an effort to stabilize the German currency in the wake of runaway inflation. One rentenmark became equivalent to one trillion marks.

2. *Hotel Savoy*: Roth's second novel—though the first to appear between covers—came out in 1924 from the respected Berlin firm Die Schmiede, publishers of Kafka and Proust. They went on to publish *Rebellion* and *The Wandering Jews*.

3. Jozef Wittlin married in 1924.

12. To Paula Grübel   *[Berlin, 15 July 1924]*

Dear Paula,

Friedl wrote you yesterday. But knowing how unreliable you are, I will repeat both her content, and her instruction to write back ASAP. I am going to Poland for work. What is the level of the Polish mark? I have 800 German marks. Can you work out the exchange? Can I live off it for 3 days *in Krakow*? Can you meet me there? I can barely stammer a word of Polish any more. Inform Frau von Szajnocha, Wittlin, Mayer! Then I will travel to Austria with you, and perhaps even farther afield, depending on money. Am bringing books. Looking forward very much to clapping eyes and ears on you again.

Warmest best regards ALL ROUND.   Your Mu

13. To Erich Lichtenstein   *Berlin, 22 January 1925*

Dear Dr. Lichtenstein,[1]

I am writing to you on the instructions of Dr. Max Krell.[2] I seem to recall writing to you once before. By mid-February I shall have completed a novel. However, I am contractually tied to the "Schmiede."[3] I will admit to you quite openly, though with a plea for discretion, that I am not satisfied with either the promotion, the payment, or the appearance of the books. Nor do I think the Schmiede will be overjoyed to learn of my new terms. So it might very well come about that you and I will have business with one another.

At the same time, I would like to write books other than novels, books that are not covered by my contract with the Schmiede. For instance, I have long toyed with a plan to write a book of cheeky and irreverent dialogs on (in the broadest sense) "questions of the day." I can imagine the book appearing under the title "Alfred and Edward," or something of the sort.

I am told you are sometimes to be found in Berlin. I will be here until March, and thereafter in Paris. If you are ever in the city, I should like to be informed. In any case, I should be grateful for the kindness of an acknowledgment.

Yours sincerely,   Joseph Roth

N 35, Potsdamerstrasse 115 a. c/o Tome

1. Lichtenstein: Dr. Erich Lichtenstein (1888–1967), reviewer, publicist, and publisher. This letter is an early instance of Roth's simoniac tendencies as an author, his self-given right to agitate, to inveigh, to two-time, and ultimately to desert publishers. (NB, such behavior on his part comfortably antedated exile and Third Reich.)

2. Max Krell worked as an editor for another publisher, the Propyläen Verlag.

3. The unfortunate "Schmiede" was where Roth's books for a time appeared. Roth's swagger is hard to take, and hard to like.

PART III

1925–1933

*Paris, Points South and East,
Disappointment, Tragedy, and Triumph*

JOSEPH ROTH WITH THE TRADEMARK NEWSPAPER

rance—the Midi, Paris, Marseille—marks nothing less than the appearance of grace in Roth's life. (And for once, not—his phrase—the "grace of unhappiness.") Something unlooked for, undreamed of, or perhaps only dreamed of, something exceeding any human measure of reason or cognition. It is one of those classic collisions between the highly intelligent and almost post-mature but somehow starved observer and the Abundant Place: other instances that come to mind involve poets: Osip Mandelstam in Georgia, and Elizabeth Bishop in Brazil. Roth for once flaps at the limits of sense—which, as witness the reproving letters to his friend and protégé Bernard von Brentano (or later to Stefan Zweig), is something he hates to do, he disdains anything incoherent, stuttering, pompous, blathering. "I feel driven to inform you *personally* that Paris is the capital of the world, and that you must come here," he writes in no. 14 to his boss-cum-friend Benno Reifenberg, "Paris is Catholic in the most urbane sense of the word, but it's also a European expression of universal Judaism." (Reifenberg got it, and later got to be the paper's Paris correspondent himself.) Roth's delirium, cooled and formed, is still palpable in the beautiful series of pieces he gave the *Frankfurter Zeitung* (they ran between 8 September and 4 November 1925), called *Im mittäglichen Frankreich*, "In the French Midi," and a projected—and sadly, rejected—book version to be called "The White Cities." I found the white cities just as they were in my dreams," he writes in the title piece, ending with a landscape of Matisse-like strength, serenity, and loveliness:

> The sun is young and strong, the sky is lofty and deep blue, the trees dark green, ancient, and pensive. And broad white roads that have been drinking in and reflecting the sun for hundreds of years, lead to the white cities with flat roofs, which are as they are to prove that

even elevation can be harmless and benign, and that you never, ever fall into the black depths.

In a life full of calamities—his father's madness before he was even born, Friedl's schizophrenia, the end of the Dual Monarchy, Hitler's coming to power—the loss of the Paris correspondent's job for the *Frankfurter Zeitung* seems perhaps the most gratuitously wounding of all. It is too tantalizing to imagine Roth's life with—in the full, officially possessing sense of the word—Paris. Perhaps his critical, oppositional spirit would have asserted itself sooner or later anyway; the novelist would have shouldered his way out past the journalist. But as it was, the *Frankfurter* gave, and the *Frankfurter* took away: for Roth, the flat roofs of the white cities were to have hurtful and malign black depths below them after all. In its unwisdom (and in the financial and organizational and political nervousness and turmoil of the twenties), this Jewish-liberal institution made the Nationalist—and later Nazi—Friedrich Sieburg its Paris correspondent, reasoning that Sieburg could do reporting as well as feuilleton. Roth in 1934 made a sour little joke about Sieburg's busily seeking God in France (it's an expression meaning something like "high on the hog"), while the Germans had happily found Wotan at home in Germany—but his feelings toward the man were not amusing or benign. Roth—hardly nature's idea of a docile employee anyway—never subsequently trusted the paper, but then you could argue that he had probably never previously trusted it either. In any case, who could blame him? He remained based in Paris, half out of protest, but demoted, casualized, cantankerous, and impatient to be done with newspapers.

The antagonistic relationship between the *FZ* and its star writer is one of the burdens of this correspondence. Lines of command at the paper were, to say the least, fuzzy. There was an editorial committee—hence the extraordinary proliferation of newspapermen's names in some of these letters (a history of *The New Yorker* would be no different, of course). Design, personnel, allegiances, politics, finance, all underwent continual change. Hence one's sense of Roth's at times loitering unhappily and unproductively around the head office in Frankfurt—he was watching his own back. Hence, too, his adoption of the slightly younger Brentano—it was so that he too might have someone to command, to patronize, to induct into mysteries, and to lead into battle. From these letters, one feels that there was any number of chiefs at the *Frankfurter*, and Roth their only Indian. It was a remarkable paper, distinguished, even unrivaled, in its roster of writers, among them Walter Benjamin—but it also had a powerful (and to Roth, never that much of a team player, rather nauseating) sense of its own distinguished remarkability. Newly arrived in Paris, or in Russia, out of sight of it, he still had some interest in its affairs, and wrote painstaking critiques and—practically!—memos to senior colleagues. A few years later, he had none. In 1931, he wrote to Friedrich Traugott Gubler, Reifenberg's successor as feuilleton editor, "It's just a paper, only slightly better than the others in Germany. It's no longer absolutely good or essential. And neither you nor Reifenberg nor Picard will be able to fix it. You will sacrifice your personal lives, the *only* important thing." And this is what he then, rather movingly, goes on to prescribe: "Always do what your wife says, spend time with her and the children, discuss *everything* with her, and don't do anything just because your obstinate man's head tells you to." The *Frankfurter*'s sense of exceptionalism—one might almost call it "manifest destiny"—mixed, of course, with relativism, kept it going, trimming as it went, through ten years of the Third Reich, until it was finally closed down in August 1943. Like some of his colleagues, Reifenberg, who stayed at the paper throughout, and was involved in its next incarnation as the *Frankfurter Allgemeine Zeitung* of today, was persuaded that they had managed to keep up some coded, clandestine resistance to the Nazis in their columns. Looking at some contributions with a view to putting together an anthology of them in the 1950s, he was forced to realize there was no resistance in any meaningful sense, not that any reader would have understood. The newspaper was trapped in a vainglorious bubble of its own making; and Roth, who after 1933 would have nothing to do with it, and broke off all relations with colleagues still there, was tacitly and belatedly vindicated in his intransigence.

It was in France, you could say, that Roth learned to fear and hate and see Germany as it was. The specimens of German-ness that fetched up in Paris—the Prussians he thought of as *boches*—and penitential return visits to Frankfurt or Berlin taught him a sort of visionary anthropology. Once Paris was denied him, and he had been to Russia, and a further visit there failed to come off, the *FZ* had only Germany and Germany and more Germany to offer him, and Roth's responses became swifter, more virulent, more instinctive, and less patient. His eye was trained by the health, glamour, and nature of a sort of anticipatory self-exile in France. Germany, by contrast, was a disfigurement, a freak show, a deeply sick patient:

> I feel Germany right off the bat, and all of it at once. Every street corner expresses the awfulness of the whole country. It has the ugliest prostitutes, the girls indistinguishable from the women who swab the floors of the *FZ* at night, in fact I think they're the same. The men are all scoutmasters on display. You see more blondes in summer than in winter. All tanned and deeply unhealthy looking. An awful lot of bodies, precious few faces. Sports shirts, no skirts. Yesterday, my first day back, was ghastly. *Immediate plummet of spirits*, the way mercury can fall to zero. The feeling as though your genitals were gone, nothing left! Skirts, where there are skirts, all buttoned up, crooked gait of the men, as though they were originally designed as quadrupeds. (no. 134)

This account matches the sarcastic horror paintings of Otto Dix. Roth tried—further driven on by the plight of Friedl, who required treatment, and finally hospitalization—to save himself in fiction. He put out a book a year: *Flight Without End* in 1927, *Zipper and His Father* in 1928, *Right and Left* in 1929. (After 1933, it was to be more like two books a year: a completely ruinous and impossible production.) The rejection by S. Fischer of *The Silent Prophet* and his own abandonment of *Perlefter: The Story of a Bourgeois* checked his progress. When the firm of Gustav Kiepenheuer took him on, and *Job*, subtitled *The Story of a Simple Man* came out to excellent reviews and—for the first time—appreciable sales in 1930, it looked as though—after seven novels!—Roth might be poised for a new career as a novelist, and he quite deliberately set himself (bought himself time and space, and as much peace of mind as a monthly stipend could buy) to write the "book of old Austria" that was to be his master-piece, *The Radetzky March*. It was serialized in the *Frankfurter Zeitung* (among his last gifts to the paper), and published in August 1932—nicely in time to be fed to the flames by enthusiastic National Socialist students in Berlin on 10 May 1933.

Dear Mr. Reifenberg,[1]

I fear this letter may give you the impression that I am so besotted with Paris, and with France, that I have lost the balance of my mind. Be assured, therefore, that I am writing to you in full possession of my skeptical faculties, with all my wits about me, and running the risk of making a fool of myself, which is just about the worst thing that could happen to me. I feel driven to inform you *personally* that Paris is the capital of the world, and that you must come here. Whoever has not been here is only half a human, and no sort of European. Paris is free, intellectual in the best sense, and ironic in the most majestic pathos. Any chauffeur is wittier than our wittiest authors. We really are an unhappy bunch. Here everyone smiles at me, I fall in love with all the women, even the oldest of them, to the point of contemplating matrimony. I could weep when I cross the Seine bridges, for the first time in my life I am shattered by the aspect of buildings and streets, I feel at ease with everyone, though we continually misunderstand each other in matters of practicalities, merely because we so delightfully understand each other in matters of nuance. Were I a French author, I wouldn't bother printing anything, I would just read and speak. The cattle drovers with whom I eat breakfast are so cultivated and noble as to put our ministers of state to shame, patriotism is justified (but only here!), nationalism is an expression of a European conscience, any poster is a poem, the announcements in a magistrate's court are as sublime as our best prose, film placards contain more imagination and psychology than our contemporary novels, soldiers are whimsical children, policemen amusing editorialists. There is—quite literally—a party against Hindenburg[2] being celebrated here at the moment, "Guignol contre Hindenburg" but then the whole city is a protest against Hindenburg anyway, against Hindenburg, Prussia, boots, and buttons. The Germans here, the North Germans, are full of rage against the city, and they are blind and insensitive to it. For instance, I quarreled with Palitzsch,[3] who is of the better sort of North German and who can only understand my enthusiasm as a sort of poetic spleen, and thereby excuses it. He makes allowances for me! Me, a poet! That much vaunted North German "objectivity" is a mask for his lack of instinct, for his nose that isn't an organ of sense but a catarrh dispenser. My so-called subjectivity is in the highest degree objective. I can smell things he won't be able to see for another ten years.

I feel terribly sad because there are no bridges between certain races. There will never be a connection between Prussia and France. I am sitting in a restaurant, the waiter greets me, the waitress gives me a smile, while the Germans I am with are frosty to the manager and the errand boy. They give off a ghastly rigidity, they breathe out not air but walls and fences, even though their French is better than mine. Why is it? It's the voice of blood and Catholicism. Paris is Catholic in the most urbane sense of the word, but it's also a European expression of universal Judaism.

You must come here!

I owe it to you that I was able to come to France, and I shall never thank you enough. In a few days I'm going to take off for Provence, and I won't write until my ecstasy has calmed down, and become the ground plan for the edifice of my descriptions.

My wife is staying here for the moment, she's unwell, I'm afraid it may be her lungs. Please write to her:

Friedl Roth, Place de l'Odeon, Hotel de la Place de l'Odeon/Paris. It's so cheap: 10 ff for a good meal, 15 ff for the night!

I'm also writing to the paper for the rest of my payment—perhaps you could remind them in accounts as well.

Greetings to you, and I kiss your wife's hands,[4]

Your Joseph Roth

1. Reifenberg: Benno Reifenberg (1892–1970), journalist, and JR's boss-cum-friend (though as he says frequently, this sort of mixed relationship is hard to negotiate; JR is forever talking to him privately in the office, or sending professional démarches to his home). Joined the staff of the *Frankfurter Zeitung* in 1919; editor of the feuilleton from 1924, Paris correspondent from 1930 to 1932, political editor from 1932 to 1943; co-founder and co-editor of the journal *Die Gegenwart* (1945–58); on the board of the *Frankfurter Allgemeine Zeitung* from 1958 to 1964.

2. General Paul von Hindenburg was elected president of Germany on 25 April.

3. O. A. Palitzsch, journalist.

4. Born Maryla von Mazurkiewicz, to whom JR had a cordial relationship.

15. To Bernard von Brentano   *Paris, 2 June 1925*

Dear Brentano,[1]

don't be annoyed! In the first place, I'm incredibly mixed up. I don't know if I'll ever write another thing. Maybe I'll go back to where I came from—you know—and herd sheep. I don't see the point in being a German writer. Here is like being on top of a tall tower, you look down from the summit of European civilization, and way down at the bottom, in some sort of gulch, is Germany. I can't write a line in German—certainly not when I am mindful of writing for a German readership.

Secondly, I've failed to do all the bureaucratic police stuff on time, and am forced to hang around waiting for a visa extension. Don't snigger—it's not the French who are to blame, it's purely my fault.

Third, don't give the O.[2] episode any more importance than it has. Don't bother your head about him, or Mr. Stark,[3] or any of the rest of them. The *Illustriertes Blatt*[4] is none of your beeswax. If someone tries to accuse you, shrug your shoulders. I can't understand your worrying about it. Ott is a fanatic of bad behavior. Be distant to him. Don't get "cross." Be "nice" to him. Be like a father, or a nobleman: remember, distance. Basically he's just a soft and decent human being, just a little "nervous."

4. Be as industrious and objective as you can. Write, write! Then

none of the others will get a look in. Why don't you have anything for me to read? You're my hope, and I'm too proud to admit you've let me down.

5. Thank you for giving me news from Frankfurt. It sounds rather favorable. I have no plan and a guilty conscience. I feel as though I've duped the paper.

6. We're writing to your wife now.

7. I'll write at greater length when I'm through with the police.

8. The mail is so unreliable here, if you could, let me know you've received this.

9. Even if I don't get to Germany, I'll always be your friend.

10. My wife sends her regards   Yours Joseph Roth

Hotel de la place de l'Odéon,

VIᵉ, place de l'Odéon 6.

You're wrong to think people are the same the world over. The French simply *are* different. Yes, they whistle and clap during war films. But trust a fanatic and a "subjective" like me: I've never heard such feeble applause.

1. Brentano: Bernard von Brentano (1901–1964), publicist, essayist, and novelist. Descended from the Romantic poet Clemens von Brentano. From 1925 to 1930, Berlin correspondent of the *Frankfurter Zeitung*. He owed his introduction to the paper to JR. There was a violent breach in the relationship in the late 1920s when Brentano swung first left, then hard right. JR was described as "foaming with rage" when BB's name was mentioned. See no. 83.

2. O episode: Ott episode?

3. Stark: Oskar Stark (1890–1970) journalist. From 1920 to 1931 in the Berlin office of the *Frankfurter Zeitung*, from 1935 to 1943 in head office, after the war with the *Badische Zeitung* in Freiburg.

4. *Illustriertes Blatt*: magazine produced from the same stable as the *Frankfurter Zeitung*.

16. To Bernard von Brentano   *Paris, 14 June 1925*
                                                 Hotel de la place de l'Odéon
                                                 6. Place de l'Odéon

My dear Brentano,

many thanks for your letter. I haven't seen your articles. It's hard to find the *Frankfurter Zeitung* in Paris, it gets here a week late, and not always then, even to Dr. Stahl, its representative here. Put some clippings in an envelope, and mail them to me. Work harder! Three pieces a week. Practice that manner that's eye-catching and load-bearing at the same time.

Thanks for your crossed fingers, my bureaucratic hoopla is looking reasonably promising just now. My wife went along to the Interior Ministry, and Frenchmen will do everything for a woman. Germans just get impatient . . .

I'm just as enthusiastic as before, and just as depressed about Germany. I can understand a German poet[1] coming here, digging himself a mattress grave, and giving up the ghost. Before we get around to making a German nation, we may find there's a European one. Perhaps to the exclusion of the Germans.

I'm taking my novel to Provence round about the 20th. I'm probably going to write a book about Marseille. My book has been translated into Russian 4 times. I have 200,000 Russian readers. And 4½ in Germany. Does that make me a German writer? I'd say of those 4½, 2½ are Russian Jews anyway.

I don't know how things are going to go on. I think I'll be back at least once, for practicalities. But I'm a different person, and it won't be for long.

Will you ask your wife whether she got our postcard?

Give my regards to Dr. Guttmann,[2] who behaved scandalously badly here—to me as well.

Regards to the great Sonnemann.[3]

Don't go anywhere yet, and don't talk about it either. I hear a school-boyish eagerness has come over Otten.

I shake your hand and remain

Your old[4]   Joseph Roth

My wife says make sure to send her best.

1. The reference is to Heinrich Heine (1797–1856), who died in Paris. In 1848 he was suddenly paralyzed, and spent his last eight years in agonies in what he called his *Matratzengruft*.

2. Guttmann: Bernhard Guttmann (1869–1959). Before 1914 London correspondent of the *Frankfurter Zeitung*, from 1918 to 1930 head of the Berlin office, then Frankfurt, retired in 1933.

3. Sonnemann: Leopold Sonnemann (1831–1909). Founder and co-proprietor of the *Frankfurter Zeitung*. JR is being whimsical/facetious.

4. Roth, who will usually sign like this in his remaining years, is just thirty years old, younger than Jesus Christ and Alexander the Great.

17. To Benno Reifenberg   *Lyon, 25 July [1925]*

Dear Mr. Reifenberg,

thank you so much for your letter. With the same post I'm sending a feuilleton to the office, entitled "On the Road in France"[1]—it's your title, and I've borrowed it—hope you don't mind. I'm putting these business things in a personal letter, because I can't trust the post, and I always worry a letter to a German official address wouldn't get there.[2] Please drop me a line at the Hotel de la place de l'Odeon, where they're keeping my mail for me, just to confirm its safe arrival.

Splendid is such an overused word, but if you were here, you'd understand why I had to reach for it. Lyon is splendid in the old way, majestic and lovely, but without pomp. The Rhone is an old wide river but frisky as a stream. It doesn't know the meaning of the word gravity, it's a French river. I walk through the streets of the town, and the country roads about—everywhere you see the Roman flowing into the Catholic, and you see (what you must never write!) the continuation of something archaic and heathen that has found a form for itself in Catholicism, but still exists.

The people are wonderful, very open, mild, with lovely irony, the women terribly delicate, always young, always naked, a lot of Oriental blood, Negro mixed race, the middle classes quieter than in Germany, politically on the left, the men practically as well dressed as the women in Paris. The women still better, silk everywhere, wonderfully adaptable material, soft, coarse, simple, imposing—all silk.

I kiss your wife's hand, and shake yours. I must say, Paris felt a little empty after you went, your old   Roth

Hug your little boy for me. He must learn French. It will make a European of him.

1. "On the Road in France": this became Roth's series of articles in the *Frankfurter Zeitung* "In the South of France," which ran from 8 September to 14 November 1925, and was to have been reworked into a book called "The White Cities." See letter no. 19. See *Report from a Parisian Paradise* (W. W. Norton, 2003).

2. wouldn't get there: a habitual anxiety of JR's. Then again, we are just seven years after the end of World War I, and the bad atmosphere between Germany and France lasted into the 1950s and beyond. Cf. de Gaulle's dictum that he liked Germany so much, he preferred there to be two of them.

18. To Benno Reifenberg   *Avignon, 1 August [1925]*

My dear Mr. Reifenberg,

I'd like in this letter to tell you about my great good fortune, only I have such a fear that my pieces aren't reaching you. It's a sort of illness, of course, but it threatens to make me sterile, and that's my excuse in perpetrating such a breach of decorum as to ask you in a personal letter to send me confirmation at the Hotel de l'Odeon that you have safely received the 6 or 7 feuilletons from France. My mail is being forwarded to me.

Even as I write this, I'm unsure whether you will get it. But even if you don't, I still hope you will somehow sense that I am enjoying—seems wrong, quaking, yearning, crying—the best days of my life. I shall never be able to describe what has been vouchsafed to me here. You will probably best assess the scale of my good fortune by the way I see how small and powerless I am, and yet seem to live thousandfold. I love the rooftops, the stray dogs that run around the streets, the cats, the wonderful tramps with their red leather complexions and young eyes, the women who are so terribly thin, with long legs and bony shoulders and yellow skin, the child beggars, the mix of Saracen, French, Celtic, German, Roman, Spanish, Jewish, and Greek. I am at home in the Palace of the Popes, all the beggars live in the most wonderful castles, I should like to be a beggar and sleep in its doorways. Everything we do in Germany is so stupid! So pointless! So sad! Come to me in Avignon, and I promise you you'll never set another article of mine. I'm learning French poems by heart for the fun of it. Kiss your wife's hand, greet your son from me in a way he'll understand, and write a personal letter to your old

Joseph Roth

19. To Benno Reifenberg   *Marseille, Hotel Beauvau*
                                         rue Beauvau, 18 August [1925]

Dear Mr. Reifenberg,

I am making one last effort to find out whether I haven't sent 6–7 feuilletons to the *FZ* for absolutely nothing, and haven't written a further 3, which I'm not sending until I get a reply from you or the board. You know as a rule I couldn't care less what they do with my stuff. But one thing I cannot be indifferent to is if all reports of a journey whose fruits are a moral victory for me, disappear without trace. I don't know if it's the post that is to blame, but I'm presuming I must have breached one of the unwritten Hindenburg laws that even decent people now follow in Germany, from what I hear. Perhaps an infraction of tone, a word, a suggestion, who knows. Anyway, I want to know. If so, then continuing this journey makes no sense—because I can't deal with events in Germany, perhaps I'm not equal to the politics of the newspaper either. I can't change my tone. Maybe the newspaper would like to be rid of me—well, fine by me. I can understand that there's no wish to put up incendiaries in a burning house.[1]

I have material for a beautiful volume with the title "The White Cities"[2] for the book-publishing arm. But I don't know whether the house will still print books that make a sound like mine. I understand the air has become fairly unbreathable in Germany. That fact, combined with the circumstance that you're not printing anything of mine, prompts me to address to you these admittedly somewhat bitter, but personally beholden lines—and address them to your private address, so as to put off for the moment a needless public kerfuffle.

I intend to wait here until I get word from you.

Till that time, I remain your—and your wife's—old

Joseph Roth

1. The office wired JR back, "No pink elephants, all articles arrived safely, write just exactly what you want, pay no regard to anything."

2. "The White Cities": which sadly never came out in that form, though the revised sequence of pieces, some of Roth's finest, happiest, and most boisterous writing, is included in *Report from a Parisian Paradise*.

20. *To Bernard von Brentano*   *Marseille, 22 August 1925*

My dear friend,

I've received one typed letter here, and another rather hasty one. A third therefore seems to have gotten lost.

If I can begin by setting your mind at ease regarding our relationship: your income doesn't stand between us, rather it connects us. A relationship between two people isn't based on bread, but it remains important that both should have enough to eat. Hunger trumps sentiment. It's important that neither of us should starve. That's why I raised the matter, and that's why I mentioned you to Reifenberg and Simon.[1] I think you're over the worst. I think I'm headed straight for it.

I have sent the *FZ* 7 articles. So far as I know, not one of them has appeared. I think I can no longer hit the democratic tone. In every line of mine the republic gets slapped around—whatever I'm writing about. The paper is cowardly. It won't print my articles, and it won't tell me why. I think its behavior is immoral. I wrote to Reifenberg to say so. If the publisher has the courage of his convictions, he will give me the boot. Then I will be free, as I was for twenty years of my life. I'll go to Mexico. If he wants to be a coward, then I'll demand that he pay me properly for his cowardice. If he doesn't publish me, I want to see money. And even so I'm going to go to Mexico one day, in the not too distant future. I've been established for too long. You see: I really don't care about an income. I don't care about a bourgeois base. It gets in the way. It makes me ill. I am ill already.

Name and reputation in Germany—what's the good of that? I can see past the nationality. But not the language. German is a dead language, as dead as late Latin. It's only spoken by scholars and poets. By Jews. In the Middle Ages a man had power if he wrote in that language. In our democracy today he's nothing. I can cope with the fact that the Germans are barbarians. But not with my inability to convert them. We're like missionaries addressing heathens in Latin, to convert them. Futile endeavor.

To move from proletarian to human is easily said. But what if I'm only having my first experience of human beings now, at the ripe old age of 31? What if I met my first humans here in France? Germany is populated by geniuses and murderers (half animals). Humans begin at Aix. I would have to live and study for another twenty years before I could write about humans. And even then I wouldn't be sure it was possible to do it in German.

Tomorrow the Socialist Congress begins here. I have spoken to acquaintances from Berlin and Vienna. It's a terrible thing to see those people in this setting. The sun shows how much dust there is on them. They have landed here, like the Lombards a thousand years ago. With

Schiller collars! With briefcases! With umbrellas! With fat flat-footed wives! And hatless! They sweat. They smell. They drink beer. They are noisier than the many Orientals who make a deafening noise here in the port city. Social Democrats always look German. Even when they're technically Lithuanians. Because the type is native to Germany: honest, hardworking, beer-bibbing, world-improving. A socialist and a democrat. "Justice!" Hope for evolution. German through and through. The aspiration of the German woman to march through a busy life on flat heels is already halfway to socialism. They all carry on as though they had to determine world history in the next decade. They have come together to fight for Ibsenite ideals. Not knowing how antiquated those are. I saw Friedrich Adler,[2] my great compatriot. A tyrannicide on his uppers. No pistol in his briefcase any more. Features shaped from the mealy dough of humanity. The monarchies are dead—here are people with nothing left to slay. They haven't a chance against industry.

I have visited so many towns in Provence, I could write a book about them: "The White Cities." But do I know if I still need to write it? It'll be settled one way or another in the first half of September. Write to me in Paris.

Regards to your wife. Mine is in bed with a fever. Brought on by the climate, obviously. I'm just off to spend the night in the old port. That's the world I feel really at home in. My maternal forefathers live there. We're all kin there. Every onion seller is my uncle.

Your friend   Joseph Roth

1. Simon: Heinrich Simon (born in Berlin in 1880, robbed and murdered in 1941 in Washington, D.C.), son-in-law of Leopold Sonnemann, the founder of the *FZ*, on the board from 1906, co-owner from 1919. Went into exile in 1934, first to Palestine, where he co-founded an orchestra with Toscanini, then the United States.

2. Friedrich Adler (1879–1960), son of the Austrian Socialist leader Viktor Adler. In 1916 he made an attempt on the life of the Austrian prime minister Count Friedrich Stürgkh, was condemned to death, and pardoned in 1918; secretary of the Second International.

21. To Benno Reifenberg   *Hotel Beauvau, Marseille*
26 August [1925]

Dear Mr. Reifenberg,

you are much too zealous in your self-accusations. It's wrong to think you should have known how nervous I am. No one can know about the level of my agitation—constant and powerful—about everything under the sun. I am never at ease. Of course I exaggerate. When I write in that vein, you shouldn't take it seriously.

For all that, I'm grateful for your letter. I sent off three feuilletons today. Not everything in them is the way it ought to be. But they are entirely honest, I think that will come across. I have seen a bullfight for the first time in my life. If you've never seen anything like that, then you can have no conception of the gruesomeness of it. I know of no French writer who has written about—much less against—these Provençal bullfights. Not Daudet, not Mistral either, to the best of my knowledge. I think they'd be ashamed, and they're scared. They're happy to write about the wind, the sky, the people, the riders, the women. Tell me why a great writer isn't duty bound to accuse his country instead of praising it. They all write as though they wanted their personal monument. And I'm not just talking about their relation to the *patrie*, but to humanity, to society, to every manifestation of life. These writers are all so appallingly affirmative. They reinforce their readers in their bourgeois—i.e., antiquated—attitudes, instead of destroying as many of them as possible. They themselves are nothing but superbourgeois. It's perfectly OK for a little burgomaster to put up a statue to a great writer from time to time. Next to the statue of the little burgomaster. Perfectly OK for the older daughter to play Schubert on the piano. Schubert composed for her.

I was depressed to hear of Willo Uhl's[1] death. He was the first person I met in Frankfurt 3 years ago, and I'm fond of his children. I got a couple of recent editions of the paper. There were only two decent feuilletons: Rudolf Schneider on "heroes" and Willo's obituary. He was such a good and cheerful goy, he stood between the sentimental Jews and the awkward ones on the board, and he was the very opposite of German democracy. It's too bad he's dead. He could never have made 60, but 45 is maybe ten years too early. What did he die of?

Slap in the middle of my lovely time in Marseille is the Social Democratic Congress. 200 Germans, 100 Austrians. The latter a nasty perversion of Germans. The Austrians look like Germans who have understood nothing. As vile as a Prussian is when he's taking his pleasure, that's how ghastly the Austrian is all his life. Degenerate *boches*.

Not that the real ones are any better. A second wave of Lombards. This time toting briefcases and sporting Schiller collars. Fat wives, heelless sandals, perms, hatless. Jews who aren't Jews, because they have taken up the cudgels for some foreign proletariat; bourgeois who aren't bourgeois, because they're fighting for a foreign class. Continually steaming with activity and talk. The conference extended into the evening in the café, big groups and long tables, all to the horror of the waiters and the exotic foreigners of whom there are so many here. Nothing is so exotic as a German. No group is more eye-catching. But the Germans are social democrats to beat the band. If you don't like Germans, you won't like social democrats either. Half citizens, half politicians, half minds, moderate beer drinkers. Good old Stahl is here. He doesn't have a clue about the true nature of this party of toothless dragons. He still gets excited about congresses. I've seen Friedrich Adler. No pistol in his briefcase any more, just checklists. Face gone flabby like dough. Once upon a time he shot Stürgkh. Beginning of the end for the monarchy. When I see Adler today, I understand Stürgkh was a martyr. Because his killer is the secretary of the Second International. They should have hanged him. One shouldn't let heroes live.

Not one of these representatives of the proletariat goes to the old harbor quarter as I, a so-called bourgeois intellectual, do. No one threatens me. They would quite rightly beat their brains out. Eck-Troll is here. Do you know him? A queer sort of idiot. He sits in a bar for three hours, and is fleeced, and they compliment him on his French, and afterwards he tells me he has done some wonderful "studies." He pulls a photograph from his wallet: wife and child. He shows the photo to the objects of his studies. A German journalist on the job. Stahl says: Come with me to the harbor quarter! Shall I take a pistol? What a fighter. Shame there wasn't a cinema handy.

If you think of bluing laundry, you'll have a sense of how blue the sea is here. The sky, on the other hand, is as pale as a sheet of paper.

There are 700 vessels in the port. I've half a mind to suddenly take one of them. My wife cries every day, if it weren't for her, I'd be long gone. It's the first time I've had a feeling for the presence of my wife. It's only in a port that you know you're married.

I had whooping cough as a grown-up as well. Look after yourself. The consequence is often swollen glands, as with me, and mumps, which is unpleasant, if harmless. Regards to mother and son. Have a look at the clipping from *Le Matin*[2] enclosed. I give you my hands.

I remain your old   Joseph Roth

I can't permit this letter to go without the following.

Last night they played *L'Arlésienne* at the opera. As in Paris, when you get a ticket, you get your "*location*" to go with it. As a result, no one finds his seat, because three-quarters of the audience have two. The foldaway seats are all full. The aisles are stuffed with people. Everyone is wandering about. Three ancient usherettes have been driven demented. But the people aren't the least bit bothered. While they're looking around, they all have smiles on their faces.

The music starts, and the foldaway seats keep clacking up and down. People are yelling. Music is a bit like sweets. A component of an evening in the theater. Music is metaphysical, and the southern Frenchman doesn't get it. The gorgeous women are loathsome, because they won't shut up. The musicians don't care about the noise. They play. When there's a quiet passage, the audience thinks it's over, and they go wild.

The musicians go on playing through the interval, all the while they're hammering at the set behind the curtain. The whole theater is like a country fair. Complete strangers start to tell me their life story, because they're bored with the music. The actors are unbelievably hammy. They speak their lines in a kind of graveyard whisper. People laugh themselves silly. Which doesn't prevent them from applauding once a speech is over. The desperate hero, resolved to take his own life, exits triumphantly, arm aloft.

Doors open and shut all the time. People pop out for a smoke. Come back, clacking of chairs. Squeaking of benches. Laughter of women. Rustling of paper.

You can't imagine the lack of respect of the French. They obviously can't understand that art is a form of reality. If you told them a fairy tale, I don't think they would understand it. I should like to know how French children behave during fairy tales.

The Viennese, who are of course besotted with theater and music, turned up in their droves. They thought the continual hubbub was somehow accidental, and kept going Sssh! For two whole acts. The locals laughed at them. Eventually the Germans gave up. Halfway through the act, all the French moved forward and took their empty seats.

Every act is an interval. The whole performance is interval. The French roll around at a tragedy the way we do at a comic routine. They haven't the least idea of art. The Germans at least show respect. It would have been good to have the Berlin police to keep order in the theater yesterday.

Inevitably, the Germans and the French are going to intermarry. They are both desperately short of what the other have.

1. Willo Uhl (1880–1925), feuilleton editor on the *Frankfurter Zeitung* since 1913.
2. *Le Matin*, conservative French newspaper.

22. To Benno Reifenberg   *Hotel Beauvau, Marseille*
                                             30 August [1925]

Dear Mr. Reifenberg,

I really don't mean to alarm you with these registered letters. They are the consequence of my morbid fear of things getting lost in the mail. I'm sure their content is in no relation to the care of their packing. The post makes a lot of money from me. I beg your pardon, and console myself with the fact that the content of this letter can't be more displeasing to you than the fact of its being registered.

It's not easy to write this letter. Not least because I find it immoral—tactless at the very least—to burden our personal relationship with matters of business. I don't want to abuse the fact that I am fond of you (and you, I hope, have a liking for me) to perpetrate the unfairness of leaning on you—influencing is too certain—in your relation to me as an employee. You'll know what I mean. True, we only know one another through work, and thanks to work. But I refuse to relegate a relationship that has outgrown the professional to the merely professional again. But what else can I do? Should I take my case to a tribunal that a tribunal won't understand, when I know a human being? That—to my way of seeing—would mean going over your head. There is still the chance that you will preserve the distinction: on the one hand, feuilleton editor, on the other, well-disposed human being. If such a thing should seem necessary to you, I would even ask that you do so. Please don't show me any sort of private forbearance. You can always give me advice, as if you had nothing to do with the firm.

I'm afraid you probably guess more than you know, and this introduction has been too clear. My stylistic affliction, not my personal one.

My tour will be over in the middle of September. I have enough material for a book. There too, I would like to ask your advice: I should like to write a wholly "subjective" book, in other words something completely objective. The "confession" of a young, resigned, skeptical human being, at an age where he is completely indifferent whether he sees something new to him or not, traveling somewhere. Someone with nothing of the "travel romantic" in him at all. And he sees the last vestiges of Europe, places that are innocent of the ever more apparent Americanization and Bolshevization of our continent. Think of the books of the Romantics. Take away their tools and props, both linguistic and perspectival. Replace them with the tools and props of modern irony and objectivity. Then you have the book I want to write, and feel almost compelled to write. It's a guide to the soul of its writer, as much as of the country he's passing through. What do you think of the idea? It's very creative, more than a novel. I think it's a form that would be congenial to the house. To put it in a nutshell, in a way that you don't like, and I always do:

Books with practical occasion elevated into the poetic sphere. Were I the publisher, that would be my motto.

There would be something else as well, which you in the house are quite rightly not keen to see, but which is generally necessary, and in books quite indispensable. That is comparison. The first chapter would be called "The Other Side of the Fence." But the book would be on far too high a level for it to contain a "critique" of Germany. Say perhaps that the critique would be on so high a level that it would no longer count as such or read like it.

What do you say?

I would like to spend two weeks in Paris, working on this book. I trust you are not party to that German prejudice that a good book cannot be written fast. Fast is the only way I can write well. The Germans write even literary books scientifically. Their feeling is scientific. That's why they write slowly. The slow working of someone like Flaubert is based on completely different grounds: laziness, namely. You must remember from your schooldays that it's possible to slog away all day with the greatest laziness inside you.

During those two weeks I would write nothing for you. Then I would come to Frankfurt with my book. And not to deliver the book, but to talk to you about the coming months.

Principally about *money*. It matters less to me than to the publisher.

Three months are up, in the course of which I should have been paid 900 marks, 300 as expenses. It might have been more "sensible" not to mention it, but it would have been craven. Frankly I am too proud to behave in such a way. Had I been in Berlin now, I would probably have called for a raise because of the inflation, even though that too is craven, and disgusting moreover. I am not in Germany now. (I almost said thank God.) And, as you know, I don't want to go back there this year.

I see three possibilities:

1. Either the firm demands my resignation and I offer it,
2. or it gives me leave to stay,
3. or I don't offer my resignation, and the ball is back in their court, whether I starve as an even more occasional contributor, or manage to go on living, as I have lived the past 20 years. You know I don't demand a steady income. Even so, the third possibility would be the worst, and it would be truly stupid of me not to try and go for the second.

Nothing ties me. I am not sufficiently sentimental to believe in categories like future, family, etc. etc. But sufficiently sentimental to feel devotion to this house and this newspaper, the last vestiges of the old humanistic culture. I am being straight with you—this is *entre nous*. I know perfectly well I couldn't work for any other German paper. I know none would have me. And I still couldn't go back to Germany. It's a tragedy, not a passing fancy. Perhaps it's the height of "patriotism" not to stand to see the tip of a pyramid not formed by a tip, but by a shaved blockhead.[1] I can't stand to see the whole of Germany turning into a Masurian swamp. If I were there now, it would drive me crazy. Everything affects me personally. If they lock up Becher,[2] it's me that's behind bars. I don't know what would happen. I'm capable of shooting someone, or throwing bombs, I don't think I'd last very long. I risk my life when I return to Germany. Physically, I can't do it.

But do you think I can say that to the newspaper? Ever since his letter to Stahl, I've had a great respect for Simon. I would like to talk to him, though it's probably too personal. He might misunderstand, because he thinks of me as unscrupulous—when all I am is shrewd. I could never tell him. I always worry he doesn't hear half of what I say. If he has ten minutes for me, eight go on all sorts of other stuff. I worry once I'm in Frankfurt again, sniff the air in the office, which has so little in common with the rest of Germany, that the newspaper can't see Germany, and that I'll weaken, and go back to Berlin, and it will finish me off. Berlin is bad for my liver, I have trouble with gall production. Should I not go to Frankfurt?

Can I spend the winter in Paris then? I wouldn't care to stay any longer than that. Can I go to some third country—Albania, maybe—and write another book? Should I forget about the 100 marks, and so free myself from Germany? Can I go to Moscow? Schotthöfer[3] is back. Russia and the East are familiar to me.

I am desperate. I can't even go to Vienna since the Jewish Socialists have started clamoring for their Anschluss. What are they after? They want Hindenburg? At the time that Emperor Franz Joseph died, I was already a "revolutionary," but I shed tears for him. I was a one-year volunteer in a Vienna regiment, a so-called elite unit, that stood by the Kapuzinergruft as a guard of honor, and I tell you, I was crying. An epoch was buried. With the Anschluss, a culture will be put in the ground. Every European must be against the Anschluss. And only those mediocre Socialist brains don't get it. So little difference between German Nationalist and Socialist policies! Between Jew and Christian! The various camps are united by their mediocrity more firmly than by any principle or ideal. Can't anyone feel that an independent Austria is still a gesture toward a united Europe? Do they want to become a sort of nether Bavaria? More than German reactionaries, I hate that obtuse German efficiency, decency, honesty, the Löbe[4] type, the accountant who has found his way into politics. Those people should have remained civil servants. But just because there are no politicians in Germany, the civil servants go into politics, and the idiots occupy the chancelleries, and because the prisons are overcrowded the criminals have moved into the police stations. I can't go to Germany, I can't!

I hope you liked my last three articles. If not, please tell me straight out. Someone who writes day and night as I do has no vanity. Nor is it vanity that is unhappy with an "appendix" to my essays. It's the formal conscience of a journalist. There is such a thing as a typographical conscience. *It insists on a preamble and won't stand for an afterword.* That would have to be in a different typeface. The newspaper is insufficiently expressive in that way. There is no smallest type size. I've just forgotten the name of it. Petit and leaded petit are too small. Formal technical resources allow for more expression. It's terribly important for the paper to have a thousand faces; it has a thousand news stories. Congratulations, anyway, on the new masthead and design. Who is it who sets the paper now? The best-looking edition was the one with the French diplomatic démarche. Who set that? I like the layout of the world news as well. If only I could have that column to myself three times a week. With specifications as to layout. Would that be possible?

How are your invalids? Give them my best, I mean it. I remain, come what may, your old Joseph Roth

1. shaved blockhead: an unmistakable limning of Paul von Hindenburg (1847–1934), World War I general and then elected president of Germany in 1925 and again in 1932; the man who in January 1933 gave the German chancellorship to Adolf Hitler.

2. Becher: Johannes Becher (1891–1958), poet, playwright, novelist, and member of the Independent Social Democratic Party.

3. Schotthöfer: Fritz Schotthöfer, worked on the *Frankfurter Zeitung* from 1900. Retired in 1943, died in 1951.

4. Löbe: Paul Löbe (1875–1967), member of the Social Democratic Party.

23. *To Bernard von Brentano*   *Paris, 11 September [1925]*

Dear friend,

I got your two letters before I left. I've been in Paris again since yesterday. I'm working very hard, starting my travel book tomorrow, and hoping to finish it by the end of the month. Hence just a few lines now. My address is the same. Please tell me *right away* that you're better. I worry about you, not just for your sake, but because it's important that decent people remain alive and in good health. My liver's already packing up. The fools aren't to remain unsupervised, and in the happy knowledge that the good people are getting sick and falling away. My relationship with the firm is being decided now. I'll probably take the finished book with me to Frankfurt.

Write if you must. I imagine you'll have been paid, in accordance with the snail's pace of everything in Frankfurt.

Send me a detailed note.

My best to your wife.

Get well.

When is Guttmann back?

Your old   Joseph Roth

24. *To Bernard von Brentano*   *29 November 1925*

Dear friend,

let's start with your affairs:

1. I've checked with R., I *won't* be able to hear you speak in Offenbach. The paper doesn't run to that kind of thing.

2. Reifenberg will bring up your 5 mss. with Nassauer.[1] There shouldn't be a problem.

3. Come here, I would be delighted. So would Reifenberg.

4. Your articles will be out soon. The film [piece?] wouldn't fit in the politics [section?].

As for me, or rather my book,[2] I've withdrawn it, and offered it to Dietz.[3] Thus far—it's too early still—no word. I wouldn't have left it with this lot for all the tea in China. R. once remarked it was a pity I'd already sold it. R. apparently upset about the rejection. Upset is about as good as it gets with him. The degree of his upset might have made a difference, but probably not much. I'm still not sure who turned it down, even though I know Dr. Claassen,[4] the editor. He's a little Galician Jewish egghead—with German education, formerly a tutor in Simon's employ. It's possible the decision was his. Everything is possible.

I've only had one conversation with Simon, which was chilly, almost hostile. He's depressed that he isn't allowed to spend any money. It's very hard for me to get a wage rise put through here. A freeze has been slapped on everything, the atmosphere in the firm is gloomy. I'm unable to suggest any more jaunts, they all cost money. There is as yet no Paris correspondent in place.[5] They are so desperate to make economies, they hope to find one who will double as a feuilleton writer, and all for 800 marks. I have half a mind to quit. Through my personal friendship with Nassauer, I might be able to get a few advances that I could earn out later. But I'm not looking for favors. I am looking for practical, material acknowledgment from the firm. But it's in no position now to treat itself to what it sees as a luxury.

I don't know what course is more sensible: to sit tight and get out of Germany, or to resign and stay out of Germany in less comfort. The whole *FZ* looks to me like a microcosm of Germany. My loathing for it is growing all the time. I don't have a publisher there, I don't have readers, I don't have recognition. But nor do I feel pain, because nothing makes me sad there; or disappointment because I have no hopes; or melancholy, because I am just cold and indifferent. It's snowing here constantly, the world looks like a German bakery, sugar-sweet and sickening. I have nothing to do with the landscape, nothing to do with this sky. Nor anything with the technology, with the paving stones and the construction of the buildings, with the society, with the art. It's very hard to change anything in the feuilleton. They keep running German nature scenes, they pile up here, and they're all taken. It's only really when I'm here that I see how poorly we fit in. I've given up the struggle. There's no point. I just want to finish my Jewish book.[6]

The German brutality of your chauffeur is no worse than the German mildness of the culture. There's nothing to choose between them.

Cultural Germany lies between Ullstein[7] on the one side and the *FZ* on the other. God punish it![8]

We'll see each other over a glass of wine.

Shall I book you a room?

Kiss your wife's hand for me.

I remain your   Joseph Roth

Please, if you can, bring me as many of the *reviews* of me as you can lay hold of. I haven't looked up Mr. Stuffer yet. Why would I? I only ever get to see Binding.[9] Yet more Bindings?

1. Nassauer: Siegfried Nassauer (1868–1940). From 1906 on the board of the parent firm that included the *FZ*, the *Illustriertes Blatt*, and the book-publishing firm.

2. My book: the never published "The White Cities."

3. Dietz: a Berlin press, which published two novellas of JR's, *April* and *The Blind Mirror*, both in 1925 (see *Collected Stories*).

4. Dr. Claassen: Eugen Claassen (1895–1955), son of a Russian emigrant; not a Jew. Head of the book-publishing firm until 1934, when he started the Goverts Verlag with Henry Goverts, later Claassen and Goverts, and from 1950 the Claassen Verlag.

5. no Paris correspondent in place: and when there was, it wasn't Roth, to his enormous chagrin.

6. My Jewish book: *The Wandering Jews* (1927).

7. God punish it: a bold variant on the German World War I refrain *Gott strafe England*!

8. Ullstein: Berlin "Konzernverlag"—synergetic and avowedly capitalist combination of a book-publishing house with many newspapers and magazines, among them the *Vossische Zeitung* and the *Berliner Zeitung*. Erich Maria Remarque's *Im Westen Nichts Neues*—for decades the best-selling book of all time—was published by Ullstein in 1929.

9. Binding: Rudolf Binding (1867–1938), poet and short story writer.

25. To Bernard von Brentano   *Frankfurt, 19 December 1925*

Dear friend,

don't waste your time thinking useless and foolish thoughts. Dr. Kracauer[1] is a poor wretch. Once every ten years he's given his head, and is allowed to visit Berlin for a week or just a weekend, but—on account of his speech impediment and his un-European appearance—he's never allowed to represent the paper abroad. He has a clever and ironical mind with no imagination, but in spite of so much understanding he remains naïvely likable. Help him to the best of your ability, take him under your wing, and you'll be able to learn a lot from him. I myself am always learning from him, I just muster the patience to wait for half an hour while he stammers out his pearls of wisdom. It's worth it, believe me.

You say something about some woman or other you claim to be in love with. This condition is known to be delusory, and ends in bed, just as pink elephants go away when you have a drink. Just call a spade a spade and I'll understand you better. If you want to sleep with her, don't come telling me you're in love with her. I might have believed it from Clemens Brentano, but not from Bernard. That's "literature"—i.e., unworthy of a writer. You must never take a woman as seriously as, say, mounting debts. Only the latter can make us lose a night's sleep. I am sufficiently old-fashioned as to hold marriage—not that I overestimate that either—in higher regard than "love." In marriage, coition isn't the be-all and end-all, rather it's a whole string of intercourse, which may as much take the form of looks and conversations, as that of so-called physical union. I appreciate that it's upsetting not to have one's way with a woman. But a fat man put on a diet by his doctor is much more upset, and with far more substantial reason. If you can unmask your "love" as a minor irritation, your unhappiness will be greatly reduced.

That's the sort of low rationalist I am.

You say some pleasant and confusing things about my influence on you and your development. Evidently, it's still insufficiently strong, while you continue to make such tangled confessions. A clear profanity would suit me better. And you as well. It's not only when one has nothing to say that one should shut up, but also when one is unable to express it clearly. You will never attain artistic perfection unless, at the instant you reach for your pen and paper, you are as sober as if someone had emptied a bucket of cold water over your head. Your job is to communicate, don't forget. Even your dim semi-lucid states have to be expressed clearly. In Germany they don't set much store by that. Only the stammerers are great poets in Germany. But you, like me, are a favorite of reason. Remain true to her, and don't allow yourself to be seduced by the wiles of sweet German pain. You'll make—fail to make—your way in life, just like me. But you'll have your satisfaction.

Reifenberg went to Munich today. He's staying till Wednesday.

Fill a couple of columns with Christmas stuff. Facts, rather than reflections. No preamble. Start in medias res. Let me have them soon, and I'll be able to get them set, without anyone's vetting them.

Keep me in mind, not in heart, and don't go crazy as a result.

Kiss your dear wife's hand for me.

Your old　　　Roth

1. Siegfried Kracauer (1899–1966) was on the staff of the *Frankfurter Zeitung* in Frankfurt and Berlin. Went into exile in 1933 in Paris, from 1941 in New York. Novelist, biographer, film theorist, and historian.

26. *To Bernard von Brentano*　　　*Frankfurt, 30 December 1925*

Dear friend,

thank you very much for your Christmas letter and present. You'll understand, I waited before writing back. Well, as far as you're concerned, Reifenberg says you can go whenever you like. I seem to remember your saying you wanted to be back ca. 11 January. There are no obstacles from the board. It's possible to get an advance from Dr. Geisenheyner.[1] Only you haven't yet let him have the story he's bought—he mentioned it to me a couple of days ago. Send it to him now, and with an accompanying letter. The best thing is pick up the advance while you're here. G. is a primitive-sensuous type, your presence, in person,[2] will be a big facilitator. Till then you can take out a loan on the money from Frau Sternberg.

There are some strange goings-on here. As far as I'm concerned, I'm going to have to remain here probably till the end of January. I don't know what I'll be doing after that either. Maybe I'll tour a few German cities. Paris is rather doubtful now, it seems. Dewall,[3] who's in charge of foreign affairs here, has proposed Sieburg,[4] instead of Reifenberg's candidate, Lachmann.[5] It's very hush-hush, not even Reifenberg must know that you know. There may be some anti-Semitic feeling against Lachmann from Dewall. There are no other candidates. Basically, Sieburg, who's not a political journalist by training, would be another writer. Apparently a better writer than he is a character. They still haven't made up their minds. Anyway, my Paris stint is under threat, because the firm would say, why have more than one feuilletonist, if he can do political reports as well. I told Reifenberg I wasn't going to stand idly by while they pulled the rug out from under my feet. He thought I ought to go on the road and do some work. But of course I am far too worried to leave the building, now there's all these rumors flying around. For the first time in his life Nassauer's ill. I heard from an indiscreet bank employee that he, Nassauer, applied for a loan, and was turned down. For the first time in its life, the *FZ* wants to borrow money, and isn't able to. I see in that the malice of the banks, trying to teach an independent paper a lesson. The paper's teetering on the brink. Should it move to the right? Throw in its lot with the hopeless Social Democrats? Democracy has vanished in a puff of smoke. Should it woo subscribers? Remain aloof, and let the subscribers come by themselves? The board is naïve, the editors rudderless. The last man, Naphtali[6] is leaving, and so is another young person, Dr. Marschek, and Feiler[7] wants to take his hat as well. They are the best rats this ship has to offer. Is it doomed to sink? Looks like it.

That's why there was no Christmas bonus. The company no longer turns a profit. It doesn't sell. No reason to call it names. The *BT*[8] can afford more than a fortnight's salary, because it's already been sold. Whereas we sell our own freedom in return for our bonuses—indirectly, of course.

With things as they are, it's bad if I stay, bad if I go. Then there's the fact that Reifenberg needs someone to hold his hand here. He's not quite a match for Diebold.[9] Geck[10] and Diebold annoy him, and in the end he's a rather haughty passive character, whose passivity may well win out, but only at the end of ten years. I wish we could just both leave. Think about it. This place lacks control and direction. I have no idea how that could be arranged. I really don't want to spend half my time in Berlin. All I know is that someone needs to be sitting with Reifenberg in his office, otherwise things will get worse. I've suggested guest writers as star turns. But with the stodginess of this outfit, there's no sense in even waiting for an answer. We could think of a plan and put it into effect by ourselves. If you were to turn up here one day instead of me, no one would say a thing. While everything's in the balance, it's still possible to get things done.

But I'm afraid it won't be like that forever, and once Guttmann's regiment has taken over, nothing will be possible any more. He's just hired another sergeant major. Gradually he's taking over the building. Nassauer's powers of attorney have been limited, and Lasswitz[11] is turning into a chief under one's very eyes. Today he's still glad of a smile and a friendly word from me, but who knows if that'll still be true the day after tomorrow? He complained to me about your standoffishness. I told him distinguished people were like that, and to prove it to him, I went in the next day to see Nassauer, who was out—as I knew he would be—and I was even more standoffish to him than you are, and told him grand people were painfully inhibited in matters of money, and that it took years of friendship to gain their trust. So he gets the picture, and I'm afraid next time you see him, he'll probably be all over you.

I keep a thousand ears pinned to the ground, I have confidants in every camp, and I'm noiseless as an Indian. Dr. Simon is in Berlin now, if you should run into him, treat him nicely.

Come soon, and kiss the hand of your dear wife.

I remain your old   Roth

1. Dr. Max Geisenheyner worked on the travel section of the *FZ*.

2. your presence, in person: a recurring idea with JR in these letters, where he connects it with the Austrian character. (See, for instance, no. 276.) I fancy it is just as true of JR, personally.

3. Wolf von Dewall (1882–1959) joined the staff of the *FZ* in 1916, correspondent in London and Ankara; after the war freelance journalist in Stuttgart.

4. Friedrich Sieburg (1893–1964), author, poet, essayist, translator. Correspondent for the *FZ* from 1923 to 1942. After 1942 press attaché in Paris for the Nazi envoy Abetz. From 1948 to 1955 co-editor of the magazine *Die Gegenwart*; after 1956, literary editor of the *Frankfurter Allgemeine Zeitung*. It was probably the greatest disappointment of JR's life that he was passed over for the Paris job in favor of Sieburg in 1925–26.

5. Kurt Lachmann, journalist. Went into exile in 1933. After the war, was a correspondent for *U.S. News & World Report* in Bonn.

6. Fritz Naphtali (1888–1961), business editor of the *FZ* from 1921 to 1927.

7. Artur Feiler (1879–1943), business editor from 1903 to 1909, domestic political editor from 1910 to 1930.

8. *BT*: the *Berliner Tageblatt*.

9. Dr. Bernhard Diebold (1886–1945), theater critic for the *FZ*, who in 1934 returned to his native Switzerland.

10. Dr. Rudolf Geck (d. 1936), feuilleton editor on the *FZ*; at the paper since 1898. Credited with first having brought JR to the *FZ*.

11. Erich Lasswitz (1880–1959), technical director and writer for the *FZ* from 1918 to 1943. Roth sometimes strikes one as the only Indian, among this collective of chiefs, and less able to make his way than he proudly/overweeningly thinks.

27. To Bernard von Brentano   [undated]

Dear friend,

you fell for the fool's mate, because you were working on the false assumption that the Schmiede was going to be even more stupid than it actually was. I read the carbon of your letter, there's nothing in it but my address. You shouldn't have even started talking to those idiots. Now it's finished. We'll have to just let them write. I don't care. I'm past the stage where I would give them anything of mine—even if it was the last thing I wrote in German. Please tell me, more precisely, what your conversation with them was. That's not a reproach to you, but a lesson. You haven't yet got that Jewish cunning, with which it's possible to keep an entire country at bay. But you might need to have it one day. Above all, *learn to speak less*.

If you're doing badly, so am I. I want to send my wife to Paris, while I go on my German tour. I'm going to be spending some 3 or 4 weeks in the Ruhrgebiet,[1] and probably go to Paris once that's done. I'm skint. I can't get by, never mind how much I earn. Germany is making me ill. Every day I feel more hatred, and I could choke on my own contempt. Even the language is loathsome to me. A country's provinces give it away like nothing else. The fake elegance, the loud voices, the yahoos, the silence, the respect, the impertinence. There is a sort of unfreedom in these people that is worse than the subordination in front of a sergeant major. I understand that the rest of Germany kowtows to Prussia. It has one method: to distract people from their lack of inner freedom by external impositions. The way you make your toothache better by slapping your face.

I saw Dr. Simon. We concluded a sort of truce. He admitted he was slightly afraid or wary of me. I suspect that hasn't entirely vanished. We were somewhat reconciled. We talked about your brother.[2] He made a very good impression, albeit still a "Catholic-Jesuitical" one. Simon feels a degree of suspicion of him too. Suspicion will always accompany admiration in him. I understand it very well, and let it pass, having encountered it a thousand times myself.

My dear friend, I'm becoming more and more solitary.[3] More manifest in the details of life, in matters of taste, food, clothing, restaurants, and pleasures than in questions of principle or philosophy. Sometimes I catch an echo of it from Reifenberg. Even my wife is withdrawing from me, for all her love. She is normal, and I am what you'd have to call insane. She doesn't react as I do, with vehemence, with trembling, she's less sensitive to atmosphere, she is sensible and straightforward. Anything and everything is capable of provoking me. The conversation at another table, a look, a dress, a walk. It's really not "normal." I'm afraid I'm going to have to forswear society, and break off all ties. I no longer believe anything I'm told. I see through a magnifying glass. I peel the skins off people and things to see their hidden secrets—after that, you really can't believe anything. I know, before the object of my scrutiny knows, how it will adapt, how it will evolve, what it will do next. It might change utterly. But my knowledge of it is such that it will do exactly what I think it will do. If it occurs to me that someone will do something vicious or low, he goes and does it. I am becoming dangerous to ordinary decent people because of my knowledge of them.

It makes for an atrocious life. It precludes all of love and most of friendship. My mistrust kills all warmth, as bleach kills most germs. I no longer understand the forms of human intercourse. A harmless conversation chokes me. I am incapable of speaking an innocent word. I don't understand how people utter banalities. How they manage to sing. How they manage to play charades. If only the traditional forms still applied! But the new informality in Germany kills everything. I can't participate. All I can do is talk very cleverly with other very clever people. I am starting to hate decency, where—as is so often the case—it's paired with limited intelligence. The merely decent are beginning to hate me back. It can't go on. It can't go on.

My novel is coming along.

I got an invitation to join Döblin's group.[4] I will accept it in a noncommittal way, out of politeness. I don't want any ties to German writers. Not one of them feels as radically as I do. Read my essay on Döblin. I think it will offend him. I can't help it. Ask him about it sometime.

Say hello to Dr. Simon. I wrote to Guttmann yesterday.

Write me at the office. I am leaving this week. If I get enough money, I'll look you up in Berlin. Otherwise I'll be there in about three weeks.

Your old friend

I'm off.

1. Ruhrgebiet: the industrial sector in western Germany. From 1923 to 1925, it was under the occupation of the French, exasperated by the German nonpayment of reparations (this was during the time of the inflation). Roth wrote a series of reportages from there. See also no. 29.

2. brother: Heinrich von Brentano (1904–1964). German foreign minister from 1955 to 1961.

3. more and more solitary: cf. the dangerously detached Franz Tunda, the hero

of Roth's 1927 novel, *Flight Without End*, which is also the novel that is described as "coming along."

4. group: the "Gruppe 1925," a Marxist discussion club, whose secretary was Rudolf Walter Leonhard, and whose members included Johannes R. Becher, Bertolt Brecht, Albert Ehrenstein, Egon Erwin Kisch, Kurt Tucholsky, and Alfred Döblin. Not a natural or congenial habitat for Roth.

28. To Bernard von Brentano   *[undated]*

Dear friend,

thank you so much for your letter. I wish you would always write with such detail and clarity. Today I got your piece on the blown-up building. It's not outstanding, but it is journalism. In such pieces I miss information. The number of workers, the buildings on either side, the neighborhood and its social setting.

Your visit to Frankfurt will probably encounter difficulties. I haven't discussed it with Reifenberg yet.

Nor can I tell you whether I'm coming to Berlin or not.

I want to turn down your suggestion regarding the *Modeblatt*. I have no desire to take on the goodness of your mother and your family for an organ I've never even seen. I don't think it's quite right. Not even with your permission. The sort of journalism that makes profit ("tacheles") from a chance personal relationship seems dubious to me. There is only one person who can take this thing on, whether for the *FZ* or the *Modeblatt*, which is you. I don't understand why you didn't do it long ago anyway.

From your wife's letter I see that Landau did come in useful. In matters of health and money, prominent Jews are always a good idea. Jewish doctors are a sort of atonement for the crucifixion.

Will you tell me what Florath is up to.

Call Reifenberg about Diebold.

Neither with Reifenberg nor anywhere else in the Lothar[1] establishment did I come upon any favor for the idea of your visit. It wouldn't greatly matter anyway. I've been there, and heard a lot. The party was arranged for and partly by Simon. It was my first experience of the Frankfurt *haute volée*. Seven counts were of the company, Unruh[2] drank champagne in an exclusive circle. Jewish and Christian bankers behaved abominably. Their wives were whores *manquées*, dreadful informality for all their efforts to stay among themselves and in costume. Panic at the approach of any outsiders. A fancy dress ball where everyone pretended not to know one another, and where all those who wanted to, rapidly got acquainted. A few didn't—and remained tiddly ridiculous outsiders. I was the only one with more pride than the counts and bankers. I sat there silently. Simon crept around me, my look drove him away, he saw bombs ticking in my eyes. A stench of living bourgeois corpses.[3] For at least a day Simon hated me. If our relationship takes account of this development, I will leave the paper.

No, my dear Brentano, this isn't a society where I want to be known and read. The aristocracy is visibly subservient to industry, industry to the banks, and turn about. It's a world dying of ugliness. If the Andrä society in Berlin is anything like that, I want no part of it. I'm afraid I'm right. These people will cling to power for another 5 years. Their manners gave them power over the proletariat. Now they themselves are unmannerly plebeians. Proles have better taste.

As of yesterday my hatred of the country and its rulers has grown considerably. I am bound to leave it.

Your old   Roth

Kiss your wife's hand. Get well!

---

1. Lothar: Hans Lothar, relative of Heinrich Simon's, working on the *FZ*.

2. Unruh: Fritz von Unruh (1885–1970), playwright, novelist, essayist. Pacifist after World War I. Went to live in France and Italy in 1932, in New York from 1940. Wrote an autobiography, *The General's Son*, in 1957.

3. living bourgeois corpses: see the ferocious party scene in *Flight Without End*, based on such experiences. JR in those days was like an open knife, a mixture of prophet, revolutionary, and sociopath.

29. To Bernard von Brentano   *Kaiserhof, Essen, 11 February 1926*

Dear friend,

your letter of the 6th was forwarded to me here today. By now you will have spoken with Reifenberg, and you will know my views on editing. But just in case, let me say again: it goes against the grain of journalism to forbid an editor to make cuts. Since I fought for this principle the whole time I was in Frankfurt, I can't very well turn around and say you shouldn't be cut. (It wouldn't do much for you either.) Not only is it right to cut and to make changes, I see it almost as an imperative. Of the 40-odd pieces I've written, maybe ten appeared "unshorn." You are no soloist, you're a choir member. You toe the line. In questions of detail, you can argue the toss if you like. But in principle you are duty bound to submit. Perhaps, with your jealous love of every single line you write, you will become a brilliant poet, but you'll never make a half-decent journalist. The subject of your article is sacred to you. Your article is means to an end. Your subject and you, the writer, are more important than your article. As much more as you are more than the air you breathe out. As far as your latest piece is concerned, it wasn't any good. Kracauer cut it. He was right to. It was loose, inorganic, the description of a path, but not the path itself. You have good ideas, good images, good turns of phrase. But they don't grow together. Your pieces are chain links without any coherence. Read French feuilletons, read Heine's prose. Learn about natural transitions. Your spade was the best piece of yours I've read. In poems, atmosphere and rhythm fuse loose things together. In so-called prose, the context must make the atmosphere.

My wife is in Paris, Hotel de la place de l'Odéon. I'm about to go on the road for a few weeks. With no money. It's terrible to set off in such a state, I'm desperate, I can't forsake my expensive habits, and the newspaper is economizing, and economizing horribly. It's no fun any more, I haven't even had an advance for March, I have no contract, I am inconsolable.

It's not pretty in the Ruhr, Nationalist like everywhere, or still worse, in Cologne. Everything is red-white-and-black, all the cinemas are showing Nationalist trash, the "black shame"[1] is proclaimed on every street corner, "the enemy is gone," our culture is under arms.

Tell Dr. Guttmann, to whom I send regards, I've written to him already.

Write to me at my old Parisian address, or at the newspaper, it'll be forwarded to me either way.

Don't take my strictures amiss. You are the only young person I have any regard for, don't go fishing for compliments from the clientele at Schwannecke's,[2] you shouldn't trust compliments anyway. If you don't live up to your own standards, no amount of compliments will help. Don't write letters in your initial excitement. Leave it for 24 hours, if you're still excited.

I didn't write to Döblin, who's not the president of the association, but to Rudolf Leonhard, who was responsible for inviting me. Between ourselves, it's no advantage to belong to such a club. There are people in it I despise. I told Leonhard that I wondered if I could praise an association whose task it was to get all decent people to emigrate. The state is not just Gessler's[3] and Stresemann's[4] and Gerhart Hauptmann's,[5] but also Heinrich Eduard Jacob's,[6] Alfred Kerr's,[7] and Rowohlt's,[8] and there's nothing in it for us.

Let's meet up when I have money again. Keep me posted.

Your old   Joseph Roth

1. "black shame": an allusion to the Nationalist campaign against the African soldiers who were a prominent part of the French occupying force in Germany left of the Rhine.

2. Schwannecke's: rather preening literary café in Berlin in the 1920s, just off the Kurfürstendamm. See JR's feuilleton "At Schwannecke's," in *What I Saw*.

3. Otto Gessler (1875–1955), German defense minister from 1920 to 1928.

4. Dr. Gustav Stresemann (1878–1929). German chancellor in 1923, foreign minister from 1923 to 1929. Responsible for the Locarno treaties in 1925, and shared the Nobel Peace Prize in the following year.

5. Gerhart Hauptmann (1862–1946), playwright, novelist, essayist. It seems the first three names here meet with Roth's approval—or at any rate are figures of substance—and the second three not.

6. Heinrich Eduard Jacob (1889–1967), writer, biographer, essayist.

7. Alfred Kerr (1867–1948), the other well-known theater critic of the day (with Ihering).

8. Rowohlt: Ernst Rowohlt (1887–1960), founder of the publishing house bearing his name; it was situated first in Berlin, and after the war in Hamburg.

30. To Benno Reifenberg   *Paris, 29 March 1926*

Dear friend,

at last, spring has come to France, and our meteorological soothsayer, the abbé Gabriel, is said to have predicted fine weather for Easter. Come and visit, there are plenty of things we can do! We can take the boat to Sèvres, past the irrigated fields of Asnières, and Sèvres-Ville d'Avray, where Gambetta died and Balzac lived. We can visit the grand, famous, and now verdant park at St. Cloud, more of an aristocratic wood, really, stand on the plateau from where one can look over the whole of Paris, the cheerful squirming of its chimneys, and the stately, dignified, and happy dance of its towers. Would you like to go to Versailles, Malmaison, St. Germain? Would you like to see the old cathedral of St. Denis? Wherever you go, you will find the earth drenched with history, a cultivated nature that, with proud grace, has yielded to human wishes; humane landscapes, endowed with common sense; paths that seem to know themselves where they are going; hills that seem to know their own height; valleys that can dally with you.

There will be many people too. Charabancs take inquisitive Englishmen all around the outskirts of Paris, travelers of the kind we are familiar with, who need to feel they have understood something to enjoy it, and can't in any case enjoy it without taking a photograph of it. It might be an idea, therefore, to head out to Normandy, by way of Rouen. It's really not far! If we're at the St. Lazare Station at ten o'clock on Good

Friday morning, we can lunch in Rouen at noon, with a view of the cathedral, the lean singing central tower of Rouen Cathedral, the old medieval city, whose bells are very powerful and very distant, and whose streets and lanes are of a bright and cheerful narrowness, of the sort one finds only in French towns.

And two hours after that, we'd find ourselves in Le Havre, the second-biggest port in France. We'd tour the old harbor together, where the little bars are: where the carousels turn, and the dance halls are packed, and where you can win—or lose—a lot of money. Then we can go on a walking tour of Normandy. People will stop and stare. Because in this country, no one goes anywhere on foot, even though the roads are as fine and smooth as parquet floors. The livestock will be grazing in the fields. Every hour, we will hear the chimes of Lisieux, Honfleur, and Pont-l'Evèque. By night, the searchlights of Le Havre stroke the dark countryside like silver hands. And always, the song of the sea.

I think we'll go to Deauville, the very ritzy, still empty, and in any case boring spa town. From there, there's a direct express to Paris. Four hours.

There, doesn't that sound good to you? Come, and come soon![1]

Your Joseph Roth

1. Reifenberg had this letter printed—see no. 33—in the Easter supplement of the *FZ*, on April 4, 1926; it is included in *Report from a Parisian Paradise*.

31. Benno Reifenberg to Joseph Roth   *Frankfurter Zeitung, editorial*
   Frankfurt am Main, 7 April 1926

Dear Mr. Roth,

I have much to thank you for, *Le Sourire*[1] and the American magazine; for your punctual Easter letter which I took personally, even though I went ahead and printed it in the newspaper; for your continuing work on the Ruhrgebiet, and the "private lives of workers"; and now for your reportage from the battlefields. I would put it to you that you change the title from "Don't Forget the Battlefields" to: St. Quentin, Perronne, La Maisonnette.[2] That gives the piece a geographical title that is a continuation of my Champagne. Hermann Wendel is writing on Verdun. In any case, I don't think the title "Don't Forget the Battlefields" is a great loss.

Dear Mr. Roth, I won't have to tell you that your departure from our newspaper is the gravest blow I have experienced in the course of these early years. I was simply *counting on you*. I need the work of men of my generation with whom I can communicate effortlessly, with whom I share ideas that I have grown up with. I would see it as a defeat if your name were now to appear in Berlin newspapers. I have said as much to the firm, and ask that you believe me when I tell you that the firm shares my view, and is very concerned to reach a solid understanding with you. If you think the suggestion that you go to Italy was a refuge, a pis aller, then you are right inasmuch as the firm is really in a tricky position with you. When they took on Mautner, they did give you a fairly firm guarantee of Paris. Then, through the physical incapacity of Mautner, which emerged only later, it was forced to take on Dr. Sieburg. It's not altogether that they don't want to send Dr. Sieburg, a noted feuilletonist, as you yourself concede, together with you to Paris. But the firm wants to keep you on at the newspaper, and your name to appear in it, come what may. Given the pithy way that you write, the dateline or subject matter of your pieces is always a secondary concern. If therefore Italy does not agree with you, I have been asked to put the following proposal to you: the firm is ready to send you as a feuilleton correspondent to Moscow, and is also prepared to send you to Spain for a time. True, we have an elderly correspondent in Spain, but he writes little or nothing any more, and we have little sense of contemporary Spain. This last proposal comes from Mr. Schotthöfer. The proposal relating to Moscow may be more attractive to you. There is, admittedly, the question whether your knowledge of Russian is good enough. You personally, Schotthöfer insists, would not only experience no difficulties, you would be received with great warmth. I still cling to the idea of Italy as the best suggestion. The problem of Mussolini and Fascism is internationally acute, and it will be a question of identifying the national component of Fascism. To date, we have heard far too little from Italy.

I would like to add (and Brentano will bear me out) that Sieburg is very unhappy about the way that he and you have by force of circumstance been turned into rivals. To my mind, Sieburg is very frail, and uncertainty has made him adept. I don't quite trust him on the surface, but I do truly believe that among the few genuine sentiments he is capable of is the desire to get along with people of your stamp.

I now must ask you to let me know your decision soon. Sieburg starts in Paris on 1 May. It would be ideal if you could keep us supplied with occasional short pieces and news stories throughout April. We are rather too insular, and have nothing about France in the newspaper. Yesterday we ran a report that 350,000 French war veterans demonstrated for Locarno, we should have been able to offer a little background on such a story.

I wish you well, and remain with warm greetings and in expectation of a speedy reply your Reifenberg

1. *Le Sourire*: a Paris-based humorous paper.
2. St. Quentin, Peronne, Maisonnette: see *Report from a Parisian Paradise*.

32. *To Bernard von Brentano*   *8 April 1926*

Dear friend,

you write me bafflingly unclear and ill-conceived letters. I worry about you. You are in a bad way, I know, Frankfurt and the firm are to blame. But you must be stronger than your surroundings at all times; remember that.

Don't worry about a hotel or spa. There are plenty of rooms, it's enough if you write me 4–5 days before you come, no earlier, no later. Most likely you have different standards than I do where hotels are concerned, but you can always move. There are plenty of quiet places on the map, some in Brittany come to mind, which Professor Hensard told me about. Just see that you get here!

As far as my position is concerned, you are entirely mistaken. You think I fear having Sieburg in Paris as a rival, whereas the situation is that the firm is compelling me to leave Paris. They won't *let* me stay there. I informed Reifenberg of my decision to stay in Paris, and leave the paper. Now the publisher proposes Italy, Spain, or Moscow, doesn't seem to be that shaken about my departure. I'm not keen to go to Ullstein, though I could. Stahl would like to have me. I don't want to surrender to the firm that has treated me badly. I don't want to turn down Moscow just like that either. I am thinking my position through very carefully.

That, for your information, is how things stand. Mr. Reifenberg doesn't seem to have told you. I don't know if he has a reason for keeping his correspondence with me secret, but I don't think so. I am writing this to put you in the picture. In any case, my trust in this Jewish firm is shaken, and nothing remains but my friendship with Reifenberg. I know he will get old and gray before he achieves anything here, and that he himself has no idea how little he has achieved. I only hope he doesn't have a bad awakening one of these days. He is anything but careful.

Give him my regards, tell him—which is true—that friendship has compelled me to share this with you, and try to be calmer and not so nervous and fidgety when you next write,

to your old   Roth

33. To Benno Reifenberg   *9 April 1926*

Dear Mr. Reifenberg,
thank you very much for your long letter, which must have been as hard for you to write as mine was for me. I am terribly cast down, I can't answer you yet, I beg you for *around 8–10 days' grace.* To leave you behind in the firm is like leaving a brother on the field. Believe me! You have

no idea how much I stand to lose in both personal and career terms if I have to leave Paris.

Change the title of my piece; change the content too, if you like. I came up with the title as a nod to yours. As of and by itself it's not very good. The article isn't very good either, by my standards. I have just now written and mailed you a good one, about Paradise.[1] I hope you print it soon—or not, after all, what does it matter?

How is your heart, and how is Jan?[2] Write me a *personal* line or two. There is nothing so cruel as having a friend in an editorial office. The friendship of the poor! You hear the chains rattle.

Be well! Paris is warm and lovely! (Won't you come here spontaneously?) My letter was meant personally, you understood . . .

Your very old   Joseph Roth, I will call myself Moses[3] from now on, just so

1. Paradise: see the feuilleton "Report from a Parisian Paradise" on the pleasures of, *entre autres*, calvados.
2. Jan: the Reifenbergs' son, after whom Roth almost always asks fondly.
3. Moses: a prime expression of JR's variable identity.

34. To Benno Reifenberg   *22 April 1926*

Dear Mr. Reifenberg,

I'm going to give you my answer today, and beg you to forgive me for having taken longer than I said. I am ill and in bed, my handwriting won't be distinguished, my style not very accomplished.

Let me tell you once again that leaving you and the *FZ* concerns me more than taking a job at Ullstein, for example. I'll be perfectly candid, and admit to you that I'd rather not write at all, than write for another paper.

The fact that the firm wants Mr. Sieburg in Paris—that's not for me to comment on. But sending me packing from Paris, because Mr. Sieburg doesn't want me there, *that* hurt.

Mr. Sieburg is an excellent feuilleton writer. Do I therefore have to suffer because a feuilleton writer decides to try and double up as a political correspondent? You can't write feuilletons with half a mind or one hand tied behind your back. And it's *wrong* to write feuilletons *on the side*. It's a bad underestimation of the whole *profession*. The feuilleton is just as important to the paper as its politics—and to the reader it's even more important. The modern newspaper is made of everything else in it before it's made of politics. The modern newspaper needs a reporter more than it needs a leader writer. I am *not* an encore, not a pudding, I am the main dish. Why won't people stop kidding themselves that a fancy-pants article on the situation in Locarno will grip readers and win subscribers. If Mr. Sieburg is to write mainly feuilletons, then I don't see why I shouldn't equally well have remained your Paris correspondent. I won't be gotten rid of just because it happens to suit a colleague. It's like a curse: how can the *FZ* not manage to retain two such gifted journalists as Mr. Sieburg and me.

I love this paper, I serve it, I am useful to it. No one asks my opinion when it occurs to someone to have me removed from Paris. They read me with interest. Not the parliamentary reports. Not the lead articles, not the foreign bulletins. But the firm persists in thinking of Roth as a sort of trivial chatterbox that a great newspaper can just about run to. Wrong. I don't write "witty glosses." *I paint the portrait of the age.* That ought to be the job of the great newspaper. I'm a journalist, not a reporter; I'm an author, not a leader writer.

I asked for a contract. Stenographers and telephonists get contracts—I don't. I asked for a raise. My pay is among the lowest in the company. I submit a book. It's turned down. Since I've been with the *FZ* it seems to me, the only respect I've encountered has come from rival papers. It really is an art to take someone as willing, and useful, and loyal as me, and alienate him.

Of your various suggestions: Moscow, Italy, and Spain, only Moscow is an adequate replacement for Paris, though I don't want to rule out the others. You will understand that my reputation as a journalist is paramount to me. It will be damaged by my departure from Paris, and my replacement by Mr. Sieburg. Only a series of *Russian reportages* can rescue my good name.

Spain is journalistically uninteresting. Italy is interesting, Fascism less so. I take a different position on Fascism than the newspaper. I don't like it, but I know that one Hindenburg is worse than ten Mussolinis. We in Germany should watch our Reichswehr, our Mr. Gessler, our generals, our famous compensation program to landowners. We don't have the right to attack a Fascist dictatorship while we ourselves are living in a far worse, secret dictatorship, complete with *Fememorde,*[1] paramilitary marches, murderous judges, and hangmen attorneys. My conscience would never allow me, as an oppressed German, to tell the world about oppression in Italy. It would be a rather facile bravery to report behind Mussolini's back, and keep my head down in my homeland, and go on subsidizing the thugs of the Black Reichswehr with my taxes. While I mounted an attack on Fascism in my feuilleton, in the political pages they might just about risk a mild whispering against Mr. Gessler. That's cowardice, as I see it.

I propose: Russia until winter, not just Moscow, but Kiev and Odessa as well; and in the winter Spain and Italy under some other aspect.

Manfred Georg[2] is going to America for the *8 Uhr Blatt*. Kisch[3] is going to Russia for the *BZ*. I can't be seen to do any less than them. There is so much going on in Russia, one doesn't have to write about the Communist terror. The presence of so much new life springing up from the ruins will give me a lot of unpolitical material.

Will you please ask Mr. Schotthöfer—and my greetings to him— what I need to obtain a Russian visa. My skin disease will take another 3 weeks or so to heal. Till that time, I would like some time in which to convalesce.

That's what I propose. I hope the company won't need to think twice, this time. I'd like a speedy answer.

With best wishes I remain

Your old   Joseph Roth

1. *Fememorde*: "Vehmic murderers"—an anthropological label from the Dark Ages for these political killings that appear in a list of shameful manifestations in the Weimar Republic.

2. Manfred Georg (1893–1965), journalist and writer. Left Germany in 1933 for Prague, then 1938 to New York, where he founded and edited the German-language progressive Jewish weekly *Der Aufbau*.

3. Kisch: Egon Erwin Kisch (1885–1948), the so-called *rasender Reporter* (roving or racing or raving reporter), one of the most prominent journalists of the time, and possessor of a suitably adventurous life.

35. To Benno Reifenberg   *Café de la Régence*
                                              Paris, 29 April 1926

Dear Mr. Reifenberg,

thank you for your letter, and your kind words on my "Paradise."[1] Entirely undeserved. There was so much more that might have been said, and my feuilleton covers only a small part of Paradise. Tomorrow, I'll send you a couple of book reviews, and in the coming days a feuilleton on the preacher Samson.

I will answer your official letter tomorrow, officially, and for the firm. I have a few counterproposals, details that might mitigate my defeat, our defeat, if the company agrees to them. Thank Picard.[2] I'm going to see him tomorrow. It's too bad I can't go to Ullstein for 1,500 a month, and write for Monty Jacobs[3] instead of Benno Reifenberg. I would have to close my eyes and think of journalism, or else write for the *Frankfurter Generalanzeiger*. Even that is better than Ullstein. Plus I've suddenly come down with something "very nasty," a serious skin condition. For a while it looked "like syphilis," the blood test hasn't been done yet. I am completely covered with red boils, I can only go out after dark, can't shake hands, I'm completely slathered with sulfur, and stink to match. You wouldn't so much as spit at me, in spite of being my friend, because in addition to being good and distinguished, you are sensitive. This illness lasts for 4–5 weeks apparently, or it may do, dermatology is learning from me, and claims it is an illness associated with hair loss, and—in me, imagine—the END OF PUBERTY! It's God's revenge, praise be to Jehovah. I already have a mattress grave, and must leave Paris. Please will you see that I get paid, it's the end of the month already. My money for May. I'm writing a separate letter to the firm and to Mr. Nassauer. Regards to him! *Is he better?* Why does the firm ignore my appeals if it cares what happens to me? . . .

I am miserable, industrious, poor, and abandoned. It's a cold spring this year. I'm itching all over. I have to stay up and work at night to keep from scratching myself, and in the day I'm wretched. The doctor tells me it may start to improve tomorrow. I'll be relieved once my extremities are in the clear again. At least it's not infectious. I'm proud of that.

Who is Professor Salomon[4] from Frankfurt? He's been in Paris, telling everyone (telling Valeska Gert)[5] that I have the most modern style of any journalist around.

This letter will—I know—make you disgusted with me, but you should fight the feeling, that's what friendship is. Of the two of us, things are easier for me, because you are certainly a finer, handsomer—what a comparative—human being than your wretched old Moses Joseph Roth

I thought Kracauer's umbrella piece was delightful up until the last 2 paragraphs. The style of the evening edition is still not right: too small.

1. This is the feuilleton "Report from a Parisian Paradise." It is interesting that JR wrote it as he did, under threat of imminent dismissal.

2. Picard: Max Picard (1888–1965), doctor and cultural philosopher.

3. Monty Jacobs (1875–1945), editor of the feuilleton section of the *Vossische Zeitung* from 1910 to 1934, when he went into exile in London.

4. Professor Gottfried Salomon (1892–1964) was a sociologist at the University of Frankfurt.

5. Valeska Gert (1892–1978) was a "grotesque dancer."

36. To the Frankfurter Zeitung   *Paris, 2 June 1926*

Dear Sirs,

I hear that you of your kindness are deliberating as to where I should send my next dispatches from, and are tending to favor America against Russia. I don't think you are seriously afraid that I might convert to Bolshevism, but your line of thinking may be that the so-called New World would be inappropriate to my habitually satirical mode, and that I would be condemned either to supply optimistic reports in an access of youthful enthusiasm, or to clam up entirely.

I am grateful to be the subject of so much consideration. However, I would be sorry if you concluded that my specific gifts would incline me to ironize Western institutions, customs, and habits, following the doubtful successes of the Russian revolution.

On the contrary: I am (perhaps unfortunately) wholly incapable of allowing any enthusiasm in me more space than my skepticism. I ask that you not infer from this "negative attitude" that I would substitute the deficiencies of one world view for those of another. I don't believe in the perfection of bourgeois democracy, but I don't doubt for a second the narrowness of a proletarian dictatorship. On the contrary, I believe in the terrible existence of a sort of "petty working class" if you'll allow the phrase, a species that would be still less inclined to allow me the freedom I require than its bourgeois cousins.

I am carrying none of the ideological baggage of the sort that most literary visitors to Russia have carried with them in the last few years. Unlike them, as a consequence of my birth and my knowledge of the country, I am immunized to what goes by "Russian mysticism" or "the great Russian soul," and the like. I am too well aware—as western Europeans are apt to forget—that the Russians were not invented by Dostoyevsky. I am quite unsentimental about the country, and about the Soviet project.

On this occasion let me admit—not to burden you with a full-blown confession—that my relationship to Catholicism and the Church is not at all as one might imagine, on the basis of a fleeting knowledge of my person, my essays, and even my books. That fact alone guarantees a certain distance, when it comes to things in Russia. Things that, incidentally, concern us more nearly than things in America. I get the impression that a certain useful calm has set in there, useful in the sense that people may finally be coming to terms with the recent past. I get a sense of things being about to change therefore in Russia, while America in a year's time will still be America, if not more so.

Since I report on actual conditions, depicting daily life rather than expressing opinions, the danger that I might be unable to send objective reports from Russia is not very great. Even in countries without censorship, my criticism was more to be found between the lines than on the surface of my pieces.

I will be greatly obliged to you if you were to see these depositions as a basis on which to make your decision.

Yours respectfully

Joseph Roth

37. To Benno Reifenberg 30 August 1926

Dear Mr. Reifenberg,

I am writing to you from the deck of a mail steamer on the Volga. I plan to stop in Astrakhan for a couple of days. I hope this finds you back in Frankfurt, having enjoyed your vacation. I shall be sending my first pieces to the paper from here, and would like you to read them as they come in. I know you won't read them after others have. I have been unable to write anything till now. I was overwhelmed, famished, continually shaking. It's taken me two months. If one were to set foot on a different star, things couldn't be more different or more strange.

I have no money. I need 42 marks per diem, excluding travel and the vast tips a visitor is obliged to leave. I am experiencing incredible things.

Almost more than I can put down, in terms of fullness and intensity. My illness is almost gone. I eat black bread and onions and for 3 or 4 days of the week, live like a peasant. The remaining days, admittedly, I spend in the best hotels I can find. I spent a week tramping on foot through Chuvash villages. I have been to Minsk and Byelorussia. I am now on my way to Baku, Tbilisi, Odessa, the whole Ukraine. A few newspapers greeted my arrival: "Revolutionary writer comes to Russia." Reviews of my books continue to appear. I have avoided doing anything officially sanctioned, even though most doors were open to me.

I live in the continual fear that it's all too much for the company. It's been paying me money since JULY and has received no copy. Perhaps you could set their minds at ease—and mine too!

Poland was in such an abject political and human state, that I've put off writing about it until I'm on my way back. I'm sorry to say that blasé German correspondents are not always wrong. For now, silence is the best policy for me.

There's no doubt that a new world is being born in Russia. For all my skepticism, I am happy to be able to witness it. It's not possible to live without having been here, it's as if you had stayed at home during the war.

Write and tell me what your dear wife is doing, and my friend *Jan*. I carry his picture in my wallet—any other photograph would be sentimental. Is he well?

In old friendship I shake your hand, and remain as ever

Your Joseph Roth

Picard didn't reply. I feel offended.

I haven't seen a copy of the newspaper for months. My permanent address is:

Moscow, Hotel Bolshaya Moskovskaya till October,

Thereafter c/o German Embassy for Joseph Roth, Frankfurter Zeitung

Moscow Leontyevsky pereulok 10

38. To Bernard von Brentano   *Odessa, 26 September 1926*

Dear friend,

you must be puzzled and irked and probably less puzzled than irked. Calm! Forgiveness! Today is the first day I have given myself off. Not that I have deserved it. I really ought to walk around and gather material and order it in my head, just exactly as I have on all my other days. I have never worked as hard as I have in Russia; and you know I have never been one for idleness. I shall be staying in Odessa for another two weeks; then through the rest of the Ukraine. At the end of October I'll be in Moscow again. You could write me Hotel Bolshaya Moskovskaya ca. 14 October, or here, Odessa, Hotel London, but only by airmail. An airmail letter takes 5 days—unless the censor happens to take an interest in it.

I feel as though I've been gone from Europe for six months. I've experienced so much here, and all of it strange to me. Never has it been brought home to me so strongly that I'm a European, a man of the Mediterranean if you will, a Roman and a Catholic, a Humanist and a Renaissance man. Everything I told you about myself in Paris was wrong, and a lot of what you told me *was right*. It's a boon that I've come to Russia. I should never have gotten to know myself otherwise. Finally I have the subject for the book that only I can write, and will maybe write while in Russia. It will be the novel I've waited for for so long,[1] and with me a couple of other people in the West as well. You would be amazed if I were to tell you the story. But you will get to read it in a year's time.

I hope my articles have got through and been printed. Write and tell me, if you will. The most important of them are still to come.

You know I'm a celebrity here. I enclose a clipping of an interview with me—it's as if I were an American shoe-polish king, or something. I am mobbed by journalists wherever I go. They don't always get things right, but I'd be the last person to object to a false echo, so long as it's just an echo. (Jesuit.)

Everything Toller[2] and Kisch have said about Russia is wrong. And all the attacks are not just unfair, but misplaced. It's like viewing a human residence through the eyes of a fly. I'm not talking about a positive or negative view of the Soviet states—I want to show you that both the positives and the negatives are completely wrong, because they are political. The issue here is not politics, the issue is culture, religion, metaphysics, spirituality. You will understand what I mean if you recall our conversations about Russia, and my exposition, and if you see the situation diagrammatically.

Me on Russia $\diagdown$ that's how I spoke then. Now I would speak
On Russia me $\diagup$ like this.

In other words, I am looking in a completely different direction. Russia is somewhere else. I was like a mariner from antiquity or the Middle Ages, setting off for the Spice Islands, in the persuasion that the earth was flat. If you know it's round, you know how mistaken the voyage was.

It's incredibly difficult to write newspaper pieces about Russia, unless you stick to processing other people's research, like Kisch. I won't do that at any price. You were right about that too, when you said the time for that sort of journalism was over. I'm glad you were right on those important things, and I was wrong. That shows me I judged you correctly, which pleases me more than merely being right about something.

I'd like to know what you're working on, how you're living. The *Frankfurter Zeitung* is nowhere to be found here, of course, unlike the *Vossische*, or the *Berliner Tageblatt*. Which means it has an incredibly exalted, if somewhat legendary, reputation.

Give my regards to Dr. Guttmann, I think about him sometimes and how useful his bitter clarity would be in reportages from Moscow. Scheffer from the *Berliner Tageblatt* enjoys an unfair prominence, as the one-eyed among the blind.

Regards to your wife, regards to Dr. Guttmann, and don't forget
Your old   Joseph Roth

1. The novel I've waited for for so long: perhaps the first glimmerings of *Job*?
2. Toller: Ernst Toller (1893–1939), prominent left-wing playwright, poet, essayist.

Leader of the Bavarian revolution in 1918, for which he was imprisoned for five years. It was news of the despondent Toller's suicide in New York that prompted Roth's final collapse in May 1939.

39. To Benno Reifenberg   *Odessa, 1 October 1926*

Dear Mr. Reifenberg,

it's hard to describe my pleasure on receiving your letter. A day ago I got an old letter (August) from Mr. Geck, asking—oh so discreetly— whether I was ill, why they had heard nothing from me. I gathered from that that 2 pieces I dispatched from Poland, and 1 letter and one book review have failed to arrive. It turns out that the Poles have an occasional, but then all the more inflexible, censorship. I wrote back right away, you'll see the letter, just asking for confirmation of arrival. I'd had a nightmare, namely that my articles on Russia were all appear- ing in the Bäderblatt.[1] It was a hideously real nightmare, my articles were on page 2, column 4, over a large ad for Bad Nauheim, and I was cross that the photograph of the Kremlin had been stuck on page 4. You said just one word: "misplaced!"—dolorously, as if on stage. Only one creature is endowed with dreams like that, namely a reporter on the *Frankfurter Zeitung*. I'm sure I'm more afraid of your restraint than you are of a scoop. What a happy awakening when your copies arrived, with that dignified, if rather flattering byline. Thank you! But isn't it too chancy to settle on a particular day? What if I have no ideas, can't write anything for 3 weeks? Have you got all 7 articles? The tenth is already done, I keep putting off making a fair copy, it's torture for me, I have to keep thinking about the blond sub with the academic qualification—geology, wasn't it? I dread misprints, two jumped up at me just now like fleas from the type.

It was very funny to read about your brother Hans. You nailed him in your article. I think of you calmly watching him, you must have been writing the piece in your head already. What material! I'm envious of both material and execution. It's an excellent piece in literary terms, almost a reportage, I can see you growing out of literature and becoming a proper journalist, and then Maryla will no longer be able to say "a smart journalist!"—How is she? Give her my regards! And your mother-in-law. You don't say anything about her, or JAN. I asked specially. What's Jan up to? How is he? Will he still recognize me? Or is he growing up too fast?

As I am myself. I won't stay as long as I thought I would. The money hurts. I would like to save it all, and spend all of it instead. I'm going to ask for damages for all the torments of this exotic journey in the Caucasus, on mule, bus, bumpy carts, for seasickness, mountain paths, Ararat—Leopold Weiss[2] rides on camelback and has his wife and child with him, and I'm dreaming of a room at the Frankfurter Hof. Oh, for running water! Hot and cold, telephone, ten bells, three lights, bathroom ensuite, fleecy towels, cars, white napkins. Hausenstein[3] asks whether there might be interest in Russia for his work on Rembrandt. I can't give him an answer at the moment, tell him it'll be another decade before they acquire an interest in Rembrandt. How little we know about Russia. Everything we say about it is mistaken. I read Lenin and Victor Hugo alternately, political authors both, chance purchases, cheap, secondhand editions. Perhaps it shows in my articles. Lenin is a great dialectical brain, Victor Hugo a great dialectical heart, and he writes a better style. I long for Paris, I have never given up on it, ever, I am a Frenchman from the East, a Humanist, a rationalist with religion, a Catholic with a Jewish intelligence, an actual revolutionary. What an oddity! (Please excuse this outburst!)

What's Dr. Simon up to? At this distance, he seems even stranger to me than he does in Germany. He is very much a Westerner, I think, the farther east I go, the farther west he seems to recede in my mind. The last time I saw him was in Paris, six months ago—five months—an eternity. Time is little, space is everything! I took his wife to Moulineux. How far Moulineux is from Russia . . .

1. Bäderblatt: literally the "bath" or "spa" paper. A low-brow, commercial supplement that features repeatedly in Roth's nightmares.

2. Weiss: Leopold Weiss (1900–1992), the *FZ*'s special correspondent in the 1920s. He converted to Islam ca. 1926.

3. Hausenstein: Wilhelm Hausenstein (1882–1957), art critic and essayist, worked for the *FZ* from 1917 to 1943. Later was the German ambassador in Paris.

40. To Bernard von Brentano   *18 October 1926, Moscow*

Dear friend,

I am back in Moscow, here for another two weeks, an airmail letter would reach me in time. In the German embassy I got an old letter of yours, with enclosure. Thank you for the feuilleton, it's good, in places very good, but unjournalistic, by which I mean it didn't have to be written. Journalism has little tolerance for an indirect form, i.e., the disguising of an observation or an event. Your letter attests to your needless nervousness. What you think about me is mistaken, what you think about my wife is triply mistaken. She doesn't dislike you. At the same time as yours, I got a letter from her where she wrote about the moving way you were waiting for my articles. (I quote: "B. is incredibly moving, the way he waits for your articles.")

It's been a while since I felt completely well. I think I'll leave Russia earlier than planned.

I hope you're well.

I shake your hand. Write soon   to your Joseph Roth

41. To Benno Reifenberg   *[October 1926?]*

Dear Mr. Reifenberg,

unfortunately I've mislaid the original of my article on petroleum. I want to ask you for certain reasons to cut the sentence where I refer to workers of the *Krupp dependencies.* If there's a lacuna, fill it. Please. The piece can come out after the one about the Jews, after or before, it doesn't matter: *The Street.*

For some weeks now, I've heard nothing from my friends. Even Brentano, to whom I wrote *an incredibly cordial letter, won't answer me.* I'd be sorry if things had gotten to that pass. I pride myself on not being wrong about people. Anything but that.

At this distance, everyone seems transformed anyway, all the Western men and Fräulein Weber as the prototypical Western woman. Only you remain tall and handsome, and Kracauer small and miserable. Dr. Simon, Geck, Diebold, Nassauer, Dr. Guttmann, and Rudolf Guthmann[1] look like mirror images to me, they loom out of the mercury. I see a framed Geisenheyner on a desk, resting his hand on the back of an armchair, Dr. Lothar is in the corridor, I can see him on the other side of the glazed door, he has lost weight, and is looking sporty in tennis shorts. For some reason, Max Beckmann[2] is often in my thoughts. His legs are stretched out in front of him as though he were sitting down, but he's standing up. I am going slightly potty, have vivid dreams, am living in tremendous isolation, in a state of not-hearing. Snow falls and melts, the wind blows, my feet are always wet, I've ordered a second pair of boots and will need a new wardrobe. I now have the ability to sit somewhere for two hours, and look at all the people, near and far, I wind them up, and they process past me, part of some mechanical toy. My wife is coming ever nearer, writing me strange love letters: lots of grumpy, dissatisfied, almost angry reviews of my articles. Perhaps she means *me* and doesn't know it. I must have become very sentimental. Hausentein is always turning his back on me. That offends me. You are closer to me as well, but generally chilly. Still a little objectivity. I am always on the point of giving in to you, but hesitate—a fox who's read Plato, the older Brentano put it. You have your hand extended but won't give it to me, your big hand. There's tension now between you and Kracauer. He is angry with me at some level. Because I'm in Russia. Cheers!

I'm working on a novel. I work very hard on my articles, writing them slowly and entirely subjectively. Each one takes me 3–4 days. Some I've torn up.

My isolation is enormous, unendurable. I need a letter now and again. People, people, all day long, politicians, journalists. No women. Hence the isolation. Nothing but men is like a desert full of sand. Lots of unimportant men. I've just been with Scheffer, the *BT*'s man in Moscow. A clever fellow, but something I don't quite like about him. He's too evangelical. He is married: a very nice, distinguished, no longer young Russian woman. She took him because her German isn't good enough to work him out. He took her because he knows next to no Russian, and sees her as something entirely different from what she is. And so they sleep together. How is it possible? I keep meeting foreign journalists and diplomats there. *All banal!* I get a lot of invitations. Don't speak a lot of Russian, but what I do say has a Slav accent, which makes me a miracle man. I'm getting vain in my old age. Tomorrow I'm going to visit a lady from the Old World, who has turned Communist. All sorts of people turn up there, and I'm very curious.

Presumably the party season is getting going in Germany. Do you remember the time when you, Kracauer, and I went to the Christmas market together? And you went to the watchmaker?[3] There is something terribly affecting about Germany when everyone goes soft, and the Jews decorate Christmas trees, and the theaters put on Christmas pantomimes.

Something astounding has happened: get this: my dear German professor, Dr. Brecht, who is going to Breslau now, hasn't written me in 6 years. At the time I was his student, I was a German nationalist, as he was. Of course I assume that as a result of what I've published, I assume he will have effaced me from his heart. Then in an old newspaper in the Caucasus, I read that he's turned 50. I write to congratulate him. And today the *FZ* forwards me a letter from him: he sends me his photograph. I was his student in 1912–13. He is completely unchanged. And he has just put me forward for a *prize for young authors*. He's read everything I've written. He is just tidying up, and he packs—he packs my papers I wrote for him as a student. HE'S PACKING THEM! He's taking them to Breslau with him! He put me up for scholarships then, and for prizes now. A German nationalist! Son of a professor, son-in-law of a professor, a friend of Roethe's![4] *There's a German professor for you.*

What do you say to that? The older you get, the better people become. At some level feeling is what counts. You can only hope to judge the Germans when you're past forty.

Alfons Paquet[5] is fondly remembered here. Give him my regards when he comes, with a greaseproof parcel in his briefcase that he leaves in the secretary's office. He picks up review copies of books, and needs packing paper for some purposes of his own.

I'd be grateful for a line, and send my sentimental greetings

Your Roth

1. Guthmann: Rudolf Guthmann, a manager on the *FZ*.

2. Max Beckmann (1884–1950), generally regarded as the greatest German painter of the twentieth century. He went into exile in Holland in 1937, and died in New York City. Reifenberg was a long-term admirer of the painter's, and wrote his biography. See also letter no. 136.

3. watchmaker: JR loved and collected (and gave away) watches. Watches and knives.

4. Roethe: Professor Gustav Roethe (1859–1926), Germanist.

5. Alfons Paquet (1881–1944), poet, dramatist, novelist, essayist. Traveled extensively, and wrote for the *FZ*.

42. To Benno Reifenberg   *23 April 1927*

Dear Mr. Reifenberg,

thank you for your letter. I'm late with my reply, because ever since Vienna I've been caught up in a steady stream of nasty banalities. The deal with the novel must have put you to so much trouble that I'm embarrassed to think about it—that, and the sheer impossibility of ever paying you back in important things what you expend on unimportant ones. What's depressing about having you as a guardian angel—as you are to several of us in that firm—is the fact that you achieve tiny results with colossal expenditure of effort. Your friendship deserves greater outcomes, just as your talents deserve a better and nobler setting. I am continually moved, but rarely assuaged. I know that a big part of Dr. Simon's decision was the consideration "you can't do that sort of thing to Roth" when even you know how little vanity I have, and how difficult it is to offend me.

Anyway, your proposal seems impractical to me. The novel—let's just say for the moment that it's a flawless piece of work—given that sort of publication will not only get no attention, but no interest, either from readers or from publishers. It will drop out of the structural, as we'd intended, and be left with the chance and circumstantial, which will do more harm than good. So, I'm against it—in favor only because I need money badly. But then something else comes into play: namely that I *don't think* the novel is at all flawless—this has nothing to do with the objection advanced above—and I am having to add another 40 pages or so of Parisian meat to the bones. I have been in negotiations with Ullstein about it. Kurt Wolff[1] has spoken to his director Meyer, whom I saw in Berlin, of the necessity of publishing me. Max Brod[2]—who will already have sent you his novel, which I started (in Prague) and endorse—has recommended me to Zsolnay.[3] If I accept your proposal, that means losing Ullstein. He's not yet decided—and I need money. I'm now embarked on another novel, which is going absurdly smoothly, a book with plot, tension, hooks, twists, something even suitable for the *Illustriertes Blatt*. I hope to bring it with me, completed. I would far prefer to have that appear as my novel with you. At any rate, you should send me money. I guarantee that you will have one novel manuscript.

I am flat broke. I was in the rotten position of having to take an advance from the *Prager Tagblatt*—I can't stand to travel on that basis. I am slow, thorough, full of fear that I might see something wrong, my so-called style is based on nothing but an exact understanding of the facts—I write badly without that—like Sieburg in the Easter issue. I don't have "ideas," only understanding. I am incapable of vacuous writing. I need

money, and won't be finished with the Balkans[4] till June. Four weeks is
not enough time to understand anything. Four weeks might do for *one*
reportage or lead piece. So I will have to live off my royalty, and when I'm
back, resume my campaign: either an unambiguous relationship with the
newspaper, or else 6 articles a month, free agent, small retainer. The firm
puts out a history of the age, not a newspaper, it has no idea of how to
treat a journalist. You've seen yourself how little the editors are able to do.
I won't spend another 3 months sitting in the Englischer Hof, twiddling
my thumbs. It's a waste.

I'll wire the address from Belgrade. I'll be there for 6–8 days. If you
have a moment, write me as soon as you get my wire.

Please tell the editorial conference that I won't be able to write anything about the Yugoslav–Italian conflict before my visit to Albania—for
fear of the trouble the Italians can make for me in Albania, where they
are effectively in control.

Best regards to Dr. Kracauer, and tell him his Parisian article caused
a real stir, and that people ask me about him—people in Berlin, Prague,
Vienna.

[. . .]

1. Kurt Wolff (1887–1963), publisher. In 1913 started the imprint bearing his own
name known mainly for bringing out Expressionist writers. The Kurt Wolff Verlag
was sold in 1931, and in 1933 Wolff went into exile, to Florence, Paris, then New York.
In 1942, he founded Pantheon Books with his former secretary and wife, Helen. (The
novel at issue here, *Flight Without End*, was duly published by Kurt Wolff.)

2. Max Brod (1884–1969), novelist, essayist, translator. Editor and friend (and execu-
tor) of Franz Kafka.

3. Zsolnay: the Paul Zsolnay Verlag, in Vienna.

4. the Balkans: Roth traveled to Albania for the paper and wrote a series of articles.

43. To Ludwig Marcuse
          Paris VI, rue de Tournon 23
          Hotel Helvetia
          Paris, 14 June 1927

Dear friend Marcuse,[1]

I owe you a long letter, but since I have only grim news to report, I'm going to keep this as short as I can. I was in Berlin, but didn't get to speak to anyone at Ullstein. Apparently it takes two weeks to get hold of anyone authorized to take a decision. So I decided to give it one last shot after my return here. Now Reifenberg has written to say he does want my novel after all. I made no great efforts therefore with Krell, the novel isn't for the *Vossische Zeitung*.[2] While I was away in Albania—as you know— Black Friday happened on the stock exchange.[3] Dr. Simon seems to have taken that very much to heart. Even though I'd only been furnished with 1,000 marks, they wired me to say they were sorry I hadn't written anything. It was a snotty, provincial, and wounded telegram, and hurtful too. I requested another 400 dollars—life is very expensive there. They wired me back that I'd had all I was going to get, the expenses account was empty, and I should come home. I got sick, got on a ship, I didn't have enough money to go via Berlin, I went straight back to Paris, sent them another rude wire, asking whether they'd meant to get rid of me, and whether that were still their intention. I came back from that trip with 14 articles, of which just 2 have appeared. I had no reply, no money, I expect I'm too expensive and too demanding for them—now that old Mrs. Simon has probably lost money on the stock exchange. I wrote to Kaliski[4] in Berlin, about Ullstein—no answer. I wrote to Lania,[5] about the *BC*[6]—no answer as yet. I am desperate, sick, penniless. I'm wondering whether to write to Dombrowski about Ullstein—whether he would write to Magnus, or whether I should wait for Kaliski to reply. The novel has gone to Kurt Wolff.

What now? Paris is more expensive than ever, I have a terrific reputation, which makes it impossible for me to hawk myself around—hence no prospects.

What are you up to? And Sasha?[7] It costs me a lot to write these sorry lines—if I had any better news, I'd have written long ago.

Greetings from your old   Joseph Roth

1. Ludwig Marcuse (1894–1971), German Jewish biographer, essayist, theater critic for the *Frankfurter Generalanzeiger*. Went into exile in March 1933 to Paris, and Sanary-sur-Mer, in 1938 on to Los Angeles, where he became professor of German literature and philosophy at USC.

2. *Vossische Zeitung*: elegantly described by Hermann Kesten as having been started by Lessing and ended by Hitler.

3. On 13 May 1927 prices on the Berlin stock market suffered precipitous declines.

4. Kaliski: worked in the Ullstein Verlag.

5. Lania: Leo Lania (1896–1961), journalist, biographer, novelist. Went into exile in 1933. Wrote an account of Willy Brandt's coming to power.

6. I.e., the *BBC*.

7. The later Mrs. Marcuse. Bronsen tells the lovely story of how they met: Marcuse was upset after being dumped by some other flame, Roth reminded him that the world was full of attractive women, and pointed to the waitress in the bar in Berlin where they were sitting. This was Erna, who, a little later, became Sasha when Marcuse told Roth that he loved her dearly, but found her Berlin speech full of embarrassing solecisms. Roth's solution was to dub her Sasha and claim she was a Russian princess; his policy with Friedl, his own wife, was not dissimilar, but much less successful.

44. To Bernard von Brentano   *Paris, 19 June 1927*

Dear friend,

thank you for your letter and review.[1] You shouldn't worry: there is nothing finer than being bribed, I've long prided myself on that condition. It's the height of morality. More than for your review, though, I'm grateful for your letter. If it weren't that the book was with Schmiede, it might be a great success. Stefan Zweig, Toller, Meier-Graefe[2] have all written to me. Do you have an address for Emil Ludwig,[3] by any chance? I'd like to send him a copy. He was here, and I would have tried to meet him if I'd been well. As it is, I read an interview with him in the *Nouvelles Littéraires*[4]—and for the first time felt something like respect for him. He's the only one who tells the truth about Germany, literature, his preferences and opinions. What's your opinion of Keyserling?[5] Absurd and completely unimportant figure! I've yet to hear a German talk the way he does—twerp. Of course, it's easy for L. to be brave. But some people can't be prevented from being deceitful or polite (as people call it), so consumed are they with the task of "representing" Germany.

The paper has treated me shabbily. Reifenberg will tell you about it, though you'll have to make allowance for his conciliatory manner. You don't see the paper anywhere, I think it must have a smaller readership than even the *Hamburger Fremdenblatt!* Ullstein has written to me again.

I'll probably be better in two weeks, go to Frankfurt, then Berlin. It's not so awful that you're in Frankfurt. The closer to the epicenter of the disaster, the calmer it probably feels. Renew a couple of old friendships, move in a society that impresses the snobs, go to a dinner club where the saddest knights in the world flank the saddest king.

Where is your wife? I send you my regards, and thank you for your kind words—I'm afraid I can't reply in kind, because I haven't read anything of yours for a while. I remain, as ever your old

Joseph Roth

1. review: a review of JR's book *The Wandering Jews.*
2. Meier-Graefe: Julius Meier-Graefe (1867–1935), art critic, novelist. Co-founder of the journal *Pan.* Supposedly matched Roth's royalty of one mark per line at the *FZ,* and the only other writer to do so.
3. Ludwig: Emil Ludwig (1881–1948), journalist, biographer, novelist.
4. *Nouvelles Littéraires*: a literary weekly in Paris, founded in 1922.
5. Keyserling: Count Hermann Keyserling (1880–1946), popular philosopher.

45. To Ludwig Marcuse   *Paris, 22 June 1927*

Dearest Dr. Marcuse,

thank you for your letter, your touching anxiety on my behalf, your friendly offer. You have no idea how little Reifenberg is able to accomplish for someone like me. Some resent me because of my talent, and others—the bosses—because I'm ornery and intractable. Even so, I will try Ullstein once more. (Keep it under your hat.) Reifenberg has written to say this and that. Then the company goes and does the opposite. At any rate, they still haven't sent me any money. If and when they do, I'll be in Frankfurt on July 2 or 3. You know exactly how things stand, and there's nothing to be done about S.[1] He doesn't like me, and takes the worse state of the newspaper as a pretext to get rid of me. I can stand it.

Will you be in Frankfurt?

Till when can I wire you for the fare to Frankfurt, if the need arises?

My wife is well. She sends her best to you both. Drop me a line. I'm feeling a bit better.

In old comradeship your old   Joseph Roth

1. I.e., Heinrich Simon.

46. *To Ludwig Marcuse*   *Paris, 28 June 1927*

Dear Marcuse,

I have to go to Deauville for 3 days for the Bäderblatt,[1] because it will bring in a little money. Unfortunately, my dear fellow, it means I won't be able to see you in Frankfurt. I'll stay there a week, and then Berlin, or else perhaps go on a tour of Germany. The business with the Foreign Ministry is awful. I'm afraid it kept several of the articles. We'll see each other after your return. I take it you'll be going via Berlin? I'll be able to tell you personally what I'm not really able to write. Your friendship, let me say this, almost frightens me. Your comradeship goes to a point I'm sure I'll never reach—and there's no point in thanking you any more, because that's not enough. Suffice to say, I won't forget it—if that does.

I hope you and Sasha have a good trip, and offer you my warmest greetings—from your grateful

Joseph Roth

Bye!

1. Cf. "A Couple of Days in Deauville," in *Report from a Parisian Paradise.*

47. To Bernard von Brentano   *Marseille, 31 July 1927*

Dear friend,

the news of your father's death has just reached me. (I go to pick up my mail every ten days or so.) I never got to meet him, but even so I mourn his passing. I imagine he was one of those characters that no longer exist in Germany, a person with the aura of the Counter-Reformation, and the old Holy Roman Empire. You know how drawn I am to such people, even if most of them don't share my politics.

I mourn his death of course not least for you, my friend, because you still needed him, and it would have been only fair if he had lived to see your literary fledging. His passing marks a turning point in your life. If you feel too alone, then accept my assurance that I am standing at your shoulder—now, and in every enterprise in which you should feel in danger or alone.

Don't take it amiss if I tell you that such moments are necessary and even fruitful. They attach us to the beyond, it's a little like going to church, which of course we don't do.

Write to me through Miss Weber—but only if you want to.

Please send the enclosed letters to your brother. I don't know his address.

Always your old   Joseph Roth
Give my regards to your mother.

48. To Benno Reifenberg   *Grenoble, 17 August 1927*

Dear Mr. Reifenberg,

I hope you are already off on vacation with wife and child. I am trundling across France, a wandering writer, a genuine minnesinger. I hope my novel doesn't appear before you get back. I must see the galleys, if you write to the office, ask them to send them to the Wagner address in Paris.

My new novel is wonderful. (Keep it under your hat: I'm ashamed to tell anyone else.) I couldn't after all muster the strength or the brazenness

to write a novel in episodes for the *Illustrierte*. All I've done is written one
called

Zipper and His Father.[1]

I'm looking forward to reading it to you! It's so wonderful when you pay
close attention, and are open and engaged!

I'll be done in 12 days.

When are you back?

I met Dr. Simon in Marseille. Very happy. He looks like a stripling—
or a stripeling—in his striped summer suit.

Kisses to Jan, and both Maryla's hands.

Have a lovely time.

Don't forget your old   Joseph Roth, and read the last two volumes of Flaubert's correspondence.

1. *Zipper and His Father* (Munich: Kurt Wolff Verlag, 1928).

49. *To Stefan Zweig*   *Glion near Montreux, 8 September 1927*

Dear esteemed Mr. Zweig,[1]

I've been in debt to you for an unconscionably long time. You sent me
kind words on my Jewish book.[2] I thank you for them.

I don't agree with you when you say the Jews don't believe in an after-
life. But that's a debate that would take an awful lot of time and space.

I'm thinking of bringing out an ampler version of the book in the
course of the next few years. Perhaps I can combine some of the research
with my reporting work for the *FZ*.

In the autumn I'm bringing out my next book (a novel, or rather, a
sort of novel)[3] with Kurt Wolff. If you wouldn't mind, I'd like to have a
copy sent to you.

With sincerest thanks and regards   Joseph Roth

1. Zweig: Stefan Zweig (1881–1942), privately wealthy writer, translator, collector,
patron. In touch with most of the leading personalities of the time—from Rilke to

Freud, see his autobiography, *The World of Yesterday*—and probably the best-selling international writer of his day.

2. my Jewish book: *The Wandering Jews*, 1927.

3. a sort of novel: *Flight Without End* (Munich: Kurt Wolff Verlag, 1927) was subtitled "a report." It marked the height—the beginning and end, really—of JR's flirtation with the so-called *Neue Sachlichkeit*, or "New Objectivity."

50. *To Félix Bertaux*[1]   *Hotel Foyot, Paris*[2]
                                              16 September 1927

I am just back from vacation for 2 days, and am deeply sorry I don't have a moment to see you before my departure. I have to go back to Germany—already, and contrary to the wishes I told you of on the occasion of our last time together. The silver lining is the fact that I will be able to meet your son[3] in Berlin—and as I am looking forward very much to showing him something that other people might not be able to tell him about, I would ask you to let me know his address in Berlin, and how long he will be there; either via the *FZ*, the Kurt Wolff Verlag, or my wife, who will probably be here for some time yet.

My regards to your wife.

Yours truly,   Joseph Roth

My wife will either be staying here or at 23 rue de Tournon. Her address is mine too.

1. Félix Bertaux (1881–1948), leading French Germanist and critic, friend of the Mann brothers Thomas and Heinrich, author of the standard work on German literature between 1880 and 1927, *Panorama de la littérature allemande contemporaine* (Paris, 1928).

2. Hotel Foyot: JR's favored residence in Paris or pretty well anywhere. See the elegy he wrote for it in 1938, "Rest while Watching the Demolition, in *Report from a Parisian Paradise*.

3. son: Pierre Bertaux (1907–1986), a Germanist like his father, specializing in Hölderlin.

51. To Bernard von Brentano   *Frankfurt am Main*
                                                 20 September 1927

My dear Brentano,

thank you for your troubling letter. Still, part of me thinks it can't be
as bad as you say, at least from what I hear from dear good Mr. Reifenberg. I know he is such an inveterate optimist, he often distorts things
the other way. But there's no call for you to become nervous. *Human relationships with newspapers are just impossible.* For every decent, confident,
self-willed individual there comes a time he must break. As far as I'm
concerned, I'm hoping to be able to give up journalism as my principal
occupation fairly soon. If you're smart about it, you'll be able to yourself
in 2–3 years. You have the talent.

I don't think you can present yourself to Ullstein, unless invited to.
Would you like me to recommend you to Katz?[1] I'll write you the warmest note of which I'm capable. He is not without influence, he's the man
who wrote those great travel pieces and started the *Grüne Post*[2] (or was it
Welt). I don't understand why you continually want to move in *Jewish circles.* If you gave the least indication you wanted to, *you'd be the big chief at
the DAZ.*[3] They are deficient in temperament, and could use men with a
line to intellect. The people there would be more grateful than Jews, they
are freer and more receptive. The concept of the reactionary has moved
again—for now. Have you not noticed that? If you only wanted to, you
would have all the necessary requisites to be an important figure—*over
there.* Whereas if you stay here, all you have to look forward to are a
couple more years of inadequate pay or poor job or scheming Jews. *There
you would be the smart Jew*—and your own man on top of that. Do you
think freedom or intellect can be found with the Reichsbanner?[4] *I'd a
thousand times rather Hindenburg than Koch*[5]—*more honest, stronger, freer.*

I'm bored, had to dash off a miserable article for someone else about
a wretched trade fair. Hope to be back in Berlin soon, and write 2 or 3
articles. Then it's Russia again—in the spring. Since my Russian pieces

were not up to my usual standard, I have to revise them continually. (But keep that to yourself.) Write to

your Joseph Roth

1. Katz: Richard Katz (1888–1968), travel writer, correspondent for the *Vossische Zeitung*. Worked for Ullstein Verlag, still a major German publisher today.

2. *Die grüne Post*: a weekly paper for country people.

3. *DAZ: Deutsche Allgemeine Zeitung*, newspaper for heavy industry.

4. Reichsbanner: liberal soldiers' union in the Weimar Republic.

5. Koch: Erich Koch-Weser (1875–1944), one of the founders of the German Democratic Party; from 1919 to 1921, minister of the interior, 1928 to 1929, minister of justice.

52. To Benno Reifenberg   *Strasbourg, Tuesday [1927]*

Esteemed Mr. Reifenberg,

1. I'm returning Holitscher's[1] manuscript by the same post. I didn't care for it. It had some potential, but for H.'s unbearable views on *grand monde*, fashion, women, prostitution, etc. A man who is only familiar with life in Berlin or Munich, is naïve, and doesn't understand the first thing about women, shouldn't write about such topics. It's just one more sorry confirmation that the German author remains hidebound and ignorant. No *homme social* he.

2. The first of my thin but full *Diaries* will go to you tomorrow. I'm pleased. Setting off deliberately from the personal, it slowly spreads into the universal. My work as a reporter is always done with a book in mind, which doesn't stop it from falling apart into separate articles. The binding is my style, is me. You will see.

3. I'm finished with the Saarland.[2] I left because I wasn't able to write anything while there. I need to fill two more *diaries*, almost a book. I have visited factories and a mine. For half a day I worked as a salesman, got drunk at night, and slept with an ugly hotel chambermaid from sheer wretchedness. But I am steeped in the Saarland, and know it as well as I know Vienna. You will see.

4. I'm going to go to Paris for a few days. My wife is very ill in St. Raphael. I may have to take her to Frankfurt. From Thursday, my address is c/o Wagner *8 rue Mignard*.

5. In about 10 days I'll be through with writing my reportage. *Where would you like me to go then?*

6. I can't get by on the money. In 4 weeks, I've gone through 500 marks. And they use francs. 6a.

7. I am very widely known—almost popular—in the Saarland. Asked to give a talk on Russia, at the request of some cultivated middle-class people. The paper is widely and attentively read. The only place where we are ahead of *BT*, *Voss.*, and Cologne. People mostly very much in favor. Complaints about the books pages. [. . .] Promotion, sales, wooing of subscribers, advertising space, all inadequate. Bäderblatt is popular. My novel much admired. Kracauer's photograph likewise. [. . .]

I think that's everything!

Best wishes, your   Joseph Roth

1. Holitscher: Arthur Holitscher (1869–1941), travel writer and novelist. He was Thomas Mann's model for the awful writer Spinell in the novella *Tristan*.

2. Saarland: Roth was engaged on writing a series of articles on the Saarland and Lorraine, which appeared in the *FZ* in 1927 under the title of "Letters from Germany."

53. To his parents-in-law   *Hotel Englischer Hof*
                                                Frankfurt am Main
                                                30 November 1927

My dear parents,[1]

thank you for the gloves and the kind letter. I'm going to be here for another 10 days, then to the Ruhr, and then probably joining Friedl in Paris. We could only go to Vienna if I managed to sell my new novel first, but the chances of doing that by Christmas are slim. Also, to get a better offer, it would be more advisable to allow its predecessor a little more time. I hope it is a success! There's no point in going to Vienna with a little money, and Hedi[2] needs our expenses even more than she needs our physical presence. I send her my very best.

My health is so-so. Next spring, I should like to take a cure in Vichy or Karlsbad.

Regards to you and the children, from your   Son M.

1. parents: Selig (1875–1958) and Jenny (Jente) Reichler (1876–1954), née Torczyner. They lived in the Leopoldstadt in Vienna, and in 1935 emigrated to Palestine, where they died.

2. Hedi: Friedl's sister; she left Austria in 1938 for exile in London.

54. To Félix Bertaux   *Hotel Excelsior, Munich*
                                            21 December 1927

Esteemed Mr. Bertaux,

I'm sorry I couldn't answer your letter before today. I'm so grateful to you for your kind words—they filled me with a childish glee. I really don't know whose verdict on my book[1] could have had more importance than yours. Only French Europeans of your stamp are still in a position to recognize the European tradition of stylistic purity—certainly not the American Germans in whose midst I write. If it hadn't been for your letter, I would have despaired at the stupidity of all the German reviewers, all of whom praised me, but for things I don't see. Except for one piece of advice, which I am unable to follow: to write in French. They all talked about my "Latin clarity." You may see thereby how far the Germans of today are fallen from their own literary traditions. It's the country where the British and American authors have the biggest print runs, and the greatest successes. Whereas I—according to my German reviewers—am a "one-off in German literature"! The feeling of not belonging anywhere, which has always been with me, was borne out.

I am glad you recognized *Rohan*.[2] *Oui, c'est ça, c'est lui!*

May I tell you I am now working on a novel on the postwar generation.[3] I hope the material will be of interest to you.

I'm going to be in Berlin in February. I will be delighted to seek out your son. Before that, though, there's a chance—a probability, even—that I'll be in Paris. End of December—I'll try to see you, if you have time.

Once again: my best thanks!

Please give my regards to your wife.

I remain, as always, your   Joseph Roth

1. my book: *Flight Without End*.

2. Rohan: presumably Prince Karl Anton Rohan (1898–1975), editor of the *European Review*, and a proponent of good Franco-German relations.

3. novel: *Right and Left* (Berlin: Gustav Kiepenheuer, 1929).

55. *To Georg Heinrich Meyer*   *Paris 16ᵉ*
                                                 152–54 rue de la Pompe
                                                 27 December 1927

Esteemed Mr. Meyer,[1]

you will have heard by now that I have concluded a new contract with Kurt Wolff. I had hoped to see you in Munich, and talk to you once more. I've been more convinced than ever, since Frankfurt, that your memoirs would be an important book. If you do write them, then be sure to mention me as your newest acquisition in nonpareil at the back.

Are you pleased with my book? Happy New Year, and a great success for *Flight Without End* from your old   Joseph Roth

1. Meyer: Georg Heinrich Meyer (1869–1931), editor with Kurt Wolff. The book JR asks after—already, before exile, before Friedl's diagnosis, he is knocking them out at a dangerous rate—is *Zipper and His Father*, which Wolff brought out the following year, 1928.

56. To Benno Reifenberg   *Paris 16ᵉ*

152–54 rue de la Pompe

27 December 1927

Dear Mr. Reifenberg,

I didn't go to the Ruhr at all, of course, but to Paris. I couldn't even stand Munich. If I had money, I'm sure I would have gone back to Frankfurt—Ruhr or no—for a day. But I didn't get the whole of the sum I was counting on. Can I ask you please to take out the rest of my 400 marks for January on the basis of the accompanying letter, and keep them for me.

Nenikekomena.[1] I am glad for once to be able to give you some good news. Through April I will be getting 700 marks a month from the Kurt Wolff Verlag. For another 4 months at least as much, if I give them my next novel ("The Younger Brother").[2] The publisher is compelled to take the book (unseen), but I don't have to give it to him. As I've since had a rueful letter of apology from Zsolnay, regretting the loss of my *Zipper* through his little "zsenanigans," I have reason to presume on Zsolnay's interest in my next book, and thus be able to get more like 800–1,200 marks per month out of Wolff. Use your loaf! So for the next 7 months, I'll be able to eat, with no newspaper work, almost like a prewar novelist. I don't like admitting to you that it's *Zipper* that is the cause of my first true independence—i.e., that I am able to live, without submitting to the censorship that any newspaper exerts. I'm glad, because it's the novel I dedicated to you—you have no objection, I take it? I'll make some changes. I'll take out the somewhat mystical conversation with P. at the end; instead, the conversation will be between me and young Zipper. Following the conversation, and ending the book is the letter to him. In the middle a dialog between old and young Zipper. The character of the actress fleshed out a little. Dedication: to Benno Reifenberg, in warm and wary friendship. (only joking) What do you think?

It appears I made a favorable (i.e., unfavorable) impression on Kurt Wolff. Hence the contract. That, and the current view that I am among the 20 or so writers who can write German. At last I am making converts, having converted myself long ago—other people are always slow on the uptake. I really don't want to write for the paper any more. Only on occasions, so I have to visit that accursed country less often. They spoil my enjoyment. But for you, I could stop just like that. Sometimes I wish you would leave, and I could follow you.

[. . .]

Viewed churches, streets, and Annette Kolb[3] in Munich with Hausenstein. Good tour guide, splendid churches, spring-summery, sparkling Miss Annette. Mrs. Hausenstein gets younger all the time. Younger and sweeter. Good eye. Child is a gifted little rascal. Flirty at bedtime. The evening at Wolff's. Mrs. Wolff well-bred. A character—not in quotation marks either.

Introduced to A. M. Frey:[4] nice. Schneider: ghastly.

Munich: Gothic and Baroque layered over Romanesque. Not a German city at all, a royal city.

Recommended Kracauer's novel.[5]

Read Hauser's book[6] on the road. Little sleights of hand. Tries to create an atmosphere by enumerating and describing other destinies, local color, and water. Doesn't understand that atmosphere doesn't grow out of humanity but out of the facts. Still, competent enough. Technically, too, in spite of alternation between 1st and 3rd-person narration. Irony. Tension. Living language, if a little porous. Gave the novel to the publisher. Will present Hauser with my objections, though I know he's not open to criticism.

Do you see Soma Morgenstern?[7] I'd be grateful for his address in Frankfurt.

Liver flushed with calvados. Otherwise OK. Writing scene of Franz Joseph's departure for Ischl. Very effective. 300 marks worth. Net.

Paris lovely, with thousands of naïve booths on the boulevards. A fair—the 12 days of Christmas. Little harlots down from Le Havre on vacation.

Christmas tree in Montmartre, little baby Jesuses in all the brothels. Currently resting happily on my laurels.

Happy New Year to you.

Tell your mother-in-law: *Szczesliwy Nowy Rok!*[8] From me.

Is Liselotte with you? Greetings to Maryla and Jan.

Your old   Joseph Roth

1. *Nenikekomena*: perfect tense of Greek *nikein* - to win or conquer.

2. "The Younger Brother": working title for *Right and Left*; perhaps as a result of JR's maneuverings/sharp practice, it didn't appear with Kurt Wolff, and he had some difficulty placing it at all.

3. Annette Kolb (1870–1967), Bavarian-French novelist of great subtlety and charm.

4. Alexander Moritz Frey (1881–1957), novelist.

5. novel: *Ginster*, by Siegfried Kracauer.

6. book: the novel *Brackwasser*, by Heinrich Hauser (1901–1955), who also wrote for the *FZ*.

7. Soma Morgenstern (1896 Brody–1976 New York), friend of JR's. Vienna correspondent for the *FZ*, novelist, and memoirist.

8. *Szczesliwy Nowy Rok*: the Polish for Happy New Year.

57. To Félix Bertaux   *Paris, 5 January 1928*

Esteemed Mr. Bertaux,

illness has detained me in Paris—and so your kind letter from Berlin only reached me today, after many detours. I'll be here another couple of days till I'm restored; if you would let me know when you can see me, I'll be very glad.

Fischer[1] has written to me, and I want to thank you for your advocacy. In the meantime, though, Wolff has bought the book from me.[2] Still, I've written to ask Bermann[3] if he'd be interested in my *next* novel (should be finished in October). I'm waiting to hear. It's about the new generation, and is called *The Younger Brother*. The generation of German secret associations, separatists, Rathenau murderers—in short, of our younger brothers, today's 25-year-olds.

The version in which you read *Zipper* was not the final one. It's missing a couple of dramatic scenes, and the conclusion, which takes the form of a letter from the author to young Zipper.

Kurt Wolff would be very happy for advice from you concerning translation rights. And I—you know this—would throw my arms around you, which I'd like to do anyway, for your wonderful humane interest in my literary fate. It makes me very proud.

I hope you found Pierre doing well in Berlin.

My regards to him, please.

I wish you a Happy New Year, and kiss your wife's hand

Your devoted   Joseph Roth

152 rue de la Pompe

Hotel St Honoré d'Eylau

1. Fischer: i.e., the publisher S. Fischer, where Roth had hopes of being published at this time.

2. Kurt Wolff: Wolff published *Flight Without End* in 1927, and *Zipper and His Father* in 1928.

3. Bermann: Samuel Fischer's son-in-law and designated successor on his death in 1934. He took the firm to Vienna, Stockholm, and New York, before relocating it in Frankfurt after the war.

58. To Benno Reifenberg   *Paris, 8 January 1928*

This letter doesn't need an answer/

contains no questions!

Dear Mr. Reifenberg, I address this letter to you at home, in the hope that you'll be resting for a few days, and not going to the shitty office. Don't worry, I've been ill myself, and only recovered consciousness about 3 days ago, with an understanding of what it all means. It's a residue of the animal in us, the hibernal instinct, strongest when the days are shortest. I could have burrowed myself into my nest, had no desire to eat, and

am perfectly convinced that I could curl up in a hole and sleep uninter-
ruptedly from December 21 to January 15. And if you don't, and you
stay awake, you fall prey to all sorts of diseases and nervous weaknesses.
Neuralgia is rampant. So you should listen to your body, and sleep. Only
an increasingly instinctless humanity has decided to begin each year at
such a time, which is what makes our years so miserable.

Yesterday I sent you a piece from "Cuneus."[1] I'm afraid it may step on a
few political toes. Maybe it could be given to a tame pol.[2] I also hear that
the *Saarbrückener Zeitung* came up with a couple more attacks on the
19th or 20th last. Send copies, if possible. If Matz comes back for more,
following the mild cuffing I gave him, then I'll beat him up good and
proper, for all my manifest disgust with these roaches.

To me the *Frankfurter Zeitung* isn't so much a springboard, more
a sort of spring mattress, of the kind we used to see in variety shows,
with zebra-striped ticking. It's my only home soil, and must do for me
as fatherland and exchequer. All I want now is time to write my books.
Here enclosed—to be returned at some convenient time—is an offer
from Fischer. He has also asked Annette Kolb—who wrote me a lovely
letter—to ask about my availability. Nor is he the only one. The Verband der Bücherfreunde has been in touch. I won a humiliating victory
over Zsolnay. He wrote me an abject letter of apology. In the event of a
good offer, I'll swap Wolff for Fischer, if less good, I'll just play them off
against each other. My stay in Paris is very important just now, because
I can follow up the translation, and make connections with the literary
establishment here. Unfortunately, my French isn't quite good enough.
The pax with S.[3] is opportune because otherwise he could have been a
(small) hindrance here. Diplomacy. Don't you hate it. It's as much trouble
as 3 books.

[. . .]

Cottage or apartment in the environs of Paris as cheap (or dear) as near
Frankfurt. Only made expensive by travel (40 marks per person, 60 for
wagon-lit, 80 for luxury train via Cologne). But why not. Polish newspa-

pers available here for your mother-in-law. (Convey regards, please.) Air is best in May. Possible trips to the Alps, etc. My wife is asking for precise details of Meudon. I'll let you know. Best New Year wishes from us both.

Kracauer demanded his chapter back. What's he doing? Best regards.

Health, luck, blessing,

Your old   Joseph Roth

Am writing generation novel.

Have a thick notebook with yellow paper set aside for you.

1. Cuneus: Latin for "wedge," and Roth's pseudonym for the politically delicate series on Lorraine and the Saarland.

2. tame pol: i.e., a colleague from the paper's political section who will vet it permissively?

3. S.: Sieburg.

59. To Félix Bertaux   *Paris, 9 January [1928]*

Esteemed Mr. Félix Bertaux,

I was thinking for a long time about your inspired translation[1] of "Neue Sachlichkeit," and came to the conclusion that "l'ordre froid" is far too good for that ugly label, which seems to have reached German literature by way of German painting. It exalts all the productions that sailed under that flag to a level they don't deserve. The French reader will be inclined to think more of that objectivity than he should, simply by dint of your splendid term. If I were you therefore, I would note that the translation ("l'ordre froid") is better than the original (Neue Sachlichkeit), and refers not to the *achievement* but the *orientation* of most of the so-called Objectives.

Please excuse the advice, and the following too. You will probably be unable to avoid connecting the absence of a truly German novel (in the French sense) with the absence of a truly German society (in the French sense). In this context, can I draw your attention to the newest novel by Annette Kolb (published 1927, chez S. Fischer)?[2] It describes nothing less than the last remnants of a cultivated German society. It's exemplary, less a novel than a symptom, last sign of life of people who no longer exist.

Enclosed, you will find the review by Franz Blei,[3] not so much for itself, as for the way it stands in for very many other reviews.

Once again, thank you for your great, humane, and just sympathy.

Ever your   Joseph Roth

1. translation: in Bertaux's survey, *Panorama de la littérature allemande contemporaine.*

2. The novel in question is *Daphne Herbst* (Berlin: S. Fischer, 1928).

3. Franz Blei (1871 Vienna–1942 New York), short story writer, essayist, humorist, editor, and translator of Gide and Claudel.

60. *To Félix Bertaux*   *Monday [early January 1928]*

Esteemed Mr. Bertaux,

just got your card! Of course. I'll be honored and delighted to read your survey,[1] even if I'm quite sure you won't have perpetrated any solecisms. You certainly have finer instincts than German literature professors, so even if you happen not to know something, you'll be correctly oriented.

I'll give you my next address in Germany—or is there any chance you can get me the proofs by Wednesday?

I enjoyed myself very much at your house yesterday, and hope to be in a position to invite you to a home of mine one day, if royalties should permit me ever to have one.

Please convey my regards to your wife. I remain your grateful

Joseph Roth

1. Félix Bertaux's *Panorama.*

61. To Benno Reifenberg   *Kaiserhof, Essen*
                                                       17 January 1928

Esteemed Mr. Reifenberg,

I got your forwarded letter, thank you! I'll answer the reader's letter
after this. If it's physically possible, I'll try and do corrections and cuts
myself. Maybe on the galleys. It'll save you the trouble, and the awkward entry into a different sentence rhythm. The question mark you
allowed to stand is part of the signals of our correspondence: a private
code emerging from our conversations—don't be surprised if others don't
get it. Why didn't Dr. Feiler go over this feuilleton? Why give it to Dr.
Drill[1]—and for how much longer does the political desk (i.e., not the editorial conference) intend to supervise our feuilletons? If it's to be a form
of censorship, then let it be according to the views of the whole board,
not the more or less reactionary—or revolutionary—views of a single
politician, whom as an individual I will not allow the right to represent
our age better than I do. (I'm not referring to Dr. Drill, whom, as you
know, I rate very highly.) I'm going to raise this matter of censorship—if
it's agreeable to you. Or I will make the perfectly reasonable demand
that the political correspondents submit their pieces to *me* for censorship.
This absurd supervision is wholly unjustified. We represent the paper no
better and no worse than the leader writers.

I enclose something for the books pages, very topical, highly controver-
sial. If you have any doubts about it, feel free to add an editorial preface.

I am writing two more articles for the books pages, namely: Gide and
the Congo[2] (in a fortnight) and on Benda's *Trahison des Clercs*.[3] Linguistic analysis in Frankfurt. Could you send me the money for the three
articles, so that I get it on or before 20/21. Because on the 23rd I will have
to be in Frankfurt again, but I need money here, before that. If so, please
wire me that it's coming, so I'll be sure to be at home.

I finally got to be introduced to *Gide*. He Olympian, I merely snotty.
He was in Berlin to give the standard talk on mutual understanding. I

told him what I thought about it. Who's covering it for us? Brentano? Was asked later what I thought of Gide. *C'est un acteur, n'est-ce pas?—* said Paulhan.[4] And I: *il est plus qu'un acteur, il est une actrice!*

Dear Mr. Reifenberg, I've long owed you thanks for your violets. It was excellent, save one clearly intentional childish note. What should have been someone's distant recollection sounded like the zoom of a fresh close-up. A "plus serré" would have fixed it. But perhaps then the lovely, mysterious to-and-fro would have been lost!

I'm uneasy about you. What's happened? *Something* must have happened! Something unexpected!

Sincerely, your old   Joseph Roth

Please don't forget money and censorship!

1. Dr. Drill: Robert Drill, with the *FZ* since 1896, dismissed in the Third Reich, died in South African exile in 1942.

2. Gide and the Congo: The travel diary *Voyage au Congo* (1927), by André Gide (1869–1951), the French novelist and essayist.

3. Benda: Julien Benda (1867–1956), philosopher, novelist, and essayist, whose treatise *La Trahison des clercs* appeared in 1927.

4. Paulhan: Jean Paulhan (1884–1968), essayist, literary critic, and director of *La Nouvelle Revue Française*.

62. *To Stefan Zweig*   *Cologne, 24 January 1928*
      Till 30th at the Englischer Hof, Frankfurt

Dear Mr. Zweig,

I was very glad of your letter. If anyone has a right to demand perfection of me, then surely you, who write so cleanly and immaculately. There's much I could tell you about my Tunda.[1] You're right, though, it was an intentional break. The book switched from the first person to the third. While one might not sense any tragic quality in the narrator, then perhaps in the "hero" he talks about. But I had qualms, I have qualms about that "tragic" component, I think our postwar man no longer has that "classical" capacity for tragedy, which is no longer a component of character but is still present in the "historical view." Which means there is perhaps tragedy in the way we view the fate of someone like Tunda, even though he himself won't see it or feel it.

At Easter another novel[2] of mine will appear, carefully written. I will send you a copy if I may. Right now, I'm busy on a third,[3] on the young generation in Germany. I have drafts going back to 1920, half-written manuscripts that I didn't have time or leisure to complete. Now I'm at least able to live respectably and write like a madman. Unfortunately, I'm still not able to give up the journalism. My articles probably get in the way of those "creative pauses" that a writer needs. But even though publishers are queuing up to offer me little 3,000-mark advances in return for 2 or 3 years' work, not one is really willing to back me, which means freeing me of the necessity of writing for the paper. I'm still waiting, in effect.

I would very much like to meet you.[4] But then I'm always back and forth, without a fixed address. I wrote to you in November when I heard you were coming to Paris (I was there in December), but I didn't get an answer, and thought you were probably traveling. But it's also possible you never got my letter. I'm going to send this one by registered mail, at the risk of interrupting your work just to elicit your signature. When will you be in Paris? I have an address there which will be valid till mid-February: Paris XVI, rue de la Pompe, 152–54. Perhaps you could write me there, and let me know your whereabouts in spring?

Yours with heartfelt thanks,   Joseph Roth

1. Tunda: Lieutenant Franz Tunda, hero of *Flight Without End*.

2. another novel: *Zipper and His Father*.

3. busy on a third: *Right and Left*.

4. In the event, JR didn't meet Stefan Zweig, the man who underwrote his last ten years on earth, until May of 1929, in Zweig's house in Salzburg.

63. To Félix Bertaux

St. Raphaël, 13 February 1928

Esteemed Mr. Bertaux,

your card has just been forwarded to me here—because I suddenly had to up sticks and head south with my wife, who was feeling poorly. I hasten to thank you, my dear esteemed Mr. Bertaux. To me at the beginning of my literary career, I know of nothing better or greater than for my words to be translated into the language I love, and the one that is used by the greatest contemporary authors. It really is reason to wax pathetic—forgive me, if this is happening to me. But let me tell you how deeply grateful I am, and that I thank heavens for the fortune that brought us together.

I will write to Kurt Wolff tomorrow about the rights for Gallimard,[1] and concerning Monsieur Betz.[2] In any case, I hope I shall have the honor of knowing my book will be scanned before its appearance by you. It's my belief that in France people still listen to the *word*—as opposed to Germany, where if you write passable German they call you French. I can't say I mind.

I am still negotiating with S. Fischer about rights to future books. I hope we come to an agreement, even though it would be Wolff's loss. But it seems to me that, in Germany, I need the full authority of the Fischer imprimatur.

I heard (while in Germany, for January and early February) that the *Nouvelles Littéraires* published an essay about me. Did you get a chance to read it?

I'm here till the 16th, and then taking my wife to some other place where they have no mistral. She is doing better today already, and sends her regards.

I hope to meet you in Paris at the end of the month.

For the time being, I remain, with regards to your wife and self,

your grateful and obedient servant   Joseph Roth

Villa Alice (Var)

Thanks again for the essay in the *NRF*!

1. Some of Roth's novels were published in French translation in the *Nouvelle Revue Française* imprint of the famous house of Gallimard.

2. Maurice Betz (1898–1946), noted French translator, of Rilke, among others.

64. To Félix Bertaux   St. Raphaël, 24 February 1928

Esteemed Mr. Bertaux,

thank you for your card. My wife is feeling better. She thanks you for your concern, and sends her regards. She is staying here while I go back to Paris today, for 2–3 days, and then probably on to Berlin, to draw up a contract with Fischer. I would be glad indeed if Dr. Bermann turned out to be the excellent person I seem to see in his letters.

Kurt Wolff has written to Gallimard. I have written to Betz, using your name—I hope that's not unwelcome to you?

Your question regarding *Ulitz*[1] refers to Franz Blei's review, I take it. Where you and I are both praised. In my view: *c'était de la politique.* Döblin: *un juif,* Musil:[2] *juif-Viennois, moi: encore moins qu'un juif. On a du nommer au moins deux Allemands de "pur sang."* Blei is a real tactician, a literary diplomat, of Semitic cunning. Ulitz is a Silesian writer, bags of pathos, big heart, small head, perspective narrowly provincial (he used to be a primary school teacher in Breslau). But at least he writes correct German. Morals: excellent. Mental capacity: below average. Industry: praiseworthy.

What did please me was the reaction of your son Pierre. I will seek him out in Berlin. He seems to have inherited his father's eye—and if he has your conscientiousness, and your extraordinary flair for a phrase, then German literature will have a rosy future in France.

Dear, esteemed Mr. Bertaux, may I ask you to leave word at rue de la Pompe 152 on Saturday 25th or Sunday 26th *when* I can see you? I'll probably be going to Berlin on Monday or Tuesday. And, as you know, to me you are both a literary patron saint and a warm and clever person who never fails to cheer me up.

Kiss your wife's hand for me!

I am, as ever, your grateful   Joseph Roth

1. Ulitz: Arnold Ulitz (1888–1971), Silesian writer and poet.

2. What Roth is saying here, its bluntness softened perhaps by being said in French, is that Blei's selection of German writers was guided by tokenism, choosing Döblin, a Jew, Musil, a Viennese Jew, and himself, something less than a Jew (perhaps by virtue of being an Eastern Jew). Blei then saw himself faced by the need to name racial Germans, and came up with two further names, one of them Ulitz's (See the essay list "Auto-da-Fé of the Mind," in *What I Saw*, where Roth lists the Jews among the German writers of the period.) The intellectualist Robert Musil (1880–1942) and Roth did not get on. In point of fact, Musil was not a Jew, not even a Viennese Jew.

65. *To Félix Bertaux*

Grand Hotel Victoria
Zurich
26 March 1928

Dear esteemed Mr. Bertaux,

thank you for your kind letter, and please forgive me for being so tardy in answering it. My wife's illness has upset all my plans. I had to accompany her to the Ticino, and am now on my way to Vienna with her. I hope to be in Frankfurt early in April. It's too bad that you're going back to Paris as early as the 3rd or 4th, and I lose the delightful prospect of seeing you and your son Pierre together.

Please send or hand in the proofs and a possible accompanying note—which I would beg you to write—to the Feuilleton department at the *Frankfurter Zeitung*. They will give you an address for me in Vienna.

My wife is feeling much better. She thanks you and your wife for your concern, sends her regards to you both, and will write as soon as she is up to it.

Please don't forget to call on Mr. *Reifenberg* at the *FZ*. And Dr. Kracauer too. There are not many such people in the whole of Germany.

I look forward to seeing the proof[1] and your accompanying words—kiss your wife's hand for me, and give my regards to your son Pierre.

Cordially as ever,   your Joseph Roth

1. Still, no doubt, of the *Panorama*.

66. To Félix Bertaux   *Lvov, Poland, 31 May 1928*

Dear esteemed Mr. Bertaux,

I hope your wife is better, and ask you for a few words to set my mind at ease.

I've been on the road for the past 3 weeks, and have only had an address to give you as of today. It will be my main address while in Poland. In a few days, I'm going to Vilnius and the Polish–Lithuanian border.

I am writing a series of "Letters from Poland" and at the same time working on my new novel. Fischer—I've grown fond of the old gentleman by now—will be pleased.

Is it possible for you to send me your survey here?

My wife is with me. Not well, but better.

In old friendship and gratitude I press your hand, and remain your

Joseph Roth

P.S. Franz Blei urged me to drop the introduction for the French edition of *Flight Without End*. What do you think? And if you agree, would you be kind enough to let Gallimard know?

The address:

c/o Madame Helene de Szajnocha-Schenk,

Lvov, Pologne

Ulica Hofmana 7/1

67. To Stefan Zweig   *Warsaw, 10 July 1928*

Esteemed Mr. Zweig,

I am late in thanking you for your book.[1] I read it on the road as I was passing through many small towns, and must thank you twofold: for your company in that somewhat bleak setting, and for the enjoyment of your book at all (the effect of it was intensified by my solitariness). I have the sense that I am closer to you now than if I had read you or met you, say in Berlin or Paris. All that remains to be sought is an opportunity and your permission to seek you out personally. Perhaps sooner rather than later, because on the 20th or 21st I'll be in Vienna, where I have to see to a (for me very tedious) formality regarding nationality.[2] I hope it won't eat up the whole 5 days I'm there. I can be found c/o Mr. E. P. Tal,[3] Vienna VII, Lindengasse 4.

The Stendhal section was I thought the best part of your book— perhaps because he is such a sympathetic figure to me anyway. But, even though I know him well, I still have a sense that he comes out as a character in your pages. It's a real *portrait vivant* that you've composed. What you are so masterly in, if I may make so bold, is the yoking of a cool and precise language to a warm and relaxed patience. You write a remarkably human literary history, but always with dignity and distance. I knew little about Tolstoy, and next to nothing about Casanova. I thank you for introducing me to the material, and assure you that I feel a colossal knowledge on every page. How industrious and exacting you are!

Superfluous to remark that I'm giving you poor words in return for good ones. But you will have seen from my books that I would be ashamed to be untruthful—and already I am ashamed to have uttered such a sentence. Please disregard it.

I wish you happiness and industry! Where will you be this July and August? Till the 19th inst. my address is as below:

c/o Frau H. von Szajnocha-Schenk

Lvov (Poland)

Hofmana 7/1.

With warm and grateful regards   your Joseph Roth

---

1. book: Zweig's *Drei Dichter ihres Lebens*, lives of Stendhal, Casanova, and Tolstoy.
2. nationality: Roth was attempting to get Austrian citizenship. See no. 69.
3. E. P. Tal: a Viennese publisher.

68. To Benno Reifenberg   *Hotel Imperial, Vienna*
                                             [July 1928]

Dear kind Mr. Reifenberg,

I was very glad of your short letter because it was yours, even though
I understood almost nothing of it. Why don't you ask to see a carbon of
it, and read it back to yourself. It has an unnatural laconicism and a hor-
tatory tone and makes it clear that you are doing your duty in running
the feuilleton section, while I am writing a novel. That's not you, that's
not your tone, and the gravitas in which you fail to say anything about
yourself is almost more pathos-laden than that of someone talking about
himself. Why not tell me? Why conceal yourself "behind your job"? I'll
tell you anytime that you are much more important than the feuilleton section, than the whole of the *Frankfurter Zeitung* and all German
Jews and the ridiculous "duty" we are allegedly performing in Germany.
You know I'm not offended or hurt by your brevity. If you'd written me
nothing but: I'm out of cigarettes!—I would have recognized you. But
now fulfilling duties and beavering away at Europe or Germany or the
whole world in those tawdry editorial offices—well, I don't recognize
you. Your latest very good feuilleton about Frankfurt regrettably starts
off with a Faustian paragraph about heaven and hell—by way of a so-
called introduction—and what you say there is unnecessary because it's
between your lines anyway, all it is is the outpouring of a homesick heart,
and it recalls the song of the archangels, and has a gentle parp of trom-
bone. What's keeping you, my friend? I don't know where to find you
any more, it's as though we were both standing in a pitch-dark room.
The cuts you undertook yourself soothe me, but just a little. You're not
cheerful, you've spent too long in that self-important office—and it's time
you knew that I'm convinced that you and you alone (not you with me or
you with Kracauer) will save the *FZ* from the fate of becoming a *General-
Anzeiger*. Germany is one *General-Anzeiger*: It's all they know.

Be well, I pray that you might not have become so humorless as to take
umbrage at my directness.

I'm not too well myself. (We'll talk.)

Your old   Joseph Roth

Regards to your folks. A word about Jan and your mother-in-law, and a smile from your wife is worth more than all the duties of German newspapers *and* books.

69. *To Benno Reifenberg*   *Hotel Imperial, Vienna*
                                             30 July 1928

Dear Mr. Reifenberg,

thank you for yours. A few more words on your article. You know I write with exactly the same intentions and the same means as you do. The reason I took against your introduction has nothing to do with that chronically misunderstood term "objectivity." You're right to be Goethean—it's the only way of writing well in German. What I was critical of was the irrelation between introduction and subject—your private view of Frankfurt can't be permitted to set the tone. The archangels' song is in *Faust* and not *Werther*—not to compare the worth of the two works, but the value Goethe wanted to give them. An article about an exhibition for instance can't be used "naïvely" as an occasion to vent one's private feelings or moods too crudely. You violate the rule that demands information. If you wrote more regularly, you would come to the conclusion all by yourself that an impulsive rush of writing will match the object maybe 2 or 3 times in the course of a lifetime, and that those times when you write freely and with pleasure are precisely those times when you have to be extra careful you don't give yourself away. Rush and pleasure have to be confined in or to the subject, for that to acquire a sort of sheen. That's the only way. But in your article, Reifenberg gets more gloss than Frankfurt—which is surely the last thing you wanted. And because you started off with Reifenberg, you used up your whole tank of fuel, and ended up pushing your vehicle by hand. You understand me, don't you? If you don't write often, it's necessary to write a *lot* to write better. You will draw such security from it that you won't have need of any mornings, or any vainglorious moods.

I am in critical difficulties.

Firstly, I will shortly have to move my old friend Mrs. Szajnocha in with me. Which means founding a household. She can't stay in Poland for many reasons—and I am her only material prop. Secondly, I need to come up with an arrangement for my wife. Where? What with? How? Where am I going to put these two women?

3. I need to begin a new life. The time has come once more when I must transform my entire existence, go away, be gone by myself—to America, or Siberia, for that matter. I am so dependent on reality that in the most ordinary sense of the word, I need to experience something, to have something to write about.

4. The position concerning my documents is tangled and difficult. You remember how I changed from being a Russian to an Austrian—well, now I have to prove that I was always an Austrian. The unorthodox means by which I furnished myself with names, dates, schools, and army career are to be tested to their destruction—and I've spent the past fortnight trying to establish my literary and journalistic existence to authorities who don't know anything about me. The earth would betray me, so I'm forced to use Olympus. Arguing that papers are *quite rightly bound* to have disappeared—hence the absence of conventional documentation. I'm living and improvising twenty novels. It's so exhausting, I haven't a hope of getting on with the one I'm trying to write. I've called a halt. My nationality is connected—via the question of passport—both to the question of household and to the questions of travel. Without a passport, I'm toast. This month, August, I shall have to find my way to a document that accords with my present identity. For the past 25 years I've been living as a sort of fantastic figment.

You can imagine how I feel. Every day I go to some office or other. Fight against the recalcitrance of the lower officials and the cunning of their superiors. Trying to make play with my "social position" and call in aid the patronage of personal acquaintances. Another two weeks of this, and I'll be done in.

My liver is playing up again.

Cordially   your old Joseph Roth

Address: c/o Tal, Vienna VII, Lindengasse 4.

No hotel, because it's very expensive, and I moved out, am only hanging on here to suggest a fixed address to officialdom for a few days.

70. To Benno Reifenberg   *9 August 1928*

Dear Mr. Reifenberg,

even though I wrote you two letters yesterday, one after the other—which I hope you received, they weren't registered—I'm writing you again today. Because, given my intense mistrust toward the world, *FZ* included, the sudden announcement of my visit to Italy[1] makes me suspicious. (1) How is it that you don't try and see me in Frankfurt, following the end of a tour? (2) Why does the board agree to a proposal of yours so quickly? I, or if you like, my suspicion, can think of the following reasons: (1) You, dear Mr. Reifenberg, have some reason not to see me right now. You're planning something, or have just done something that you assume I wouldn't approve. (2) The board thinks Roth shouldn't be running around drawing money, unless he's been given something to do. (3) The board is able to sell copies in Italy again, and thinks Roth is sometimes tame enough for Bäderblatt articles, and maybe we could use him to try and sell space and subscriptions in Italy. You see what sort of things are apt to fly into my mind when someone does me a good turn. What pains me the most is of course (1) that you might have some personal grounds, and that makes me ask openly and suspiciously: *if* you go on vacation, *who* is filling in for you? Whose job is it to unpick the little bit that has been achieved? Please tell dear Kracauer that I don't trust him, ever since the books pages under his command have been opened to the tone and the feeling of Fred Hildebrandt.[2] If Kracauer carries on like that, out of laziness or apathy or whatever, then I promise I will wreck his literary career for him. Please give him my regards, I remain personally very fond of him! Dr. Morgenstern seems to be personally offended with me, I haven't seen him for a long time. And now *you* pack me off to Italy. Faced with so much kindness, *timeo danaos*, I start to scent mischief.

You're none too well, I know. You run around with a heavy heart, and need to groan: Oh Lord! at least twice a day—and that takes some doing. And it's not the case that you can shake off that sort of thing easily. Cycling doesn't always help. You're stuck on a horrid treadmill, and you won't mind my giving you the truth. I make no demands of you, as you know, only that you don't go to the trouble of being diplomatic with me, because I won't even believe the unvarnished truth.

Warmest regards to all at home, and no one in the office.

Your old   Joseph Roth

1. Italy: JR visited Italy for the paper in 1928, and wrote a series of articles called "The Fourth Italy."
2. Fred Hildebrandt, the feuilleton editor of the *Berliner Tageblatt*.

71. To Benno Reifenberg   *telegram from Vienna, 22 August 1928*

reifenberg grueneburgweg 95 frankfurtmain
wire deputy prior departure what I should write if not italy stop paris hotel foyot stop propose resigning because simon hindrance to my participation on paper till tomorrow Vienna stop in event of future difficulties am prepared to write publicly against paper have received request cordially   roth

72. *To Benno Reifenberg*   [1928?]

Dear Mr. Reifenberg,

I wrote you at home a week ago.

I would like, not a reply, please don't go to any trouble, but just a con-firmation. Since the 2nd I've wanted to go to Essen by way of Cologne. But I am incapable of traveling, of writing, am completely crushed, fight-ing an illness I won't allow to break out, days in bed, curing myself with raw onions, and tired, terribly tired.

A little patience still, please. I'm writing two more letters.

Cordially,   your old Joseph Roth

Big successes. Offer from S. Fischer.[1]

1. This seems doubtful, or at least overstated. The closest Roth got to being pub-lished by Fischer was when a chapter from his unfinished novel *The Silent Prophet* was printed in Fischer's "house" magazine, *Die Neue Rundschau*, in 1929.

73. *To Stefan Zweig*   *Hotel Englischer Hof*
                                                          Frankfurt am Main
                                                          26 November 1928

Dear esteemed Mr. Zweig,

after a long stay in Italy and France, I happened to pick up a news-paper, where you mention me in connection with another book. After a long time, it's the first positive sign from you, and I hasten to thank you for it. I have the faint hope that fate might favor our meeting, if I tell you a little more.—Tomorrow I am going for 2 days to Vienna, where my address remains c/o E. P. Tal Verlag, Lindengasse 4, VII. Thence to Berlin to deliver my new novel[1] to S. Fischer, I finished a week ago, after 8 months of work. I heard once indirectly, that you expressed the wish to see a *manuscript* of mine.[2] It is yours whenever you want, I'll be in Berlin ca. 1–2 December. Then a day in Frankfurt Englischer Hof, then 1–2 weeks Paris 6ᵉ, Hotel Foyot, rue de Tournon.

After that I don't know. I can't work so much for the newspaper any more. I have major projects in mind, and nothing to keep me fed, if I don't write articles.

How have your recent books fared? Are you satisfied?

A line from you to one of my addresses would make me happy, a meeting with you would be the fulfillment of a long and deeply held desire.

As ever your   Joseph Roth

1. new novel: either (probably) *The Silent Prophet* or *Right and Left*. When Fischer declined, Roth took himself off to Gustav Kiepenheuer Verlag, Berlin.

2. a *manuscript* of mine: Zweig was one of the leading autograph collectors of the day.

74. *To Félix Bertaux*   *Hotel Imperial, Vienna*
                                          29 December 1928

Dear esteemed Mr. Bertaux,

I want to wish you and your wife a Happy New Year! Tomorrow I'm setting off for Zurich, and from there to Marseille. Maybe I'll be in Paris in the course of January. Then I will have the great pleasure of seeing you. If not, I'll send you 3 or 4 of my articles on the Saarland from Marseille. Some were unavailable from the *FZ*—the issues sold out—and I've had them copied, though I don't know if a manuscript is any use to you.

Fischer didn't like my novel. I won't therefore get it published— because I don't want the publisher to bring out a book of mine without conviction. Perhaps Fischer, who even as I speak is thrilling to Gerhart Hauptmann's new novel *Wanda*, is getting on a bit. The people around him are marionettes!

Your son Pierre will have written to you about me. His development is really exceptional, he is becoming terribly clear and wise and warm-hearted: a young *Mensch* in the old, almost lapsed sense of the word. We became very close, and I will be delighted if he can accompany me to Russia in the spring.

Goodbye, dear Mr. Bertaux, and please give Mrs. Bertaux my regards,

Ever your grateful   Joseph Roth

---

75. *To Benno Reifenberg*   *6 January 1929*

Dear Mr. Reifenberg,

I got your kind letter today—thank you. I know how hard it is for you to send me money, but still I have no option but to take it. I am simply too wretched. Thank you for the improvisation too. It's in your best vein. What else can I write you? Yes! I would like to have written an introduction to my *Panopticum*,[1] making the entire book over to you. But in the meantime, misfortune struck, and I had to content myself with a hasty dedication, for which I ask your pardon.

Best regards to you and yours, especially Babuscha.[2] I am still a wreck, a long way from being whole. Who knows if I ever will be again.

Ever your old   Joseph Roth

1. A collection of Roth's feuilletons that appeared under the title *Panoptikum: Gestalten und Kulissen* (Munich, 1930), all part of a deal with the *Münchener Neueste Nachrichten*. See no. 84.

2. Babuscha: Maryla's (Polish) mother, of whom JR remained very fond.

---

76. *To Stefan Zweig*   *Hotel Beauvau, Marseille*
                                               15 January 1929

Dear esteemed Mr. Zweig,

as Ernst Tal was away for the Christmas holidays, I didn't get your wife's[1] kind note in Vienna, but forwarded to me here. Please kiss her hand, and thank her for the answer to my first telegram, and beg her forgiveness for the second.

I had so looked forward to meeting you at last. All these wretched obstacles that make us slip past one another.

I heard you were going to Russia again.[2] I am to visit Siberia in early April. Will you let me know when you set off? I'm sure I'm going to be here for the next 10 days. I must finish my Jewish book—a revised version is to appear with Kiepenheuer, including a new section, called: The Jews and Their Anti-Semites.[3] I am also finishing a new *Zeitroman* that's been on the go for a long time.[4]

I'm delighted to hear of your success with the Volpone adaptation.

Let me say again how much I long to see you in the flesh. I have a sense of your humanity, even though—as you will know only too well, all the literary dogs are yapping. Just because would be too easy. No. There is something else in you, a humane heart surely, and a fine humanistic contempt. Happy New Year to you,

Cordially your   Joseph Roth

1. wife: Friderike Maria von Winternitz-Zweig.
2. Zweig had been to Moscow in 1928 for the Tolstoy centenary celebrations, where he had met Maxim Gorki.
3. The Jews and Their Anti-Semites: long mooted by JR, but it was never written.
4. This sounds like *Perlefter: Story of a Bourgeois*, which remained unfinished, unpublished in Roth's lifetime, and untranslated.

77. *To Félix Bertaux*   *Hotel Beauvau, Marseille*
                                            18 January 1929

Dear esteemed Mr. Bertaux,

I enclose a couple of my old articles—copies, because as you will see from the *FZ*'s letter to me, the numbers in which they appeared sold out. Is it too late?

Forgive me for keeping you waiting so long. I have a lot to do just now, working on 2 books at once, which must be finished before I leave for Siberia.

I got a charming, clever, and very intimate letter from your son Pierre. He is some fellow, as they say in Germany.

Always your grateful   Joseph Roth

P.S. I can't find Reifenberg's letter just at the moment. I'll send it later.

78. *To Pierre Bertaux*   *Hotel Beauvau, Marseille*
                                           26 January 1929

Dear friend,

your letter came, like a good friend, like a personal envoy of yours. Thank you! As you say, I'm sitting in the southern part of Europe, feel happy and at home, and not the least bit romantic. You came up with an excellent definition of modern man, showing the true measure of difference between the past and future type. Incidentally, the one who's never surprised by anything is a type that has existed before. It's not my sense that Alexander the Great felt romantic emotions—which after all began with Napoleon—when he was in Egypt. Nor did Caesar. In the Middle Ages, people shuttled between Padua and Krakow. And we'll be going to Moscow in just the same fashion. What's insufferable about Germany isn't the technology so much as the romantic cult of the technology. The German is always a small-town person, so he always finds something to gawk at. Really, the Tartarins[1] belong in Germany far more than they do in your land. See how every German is equipped with all kinds of gadgets and portable knickknacks, forever on the hunt, the police are kitted out à la Tartarin. The most important difference between the American and the German is that the former uses the technology as naturally as a baby drinks milk, while the latter is incapable of making a phone call without lyrical commentaries on what a great thing the telephone is.

That's what preserves Germany from ultimate Americanization. We're half ashamed of still being Europeans, and are not capable of becoming Americans. (That's part of the German misfortune.)

It's a wide field.

Outside it's bright and clear, a mistral blowing, typical Marseille weather. I'm writing this in a café, excuse the scruffiness of my writing, and this letter. I'm hard at work, writing two books simultaneously (my novel and the "Jews and Their Anti-Semites"), and articles 4 times a month. My wife isn't quite well, is in bed, sends her regards. I've become very moody, toying with my novel, assaying various willfulnesses, all to loosen my stiffness. Like a form of gymnastics.

I hope your work is going well. I hope to be here 2 more weeks. Please write, and don't mind my irregular replies.

In old cordiality ever your   Joseph Roth

1. the Tartarins: see Roth's piece on Alphonse Daudet's delightful book in *What I Saw.*

79. *To Stefan Zweig*   *Hotel Foyot, Paris*
                                                        27 February 1929

Esteemed Mr. Zweig,

your kind letter has been in my correspondence file for a month now. I was delighted by it. It's a kindly proof of the humanity I sensed in you, and a generous present to a near-stranger who is unable to reply in kind. I had other reasons, admittedly, that kept me from writing to you: a pro-tracted illness of my wife's (who is still not completely well), a flu that laid me out, and the aggravation of a chronic stomach ailment, and on top of everything else 10 hours a day working on my book, of which 30 pages remain to be written, and which I hope to finish by the end of March. Even if there hadn't been all those distractions, I would have sat over my piece of paper just as perplexed as I'm sitting over it now. I don't know what entitles me to your great trust, and to what extent I may reveal my (unexpected) self-confidence without making myself ridiculous to you, by answering a personal letter of yours as though I'd all along been entitled to receive such letters. By making me a present you embarrass me.

The book I'm working on now isn't the one I told you about then. I traveled to Marseille for material for the book that is to come after this one. What I am working on now is the story of a German bourgeois up to 1928.[1] As you see, I work hard. I have the feeling it takes a great deal of talk to get one out of the stage of being utterly misunderstood into merely partial misunderstanding. The only reason I work though is material. I must succeed in producing the minimum from my existence, without regularly writing articles that undermine my health. So that my life isn't too grotesquely abbreviated, I should like to find myself a free man in a year's time. And for that to happen, I have to write every day. But that's a change. It's impossible to fix myself. I have no such thing as a stable literary "character." I am not stable in other respects either. I haven't lived in a house since my eighteenth year, aside from the odd week staying with friends. Everything I own fits into three suitcases. It doesn't strike me as at all odd, either. What is odd, though, to me, and even romantic, is a house, with pictures on the walls, and so on and so forth. In a fit of mindlessness, I took on the responsibility for a young woman. I need to keep her somewhere, she is frail, and physically not up to a life at my side.

You write true things about Marseille. I want to write a (commissioned) article on the city for the *Wiener Neue Presse*,[2] and then you will see how much our views coincide. Marseille has another side: the terrestrial one. The city is even more colored by Provence than it is by the sea. I spent months living and working among peasants. The city quite lost its maritime aspect and acquired a wholly continental character. (Please excuse my skewed handwriting.)

1. Hermann Kesten thinks *Right and Left*, but this is more likely *Perlefter: Geschichte eines Bürgers*, a satirical novel that Roth began and abandoned. The manuscript surfaced only recently; there is no English translation.

2. *Presse*: JR means the *Neue Freie Presse*, for which Zweig made his literary debut, and remained a regular contributor.

80. To Félix Bertaux   *Hotel Foyot*
                                                          Paris
                                                          27 February 1929

Dear, dear Mr. Bertaux,

I begin this letter with a burdened conscience. I didn't answer your kind letter, but put it off, day after day. My wife has been in bed for weeks, I was unable to leave the room in Marseille, and have become ill myself. I have been working on my novel 12 hours a day. Finally, I came back here, because I didn't want to see a doctor in Marseille, and my wife's state was getting worse all the time. She has a swollen cheek (this is to do with her general frailty) and will perhaps have to undergo a minor sinus operation. The doctor who will come this afternoon will make the decision.

Dear Mr. Bertaux, I am so indebted to you that every word I write seems hollow and formulaic to me. I cannot tell you what it would mean to me to be read by a generation of young Frenchmen. If I were a master of pathos à la pacifist Curtius,[1] and "Europeans" of that ilk, I would beat my breast with pride. But I have not those means to hand. I am not one to overestimate "nations" or the relations between them, and don't feel called to "represent" anything at all. My modest personal relationship to "France" (every other word has to go in quotation marks, that's how damaged I feel they are) is approximately this: the fond hope that simple human freedom will never be lost in this country, as it has been in others. Maybe I can convey to the odd young Frenchman what a terrible thing unfreedom is for the individual. By way of warning!

I'll be staying here for about 4 weeks, to write the last 30 pages of my novel at a page a day. Is there any possibility of our meeting? Perhaps we could have lunch somewhere (although my stomach is bad, and I'm not much of a companion at mealtimes)?

My wife sends her regards to you both.

What news of Pierre?

I kiss your wife's hand, and salute you cordially,

your grateful Joseph Roth

1. Curtius: Ernst Robert Curtius (1886–1956), German essayist and thinker on European matters.

81. To Félix Bertaux

Hotel Foyot, Paris
Friday
[postmarked 1 March 1929]

Dear Mr. Bertaux, mon ami,

thank you. I'll be waiting for you tomorrow then at half past 12. I'm sending you a note, because I'm having so much trouble with the telephone. 12 young Germans, teachers or students, aspiring Curtii the lot of them, have broken into the hotel, and spend half the day on the phone, forging pacifist links with France.

Thank your wife for me. Mine will be very pleased.

Till soon,

Ever your   Joseph Roth

82. To Pierre Bertaux

7 March 1929
Hotel Foyot, Paris 6
rue de Tournon

Mon bien cher ami,

it's not enough to "thank you sincerely." It may be more to tell you that your letters are a real comfort to me—as they say, a *reconfort*—and that I have a physical sense of your friendship. It's correct that one may not share griefs, that only redoubles them. But there is an infinite solace in that redoubling. My grief leaks out of private things into the public realm,[1] and that makes it easier to bear, just as, for instance, a war appears more bearable to an individual than a bout of pleurisy.

So far as my wife is concerned, her present illness is only an acuter version of her chronic weakness, a complete lack of resistance, in which I am not without blame. There are various causes. These things, of which

I have been unable to speak for months, if not for years, oppress me more than the form of the illness itself. Perhaps in another ten years I will be able to write about them, if I am still a writer then. For now, I drag them around with me, and torment myself.

Ernst Weiss,[2] whom you mentioned, is to me a sort of *cas typique*, if you are interested in Prague and the Jews of old Austria. He is from the ghetto. A man who sailed past foreign shores as a ship's doctor, without ever setting foot on them, who stayed in his cabin to write. A mind that is ashamed of being a mind, and so instead, without realizing it, plays a "folly." It seems to me the man is incompetent, crippled, infantine, never left puberty, and dwells in it still happily. Read his books *Nahar* and *Animals in Chains*. You will see that this highly gifted writer joined the expressionistic bandwagon for no very good reason, other than his shame at "normality." He always lacked courage. He was always ashamed of having courage. Courage is a brother of sense, and Ernst Weiss chose folly instead. He was a German writer. The best thing he's written is the novella *Franta Slin*.

Have you met *Mrs.* Coudenhove?[3] A rare instance of a *robust hysteric*. It's not possible to like her, because she's so ill-mannered. But she's head and shoulders better than her husband and the pan-Europeans, and the society where she is disliked. She is a pan-Jewess. A daughter of Jehovah's.

You will have enjoyed stammering with Kracauer. He's a sweet boy, only cowardly, extraordinarily cowardly. He's capable of betraying you, and becoming a bastard out of cowardice. A beaten-up-on (outside) and pampered (indoors) Jewish boy.

You can tell me what your "project" is. I won't be in Berlin till mid-April at the earliest, I'm working on my novel till the end of March.

My wife sends cordial regards.

I had dinner with your father, and mean to telephone him one day soon. He is dear, distinguished, and moderate, as always.

Write me soon. I suffer from the idée fixe that the post is unreliable.

In friendship, your grateful   Joseph Roth

1. into the public realm: this strikes me as a remarkably acute self-diagnosis. There is something terrible, even tragic, about JR's susceptibility or responsiveness to public events, from the mid-twenties into the thirties; one feels it continually exceed its "cause."

2. Ernst Weiss (1882–1940), doctor and author. He committed suicide in Paris on the eve of the German occupation. Several of his novels have been translated into English, most recently *Georg Letham: Physician and Murderer,* in 2010.

3. *Mrs.* Coudenhove: Ida, wife of Richard Count Coudenhove-Kalergi, founder of the pan-European movement and the European Parliamentary Union.

83. To Pierre Bertaux   *Hotel Foyot, Paris*
                                                          28 March [1929]

Dear friend,

thank you for your letter. I hope to see you here before my departure for Berlin. So it won't be possible for you to come to Russia—I shall feel lonely on my trip, having prepared myself with the thought that you would be coming with me.

Your description of your meeting with Brentano was very amusing. I know exactly that you will have gotten excited to no end with him, because he is one of those people who will go on and talk to others, using *your arguments*, and simultaneously bad-mouth you. If Brentano is as unhappy as you say he is, then with every reason. No one has merited unhappiness as much as he. I only fear he won't be unhappy enough. Another thirty years of life for a creature like that are in my view too many. In thirty years, he can wreak much more destruction. He is one of three or four people I would happily murder, with no more compunction than putting out a cigarette. I don't know if you're acquainted with the feeling that removes any so-called humanity in you, and renders absurd the notion that killing a human being was anything special. Sometimes I feel the murderer in me is as natural as the writer, and if I were arrested and put on trial, I would be utterly perplexed.[1]

I'm fairly sure that my name will have been sufficient cause for an argument between you and him. I am a red rag to him, just as he to me is a slavering dog. His brain is mad, his heart is weak, his tongue is glib and stupid. I have no sort of magnanimity or "Christian feeling" for those who dislike me, and not sufficient dignity. I will hurt them as much as possible, with cunning and violence, and am only waiting for the opportunity of murdering them in a deserted alleyway.

Yesterday I finished my novel. I'm happy with it. Did the silent prophet make sense in the *NR*?[2] I fear it may have made a muddled impression.

You should work or let yourself go. You are one of those people who never lose their senses, and whose brain will keep going even after your (physical) heart in the hour of death.

Greetings in old and cordial friendship.

(Do you ever see Bermann? He doesn't answer my letters.)

Joseph Roth

1. Roth's friend, sometime roommate (see no. 313), and editor, Hermann Kesten, is troubled by this letter, and gives it a long note, to the effect that one shouldn't take it seriously, and that Roth never actually hurt a fly. According to Kesten, Roth turned on most of his friends at some time or other, but more in the spirit of a literary joke, playing with them as with the characters in a novel. "He was more concerned with artistic truth than with reality. Roth had a very strict artistic conscience." While accepting this—especially the last sentence—one shouldn't shy away from accepting that Roth all his life was quick to take offense, and was, as Irmgard Keun and others noted, a ferocious, gifted, principled, and implacable hater.

2. in the *NR*: the *Neue Rundschau* ran a chapter of JR's "Trotsky novel," *The Silent Prophet*.

84. To Stefan Zweig   *Hotel Foyot, Paris*
                                                        Friday
                                                        29 March 1929

Dear esteemed Mr. Zweig,

I hope you're back at home already, and that this letter, which for once I haven't sent registered, won't get lost in following you about. I read a short and admiring article on your talk in Brussels.

I finished my novel the day before yesterday. I'll be happy to give you the manuscript.

Thank you for your kind offer to promote *Flight Without End* in Russia. With its content and its philosophy, I fear that won't be possible. On the other hand, you could certainly help me in France. *Flight* is appearing from Gallimard this year—and if you were to mention me to your literary friends in Paris, along with *Fuite sans fin*, I would be very grateful to you.

I feel some compunction in voicing such a request. The least resemblance to those individuals who seek your literary patronage is something I would like to avoid.

I'm still not sure when I'm going. Now the *Münchener Neuesten*[1] have sent me an invitation, obviously they want to get me on board. I have so little money, and hate all newspapers equally, I wonder if I shouldn't take their offer when it comes.

It would be good to talk to you. I hope to be in Salzburg at the end of April.

With cordial greetings from   your Joseph Roth

1. The conservative daily the *Münchener Neueste Nachrichten* made Roth an offer, which he, cash-strapped and at various times eager to get away from the *FZ* (or from newspapers altogether, he wasn't sure), briefly accepted. See nos. 75 and 90.

85. *To Stefan Zweig*   *Berlin, 2 September 1929*

Esteemed Mr. Zweig,

I don't want you to think there's any trivial interruption in our correspondence. Since we last saw each other, a lot of very grim things have happened.[1] My wife was taken to the psychiatric hospital at Westend in a very bad state, and for some weeks I've been unable to write a line, and compel myself to scribble just enough to keep body and soul together. I'll spare you any more detailed account of my condition. The word "torment" has just acquired a very real and substantial content, and the feel-ing of being surrounded by misfortune as by high black walls doesn't leave me for a second. I had hoped to be able to give you my manuscript in pleasanter circumstances. I am sending it to you now under the very worst and most grievous. Be well, and drop me a line c/o Kiepenheuer Verlag, Altonaerstrasse 4, Berlin NW 87.

Sincerely and warmly   [Joseph Roth]

1. Friedl's weakness and unhappiness had lately taken the form of erratic behav-ior, hearing voices, and physical frailty. There were various diagnoses, culminating in schizophrenia, and JR for the rest of his life was frantically trying to get her cared for, long after he saw that a cure was unlikely. From here on in—not to deny that both may have had their attractions for him before—he was never off the twin treadmills of alcohol and work. The "manuscript" he mentions here to Zweig may have been that of *Job* (published in 1930), which has harrowing descriptions of the dementia of Deborah, the wife of the central character, Mendel Singer. Zweig, as with Roth *passim*, gave all the help he could.

86. *To Stefan Zweig*   *Berlin, 16 September 1929*

Esteemed Mr. Zweig,

I have just gotten a copy of your *Fouché*.[1] I would have liked to wait to thank you for the book, your inscription, and your warm and friendly letter, but I have no idea when I'll be able to concentrate in front of a piece of paper. It seems impossible for all eternity, and impossible the hope that I might amount to more than any Tom, Dick, or Harry, and owed more obligations to the world than to my suffering nearest and dearest. Thank you again. Maybe I'll find the strength to come to you in Salzburg, and shake your hand. Most probably mutely, but a little closer to you.

Your humble servant   [Joseph Roth]

1. *Fouché: Joseph Fouché: Bildnis eines politischen Menschen* (1929).

87. To Stefan Zweig   *Hotel am Zoo, Berlin*
                                                        17 October 1929

Esteemed Mr. Zweig,

in the middle of my wretchedness, I hear that you are being prodded
to write about my book. I hasten to tell you that your silent friendship
is much more precious, valuable, and dear to me than the trouble you
would be put to even to write to an editor on my behalf. Please don't
trouble yourself! My books are not destined for popularity in any case!

Thank you for the *Fouché*, your language glittering as ever. In my
rush I can think of no more felicitous phrase: brilliant, dazzling history.
I know there is more there, more heart, your good, tender, noble heart,
which I love.

My wife is beginning to improve. Three days ago they operated. She
is still in danger. I am beset by worries, coarse and trivial for the most
part, but by higher ones too, completely befuddled, and with a bad liver.

Ever your grateful old   Joseph Roth

88. To René Schickele   *10 December 1929*

Dear esteemed Mr. Schickele,[1]

thank you for your dear kind letter. Why are you surprised by my
inscription—as it seems you are? Brandeis is the main character in my
next novel, "No Entry, the Story of an Immoderate Man."[2]

I am writing in a desperate plight. Yesterday I fled to Munich. My
wife has been very sick since August. Psychosis, hysteria, suicidal feelings, she's barely alive—and I'm chased and assailed by black and red
demons, without a mind, unable to lift a finger, impotent and paralyzed,
helpless, with no prospect of ever getting out. Perhaps I can crawl away
somewhere in Salzburg for a couple of weeks, alone with my misfortune.
I don't know what the coming days will bring, but would like to see you.

Kind regards your   Joseph Roth

1. René Schickele (1883–1940), Alsatian novelist, essayist, and magazine editor (*Die Weissen Blätter*, 1915–19). In 1932 went into exile in France, where he died—like D. H. Lawrence—in Vence.

2. It seems Roth wanted to take Nikolai Brandeis (who appears halfway through *Right and Left*, and takes it over) and put him in another book, to be called *Eintritt verboten*, which was never published, and perhaps never begun. Tunda, Baranowicz, Mizzi Schinagl, Trotta, Kapturak, and many others—Roth has a way of injecting names and characters into more than one book; it is one of the things that make his writing seem more like a whole world than something merely excogitated.

89. To René Schickele   20 January 1930

thank you for your dear good letter, and kind invitation, which I gladly accept. Only I cannot leave Berlin before my wife's situation has stabilized, at least to the point that I know where she'll be looked after. At the moment, she's with a friend.[1] Every day I need to scrape together money for her, for the nurse, for other necessities. I'm angling for a big travel assignment, so I can leave a couple of thousand marks here, at least in prospect, and wander off. The other thing, the emotional pressure, I shall have to deal with alone. Being an author is actually no help at all. That may be my official designation, but privately I'm just a poor wretch who's worse off than a tram conductor. Only time and not talent can provide us with distance, and I don't have much time left. A ten-year marriage ending like this has the effect of forty, and my natural tendency to be an old man is horribly supported by external misfortunes. Eight books to date, over 1,000 articles, ten hours' work a day, every day for ten years, and today, losing my hair, my teeth, my potency, my most basic capacity for joy, not even the chance of spending a month without financial worries. And that wretch literature! I come from a time when you were a Greek and a Roman if you followed an intellectual occupation, and I stand there now like a stranger in the midst of this ghastly Anglo-Saxonism, that sentimental Americanism that rules the roost in Germany. I am sorry you've had such a ghastly boring thing yourself.[2] Go to a miracle man, not a doctor! Believe me, it just needs time and rest to cure it. One day it'll go away as suddenly as it came. I'll give you a couple of weeks' notice before coming. How long will you stay in Badenweiler? Are you not going to leave?

Kiss your dear wife's hand for me.

In heartfelt warmth, your sad   Joseph Roth

1. friend: the journalist Stefan Fingal.
2. ghastly boring thing yourself: Schickele suffered from eczema and asthma.

90. To Stefan Zweig   *Hotel am Zoo, Berlin*
                                        1 April 1930

Dear and esteemed Mr. Zweig,

for a long time I held off replying, because I was going to wire you any moment that I was on my way to Salzburg. Now I can confirm that I'll be on my way on Thursday or Friday. I'll wire again before I leave, and ask you for telegraphic confirmation. Maybe I'll stop off in Magdeburg for a couple of days.

Last week I finished a novel for serialization in the *MNN*.[1] For the past three days I've been back on *Job*, and find myself continually interrupted: by farewell visits. I've always found it hard to break with a place I have no great feelings for. This is my ninth month in Berlin, and it's been the worst time in my life. Never have I cared less about people. Never did they seem more intrusive and less inclined to leave me alone. And they can't have given much for what happened to me.

On account of your absentmindedness, I now own two copies of your pretty volume of stories. I took it as an omen, and read them again. I envy you your lovely epic calm, and that superior dignity which is probably a result of so much knowledge of the world and of people. How serene is even the saddest thing you have to say! It's not for nothing that you have so many readers—and how modest you remain in your private literary demeanor. I am very glad to have come to your attention.

Soon you will get the first galleys of *Job*. I hope it gives you a little of the pleasure it gives me. I hope to be done at the end of April.

Personally, I am terribly sad. Ten years of my sad marriage can't be gotten over just like that. I was so cut off from humanity, my wife was my only channel to the world outside, the social part of myself. My own glumness scares me.

Till soon! With cordial gratitude   your Joseph Roth

1. *MNN: Münchener Neueste Nachrichten*. Roth was to furnish the paper with a novel for serialization, for which he was to be paid 20,000 marks. Along with the manuscript he included a page where he had scribbled a dozen times: Must finish novel in three days! Must finish novel in three days! Disconcerted either by this page, or by the rest of the manuscript, the newspaper tore up the contract with Roth; it wasn't possible, they argued, to complete a story of the requisite quality in three days. Kesten admirably notes that nothing from Roth's pen was ever as bad as what the *MNN* liked to publish.

91. *To Stefan Zweig*   *Hotel Stein, Salzburg*
                                         Monday, 14 [or 18] April [1930]

Esteemed Mr. Zweig,

I hope you're back already. If possible I would like to see you today. I write until 2 p.m. After that I'll be in the hotel. Perhaps you could drop me a line if you are able to see me.

Looking forward to seeing you again,   ever your Joseph Roth

92. *To Hedi Reichler*   *Hotel Stein, Salzburg*
                                         30 April 1930

Dear Hedi,

enclosed is a letter from Dr. Lichtenstern, who is the director of the sanatorium *am Rosenhügel*, and who knows Friedl. Find out when her consultation hours are, I think they're 3–5 in the afternoon, you can find out over the telephone. Mme von Szajnocha has put her in the picture. She can help in various ways, choice of home, expenses, prescriptions, perhaps a particular nurse. She is a wonderful human being, and very devoted to Friedl. Perhaps you or your husband could see your way to visiting there. You have to wait for her a long time, she's very much in demand, and it's not possible to keep her for very long either. Don't be put off by her manner, she's not really brusque. She'll certainly help.

In your last latter I missed an answer to my question how Friedl was with Dr. Schacherl; and whether he risked making a diagnosis. I will write to him, but need to know first whether he agreed to take an interest in her case. You could also ask Dr. L. about orthopedic treatment.

I will know in a few days whether I'll be able to come to Vienna. I'm expecting news from Berlin. I'll write you in time. (I'm feeling better, they're giving me a course of injections.) I should also like to know about *arsenic, insulin,* and *glucose.*

I have gotten in touch with a psychiatrist in Marbach. I'm expecting a detailed answer from him about the prospects of a cure.

If Friedl happens to talk about me, whatever she says, good or bad, true or made up, the conversation should be carried forward at all costs. Not: "You're wrong!" or "That's nonsense!" Respond to everything. Please. Promise.

I'm going to a lot of trouble, but don't get impatient, and please write in as much detail as you can.

Regards and kisses   Your Muniu

There'll be more money coming on the 1st. Let me know how much Kiepenheuer sends.

---

93. *To his parents-in-law*   *Hotel Stein, Salzburg*
                                                    3 May 1930

Dear parents,

Dr. Schacherl has written to Stefan Zweig about Friedl. It appears that the doctor is of one mind with me. Friedl seems, thank God, not to be suffering from any form of dementia. She probably has a hysterical psychosis. If it wasn't that she was so intelligent and so acutely sensitive, the whole thing might have been over in a few weeks. But she is obsessing on a certain point, can find no way out, and, out of despair at this, so to speak, is losing her mind.

I am passing this on to you right away to get your hopes up. Dr. Schacherl is an outstanding diagnostician, and a reliable fellow. Chin up, Friedl will one day speak clearly again. For the time being, her sickness is fed by her physical frailty. I'm in favor of mixing *Hepathrat* into all her food where it can go unnoticed. If her heart is sound, she can drink good strong coffee. Instead of Luminal, ask for *Luminalettes*, where the dosage is far lower. A little of that could go into her food as well, so that she keeps ingesting it at a low level throughout the day. Episodes of disquiet cost her strength, whereas the Luminal doesn't hurt and will only keep her from weakening further. Her weight has to go up to 55 kilos again. If she can tolerate liver and will eat it, give her liver, as much as possible, and slightly underdone. It's not just a matter of nutritious things, as of such that will replenish her stock of blood. Hence the Hepathrat and the liver. Perhaps she will take blood soup. I am just now in correspondence with a psychiatrist in Marbach about the possibility of blood transfusions. Friedl is seriously anemic, i.e., she has too many white blood cells. Perhaps you might ask Dr. Schacherl on the telephone whether she could be given a *hormonal preparation*. In any case, her physical condition is of paramount importance. Concern yourselves as little as you can with her mental symptoms. Tell Friedl whenever you can that her confusion is caused by a glandular imbalance. She will understand. She understands everything, it's just that she doesn't respond in the right ways. It will come as a huge *relief* to her to learn that her confusion has a physical basis. Her thoughts should be deflected away from obsessing with some emotional conflict to a solicitude for her physical well-being. (Please write and tell me you understand this!) As long as her weight is under 50 kilos, she is at risk. Please ask also whether short spells of ultraviolet irradiation may be indicated. According to what Professor Kretschmer tells me, such attacks often heal quite suddenly, even after a long time. So please, please, don't lose patience! So long as I can manage to bring in enough money, I'm sure Friedl will get well without an asylum.

I hope to be in Vienna for a day or two, on around the 6th or 7th or 8th. Please don't tell Friedl. If it's not too much trouble, why not give her a canary to keep in her room. It might distract her. You can always give it away, and they don't cost much. Can you run to a canary?

It does no harm to speak of Friedl's *physical infirmity* in her presence. That will stir her will to live. Please follow the instructions of this letter as well as you are able.

I embrace you both   your M.

94. *To Stefan Zweig*   *13 May 1930*

Dear esteemed Mr. Zweig,

I should have written to you long ago, I've been living in such turmoil since leaving you that I only do what I physically must to survive, and thus dash madly from one bit of drudgery to the next. But I want you to know that I think of you often and gratefully and with an affection that I haven't mustered for anyone in a long time, and that has the effect of rejuvenating me.

Today, just an hour ago, I learned that a woman friend of mine yesterday shot herself. She was staying here in the hotel, had failed to find me yesterday, and I'm convinced I could have averted her death. All around me are suffering and death, and I could weep at my inability to find a little bit of goodness in myself, to save the life of a single human being.

It's not my intention to drive you to sorrow, but it's how I feel all the time. You had the ability, as long as we were together, to tickle a little cheerfulness out of me. You are clever and good.

Drop me a line, but only if it doesn't get in the way of your work. Keep your fondness for me, as I do for you.

Cordially your   Joseph Roth
Hotel am Zoo
Kurfürstendamm 25
Berlin W.

95. Benno Reifenberg to Joseph Roth   *14 May 1930*

To Mr. Joseph Roth, c/o Gustav Kiepenheuer, Altonaerstrasse 4, Berlin NW 87

Dear Mr. Roth,

I wired you yesterday. I wouldn't have waited so long, if I hadn't thought the correspondence between me and Kracauer about your renewed engagement for us would have been over sooner. Let me tell you then, while the correspondence is still inconclusive, how things stand.

1. If the *Frankfurter Zeitung* is to work with you again, then it can only be on condition that we once again enjoy an exclusive right to your journalistic work. We will not and must not share a Joseph Roth with other papers.

2. The tedious business with the *Weltbühne*[1] must be put to bed. What you may not appreciate is that the entire editorial board here saw your article as a defamation of the *FZ*, and you are therefore facing an extraordinary degree of suspicion and resentment. I had thought it might be possible to level off the affair by an open letter to you, and your subsequent reply. However, voices were raised to the effect that you should resolve the matter—where it began—in the *Weltbühne*. I can't do anything without my colleagues, not least as I am no longer in charge of the feuilleton section, but rather, as you know, have become the Paris correspondent of the *FZ*. I wrote therefore to Heinz Simon, and asked him to take a hand in the matter. I hope he will be able to give you a final decision quite soon.

I don't need to tell you how much I look forward to seeing you here again. We're well. Babuscha is with us of course. Jan has grown, and is as charming and delightful as ever.

In old cordiality   Your [Benno Reifenberg]

1. *Weltbühne*: *Die Weltbühne*, a highbrow weekly magazine founded in 1905 in Berlin by Siegfried Jacobsohn. Following his death, in 1926, it was edited, briefly, by Kurt Tucholsky, JR's bête noire, and then by Carl von Ossietzky. JR remained rigidly unsympathetic to its politics and style.

96. To Benno Reifenberg   *17 May 1930*

Dear Mr. Reifenberg,

I just came back from Vienna, to find your letter waiting for me.
The enclosed letter will probably say more to enlighten you about my
state than I could. I have taken my wife back to the sanatorium outside
Vienna. You may imagine what a week's stay there meant for me. When
I am in Paris you will have a chance to see for yourself how little of me is
left for any newspaper to have. I am completely indifferent to all matters
of public interest. As Kiepenheuer's 50th birthday is on 10 June, I can't be
in Paris before then. How long will you remain in the city in summer?

Max Picard should be there. Give him my best. We've been exchanging letters for a while, on the subject of you and me.

I wouldn't be able to take anything back in the *Weltbühne*. I am not on
terms with the *Weltbühne*. I want nothing more to do with those *scum*.

What I wrote at the time was that my views were not identical with
those of the *FZ*. Which is true. I do not have any sort of philosophical
solidarity with the likes of Dr. Drill and Junge[1] and Schotthöfer, nor do
I aspire to it. Do you consider that offensive?

Kiepenheuer won't be happy to have me on an exclusive contract to
the *FZ*. It would mean he couldn't pay me anything. But we'll see about
that. For the moment, I've asked him to call off other negotiations that
were in train. Since he is paying me a stipend, I take it he won't want to
stand idly by for long. He gives me everything, my wife too, he has been
very good to me.

I look forward to seeing you in Paris.

Warmest regards to Babuscha, Maryla, and Jan.

Where are your political sympathies just now?

Tomorrow I'll look for Kracauer.

Most cordially your   Joseph Roth

1. Junge: Karl August Junge, journalist, with the *FZ* since 1903.

97. To Jenny Reichler   *Berlin, 18 May [1930]*

Dear mother,

just back today from Frankfurt. Thank you! In two weeks I'll be finished with the novel. I hope to get an extra 200 marks then, and send
them to you, an article has come out in America. I'll write from Baden-
Baden next. I've got an invitation there. My health is fine. Apart from
that, I'm living off *rachmones*.[1]

Give Friedl my best, write me again, and don't be cross with me if I
don't write. I have thought of a way of earning 2,000 marks at one fell
swoop. I have an invitation to write a novella for a Dutch periodical.

Warm embraces from   your Muniu

1. *rachmones*: (Yiddish) charity.

98. To Gustav Kiepenheuer on his fiftieth birthday[1]

I have covered many miles. Between the place where I was born, and
the towns and villages I have lived in in the last ten years—and lived
in only, apparently, to leave them again—lies my life, amenable more
readily to spatial than to chronological measurement. The years I have
put behind me are the roads I have traveled. Nowhere, in no parish reg-
ister or cadaster is there a record of my name or date of birth. I have no
home, aside from being at home in myself. Wherever I am unhappy is
my home. I am only ever happy abroad. If I leave myself even once, I will
lose myself. Therefore, I take great care to remain within myself.

I was born in a tiny hamlet in Volhynia, on 2 September 1894, under
the sign of the Virgin, to whom my given name of Joseph stands in some
vague relation.[2] My mother was a Jewess of strong, earthy, Slavic con-
stitution. She would often sing Ukrainian songs because she was very
unhappy (and where I come from it is the unfortunates who sing, not the
lucky ones, as in Western countries. That's why Eastern songs are more

beautiful, and anyone with a heart who listens to them will be moved to tears). She had no money and no husband, because my father, who turned up one day, and whisked her off to the west with him—probably with the sole purpose of siring me—left her in Katowice, and disappeared, never to be seen again. He must have been a strange man, an Austrian scallywag, a drinker and a spendthrift. He died insane when I was sixteen. His specialty was the melancholy which I inherited from him. I never saw him. But I remember when I was four or five, I had a dream of a man in whom I saw my father. Ten or twelve years after that, I first saw a photograph of my father. I had seen the face before. He was the man in my dream.

At the sort of tender age when other children are just learning to walk, I was already traveling on trains. I came to Vienna early in my life, left it, came back, went west again, had no money, lived on handouts from well-off relatives and from giving lessons, started to study, was keen and ambitious, an odiously good boy, full of quiet malice and poison, modest out of conceit, jealous of the rich, but incapable of solidarity with the poor. They seemed stupid and clumsy to me. I dreaded any sort of coarseness. It made me very happy when I found an authoritative confirmation of my instincts in Horace's *odi profanum vulgus*. I loved freedom. The times I spent with my mother were my happiest. I got up in the middle of the night, dressed, and left the house. I walked for three or four days, slept in houses whose state I didn't know, and with women whose faces I was curious to see, and never did. I roasted potatoes on summer meadows, and on hard autumnal fields. I picked strawberries in forests, and hung around with a half-grown rabble, and was thrashed from time to time, so to speak, by mistake. Everyone who gave me a thrashing would quickly beg my forgiveness. Because he feared my revenge. My revenge could be terrible. I had no particular affection for anyone. But if I hated anyone, I would wish his death, and was prepared to kill him. I had the best slings, I always aimed for the head, and I didn't just use stones, but also broken glass and razor blades. I laid traps and snares, and I lay in wait and lurked in bushes. When one of my enemies once turned up armed with a revolver, admittedly without ammunition, I felt humiliated. I started off by flattering him; gradually, in the teeth of my true feelings, made myself his friend; and finally bought the revolver from him, with bullets I had been given by a forester. I persuaded my friend that the ammunition on its own was much more dangerous than a weapon without ammunition.

Tender feelings came to me later, and not for long. My first noble stirrings were roused in me by a girl when I was in my second semester as a student of German. The girl in question came from Witkowitz. At sixteen, she had fallen prey to an engineer, and got pregnant by him. Luckily, the child she had was stillborn. The engineer didn't care about her. So she went to Vienna, as a governess with horrible, stupid people. What else could I do, but be noble? I rented a room for the girl, induced her to abandon her ghastly blond charges in their sailor suits, and decided I would make a live baby with the poor girl, and challenge the engineer. To that end, I sold my coat, and took an advance from a lawyer whose son I was teaching. I traveled to Witkowitz, found the engineer, he arranged to meet me in a café, after he received my blunt little note. He had a pointed black beard, crooked upward-slanting eyebrows, glittering eyes, a fine, brown complexion, slender hands, he reminded me of the devil. On his calling card it said: Lieutenant of the Reserve. He bought me a cup of coffee, was friendly, smiled, admitted that he slept with the daughters of all his foremen one after the other on principle, but didn't have time to busy himself with them beyond that. He took me to a brothel, bought me three girls at once, and said he was prepared to turn one of his Witkowitz damsels over to me. He bought me drinks, took me to the station, we embraced as we parted. Unfortunately, he was carried off by the typhoid epidemic of 1916. He was one of my earliest friends.

I got back, the girl had found a new job by now. She wrote me a nice farewell letter, from which it appeared I wasn't the type for her. Quite rightly, she was still in love with the engineer. Thenceforth, I started looking for women in the Stadtpark, the Volksgarten, the Vienna Woods. With modesty and false timidity, I tried to win the pity, and then the love, of the mothers of my pupils. I was especially popular with the wives of lawyers, as their husbands had so little time for them. They gave me shirts, underpants, ties, took me with them to their boxes at the opera, in their carriages, and went away with me to Klagenfurt, Innsbruck, and Graz. They were my mothers. I loved them all dearly.[3]

When the war broke out, I lost my pupils one by one. The lawyers joined up, their wives grew moody and patriotic, and began to express a preference for war wounded. I volunteered for the 21st Jaegers. I didn't want to have to travel third class, to salute incessantly, I was an eager soldier, got to the line too soon, I reported for cadet school, I wanted to be an officer. I became an ensign. I stayed on the eastern front till the war ended. I was brave, strict, and ambitious. I decided to remain with the army. Then came the revolution. I hated revolutions, but had to make way for them, and, since the last train had just left Shmerinka, I had to march home. I marched for three weeks. Then for another ten days I followed roundabout routes, from Podwoloczysk to Budapest, from there to Vienna, where, because I didn't have any money, I started to write for the papers. They printed my nonsense. I lived off it. I became a writer.[4]

Soon after, I moved to Berlin—I was forced to go by the love of a married woman and my fear of losing my freedom, which was worth more to me than my uncertain heart. I wrote the stupidest things, and so made a name for myself. I wrote bad books, and became famous. Twice I was turned down by Kiepenheuer. He would have turned me down a third time too, if we hadn't gotten to know each other.

One Sunday we drank schnapps. It was bad schnapps, it made both of us ill. Out of sympathy, we became friends, in spite of the difference in our natures, which are such that only alcohol is capable of bridging them. Kiepenheuer is a West-Phalian, you see, while I am an East-Phalian. There hardly exists any greater contrast than that. He is an idealist, I am a skeptic. He loves Jews, I don't. He is an apostle of progress, I am a reactionary. He is ageless, I have been old ever since I can remember. He is turning fifty, I am two hundred. I could have been his great-grandfather, if I wasn't his brother. I am radical, he is conciliatory. He is polite and vague, I am ferocious. He is an optimist, I am a pessimist.

There must be some secret connection between us somewhere. Because sometimes we do agree. It's as though we each made concessions to the other, but we don't. Because he doesn't understand money. That's a quality we share. He is the most courtly man I know. So am I. He got it from me. He loses money on my books. So do I. He believes in me. So do I. He waits for my success. So do I. He is certain of posterity. So am I.

We are inseparable; that's his advantage.

10 June 1930   Joseph Roth

1. This, the "Kiepenheuer letter," is the only thing even resembling a CV that we have from Roth, and for all its dissemblings and dissimulations, it is a revealing document. The one big falsehood of this letter is made up of what are actually lots of tiny truths, concerning his parentage, his fatherlessness, his precocity, his restlessness and rootlessness, his uncertain affections, his haphazard progress ("I started to write for the papers. They printed my nonsense."), his snobbery and affections across social and ethnic lines ("I don't"), his underlying, adamantine confidence ("So am I").

2. in some vague relation: in the circumstances of JR's life, I find this bittersweet joke positively heroic.

3. This tale has elements of JR's story "April" (1925), where the "engineer" is a railwayman.

4. I became a writer: cf. JR's story "Rare and ever rarer in this world of empirical facts . . ." in Collected Stories.

99. To Stefan Zweig   Hotel am Zoo
                                              Berlin
                                              20 June 1930

Dear esteemed Mr. Zweig,

I no longer ask you to excuse my long and ill-bred silence, that's how well I feel you know me already, and know what my not-writing to you signifies. It means I am still unable to find the requisite distance from myself, and that it is difficult for me to give you any sort of objective report. Perhaps it's best if I stick to externals, then at least I won't make any mistakes.

Over a week ago, Kiepenheuer—who's since left Berlin—and Dr.

Ruppel of the *Kölnische Zeitung* were negotiating over my trip to Russia and Siberia. The *Kölnische* should have decided already, but it still hasn't, and I'm waiting impatiently. It's the most important factor governing the next few months for my wife and me. Dr. Ruppel (the feuilleton editor) claimed the general editor was very keen on my working for the paper. So long as he's not lying or exaggerating—and he doesn't look the sort—then my chances are good. Unfortunately, the general editor is away on vacation. He promised to confer with Dr. Ruppel about my trip on the telephone, and it seemed the decision must be made even before his return (set for early July). I await it every day. If the trip is declined, there will be other reasons I can't even guess at. There's nothing to be done about them. The Russian correspondent of the *Kölnische* was apparently based on the Turksib.[1] To improve my chances—and to the universal horror of all who are familiar with the country and my style— I asked for only 10,000 to 12,000 marks—for five months. I didn't dare ask for more. How I'm supposed to get by on that, I have no idea. I have to leave at least 3,000 marks for my wife. The water is up to my neck. Kiepenheuer's expensive authors, Feuchtwanger[2] Zweig[3] Glaeser[4] Heinrich Mann,[5] are coming in with their new manuscripts, drawing vast sums, and Kiepenheuer is *rightly* stopping my advance. I'm getting an unreasonable amount, I need 1,200 for my wife, 800 for myself, monthly, and I have already had 22,000 marks advanced to me. Since last week I've started writing articles again—stupid of me, given my state of exhaustion, and lack of inspiration—and Kiepenheuer's newspaper distribution company sells them. But I can't make more than 500 marks a month from reprints. If Cologne doesn't come through, I don't know what to do. It'll just have to come through. In October I'll find out how *Job* does. If only it would sell 15,000 copies! Generalkonsul Pflaum[6] has died. But the Munich people may go on paying me till August. Provided I am able to produce articles for them, which of course is now triply impossible. I'm no longer equal to this schmonzes.[7] I have trained myself so that I can only think on a larger scale now, and it takes me a long time to tear a pretty little piece out of something else. Which of course I then hate.

So you can imagine I'm sitting on coals. My wife's costs are fixed, I can do nothing to reduce them. I will work to the limits of possibility, even if it kills me. If it's possible via the Concordia[8] to get lower rates—as your wife wrote to me—without her having to go to a different institution, then I'd be very grateful to you. It probably won't be possible to work with Sarnetzki[9] at the Cologne paper. It's the board that seems to want me. At the moment I am preoccupied with the old business of my wife, and with the visit to Siberia. I am impatient, suspicious, mean, I can't stand myself. It's the easiest way to writer's block.

Now I notice I must no longer ask forgiveness[10] for not writing, but for writing. I have written some disgusting things to you today, and I beg your indulgence. If I were with you, no doubt your kindly eye would see more than I am able to write here and now. Please view this letter as strictly a news communication. If anything changes, I'll let you know. I promise to write to your good wife soon.—I hope you're well, and wish you all the best. Think of me, as I think of you. The thought of good friends has great power. I hope you feel me thinking of you.

Cordially, always, your old   Joseph Roth

1. Turksib: the Turkestan-Siberian Railway, under construction from 1927 to 1930.

2. Feuchtwanger: Lion Feuchtwanger (1884 Munich–1958 Los Angeles), novelist, playwright, essayist.

3. Zweig: Arnold (no relation) Zweig (1887–1969), writer, playwright, essayist, and man of the Left.

4. Glaeser: Ernst Glaeser (1902–1963), writer and journalist. Went into exile in 1933, only to return to the Third Reich in May 1939.

5. Heinrich Mann (1871 Lübeck–1950 Santa Monica), writer and essayist. Older brother of Thomas Mann. Shared a house with Roth and Kesten for a time in the south of France.

6. Generalkonsul Pflaum: director of the publishing house Knorr & Hirth, which brought out the right-ish *MNN*.

7. schmonzes: (Yiddish) nonsense, tripe, balderdash.

8. A literary association in Vienna.

9. Sarnetzki: Detmar Sarnetzki (1878–1961), feuilleton editor at the *Kölnische Zeitung*.

10. forgiveness: typical of JR's exquisite courtliness, the obverse of his occasional uncouthness.

100. To Stefan Zweig   Hotel am Zoo
Berlin
27 June 1930

Dear very dear Mr. Zweig,

the *Kölnische* (in the person of Mr. Neven DuMont)[1] seems to rate me, but not Russia. I replied I would probably have to accept a tour around Germany. Even though that brings in little money, and Russia would have freed me from more than just the material pressure. I could have become a different person there. On Monday I'm going around to Theodor Wolff,[2] and on Tuesday to Ullstein. But the world has been divvied up among those journalistic pashas called special correspondents. There's probably nothing to be done. Please give my regards to Mr. Sarnetzki anyway.—My wife is no better. I am not just grateful to Dr. Schacherl, I have become humanly fond of him. This fine man tries everything, even though experience must tell him it's hopeless. If you get a chance to tell him how I honor him, please do so. Though I'm afraid it may all become too much for him. This week, a friend of my wife's, one Professor Kuczynski (Gelbfieber) made inquiries of him via a mutual colleague in Vienna—and I'd like him not to be overrun like that.—I'm compelled to stay in Berlin. I'm getting hold of all the money I can, with more expertise than I thought I had. Berlin is apt to be forgetful. If you're not here, you can't do anything.—I'm glad you're not bringing a book out in autumn. You don't have to gallop the whole time, as I do. Miss Baker[3] was admired everywhere, is read with interest, and the book will be one of your great successes, even if you wait till spring. May God continue to give you good fortune, I am always on your side.

You are so kind to me, you tell me you no longer get on with contented people. But I know that you need such, and that unhappy people are unlucky. For months your friendship is the only comfort I have felt. (Many times I simply haven't written, because I am unable to concentrate.)

With kind regards, your old   Joseph Roth

1. Neven DuMont: Alfred Neven DuMont (1868–1940), editor of the *Kölnische Zeitung*.

2. Theodor Wolff (1868–1943), editor of the *Berliner Tageblatt*.

3. Miss Baker: Mary Baker Eddy (1821–1910), founder of the Christian Science movement, and subject of one of Stefan Zweig's three-for-one biographical excursuses, where she is paired—or trebled?—with Freud and Mesmer (*Heilung durch den Geist*, 1931).

101. To Stefan Zweig   *Hotel am Zoo*
                                                          Berlin
                                                          17 July 1930

To Mr. Stefan Zweig, Kapuzinerberg, Salzburg

Dear esteemed Mr. Zweig,

yesterday I thought it might be possible to visit you for a day in Salzburg. I would rather have spoken to you than telling you scraps of things that I am unable to put on paper. But then I get a letter from the *Kölnische Zeitung*, in which they agree to my conditions. So on Monday or Tuesday I'll head off for the Ruhr after a short stay in central Germany. It's a grisly job, which will take me at least 8 weeks, but it's the only thing that'll bring in a bit of money at the moment. I'll be getting 2,000 marks cash down, of which I'll be able to send 1,000 to Vienna. That's all I care about at the moment. Should I write to Dr. Scheyer in Vienna direct, to ask him if I can join Concordia? Is that correct?

I got a kind letter from your wife, suggesting in various ways a period of recuperation for me. I can't accept any of them. I have to earn money in the period before the book comes out, because the publisher won't give me another penny.

Letters—and I hope you will write me soon—will reach me from now on c/o Kiepenheuer Verlag, Berlin NW, Altonaerstrasse 4. Mrs. Olden, who left for Salzburg yesterday and to whom I said I would be there on Monday, will give you my best wishes.

In old sincere friendship   Your [Joseph Roth]

102. To Benno Reifenberg   *Hotel am Zoo, Berlin*
                                              17 July 1930

To Mr. Benno Reifenberg, Paris, c/o Frankfurter Zeitung
Dear Mr. Reifenberg,
I believe I owe you the following notification: I will shortly have to undertake a brief German tour on behalf of the *Kölnische Zeitung*. I know that various parties are interested in my renewed work for the *Frankfurter Zeitung*; while various other parties have expressed themselves against it. The Kiepenheuer Verlag, to whom, as you know, I have sold my journalistic work, is unable to go on paying me if I don't take this opportunity, which will bring in quite a lot of money. I know that various parties, in particular your good self, will be disappointed to see me suddenly appearing there. But there is nothing I can do about it. In any case, I think I owed you this notification.
Give my regards to your family.
I am not doing well. I am a little surprised not to hear from you.
Cordially your old   Joseph Roth
Address: c/o Kiepenheuer Verlag, Altonaerstrasse 4 II

103. Benno Reifenberg to Joseph Roth   *[Paris] 25 July 1930*

To Mr. Joseph Roth, Kiepenheuer Verlag, Altonaerstrasse, 4 II, Berlin
My dear Roth,
thank you for your letter, though it saddened me to think that I must look to find you in other newspapers and not in ours, which is really the only possible one for you. Mr. Jedlicka[1] told me you were sad about my silence, but there must be some misunderstanding there, or else you didn't get the letter I sent you in Salzburg. You see, I was waiting for news of you, not least as I was hoping to see you here in Paris among us. I am alone, Maryla and Jan have gone to the seaside. I should like to talk to you, and hear how life is treating you, and what you're writing. I was

delighted to see that we're at least going to publish the serialization of your novel, of which Jedlicka gave me a passionate account

Be well, drop me a line to let me know you've at least gotten this, and then I'll write you again at greater length.

Unaltered your   [Benno Reifenberg]

P.S. I enclose an article on the Delacroix exhibition, perhaps it—the article—passed you by. I visited the exhibition many times.

1. Jedlicka: Dr. Gotthard Jedlicka (1899–1965), art historian, writer for the *FZ*, professor of art history at the University of Zurich.

104. To Benno Reifenberg   [1930]

Dear precious Mr. Reifenberg,

it was very nice to hear from you, and to see Jan again. Unfortunately, you're right: not since the time of the inflation have I been so wretched as I am now. I find the politics quite paralyzing. It's so hard to write. I have no money, I mean really NO MONEY, I get by on 5 marks a day. And I'm drinking. And my strength is fading. Just this novel now—then I'm off to Zurich by way of Frankfurt, I stand to pick up 2,000 marks when it's done.

Kiepenheuer doesn't want the Hausenstein book. I've made inquiries at Rowohlt. Please, could you dictate your letter again, without referring to the rejection by the Frankfurter Societätsdruckerei[1] and Fischer! So that I can show it to Rowohlt, and maybe to Tal in Vienna.

Your article was very sensible and radical. Thank you! Do you write much? When is your family joining you in France?

What are our friends doing?

H.S.[2] was here, but didn't come and see me. How are you managing to work? Tired, grumpy, optimistic?

Please give my regards to Gubler,[3] and to Picard, if he's there.

Your old old   Joseph Roth

1. The publisher of the *FZ* (and book publisher).
2. H.S.: Heinrich Simon.
3. Gubler: Friedrich Traugott Gubler—see no. 118.

105. To Stefan Zweig

Hotel Englischer Hof
Frankfurt am Main
22 September 1930

To Mr. Stefan Zweig, Salzburg, Kapuzinerberg 5

Dear esteemed Stefan Zweig,

I must yield to your wish that I not address you as "Mr." if you think it impedes the friendliness of our communications. That it honors me, I need not say.

Thank you for reading *Job* once more. I for my part find it superfluous to have written it. I have no ties to it any more. I am tired of it, or I am simply tired. I don't think the book can engage me any more than I can engage myself. Believe me, I've been a burden to myself for years, sometimes intolerably so. If you do write about *Job*, please don't go to any trouble, your name will do by itself. I would be sorry if you were to contribute something that would hardly be understood in Germany, and would certainly not be appreciated.

I can hardly tell you how unwillingly I have attached myself to the newspaper again. What else could I have done? Kiepenheuer's money goes on Vienna, there's almost nothing left for me. I've lived the past 3 weeks on borrowed money. Even though I've written 50 typewritten pages for the *Kölnische Zeitung*, the proprietor tells me it's not enough, and I have to write another 3 articles if I am to claim the remaining 1,000 marks he offered me. What shall I do? I wrote to him that he is right if he pays by the line, and I am right in that I leave out lines. So I will not have the 1,000 marks. I know of no other solution than the deal with the *Frankfurter Zeitung*. Perhaps you don't know what it's like when you can't wait for a book to succeed because you have no money at all. I will hardly be able to finish my recently begun novel in the next months. But for the *Frankfurter Zeitung*, I will have to knock out 4 articles a month, and sometimes more.

Horovitz[1] of the Phaidon Verlag offers me 3,000 marks for a book. It's to be called "The Orient Express," and is to be about the train, the passengers, the hotels, and stopping-off places. First I had to get Kiepenheuer's permission for this breach of faith. He isn't able to give me any more money, but the Horovitz money won't be here for another ten days at the earliest, and who knows if the contract won't be such that I can't put my name to it. This year, apart from *Job*, I have written a ragged novel, 50 solid pages for the *Kölnische*, and about 80 articles, and I'm sitting there in perplexity, thinking it would have been better not to work and not have gotten sick, as I have. I literally can't wait for *Job* to succeed. It won't happen before January, and that's fully three months away.

In case I am able to come to an agreement with Dr. Horovitz, that'll see me through 2½ months maybe, but then I'll need to work again, because he wants his book on March 1.

Thank you very much for the Mesmer. I'd like to read it tonight, and send you notes on it tomorrow. I don't think you've forgotten how to write quickly; rather, I think it's the fault of the material, if you have to do lots of revisions. I'm dying to see your Freud. When will that be ready?

I mentioned the Insel Verlag[2] because I'm afraid Kiepenheuer will run out of money, and I need to live. I am too sick to live plainly. I can't mortify myself in literature without indulging myself a little physically.

Cordially ever   your [Joseph Roth]

1. Horovitz: Bela Horovitz (1898 Budapest–1955 New York), founder of the Phaidon Verlag in Vienna and, later, in exile, the Phaidon Press in London. Roth's book on the Orient Express was never written; instead Horovitz agreed to take on the second edition of Roth's novel *Hotel Savoy* (first published in 1924 by Die Schmiede.)

2. the Insel Verlag: publisher of Zweig, among others (Rilke). Roth's scorched-earth policy with publishers means he is already thinking of moving on.

106. To Stefan Zweig   *Hotel Englischer Hof*
                                          Frankfurt am Main
                                          Tuesday [23 September 1930]

Dear esteemed Stefan Zweig,

I've been trying for a week not to write this letter, now, after a conversation with Kiepenheuer I have no alternative. My wife has been taken to a sanatorium again, I am waiting for a call from Vienna. Kiepenheuer can offer me no further advances. I want to be gone, even before the 3,000 marks from Horovitz get here that I mentioned to you yesterday. Every wasted day is precious. Please please excuse me for introducing such ugliness into our friendship. I urgently need to send money to Vienna, close my tab here, and leave, far away, I don't know where. I enclose a letter to Dr. Horovitz, asking him to send you the 3,000 marks. And I'm asking you now please to send me part of this amount here, or get it transferred even more quickly. All my endeavors with my wife have failed. I'm exhausted, finished. You will forgive a man in my condition the crudeness of misusing a truly noble friendship. I've just been interrupted. The call from Vienna. Another change of plan, I need to send money there, the last vestiges of my peace of mind depend on it. Please will you ask Dr. Schacherl to intervene, I'll wire you at the same time. Excuse my abruptness, I must stop.

    Cordially,   your humble Joseph Roth

107. To Bela Horovitz   *Hotel Englischer Hof*
                                          Frankfurt am Main
                                          Tuesday, 23 September 1930

Dear Dr. Horovitz,

would you have the kindness to send the 3,000 marks (three thousand) owing to me as per our contract to Mr. Stefan Zweig.

I don't know whether I'm going to be in Paris—where I'd originally asked you to send the money—hence this change of arrangement.

Humble greetings from   your Joseph Roth

108. To Stefan Zweig   *Hotel Englischer Hof*
                                          Frankfurt am Main
                                          Thursday [September 1930]

Dear highly esteemed Stefan Zweig,

there was more to your Mesmer than I first thought, and I have only just gotten to the end of it. There's no point making separate notes. Things that were strikingly wrong or that I very much disliked I didn't find, and you'll be able to see to other things yourself. The proof is very bad and full of errors. Lots of things are thrown together, with commas where I'm sure you didn't put any. The beginning is a bit sticky, not like a beginning, stylistically more like a middle. You can't easily make your way into it. It's more as though you've opened it somewhere at random. I would shorten the sentences and break them up. Soften the tone a bit. Start to tell what is an extraordinary story. You assume too much of the reader at the outset. Even so, it's not *medias in res*, so much as *medias in scientias*. But then, but then! It's much better than Christian Science, and on the last pages it's quite splendid. Some passages made me shiver. "Where now, old man?" That got me. And the final paragraph—apart from the use of imperfect instead of perfect—is of a really classic beauty, reminded me of Burckhardt's[1] prose, it has that lightness and massiness of something really good. Habitual mistakes: you put "as" for "than" in comparisons, you don't use the semicolon enough, you connect syntactically things that are connected only in thought, and you are careless with tenses. Recherché comparisons, analogies, etc. are too frequent and rarely clinching. A half-resemblance, say, to Columbus, you try to make into a whole. Sometimes the wealth of associations at your fingertips tyrannizes you. But then. Then. You display more concentration than ever before. Another writer would have spun it out to 1,000 pages. And that must be praised, especially in you: to know so much, and throw so much away! Dear, dear, esteemed master. In the first 30 pages you should make your richness, your glitter, your fullness more *porous*, softer, gentler, and also harder. In your beginnings—and I know that's to do with your kind nature—you are incapable of restraint. At the beginning you come across as positively voracious—but you take the reader's voracity away. The wonderful last paragraph, I wish it were longer, and I wish the style and feeling of it were somehow also longer.—By the way, this is not an objective critical wish I'm expressing here. It's my own feeling.

My cordial thanks.

This morning I got your letter, last night your wire. Do you mind if I talk about money one last time. I've got to do that job for Phaidon. I'm going to be seeing you. I refuse to borrow money from you while I'm capable of earning it, and as long as I don't share your optimism that things will look up for me. I've just had to send 1,000 marks to Vienna, my wife is in Rekawinkel,[2] and once again the doctor there doesn't think it's schizophrenia. So quite plainly and objectively this situation can go on costing me enormous sums—and as Kiepenheuer can't pay me any more, and as my wife remains my first priority, because I can't forget about her—then I can't, in banal self-interest burden our friendship with that crap that money is. I'll work till I drop. My letter to you must have been terrifying, I can't remember, it was a terrible situation. Calls from Vienna, appeals to Kiepenheuer, who refused, I couldn't catch myself, I lost my bearings, please forgive me. And I know, I know exactly how much good you do, and that there are other people as well, and that my torments mustn't be overstated, even though I can feel them garroting me, I can see my last hour before me *all the time*. But you know about a lot of these torments. And they are all equally important. And I should like to loan Lidin[3] some money myself, and please let him know that he can count on me.

I've just announced my visit to Königstein,[4] where Dr. Simon is lying ill. He is the only one who knows Pagenstecher. I will try, if his fever isn't too high (pleurisy) to talk to him about Lidin. I know it's possible to get the price reduced. I'll wire you if there's any chance of that. But in any case I'm at Lidin's disposal.

I've just heard that Landauer,[5] Kiepenheuer's managing editor, is coming here, either tonight or tomorrow morning. It seems I am in conflict with the firm after all. It's shitty that money can wreck something, and that it's such a force. Maybe I'm being unfair. But my wife is so important, if I am to remain alive! Perhaps you won't accept that either. You don't know what it's like.

I'm going tomorrow, first to Cologne. My mail will be forwarded. I'm meeting Reifenberg in Cologne. My next six months will be filled with shit work, for the newspaper and God knows, all for money. But maybe I'll be able to get a trip to Russia out of the *FZ*. And that would rejuvenate me.—Do you still want to do that?

I get the feeling your wife is mixed up. I wrote her yesterday. Kiss her hand for me.

Cordially as ever,   your old Joseph Roth

Another thing: sometimes you have this construction "in the same measure as . . ." That's not good. "as well as . . ."

And: too many gerunds (verbal nouns), even where authentic nouns are available. As for instance "being near" instead of "nearness" and so on . . .

1. Burckhardt: Jacob Burckhardt (1818–1897), considered one of the greatest historians of the nineteenth century.

2. Rekawinkel: small woodland spa in the hills outside Vienna.

3. Lidin: Vladimir Lidin (1894–1979), Russian author, residing partly abroad. Typical of JR: to be dependent on charity himself, and simultaneously extend it to others.

4. Königstein: spa outside Frankfurt.

5. Landauer: Walter Landauer (1902–1945), publisher, first with Die Schmiede, then from 1928 Kiepenheuer. Went into exile in 1933, became (with Roth's support) editorial director of the German exile publishing part of the Dutch firm Allert de Lange, in Amsterdam, who, with Querido, and later De Gemeenschap, published Roth's literary output. Murdered in Bergen-Belsen.

109. To Jenny Reichler   *Dom Hotel, Cologne*
                                            Sunday [September 1930]

Dear Mother,

in November there will be money coming from America at last.
1,000 dollars initially, but that will do for a start, and I hope that you
and Friedl will feel better as well.—I'm going back to Paris till then, to
resume working for the newspaper. Write to me at Hotel Foyot, 33 rue
de Tournon, right away please.—Don't worry if Friedl blames you for
all kinds of things, and don't be offended, just go to her.—I am hopeful
that I might finish my novel, and be in Vienna soon.

Hugs from me, and kisses, especially to dear father.

Your son.

110. To Jenny Reichler   *Hotel Englischer Hof*
                                            Frankfurt am Main
                                            Saturday
                                            [September/October 1930]

Dear Mother,

thank you. I'm going to Strasbourg till tomorrow evening, Hotel
Diebold for any wires. Please write and tell me if Dr. Schmitt made a
good impression on you, and if you're prepared to entrust Friedl to him.
I'm loath to trust my own judgment in such an important matter.

What does Father think? What about Sandi?[1]

Hugs, your M.

As soon as I hear from Dr. Schmitt, I'll pass on his opinion.

1. Sandi: Alexander Pompan, Roth's brother-in-law, husband of Friedl's sister Hedi.

111. To his parents-in-law   *Hotel Foyot, Paris*
                                                Friday
                                                [October 1930]

Dear parents,

I didn't learn that it was Yom Kippur till I was back in Paris. Otherwise, I'm sure I wouldn't have been so crass as to announce my trip to you on that day. Please forgive me.

Write to me here. I have jaundice, and was very sick when I came back.

May God help us finally.

Hugs   your loyal son

112. To Stefan Zweig   *Hotel Foyot, rue de Tournon*
                                         Paris, 8 October 1930

To Mr. Stefan Zweig, Salzburg, Kapuzinerberg 5
Dear esteemed Stefan Zweig,

on the way to Paris I fell ill in Strasbourg. That's why I haven't written to you for so long. I thought long and hard about your last letter. Perhaps you're right in what you say about my wife. I still haven't gained any perspective on it all. At least I've gotten this far, that I can no longer continue to be as sensitive to her condition as I am now—not if I'm to go on myself. I'll write you in greater detail later. I just heard from Lidin, whose letter followed me here, it probably crossed me at Wiesbaden. He's still in Paris, it seems, and I'm seeing him tomorrow. I'm leaving on the 13th. A tour of German cities for the *Frankfurter Zeitung*. My book is out the day after tomorrow. I assume you've been sent a bossy letter about your review from the publisher. I hope you won't blame me. I'd be very glad to hear from you again before I leave.

In old cordiality   your Joseph Roth

113. To Jenny Reichler

Hotel Foyot, Paris
Thursday
[October 1930]

Dear Mother,

thank you for your letter. Milan Wileder's[1] visit appears to have been very useful for Friedl. Even though she didn't react, I'm sure she will have felt something. If there's another occasion, please describe it for me in just as much detail. Thank Hedi for writing, and for the article. I don't think there's anything to be done about my sadness. I'm through with life, for good. I can't wait around any more for miracles. I have become an old man, and have gotten used to the absence of joy. In my own life, that is. If Friedl pulls through, I will be far older than she is. Just as soon as I feel really old, she will snap out of it, I know she will.

Hugs from your loyal son   Joseph

1. Milan Wileder: an old (female) friend of Friedl's.

114. To Stefan Zweig

Hotel Englischer Hof
Frankfurt am Main
23 October 1930

Dear esteemed Mr. Zweig,

thank you so much for your kind letters. Of course I found myself staying longer on the road than I should have done; but perhaps it was necessary after all. I haven't seen the announcement for my book. If you should happen to have a copy, please send it to me, but you must stop getting annoyed about it. Every word you write about me is written out of friendship; and because I am waxing metaphysical, let me add that only things that are done out of friendship have any effect.

I am compelled to dictate this, and am sorry that I am therefore unable to respond to what you wrote about your family. I'll get on to it as soon as I can. Please tell your dear wife that I am grateful for every word she writes to me, and that I will write to her in the next few days also.

The thought of the Balearics is extraordinarily tempting. Who isn't disgusted by politics? You're right, Europe is killing itself, and in a peculiarly slow and horrible way, because it is a corpse already. This ending is devilishly like a psychosis. It's a psychotic's suicide. The devil really is in the saddle. But it's the two extremes I don't understand, for that I'm too much the contemporary of Franz Joseph, I hate extremism; it's the most fiery and disgusting tongue of this flame. Do please send me your Freud (and I'm glad you shortened the first part of the Mesmer).

You're quite right, of course I have to visit the small towns; that was the newspaper's proposal too. Maybe if I'd visited them before the election,[1] the result wouldn't have come as such a shock to the paper, and to others. I'm still unable to share your optimism with regard to *Job*; I know the book has captured hearts, but according to Kiepenheuer's calculations, it won't actually make any money until mid to late January.

Your telegram reached me too late, because I got to Frankfurt later than I'd planned. I am writing to the Insel Verlag, to ask them for the Chinese novel;[2] thank you for the tip.

I'll make sure that Dr. Moritz Scheyer gets sent a copy of *Job* too.

In old cordiality   your [Joseph Roth]

1. elections: the Reichstag elections of 14 September 1930, in which the Nazis won 107 of 577 seats (in 1928 they had just 12) and the Communists 70 (as against 54 previously).
2. Chinese novel: *Kin Ping-Meh*, published in German translation by Insel in 1930.

115. *To Stefan Zweig*

Hotel "Der Achtermann" and Niedersächsischer Hof
Currently in Goslar, 20 November 1930

Dear esteemed Stefan Zweig,

thank you very much for the Rocca.[1] The same day I got a very sweet letter from him. I'll reply today. I don't quite understand what sort of issue the *LW*[2] is putting together, and fear it may not be the ideal set-ting for Rocca. Willy Haas[3] is among the very few life-forms whom the Germans view correctly—and his scandalous reputation of course rubs off on any magazine he edits. I'm sure Kiepenheuer, or Dr. Landshoff,[4] would be prepared to put out a magazine like that, from business consid-erations alone. If the plan with the *LW* doesn't work out, maybe we can take it to Kiepenheuer?

Please God you're right about the print run for *Job*. So far, 8,500 copies have been sold, which is a lot for me. But not enough in view of the money problems of the Kiepenheuer Verlag. Neither Feuchtwanger nor Heinrich Mann is selling well. Glaeser is hovering around the 15,000 mark, he'll probably get to 30 in the end. How I'd love to be working on my novel on the Dual Monarchy now! But I need at least 2,500 a month, and I bust a gut to make 1,000, and not even that, because I can't man-age 1,000 lines a month for the *Frankfurter*. That's almost 50 a day, one would have to be a steam press to manage that. And the traveling on top of everything, and putting up in towns that defy the imagination. It's a terrible thing, you know, never having more than 50 marks in your pocket. Kiepenheuer can only ever manage installments of 100 or 150 marks, just enough to pay the hotel, and the train fare and the next hotel. I never have enough to be able to settle somewhere for a fortnight, say. Unfortunately, I've also signed with Phaidon. Vienna needed another 1,000 marks, and it was a moment when Kiepenheuer had nothing at all. But the contract is more favorable, because I asked for and got only half the advance, and in return secured the right to hand in a different travel manuscript instead. So what I'm thinking of is a "New Harz Journey," which is due to come out in the *FZ* anyway. Of which I haven't written a line. I can hardly access the newspaper tone any more—my head is full of the novel ("The Radetzky March," it'll be called), set in the Dual Mon-archy from 1890 to 1914.[5] I'll tell you the plot sometime we're together.

Before that you must permit me to talk you through the ghastly money business. Since Phaidon paid only half the advance, I have 500 in hand. Of those I have sent you none. So I have committed a sort of fraud, admittedly you're a friend, but in a way that's even worse. You will have counted on the money for other charitable purposes—which means other people will be suffering on my account. You will know how that torments me, first of all my deception, and second the sufferings of others. The worst was the airiness with which I borrowed from you, on the basis of a promise that turned out to be false. You were perfectly right: I've lost my head, I can't do sums, I am beset with astronomic debts, and I commit one deception after another. Complaints keep rolling in, my lawyer, Dr. Wolf in Vienna, Teinfaltstrasse, who gets nothing from me either, has his hands full with them, and I don't even dare write to apologize to him, that's how much I am in his debt. For my peace of mind I urgently need you to give me in writing that you'll let me owe you those 2,000 marks until February or March—and that, in spite of your generous fastidiousness. I've put Kiepenheuer in the picture. He knows I need that amount for you. If you want to upbraid me, please do it, I've earned it a thousand times over, perhaps it's best that it be said out loud, lest it fester unspoken between us.

A set date? In circumstances like mine? The *FZ* would be angry with me forever after if I left them now, as it was they put me through humiliations to get the 1,000 marks, they think they were generous in forgiving me the episode with the *MNN*. And then how? How? I need 1,000 marks, my wife needs 800, Kiepenheuer can't run to more than 500. I need to pay off 200–300 a month. The *BT* and the *Vossische* don't want me, I'm not famous enough for them.

Dear Stefan Zweig, in your friendship and good nature you are apt to confuse your prestige with mine, your freedom with my captivity. Let's talk about it sometime. I'll be in Mitteldeutschland till 10 December, within easy reach of Leipzig or Dresden, just wire me when and where. I can be with you in 24 hours. *My address is still c/o Grübel[6] Leipzig Gohliserstrasse, 18 till December 10.*

I think it's perfectly natural that you treat Freud with kid gloves. The only risk is if that became *evident* in your book. It's a matter of technique. If it became evident, then it would be private. And if one couldn't make it completely invisible, in my opinion a few words of private explanation would be called for. That would be *honest*. I don't want anyone to accuse you of special pleading. Of course that's what it is, objectivity is filth, but it mustn't show.

Another thing. A propos Rocca, you say: "his German is as good as mine, and almost as good as yours." Please not to say anything like that again! It's painful for me to have to blush, and then explain it to myself by reference to one of your magnanimous outbursts. You know and I know the sort of writer you are—it's far harder to compliment you, because everything is far too obvious. Anyway, all this is much too official, and would fit better in my dealings with Thomas Mann (who is on record as having said something unkind about me, and claims only ever to have read 2 or 3 articles of mine, what do I care!). Please excuse this petition, and accede to it!

Cordially as ever,   your old Joseph Roth

1. A book of essays on German writers by Zweig's friend Enrico Rocca.

2. *LW*: *Die literarische Welt.*

3. Willy Haas (1891 Prague–1973 Hamburg), Communist critic, essayist, and editor of the *LW*.

4. Landshoff: Fritz Landshoff (1901–1988), co-proprietor of the Kiepenheuer Verlag; started the German exile publishing house Querido in Amsterdam in 1933, and later fell in with Bermann Fischer in New York.

5. First mentioned here.

6. Grübel: JR's maternal uncle, Salomon Grübel, a hop dealer, who left Brody for Nuremberg, and later settled in Leipzig.

116. To Jenny Reichler   *Hotel Fürstenhof*
                                            Leipzig
                                            Thursday [1930]

Dear Mother, I'm feeling a little better.

Please address any further news *to Grübel*, because I'm going in a few days. Thank Hedi for writing. I have to produce 5 articles by Christmas, and am incredibly busy.

I hope to spend Christmas in Paris, a friend has invited me.

The translations of *Job* will only begin to help in spring, once the book has appeared here and there. Admittedly, the only countries that matter are America and England, all other currencies are inconsequential. The only hope for all of us is a film version in America.[1]

Please give me details about Friedl.

Warm hugs   your son

1. a film version in America: this came to pass, only 4 years later, and far too late for JR. See no. 256.

117. *To Stefan Zweig*   *Hotel Foyot, Paris*
                                               27 December 1930

Dear esteemed Stefan Zweig,

I was an idiot: I thought you'd be in Frankfurt already, and wrote you there. Well, my best wishes for Christmas and New Year, and thank you both for the evidence of your friendship. Let's arrange to meet at last:

until 12 January I'll be in Paris,

from the 12th to the 15th in Frankfurt,

after the 16th I'll be in Paris again.

Name your date! Everything else (Spain) can be settled verbally. I need your advice more urgently than ever. My homesickness for you, for your wife, for your clever words (for months I've been talking to dogmatic fools) is very great. Yes, I am sentimental. Alright! A rendezvous, with place and date.

Enjoy your proofs.[1]

Your old   Joseph Roth

Thank your wife, and kiss her hand tenderly for me!

1. Of *Heilung durch den Geist*, the Freud, Mesmer, Baker Eddy book.

118. To Friedrich Traugott Gubler   *Marseille, 31 January 1931*
                                                       As of: Hotel Foyot, Paris 6ᵉ

Dearest Gubler,[1]

I owe you so much news, I can hardly hope to fit it all into one letter. I'd better try and give you a situation report:

After being in a terrible state in Paris unbeknownst to anyone, even Reifenberg, I have fled here, and am fleeing farther, to Antibes. I am fleeing from bills. Lately three suits have been brought against me. Kiepenheuer wants his novel, and threatens to suspend payments. Phaidon wants his "Orient Express," or, failing that, the return of 2,000 marks. A bond I gave my father-in-law falls due on 15 February (for 1,000 schillings). I owe you 1,270 lines. Everything is collapsing around my ears. I have drunk a lot, eaten hardly anything, then the flu wiped me out. Only in the past week, since I've been here, have I started to come to terms with my situation. I hope to find some peace in Antibes. I have 100 francs a day. By 15 March I must have 4 chapters of my novel done. But how am I going to manage to write in this condition? I hope I'll be better in Antibes.

I owe you more than lines, namely my collaboration. If you still feel able to, trust me. I will send you 3 pieces a month. I want to write "Ghost of the Present." (Using quotations from Picard.) Get P.[2] to send me a paperbound copy of his *Menschengesicht*. Use the Hotel Foyot address, because I have no idea where I'm going to be here.

One of my worst persecutors is Hermann Linden,[3] to whom I can't go on owing 500 marks. Ask him to tell you the story. Promise!

I still have to tell you I don't like the paper. Your nonsensical explanation, the whores of the present age, and cheek by jowl with the *Tagebuch*. It hurts me to see you and yours enmeshed in that kind of thing. I've come to the conclusion that you'll only wear yourself out there, to no purpose. It's just a paper, only slightly better than the others in Germany. It's no longer absolutely good or essential. And neither you nor Reifenberg nor Picard will be able to fix it. You will sacrifice your personal lives, the only important thing. It's a job for people who a priori have none, i.e., the likes of Brentano. Always do what your wife says, spend time with her and the children, discuss *everything* with her, and don't do anything just because your obstinate man's head tells you to. I can feel you slithering into triviality and shit. There is nothing more important than being a private person, than loving your wife, taking your children on your lap as you did when we came for you. Public affairs are only and ever shit, whether it's the nation, politics, the newspaper, the swastika, or the future of democracy. You should live like a peasant, and if you don't make or do anything yourself, or don't feel like it, then redouble your love for family and friends. In Paris I saw Picard separating me from Reifenberg: his identity with the paper. (Kracauer has finally become a buffoon.) I can't have a relationship with a person who is prepared to sell my private friendship for the sake of some public totem. I can no longer tolerate do-gooders, people who, when their wife has a pleurisy, still find time to save the world. Don't get drawn into all of that. It's only God whom one may serve over and above one's chosen ones. Not the "nation."

Forgive the homily. Forgive lots of things! Give your wife my very very warmest regards. Spend time at home with her. Don't get annoyed, everything's OK, so long as your family stays healthy. It's irreligious, ungodly, and collectivist to take thought for public matters! Leave that to Glaeser and (pause) to Brentano.

I haven't told you all my worries. I can't. We'll talk.

I remain your old devoted   Joseph Roth

Do you want to entrust Kesten's new book[4] to me? You know I won't trash it. The fellow's my discovery. And toward myself I'm not incorruptible. I tell you plainly, and I won't mind if you tell me back that you don't trust me. You know I'm not objective. I hate good books by godless fellows— Kren's[5] next book, for example—and I love bad books by reactionaries.

I'd also like to write, if you're agreeable, on *Stifter* and *Lampel*.[6]

1. Gubler: the Swiss Friedrich Traugott Gubler (1900–1965) took over as feuilleton editor on the *FZ* from Reifenberg in 1930, when R. became Paris correspondent.

2. P: Max Picard. The book is called *Das Menschengesicht* (The Human Face).

3. Hermann Linden (1896–1963) edited a 1949 selection on the life and works of Joseph Roth.

4. new book: Kesten's novel *Glückliche Menschen*.

5. Kren: Ernst Křenek.

6. Lampel: Peter Lampel (1894–1965), painter and writer.

119. To Jenny Reichler   *Thursday*
                                                         [early February 1931]

Dear Mother,

thank you!

I'm going to join Stefan Zweig in Antibes.

After you get this, don't write to me here, but to Paris 6ᵉ rue de Tournon, Hotel Foyot. They'll forward my mail. I'll wire you from Antibes, after the 10th.

It's still cold. I hope to get better in Antibes.

Hugs   Your son

Give Father my regards. He's not to start conversations with Friedl, but wait to hear what she says. Don't provoke utterances from her.

120. To his parents-in-law   *Hotel du Cap d' Antibes*
                                                         Antibes
                                                         6 February 1931

Dear Parents,

thank you! Go on writing to me at the Foyot, I'm not sure whether I'll be able to stay on here. Perhaps it'll be good for me, I'm already feeling a little better. But my worries even eclipse my illness. I have to write a novel with a completely skewed head, Lord knows whether I can manage it. With all my debts, I had to stop writing for the paper, there's a financial black hole, but what can I do, I can't tear myself in half. Very good news that Friedl's putting on weight. Maybe God will help, and she will become herself again. Is her expression changed? Her gaze? What does Father say? People ask after her everywhere in Marseille, in all the hotels and restaurants.

Impossible to ignore the way pain has aged me. I'm going gray.

If I don't write, don't worry about it. I'm working.

Cordially, your   Muniu

121. To Friedrich Traugott Gubler   *Hotel du Cap d' Antibes*
Very personal   *Antibes (A-M.)*
Please deliver immediately!   *Sunday*
                                             [February or March 1931?]

Dear, dear friend,

thank you! I would surely write more, letters and articles both, which come to the same thing, if it wasn't that I'm caught in a terrible fix. I can't settle. I've fallen in love with a 20-year-old girl.[1] It's impossible, it's a crime, I know it, to attach this girl to me, and to the dreadful tangle of my life. But I can't desist. Even if I were free to marry her, her family— very rich, very Catholic, German-hating Flemish barons who suffered under the occupation—would never allow it. The girl (still underage) wants to leave her family after she comes of age in July. It will be a huge scandal there (in Bruges). I am perpetrating a cretinous stupidity at my age but for the first time since my wife's illness, I feel *alive* again. It's not something I can turn away. I think you'll understand. My novel is going nowhere, I don't have any income, I'm quite evidently insane. I can't work, and yet I know I'll become completely sterile if I can't have that girl. And then there's my still warm feeling for my wife. I would never have thought I could be so foolish as this. And the knowledge of my own folly gives me happiness to cancel out my unhappiness, and I am more confused than ever. Dear friend, it's possible I'll need your calm, and your kind and helpful heart. Will you promise them to me! Don't mention this to anyone, except your good wife!—What shall I do? I have three chapters. I must be finished in July. I'm not enough of a novelist to go around thinking only of my book. With all my skepticism, for all my self-analysis, I'm in love. I'm incredibly fortunate. I need it as a thirsty man needs water. And I know it's poison.

I'm going back to Paris today, Hotel Foyot, rue de Tournon 33, and then Brussels for a few days. Letters please to Paris.

In cordial friendship

your old   Joseph Roth

Will you help me if I need you?

1. 20-year-old girl: a wildly improbable, but wholly true story. Research by Dr. Els Snick in 2008 revealed her identity as Maria Gillès de Pélichy. See Wilhelm von Sternburg's biography of JR.

122. *To Stefan Zweig*   *Hotel du Cap d'Antibes*
                                                                    Antibes
                                                                    24 March [1931]

Dear esteemed Stefan Zweig,

I hope you're safely resettled in Salzburg, and enjoying a second spring. Here it's finally exploded. Landauer has told me it doesn't matter, and I should stay here, so obviously *Job* is still selling, and I'm happy to stay. The guardian has arrived, with long beard and big belly, a clueless man, dimmed by Catholicism. The little girl slips into my room at night, even though he's sleeping next door, prays, crosses herself, and starts to sin. The guardian has no idea what she's done with the dog. He says she's right, it was wrong to try and get such a big animal to sleep in a bed, it remained a hunting animal, and was possibly infectious. He reads your books delightedly, he's a historian, a beer table pontificator, he loves the little girl to bits, believes everything, is completely unaware of the erotic nature of his relationship to her, prays before and after meals and half an hour before bedtime, busies himself with gardening, drapes cloaks and

things round sick trees, and doesn't hold with shooting rabbits because
he feels sorry for them. Goes to Mass every morning at 6 o'clock, sings in
church twice a year, wears a shirt for a week, always in black, too tight
pants. It's getting more and more obvious. The mother is the lady mayor
of the place, spends half the day praying, cries the other half, and has a
relationship with a priest, who out of jealousy intrigues against the girl.
The girl's father hated the mother, and kept getting her pregnant to get
him off sleeping with her. He was afraid to go to brothels, in case someone saw him, or he got sick. I'm convinced he died of secondary syphilis.
In his fever, he ripped up the girl's clothes and blabbed about everything.
Then the mother started hating her. The church is involved in everything, the whole house, makes everyone blind and deaf and hard. The
girl is so soft at night, when the sun rises—different again, and her sex
uncertain. She cries a lot, is sensuous and inventive, extraordinary predi-
lection for perversities, extremely sensitive to pain in normal intercourse,
probably all stemming from her sensitive psyche. Three Catholic hymens
before the real one, a shouter, and I practice the art of deflowering whilst
feeling little pleasure. How can I desist from such an interesting hobby?
A great aunt of hers was canonized. She wore armor day and night. The
bank employees have all propositioned her. Mr. Bridgemann is starting
to hover around her, but for once I'm man enough not to be the *amuse-
bouche*. Silent loathing between Bridgemann and me. He started it, of
course. He doesn't know what to do. Day before yesterday a magician
came. When he went around afterwards to collect money, B. got up,
borrowed 100 francs from the porter, and gave them to the little girl (to
make sure she saw), to present them to the magician, B. was sitting too
far away. Merci!, she said, and "c'est vilain," and she pocketed the money,
quite the chatelaine, which doesn't keep her, when it gets dark, from
draping her arm across my black dress trousers, she in her light-colored
dress. Sella sees and grins at me. The guardian sits there and sees nothing at all. (The Danes want me to pass on their regards to you, the one
they like best of yours is *Amok*.) The curé comes here for lunch, Sunday
is sanctified, the little girl is to sell liqueur. Mme Burke has bought and
read *Job*, and taken me violets up to my room, with the classic line: flow-

ers say what the mouth denies. I'm starting to enjoy myself. Only I miss you, your shrewd eye, your shrewd heart. Am writing the fourth chapter with the regimental doctor,[1] in bold, strong lines. Very good, I think. Don't worry about me! I'm more of a writer than I'm prepared to admit. Tear this letter up when you've absorbed it all. Give my regards to your wife, I can't write to her yet, she's a woman. I feel very much a man, and empathize with manliness in all forms. The red-haired Irishwoman is stricken with yearning for you, she says she has dreams about you.

Write back soon, even if it's just a line or two. My wife is doing badly. Credit to the girl, even so, that I'm not as burdened by it as usual. I may be a sonofabitch, but defloration in a literary setting, that's worth something to me.

In old and late friendship   Your JR

1. regimental doctor: Max Demant, the Jewish doctor in *The Radetzky March*.

123. *To Stefan Zweig*   *Hotel du Cap d'Antibes*
                                             Antibes
                                             4 April [1931]

Dear esteemed Stefan Zweig,

just a few words. I'll write in greater detail once I've finished the 4th chapter. Everyone is thinking of you, and sends you their best. A horribly swaggering Remarque is here with hangers-on, Adolf Loos[1] very poor and embarrassing, with miserable wife in tow. I wish you happy Easter, good luck with your work, and I look forward to hearing from you, whether my letters are shorter or longer.

The enclosed is for your wife.

In continuing cordiality   your JR

1. Loos: the Viennese architect (1870–1933), known for his buildings in Vienna and the Czech Republic.

124. To Stefan Zweig   *Hotel du Cap d'Antibes*
                                  Antibes
                                  Saturday [11 April 1931]

Dear Stefan Zweig,

I'm going into Antibes, and think I'll stay there all day. I'm sorry I'm so unbearable, I can feel you holding it against me. But part of it—you give me the right to be frank with you—is the result of the tension between the three of us, your good wife, and you, and me. It always hurt me, as a friend, once I'd given myself permission to feel it at all. You seem to want to stifle my frankness—and for me that's what friendship consists of. I feel you holding many things against me that you are unable or unwilling to say. I am too straightforward for that, you are more complex and mature, and I can't bear it. I hope our friendship—it is in danger—won't break, either over a wife or over less. To me friendship is as high an ideal as freedom, and I want to keep them both.

I feel a little feverish, and I beg your pardon for possible bad behavior. My writing is brittle and harsh, I'm sure I could find better expressions.

I would have left long ago, if a poor person weren't keeping me here. You know it well, and you know too that I cannot leave, of my own.

I'll write from Antibes.

I embrace you in love and friendship   your JR

125. To Stefan Zweig   *Hotel Foyot, Paris*
                                  22 April 1931

Dear esteemed Stefan Zweig,

I am still on my 4th chapter, and have been here since the day before yesterday. Your good letter followed me here. The auction of Flaubert's estate in Antibes didn't contain anything remarkable. But the Maupassant manuscript the dealer in Nice wrote you about seemed, in spite of its high price, very interesting.—My life currently has more tensions and complications than I am able to set down. I may tell you about them, in some confidential hour. Will we have one again, ever? I have to go to Poland in the next few weeks. My dear old friend is iller than usual.[1] My wife is still silent, and the letters of my in-laws, which continue to speak of cure and a resumption of marriage, hurt me; just like their reports of my wife's apparent happiness when they mention me in front of her. Miss Prensky,[2] in Flanders for 3 weeks, was at least able to relax her. I am grateful to her. I will go and visit her. Even there there are complications I can't write to you about. The novel remains my chief concern. Being or staying in the mood for it: the tensions help and simultaneously hinder. I feel something important coming, and at some deep level of myself am calm, though agitated on the surface. I am sending your *Cure through the Spirit* to my Polish friend. She is very eager to see it. Here, another good friend of mine read it in 2 days, with great enjoyment. I am to tell you!

Write in full consciousness of your mastery! Your novel! It's to be your masterpiece.[3] Please don't tell anyone I'm here. I want 10 days of quiet. Give my fond regards to your wife.

I am your old friend   Joseph Roth

1. JR is referring here to Mme Szajnocha.
2. Prensky: Eva Prensky, translator and literary agent in Paris. In 1941 she was picked up in Nice and put into a concentration camp by the Gestapo.
3. masterpiece: the posthumously published and never properly completed *Post Office Girl*.

126. *To Stefan Zweig*   *Hotel Foyot, Paris*
                                 5 May 1931

Dear esteemed Stefan Zweig,

terrible, in the most literal sense indescribable things are happening in my life. Since my last letter I've been bedridden. I'm completely shattered. I am incapable of writing. For the first time in my life, I feel that even a letter requires some form of crystallinity. The confessional beckons. Even

in Notre Dame confessional chairs are set up before Christmas and Easter with the simple legend: German, English, French, etc. I am writing
in a tearing rush, with fever, with sick, inflamed eyes, and I beg pardon
for the rapidity, and ask that you be assured of my sincere friendship.

Ever your old   Joseph Roth

127. To Friedrich Traugott Gubler   *Hotel Foyot, Paris*
                                                       6 May 1931

Dear friend, heartiest thanks,

I am in a terrible situation, experiencing terrible things, not since my
wife fell ill have I gone through such a terrible time as now. I am waiting
for decisions to be taken, and then I'll come to Frankfurt. Please don't
mention anything to anyone in Berlin. I shall tell you what it is impossible to write. Life has become awful for me, a simple torment. My script
is so skewed, and my style so abrupt, because I have pain in one eye,
which has been inflamed for days.

My regards to your wife. Hugs!

Your old   Joseph Roth

128. To Stefan Zweig   *13 May 1931*

Dear esteemed Stefan Zweig,

in addition to all the other things *you don't know about*, I have an eye
inflammation that stops me from writing. Thank you so much for your
letter! I feel bad in every respect. Please say so to Mr. Latzko,[1] whose
book and letter I received. I will ask Gubler at the *FZ* to let me review his
novel. Please excuse the handwriting. I am writing with half-open eyes.
I look like a bloodhound. Flanders has taken a wholly unexpected turn.
The little girl has blabbed, and been put in a nunnery where she will

probably die. I've had a letter from a monk. Life is so much finer than literature! I feel sorry for literature! It is a SWINDLE!

In old cordiality   Your J.R.

1. Latzko: Andreas Latzko (1876–1943), novelist and pacifist.

129. To Stefan Zweig   *Hotel Foyot, Paris*
                              Whitmonday [24 May 1931]

Dear, esteemed Stefan Zweig

I am writing to you in a pair of dark glasses, prescribed by the doctor, very unpleasant, cornea apparently damaged. (Excuse any abruptness!) My heart is *not at all* full of Flanders. Though must have contributed to physical malady. I couldn't stand to have yet another woman suffer on my account. (She would be the fourth.) The second psychotic, this one channeled into Catholicism. Eye is just expression of spiritual depression. Other things, not to be written down. Quarrel with Kiepenheuer, who wants to have my wife put up somewhere more cheaply, sends me no money (but I have some from the *FZ*), has fucked up French edition of *Job*, just because Valois, a publisher of the very last rank, offered 100 francs more. Translation putrid. Living with the sense of always working in vain. Many reasons not to get away. Can't go on a train with my eye this way. Even so, must meet Landauer next week in Frankfurt.

Very cordially,   your old Joseph Roth
Please don't forget:
Otto Zarek's[1] address.
Thank you!

1. Otto Zarek (1898–1958), novelist, biographer, journalist. A friend of Zweig's, he emigrated to London.

130. To Stefan Zweig   *Hotel Foyot, Paris*
                                                          3 June 1931

Dear esteemed Stefan Zweig,

I'd rather not dictate, I can't find anyone to take it anyway. Spending half the day in hospital. Sometimes they rip out my eyelashes, at others they inject me, and rub me, and hold my eyelids open till I can't think any more. In this sort of condition, pity for publishers is about the furthest thing from me. As a sick man, after 10 books[1] and over 4,000 articles, I think I have a right to a suit, a pair of shoes, food, hospital fees. Publishers shouldn't publish crap, and they shouldn't make dilettantes famous. I need to go for treatment every day for at least another 12 days. I know I'm thinking like a sociopath, but unfortunately it doesn't help much. If there were some lousy idea that would help me make money, do you think I'd hesitate. I have to be healthy and free and able to work. I can't stand this imprisonment. I've gotten so indifferent to everything.

Cordially   your old Joseph Roth

1. No exaggeration. *Hotel Savoy* (1924), *Rebellion* (1924), *April* (1925), *The Blind Mirror* (1925), *The Wandering Jews* (1927), *Flight Without End* (1927), *Zipper and His Father* (1928), *Right and Left* (1930), *Job* (1930), *Panopticum* (1930). A few of these, admittedly, are "only" novellas, but even then Roth doesn't list either his first book, or the nixed "White Cities," or the abandoned *Perlefter* and *Silent Prophet*. To get to 4,000 articles, he would have to have written nigh on one a day—not impossible, for him, then.

131. To Stefan Zweig   *Hotel Foyot, Paris*
                                                          27 June 1931

Very dear, very esteemed Stefan Zweig,

I have one good and one bad conscience simultaneously, because I avoided writing to you while my eye wretchedness was so bad that I could have done nothing but wail to you. For two days now, no dark glasses, on the other hand, a pair of normal ones that are here to stay, a symptom of aging I can't do anything about. My left eye still very weakened by the inflammation. I myself still very confused, an illness I couldn't suppress is a shaming defeat for me.

Day after tomorrow I go to Frankfurt, after that Berlin.

Unable to work on the novel.

Where are you now?

I lost Otto Zarek's address again. Do you have it?

In old cordiality　　　　your old Joseph Roth

132. To Jenny Reichler

Hotel Foyot, Paris 6ᵉ
29 June [1931?]

Dear Mother,

please write me the name of Father's illness.

I have money for Friedl till *August*.

Sorry to write such a scrappy note.

Kiss Father for me.

When I come, I'll wire ahead.

Most cordially　　　　your son

133. To Jenny Reichler

Hotel Foyot, Paris 6ᵉ
Thursday [1931]

Dear Mother,

it takes longer than last time to shake off my jaundice. I am so feeble, please forgive these short and illegible notes.

Please, go on writing to me at this address.

By the 15th I shall have to be writing again. I hope I'm restored by then.

If Friedl were to get better at last, then I would get better too. It's brutal, I can't stand it.

Hugs to you both　　　　your son

134. To Benno Reifenberg   *Hotel Englischer Hof*
                                              Frankfurt am Main
                                              Thursday [1931?]

Dear Benno Reifenberg,

I feel Germany right off the bat, and all of it at once. Every street corner expresses the awfulness of the whole country. It has the ugliest prostitutes, the girls indistinguishable from the women who swab the floors of the *FZ* at night, in fact I think they're the same. The men are all scoutmasters on display. You see more blondes in summer than in winter. All tanned and deeply unhealthy looking. An awful lot of bodies, precious few faces. Sports shirts, no skirts. Yesterday, my first day back, was ghastly. *Immediate plummet of spirits*, the way mercury can fall to zero. The feeling as though your genitals were gone, nothing left! Skirts, where there are skirts, all buttoned up, crooked gait of the men, as though they were originally designed as quadrupeds. Refreshing humanity among the little people, far more kindness than in France. All the little employees at the *FZ*, very, very human. Silent suffering, you get a sense of what these people have to live through. Somewhat perversely: a touch of patriotic feeling. Envy of France. Arch-envy, like arch-enemy. The former more appropriate than the latter. Saw Peters.[1] Equanimity and nobility at the same time. Like a pair of scales that always hold exactly identical weights, but sometimes I think: perhaps the pans are empty? The needle hardly moves. (Not like mine.) Complete absence of crests and troughs. Eat with him on Friday. Englischer Hof completely empty. Great rejoicing at my presence, tipper, unrest-creator, asker-after-more. Page boys get errands. Arrived like a prince in Sleeping Beauty's castle. No sleeping beauty, though, bought a street girl from the Alkazar perfumery. Wouldn't stop kissing me. Felt as though I'd been blessed by the Holy Fathers or something. Convey my regards to all at home.

Your old   Joseph Roth

1. Peters: Hans Otto Peters (1893–1943), a landscape painter.

135. *To Stefan Zweig*   *Hotel Englischer Hof*
                                                Frankfurt am Main
                                                4 July 1931

To Mr. Stefan Zweig, Salzburg/Austria, Kapuzinerberg

Dear and esteemed Mr. Zweig,

may I trouble you to forward the enclosed letter to Otto Zarek, whose address I've lost again.

My eyes are much better. Unfortunately, I wear glasses now. It will take another 3–4 weeks before they're completely healed. Apparently I have an astigmatism.

I'm going to Berlin now. The only hope for Kiepenheuer and me is the American edition of *Job*.[1] Perhaps you'll run into Mr. Huebsch. Give him my best regards; I'm going to miss him in Berlin.

Have to stay here though to settle the question of what to do with the advances I've had from the *Frankfurter Zeitung*. Ghastly business.

Because of my eyes, I won't be able to get going on the novel for another 2–3 weeks. I'm staying in Berlin for about 3 weeks.

Very cordially your old   [Joseph Roth]

1. American edition of *Job*: it was published in 1931 in the translation of Dorothy Thompson, by the Viking Press (director, Ben Huebsch). The Thompson translation is still in print.

136. *To Benno Reifenberg*   *Hotel Englischer Hof*
                                                Frankfurt am Main
                                                6 July 1931

To Mr. Benno Reifenberg, Paris 5, Place du Panthéon

Dear Benno Reifenberg,

I went to the Städel.[1] It was the last day of the exhibition, Peters made me go. Formed a dismal impression of contemporary painting, without exception. Even in the case of Beckmann, there seemed to me to be a vast gulf between him and the ancients, a kind of porosity. I think painting, even more than literature, has become impossible. Of course the gulf between Beckmann and the rest is almost as great as the one between the classical painters and Beckmann. Even so, it remains perplexing to me how I, not understanding anything about painting, will find myself physically affected by an old painting, while it takes effort of brain and imagination on my part to be moved by a good new one. Old paintings *look at me*, they come to me to take my hand and squeeze my heart. For a moment it crossed my mind that B. is overestimated. But probably all this is very amateurish.

Went back with Peters. Saw many fine watercolors, and felt a great deal of space in them. I had the feeling that in this inadequate period, a delicate painter like Peters is more expressive than someone more vigorous. Saw two good paintings of his that he wants to show you, shattering pictures, but as delicate as watercolors.

Will you please mail the enclosed letter to Mrs. Vallentin.[2] Don't forget. Regards to all at home. I won't write to you from Berlin again.

Your old   Joseph Roth
Will you send my *Job* to Heilbronn?!
Yes?!

1. Städel: the museum in Frankfurt.
2. Mrs. Vallentin: Antonina Vallentin (1893 Lvov–1957 Paris), wife of the politician Jules Luchaire, she kept a high-powered literary salon in Paris, and worked as an agent on JR's behalf.

137. *To Stefan Zweig*   *Hotel am Zoo, Berlin*
                                                           8 July 1931

To Mr. Stefan Zweig, Salzburg/Austria, Kapuzinerberg
Dear esteemed Stefan Zweig,
I think I may soon go somewhere where the air is clean to work on my novel. It has to be finished by the end of September, because after long

negotiations I managed to get my advance from the *Frankfurter Zeitung* commuted to royalties for the serialization.[1] Which means that I will receive immediate payment for articles—if I should manage to write any; but the novel still needs to be finished before October. There was no better solution possible, in view of the short time, and the limited resources of the book publishers.

That's a terrible thing that happened to you. Of course you won't learn from it, and that's quite right. You won't change any more than those people who exploit you will change. That's all as it should be.

Perhaps we can meet over the summer, but I won't know for another 2 weeks or so. Things need to be straightened out here first.

In haste and old cordiality   your old [Joseph Roth]

1. *The Radetzky March* was serialized in the *FZ*, beginning on 17 April 1932, before Roth had finished writing it. The book was published by Kiepenheuer in August 1932.

---

138. To Stefan Zweig   *Frankfurt am Main*
                                                28 August 1931

To Mr. Stefan Zweig, Salzburg, Kapuzinerberg 5
Dear esteemed Stefan Zweig,

Don't expect to hear from me for a while. Mr. Landauer of the Kiepenheuer Verlag will call on you. I was doing badly for a long time. I seem to be doing better now. I'm working very hard. I need to write almost an article a day for the paper. I hope it doesn't stay that way.

Write to me as before to the Englischer Hof.

Very cordially   your old Joseph Roth

139. To Stefan Zweig   *Frankfurt am Main, 2*
                                          September 1931

To Mr. Stefan Zweig, Salzburg, Kapuzinerberg 5

Dear esteemed Stefan Zweig,

thank you for yours of the 31st.

Landauer has been here since yesterday. We talked about you a lot, very warmly. He's not paying me any more money, because of the large advance I had, and I'm just negotiating with him about the possibility of getting to finish the novel without writing more articles. I need at least 1,000 marks a month. You can hardly imagine what (even without the 1,000 marks) the prospect of financial independence means, especially for these weeks. When I heard the news,[1] I felt as if I'd just gotten my exam results. I'll let you know in a couple of days where I decide to go.

My wife has been in a state that makes it impossible for me to go to Austria.

Nor can I hide anywhere.

I have a horribly bad conscience. But if I am to finish the novel this year, then I can't go to Vienna. It would set me back weeks. I've been stuck of late anyway. Maybe it will flow again next week.

Cordially,   your old Joseph Roth

1. the news: an advance on the American edition of *Job*.

140. To Jenny Reichler   *Thursday [1931]*

Dear Mother,

I was very glad to see Friedl's handwriting is unchanged. Please don't take anything away from her, she's sure to notice if something's gone missing.

Warm hugs   Your son

Happy New Year!

141. To Friedrich Traugott Gubler   *[September 1931]*
                                                       Request proofs!

(The Palace of Scheherazade.) by Joseph Roth
Dear friend,
this is the best thing I have written for the paper for years, it's about
Alcazar, and I want to dedicate it to you. You must decide if it's alright to
put f.t.g.[1] over it. Otherwise I'll include it in a book, with the dedication.

Am in Paris, hope to rent a furnished apartment.[2] Unable to give you
further personal details just now. Need money, am very sober, sensible,
and content.

Did your son go to Switzerland? Please write to confirm,
your old   J.R.
Warm regards to your wife!   Foyot, rue de Tournon

1. I.e., Friedrich Traugott Gubler.
2. furnished apartment: this, for JR completely outlandish, aspiration perhaps hints
at the new woman in his life (and her children), Andrea Manga Bell. See no. 143 and
note.

142. To Stefan Zweig   *Friday, 25 September [1931]*
                                               Paris 6
                                               Hotel Foyot

Dear and esteemed Mr. Stefan Zweig,
my friend Landauer has just written me that the Insel Verlag is in
trouble, and is entering a partnership with the Deutschnationale Handlungsgehilfen Verband.[1] He doesn't dare mention it to you himself, and
wonders if it is appropriate for me to tell you. In accordance with my
principles, I have no alternative but to do so immediately. I should count
myself overjoyed to share a publisher with you, for whatever reason.
Please think about it.

I'm doing badly, in spite of America.
Your very old   Joseph Roth

1. The Deutschnationale Handlungsgehilfen Verband was a highly conservative commercial organization that had recently bought up the Langen-Müller Verlag in Berlin; it was rumored to be interested in buying the Insel Verlag.

143. To Friedrich Traugott Gubler   *Hotel Foyot*
                                                       Paris 6ᵉ
                                                       Thursday, 8 October 1931

Dear friend,

thank you so much for your letter. I hope to get the account from you one day soon. It's very important for me, I need MONEY *urgently*, and I must get my finances straightened out. I've had nothing from America yet. America itself is probably under just as much pressure as Kiepenheuer; sometimes I'm egocentric enough to suppose that it's me and my success that have sparked off the world financial crisis. Certainly, every one of the laws of this horrible world had to be overturned for me to have a success.

That's how I'm living, beset with money worries, and worries too about what's to become of my wife. She's become more lucid of late, asks after me occasionally, and I don't have the strength to go to Vienna. What will that do? And if my wife becomes completely lucid, do I then go back to her? My present is murky, and my future inscrutable. I have worries in all directions, sometimes I feel I have ten horses running every which way, and it's up to me to hold them together. And I myself am just a silly horse, running away from myself.

What a fine Shakespeare review you wrote there, my friend! My, you're a real author! I wouldn't have made the piece on the Taunus so lyrical, though, I think lyricism needs to be masked or stifled.

Hauser's article was an unbearable show of fresh youthfulness and civilizational insolence. Style was false too, not just putrid. Sieburg: dazzlingly masked gaucheness. Picard's graphology as ever an honest sermon, pen in hand, a sweet, great man. (He doesn't answer my letters.)

Your little girl will get better, just give her time, and I dreamed about your son yesterday. He was sitting on a swing that was a ship, and said: I'm on Lake Constance!

I couldn't leave Mrs. M.B.[1] At the last moment, my heart felt sore, and my conscience, which is situated somewhere in its vicinity, did too—and now I'm thinking I can make amends with the one for what I did wrong with others—and with myself, for that matter—(and she says to send you her regards, and sometimes we both say affectionate things about you together).

When will I see you next? I only want to write good and lovely things that make for greater clarity in me, and perhaps in the odd reader.

Give Simon Heinrich my best. I like him, the more I think of him.

Write to me, I like to hear from you.

Say hello to Křenek.[2] Tell him he's worthy of me.

Do you know J. P. Hebel's *Essay about the Jews?*

Should be reprinted each time there's a pogrom. It begins roughly like this: "That the Jews are scattered among the host peoples and . . . live from the sweat of their brows is well known to the Lord, and grieves him . . ."

Very cordially, your old and ever older   Joseph Roth

1. Mrs M.B.: Andrea Manga Bell (born 1900 in Hamburg). Father Cuban, mother from Hamburg. After World War I, married Manga Bell, the king of Duala (former German Cameroon, whose father had been killed by the Germans), lived with him in Versailles, but then didn't accompany him back to Duala, but ran a women's magazine in Berlin. Was JR's companion from 1931 to 1936. In a further, scarcely credible twist in her story, she was convinced that her ex-husband, then a member of parliament in Cameroon, murdered their son on his arrival there. See *Der Spiegel*, edition of 24 August 1950.

2. Křenek: Ernst Křenek (1900–1991), composer (of the opera *Jonny spielt auf*) and author. Wrote for the *Frankfurter Zeitung*. Went into exile in the United States in 1938.

144. To Blanche Gidon (written in French)   *25 October 1931*

Dear Madam,[1]

thank you very much for your letter. I can understand you very well on the telephone, which is what matters, because I don't say much myself. Thank you for your invitation. My *amie's* illness will probably keep me from accepting it. She is alone and bedridden, and I can't very well leave her on her own in the middle of the day. But I hope she may be up and about by Thursday, in which case I'll send you a *pneumatique*. It would be nice to see Mr. Poupet[2] again, and I would very much like to make Mr. Gidon's acquaintance! Mr. Reifenberg told me a lot about you. But with my worries—too much for a single man, and for 2 years now—I am a gloomy sort of guest, upsettingly poor, and with remote and eccentric thoughts.

Please Madam, forgive me this rather hand-wringing declamation!

With best wishes   Joseph Roth

1. Blanche Gidon (born 1883), French translator. Married to Dr. Ferdinand Gidon (died 1954), well-known radiologist, who fell victim to his occupation. The Gidons were devoted friends of Roth; he met many French authors in their house in the rue des Martyrs. Mrs. Gidon was responsible for rescuing JR's papers on his death, which were later transferred to the Leo Baeck Institute in New York by Fred Grubel, JR's cousin. The works of his that she translated include most of what he produced in his last 6 or 8 years: *The Leviathan, The Bust of the Emperor, The Triumph of Beauty, His Apostolic Majesty* (stories that appeared in various newspapers and journals), *The Radetzky March, The Hundred Days, Confession of a Murderer, Weights and Measures, The Emperor's Tomb.*

2. Mr. Poupet: the director of the publishing house of Plon, in Paris.

145. To Stefan Zweig   *28 October 1931*

Dear esteemed Stefan Zweig,

don't make me itemize the sorrows that are besetting me. Sick girl-friend, creditors, pharmacies, doctors, I myself am still going to the clinic twice a week on account of my eyes, I avoid people, have destroyed six completed chapters, they were rotten, now I'm rewriting them, Kiepenheuer doesn't know.

When are you coming? When *will you be finished?* Do you know the rumors about the Insel Verlag are getting more insistent?[1] Do you know how proud I would be if my friend Landauer were to be the steed for us both?

Very cordially, please don't put down my silence to lack of friendly feeling,

your old Joseph Roth

1. See no. 142.

146. To Benno Reifenberg (written in French)

Hotel Foyot, Paris
[postmarked Paris,
31 October 1931]

Dear friend,[1]

I won't be coming to Koslowski's today, but I will be at the Coupole at around 10 p.m. I would like you to come because I am fond of you, my dear friend, and because I would like to see you. I am very unhappy these days, in French you can say such a thing.

All yours, as ever.

Bring the special edition of the *Frankfurter Zeitung*, if you will. I saw the announcement of Gerhart Hauptmann's idiocies, and sundry others as well.

Heil, Temp et Tucho![2]   Joseph Roth

1. Writing to Reifenberg *in French* is some suggestion of Roth's alienation from developments in Germany ("Gerhart Hauptmann's idiocies"), and even from his old friend and sometime employer and sort-of successor.

2. Heil, Temp et Tucho: obscure, but perhaps a boisterous toast wishing for health, wealth, and time? Like the Spanish *salud y pesetas*.

147. To René Schickele   *Hotel Foyot, Paris*
                                            3 November 1931

Dear esteemed Master Schickele,

I have just set down your new book,[1] Fischer had it sent to me. It stuns me with its strength and clarity. I needed to tell you right away. These days, I fear not that many people will tell you. You are among the last of the real writers in Germany, dear René Schickele. I have always liked and admired you, and now, at the end of three days with your book, I like and admire you doubly.

Yours aye   Joseph Roth

1. *Der Wolf in der Hürde*, third part of the trilogy *Das Erbe am Rhein*.

148. To Benno Reifenberg (written in French)   *Joseph Roth*
                                                  Hotel Foyot, Paris 6ᵉ
                                                  Saturday [postmarked:
                                                  Paris, 7 November 1931]

Dear friend,

I hope you'll have the money for me today from the *Frankfurter*.

If not, could you help me out with 100 francs (this evening at 7 at Mahieu's),[1] to get through the terrible Sunday that is approaching, always the worst of my days?

If you can't come to Mahieu's in person, please leave the money with Mr. Wolfe, who seems reasonably trustworthy. Don't you think? I've been full of cognac since morning.

In this state of mind and body, I haven't managed to telephone you. Otherwise, I hope you've gone out sad and lonely, just as I have stayed in to drink, sad and lonely and full of literary and humanitarian duties.

Always your devoted friend, and with cordial greetings for the ladies (that's German, I know)

Joseph Roth

1. Mahieu's: a café on the Boulevard St. Michel.

149. To Félix Bertaux
20 March [1932]

My dear friend,

I am moved by your concern. I was sick and miserable for a long time, and I'm working desperately on the *Radetzky March*. The material is too much, I am frail, and unable to shape it. On top of that there's the material misery in which I'm obliged to live. Otherwise I'd have been in Paris long ago. Maybe I'll manage to be there in early May. It's indescribably hard to live here, for me in particular, and in every respect. Things were better for me during the war.

I embrace you and Pierre, and please greet Mrs. Bertaux humbly from me. More after the novel is done (another 2 weeks, with luck).

your old Joseph Roth

c/o Kiepenheuer Verlag

Kantstrasse 10

Charlottenburg Berlin

150. To Friedrich Traugott Gubler
Sunday

Dear friend,

your letter cheered me up. I am unhappy, confused, wholly unable to leave the four walls I've thrown up around me and the book, though it feels more like a mountain range in which I wander about in terror. One day, everything comes off, the next day it's all shit. Tricky, treacherous

business. I don't even want to talk about the fact that in material terms
I'm short of practically everything, I have nothing to eat unless someone
asks me out, basically I don't care. I've tried to take refuge in the prewar
era, but it's desperately difficult to write about when you feel the way I
do. I'm very much afraid I'm a bodger. I take a few minutes off to scribble
you these lines. Please remember, it's as important to me as the book, and
as my whole life, that you not forget me (you and my few friends, Picard
and Reifenberg, give them both my best wishes), and not be forgetful
yourself. I will devote myself entirely to you when I'm finished. Promise!

I love you all, please bear it in mind.

your J.R.

151. To Friedrich Traugott Gubler   Wednesday

My dear good friend,

I'm taking a quarter of an hour off, to reply to your kind letter right
away, because I'm very worried. Your idea of getting episodes in Goethe's
life written up by various hands worries me. With all due respect for
those involved, it can't be more than something confected and "made
up," and I fear both for the subject and for those working on it. It would
pain me if you and Reifenberg and Simon wound up in some distant
relation to purveyors of "biography." And as far as *I'm* concerned, I can
on no account be involved. I don't dare "identify myself" with anything
that Goethe experienced. If I should have the honor to be involved in the
whole project, then I will willingly break off my novel. Nothing would
sooner induce me to break it off. But all I can write is this: how I was
young, and used to walk past the Goethe statue in the Volksgarten in
Vienna every day, and the pigeons cacked on its head, and I froze with
respect, and took off my hat, without anyone there to see. It seems more
proper to me if everyone were to write about his own *personal encounter*
with Goethe.[1]

I'm working like a fiend, it's horrible, I am incredibly afraid the novel
will end up no good. I have a feeling for what is good, but whether God

will give me the strength to actually make it good is something else. In two weeks a big section of the book will be set, and I'll send you a copy.

(Request for news. *What's going on with Reifenberg?*)

I see Křenek wrote about Sochaczewer.[2] Why didn't you wait for my piece? Really, please, please: can you keep all those books you've set aside for me till I've finished my novel. The thing Krenek's writing about, "the moment where objectivity threatens to turn into penury is not far off, and soon . . . etc. etc." I wanted to write exactly the opposite about Sochacz's novel. Where does the optimism come from? Where, tell me? Those so-called activist bastards just get cheekier all the time. "Subjectivism" is more arrogant than ever! Can I reply to dear Ernst Křenek, with all the love I have for him through you (in spite of "the malignant rabbit")?[3]

Where is your wife? Is your daughter better? Where is Picard? Are you on good terms with Reifenberg? Be good to him! He is a wonderful man. He is honorable, even if he's not always truthful! I want to see you all again! I am desperate and poor and beset with a hundred worries that I can't write about now.

Hugs,   your old Joseph Roth

1. There is perhaps no better instance of Roth's superb and aggressive pure-mindedness (which was certainly the death of him as much as anything else) than this refusal to participate in such a venture, which so characterizes our "postmodern" epoch.

2. Sochaczewer: Hans Sochaczewer, brother-in-law of Arnold Zweig, an author with the Kiepenheuer Verlag.

3. "the malignant rabbit": someone's nickname? But whose? JR's, FTG's, or "Kren's"?

152. *To Annette Kolb*   *Gustav Kiepenheuer Verlag, Berlin*
                              5 July 1932

Dear esteemed Ms. Annette Kolb,

your kind letters come chasing after one another so charmingly quickly, I barely have a chance to reply. Today your sweet photograph came—thank you so much. If I had a bed, I would hang it up over the bed, if you didn't mind. It's a very nice picture, suffused with a sort of Whitsun earnestness.

Practical things, now:

1. Of course Kiepenheuer would publish a book that promised to sell. But no one here speaks English—I don't myself—and when I try, I sound like a bad imitation of an American Yid. Is it too much trouble to ask you to write out a typed summary of the book and send it to me? Some other interested parties might turn up.

2. My *Radetzky March* still isn't quite set. You'll get it right after I've revised the proofs, at the end of July.

3. Would you be so good as to say that to Mr. Poupet? He'll get the book right away, as soon as he offers any sort of advance; because:

4. I can't tell you how bad I feel. If you'd known me 12 or 13 years ago, I would just have had to tell you: as bad as 13 years ago, and you'd have understood. Today I have misfortune behind me and alongside me, gray hair, a bad liver, and I'm an incurable alcoholic (which is worse than 13 years ago).

5. Since I quite deliberately no longer look at articles of mine in print, I can't tell you when they appeared. But the *Frankfurter Zeitung* office will send you whatever you ask for pretty quickly.

6. Those are all the "practical" things that come to mind.

Please drop me a line! I get the sense that [. . .] is messing you about by turning you off Ireland. But you can't blame Jews for anything nowadays. They are pushed in the direction of "money"—and that's the only thing they can try and cling on to. [. . .]

I kiss your dear hands

your old Joseph Roth

153. Benno Reifenberg to Joseph Roth   *11 July 1932*
To Mr. J. Roth, c/o Kiepenheuer Verlag, 10 Kantstrasse,
Berlin-Charlottenburg 2

Dear Roth,

The Radetzky March is the first novel I read in serial form in the paper from beginning to end. Sometimes I even waited for the Reich edition to come out, so that I could read the following installment the evening before.

I am a bit tired of the political work, and am going to Tutzing to spend 4 days with Hausenstein. Will I find you in Frankfurt? Please write and let me know

[. . .]

Your old   [Benno Reifenberg][1]

1. It's hard to imagine a more gallant letter than this, and yet—dictated; addressed to Roth at his publisher's—it marks another stage in the decay of a friendship.

154. To Stefan Zweig   *7 August 1932*
                                          Baden-Baden
                                          c/o Fabisch, Yburgstrasse 21

Dear esteemed Stefan Zweig,

I'm not sure that after such a long time, you don't have the right to set this letter aside, unopened. In 4 months this is the first week—a friend has invited me, and I'm going to be here another week—that I can draw breath. The last 4 weeks, when I might perhaps have been able to do so, I was tormented by a horrible stomach catarrh, slowly getting better now. Better, but I fear probably never well. Like my eye inflammation back then, it's just another physical expression of the catastrophic situation of my life. Imagine, my novel had started to run in the paper before it was even finished. And, so to speak with the hot breath of pursuing time on my neck—of course to paralyzing effect—I had to go on writing, revise, correct, and finally put in a flimsy ending. A Hamburg book club bought the book for August. I have to correct and revise, all at the same time, for 8 bloody hours a day and I'm completely enfeebled by it. My hands are still shaking. The whole time since I left Paris, I've had to spend 4-week stints with various friends and acquaintances, and you know how ghastly that is for a habitual hotel dweller like me. The publisher was paying me 5 marks a day. I've had to stop paying back all my most pressing debts. Which made them press me all the more. There were places I couldn't even show my face. I owe the *Frankfurter Zeitung* 400 marks, I don't have the patience to write articles any more. The only thing I've managed to keep up are the monthly installments for my wife's hospitals. Kiepenheuer can only keep going as long as its Jewish bankers stay in Germany. But everything suggests they're pulling out of Berlin. National Socialism will strike at the core of my existence—apart from the fact that the booksellers are terrorized, inasmuch as they're not Nationalists themselves, and want nothing to do with writing that strikes them as "cosmopolitan" or western European, and so on and so forth. I'm convinced nothing will befall the cheeky chutzpah-Jews, but the conservatives will suffer—never has it been as true as now: dog will not eat dog. I bet the Hungarian Jews will end up practicing censorship in the 3rd Reich just as they do in Russia and in this fucking democracy. Too bad we lived to see it. Every janitor is a reactionary today, and mixes me up with Tucholsky,[1] who is his cousin! A few weeks ago, I was talking to some Nazis about you—and it took 10 minutes before it dawned on me they had Arnold Z.[2] in mind! Not that they like you any better, because you're such an "internationalist"! They just get annoyed that someone is known all over Europe, and they detach Germany from Europe to the degree that writers with a European reputation are enemies to them, as if they'd been French. It's so disgusting, I tell you, you can't breathe it, never mind write it! It's hideous to be assorted with the Left, against one's will, against one's being, lumped together with something like the *Weltbühne*. That hideous arrest of Ossietzky's,[3] when all the Jewesses drove down the Kurfürstendamm in their magnificent cars—and the poor goy paced back and forth in his cell, and Toller gave a speech *outside*. I was the only one (aside from H. Mann) not to participate, in my case it was out of disgust, H.M. was pressed for time. It's meaningless, everything's become meaningless! I have the strong sense that for me personally there is no future.

Farewell! If you're not angry, drop a line to your old

Joseph Roth

1. Tucholsky: Kurt Tucholsky (1890–1935), editor of the *Schaubühne* and the *Weltbühne*, satirist, novelist, essayist, went into voluntary exile in Sweden in 1929, where, depressed by European politics, he died by his own hand in 1935. For some reason, Roth always loathed him, even when he was farther to the left than currently, when he seems at least in part to be blaming the Jews for having brought their imminent misfortune upon themselves by dabbling in radical politics.

2. Arnold Z: Arnold Zweig, the Communist author of *Sergeant Grisha*, not to be confused with Stefan Zweig, with whom he was not related.

3. Ossietzky's: Carl von Ossietzky (1889–1938), Tucholsky's associate on the *Weltbühne*. Among the first prominent victims of the Nazis, he was put in a concentration camp in 1933, was awarded the Nobel Peace Prize in absentia in 1935, and died in police custody in 1938. It is uncomfortable to feel JR's rabid loathing for such a man.

155. To Benno Reifenberg   *28 August [1932]*

Dear Mr. Reifenberg,

you helped me out of one of the biggest calamities of my life, and I want you to know, and to remember that you not only materially alleviated my condition, but—on a human level—picked me up and in a Picardian sense improved me. Please will you tell the firm, and Dr. Heinrich Simon, that his responsiveness was a real act of nobility, which continues to honor and ennoble me, after first of all helping me. Please, promise to tell Dr. Simon. The old god will help the old paper. He's not to despair.

So far as I know, Gubler is not in Frankfurt, so I must ask you to forgive me if I leave the ethereal heights of politics where you are now situated, to revert to the depths of the feuilleton, where you once used to publish my glittering pieces in a sort of second *Morgenpost*. Everything avenges itself. Now you need to pay attention, and work out with me:

I have had 350 marks in advances.

I need another 300 marks, with articles *already written*.

Therefore I have to write 650 lines.

Now, pay attention.

Yesterday I sent off one article for the books pages; today a piece for the Bäderblatt.

Makes perhaps 250 lines. Which means I must still write 400 lines.

I will send these within the next 3 days, all glittering pieces for the feuilleton.

But then I must have the money, so that I can pay this fucking hotel. Coming to Frankfurt for 2 days, then Switzerland.

I have to live like a dog till 20 September.

Would you kindly write back right away, so that I may be sure you've grasped my muddled calculations. I need to be perfectly sure of that.

Thank you very much. (Which is a stupid thing to say, but never mind.) I can see I am abusing your friendship, but console myself by thinking that behind that is our *comradeship* which can't be abused.

Your old muddleheaded   Joseph Roth

156. To Ernst Křenek   *Hotel Schwanen, Rapperswil am Zürichsee*
                               as of: Englischer Hof, Frankfurt/Main
                               10 September 1932

Dear esteemed Mr. Ernst Křenek,

thank you for your letter and your oeuvre, both! Where may I send you the book?

One sees accounts of your plans in the papers, here and there. May God give you health, money, and luck! I think of you often. Not only, by any means, when I read something of yours in the *FZ*. Oh, it remains

Joseph Roth, age three

Joseph Roth's student ID at
the University of Vienna

Joseph Roth's military training company

Friedl Roth with dog

Joseph Roth in Paris, with two friends from Brody

Joseph Roth with the trademark newspaper

Joseph Roth with Heinrich Wagner

Joseph Roth with Bernard von Brentano
in the Jardin du Luxembourg, Paris

Joseph Roth in Albanian folkloric costume, in 1927 in Albania

Joseph Roth with Friedl in Berlin, in 1922

Joseph Roth with Paula Grübel and a friend

Joseph Roth in the company of Dutch writers in a café in Amsterdam in 1937

A signed portrait of Joseph Roth

the "decentest rag." I'm bad, I'm very bad. I can't manage any more in the muddle of my personal life. Yes, it's in lockstep with "public affairs." We Austrians, eh? We have no more business here. We live and think and write in Middle High German.[1] Your music is like that. I don't know a lot about music. But, among 20 "modern" tunes that a girlfriend sang to me, I still managed to pick out yours. I wasn't nice to you. I'm often drunk, or half-seas. Forgive me! My solidarity with you is always greater.

As far as Austria is concerned: your life there may be harder than mine in Germany. Because in Germany, I can always still pin my hopes on Austria. But when I open an Austrian newspaper, I get the impression that things there are looking pretty German. The Prussian boot, the hysterical boot, the bossy boot: mean, perverse, and decadent. It will trample all over Austria too. Down with the Anschluss! Too bad that France is our salvation. German salvation. Write me if you get a chance, tell me Austria's not yet as bad as its newspapers. (Germany is a sight worse than its newspapers.)

Your old   Joseph Roth

1. Middle High German: Professor Brecht, with whom Roth studied in Vienna before World War I, believed in and advanced an idea of Austria not as a corrupt and negligible appendage ripe for a tacit or explicit Anschluss, "a sort of nether Bavaria," as JR says in no. 22 (when arguing not against Nazism, but Socialism), but as an older, better form of Germany, "the land of the older form of German culture, a culture that has preserved many ancient German traits . . . a land of the soul and the spirit, full of tolerance, protean, rich and colorful, eluding definition, yes, opposed to definition, like the Middle Ages, like the life of the Catholic Church." Bronsen, who notes that Roth was not easily influenced by others, took Brecht's lectures to heart. Without this Austrocentric, *in excelsis Austria* creed in mind, it is difficult to make sense not just of JR's tone to Křenek here, but of his overall faith in Austria, his opposition to Germany, perhaps even his late upsurge of Royalism. See, for instance, no. 210 or no. 217. Even the mystic believes in something for a reason.

157. To Stefan Zweig   *Hotel Schwanen*
                                                    Rapperswil am Zürichsee
                                                    18 September 1932

Dear esteemed Stefan Zweig,

I'm sending this letter by messenger, ideally I'd have wired it, to thank
you for your friendly, spirited, and moving letter, and to beg you to pardon a quite unpardonable oversight on the part of my publishers. Because
of course I'd set your name at the head of the list of persons due to receive
"reading copies" two or three weeks ago. I also sent a slip with a personal
dedication to put in the book, which has been out now these past 5 days.
How your good luck message shames me. Believe me, I know all too well
that my book hasn't turned out the way it should have. Of course I can
tell you exactly why and wherefore. But what would be the point? I felt it
while I was writing. I didn't write you that whole time. I know you have
no fondness for wailing walls. They don't bring luck. Any friendship
with me is *ruinous*. I myself am a wailing wall, if not a heap of rubble.
You have no idea how dark it is inside me. My dear, admired friend, you
have the grace of luck and of true golden joy in the world. Your senses
are open to what is right, there is something in you of Goethe's understanding of life. Don't forget that since my bleak childhood I've been
groaning up at the brightness, I'm not sure if, for all your knowledge
of me, you can have felt all that. Because you are lucky enough—I've
wanted to say this to you for a long time—not to be able to see certain
depths of darkness, yes, you avert your eye. You have the grace to be able
to avert your eye from darknesses that would do you harm.[1] (Interest-
ingly enough, your wife was able to feel it in me, sometimes when you
had lost your temper.) I know my shortcomings in this novel, how I cried
to the story itself to help me, embarrassing help for my "composition,"
which was rotten and deceitful of me. That's why I tinkered away at it
for so long, two years, that's no proof of health, strength, and productivity. Yes, I must ask you for forgiveness: your critical judgment let you

down when you read my *Radetzky March*. It's flattering for me: it let you down because of your feeling for me. I promise you: I don't deserve it, and it's *harmful to you*. And that's why I didn't write to you. You're a good person. But I didn't want to disturb the harmony that's a part of your goodness. You must remain happy, serene, so childishly serene in a perfectly naïve way, to be good, to be truly good. Basically, you don't *like* people like me; and quite rightly: because they harm you. I first met you under other circumstances. (Believe me, it hurts me that I owe you money, for instance!—and it hurts me too that I am telling you this, I know exactly how much, I have it written down. I also know that you would otherwise give it to much more deserving individuals. I want to pay it back to you in slow installments.) I tell you all this, shamelessly. I hope you will understand. Yes, you will understand.—I want to make an end. If there weren't such a danger that I'd be mistaken by decent people for a "Romantic" in double or triple quotation marks): I'd like to become a monk. Assuming a modicum of grace.—*Physically* I'm fucked. I've got no money. I owe enormous amounts. I can't take on any more debt. Even the stupidest article takes me three days to write. And (*entre nous*) the FZ has asked me to write less. They just can't pay me.—(Strictly, *entre nous*.)—Well, there's the wailing wall again. Throw away this letter! It'll only bring you bad luck!—From now on I'll just write about public affairs. You must have seen the article in the *Völkischer Beobachter*,[2] where you are named with little shits way beneath you, I'm sure you must have seen that.—Well, greetings! I'd like to see you again—and I'm a little afraid of it.—To tell you something of a "practical" nature: I'm here till 1 October.—I'd like you to confirm receipt of this letter.—I have many more things I could tell you, and can't think of anything.—Otto Zarek's novel is in *Sport und Bild* or God knows the hell where. I saw one of the installments. In person, Zarek is much more sensible than you'd suppose from that installment. It seems to me he's allowed Berlin to get to him. Even so, I've asked to review the book for the FZ, because he understands a lot about human predicaments. Is it coming out in autumn? Do you happen to know? (I don't have his address.) Plus: I'd like to ask you to confirm the safe arrival of my book. I need to know whether Kiepenheuer carries out instructions.

your very old Joseph Roth

1. darknesses that would do you harm: as often in these letters of JR's to Zweig, he packs a catastrophic punch. Bronsen describes "the congenitally cautious and reticent Zweig, who liked to take himself for an Erasmus, but was no more than just a law-abiding citizen, in whom a plausible witness attested to 'a weakness for anything demonic, at a safe distance.'" The witness is Robert Neumann, friend to Zweig and author of the wonderfully entitled *Meine Freunde die Kollegen*.

2. *Völkischer Beobachter*: (People's Observer), the organ of the Nazi party, founded in 1920.

158. *To Stefan Zweig*   *Hotel Schwanen*
                                               Rapperswil am Zürichsee
                                               18 September 1932

Dear, esteemed Stefan Zweig,

in my letter I forgot to tell you that I owe you a couple of scenes in my novel,[1] you will know which ones they are, and that I am deeply, deeply grateful to you, for all my dissatisfaction with the book as a whole.

Cordially   your Joseph Roth

1. Scenes in my novel: the ominous gathering of crows in the trees presaging the beginning of World War I seems to have been Zweig's idea, for one. (Roth already had geese.)

159. *To Stefan Zweig*   *Hotel Schwanen*
                                               Rapperswil am Zürichsee
                                               23 September 1932

Dear esteemed Stefan Zweig,

I am most reluctant, of course, to write this: Mr. Landauer (he of the Kiepenheuer Verlag) insists that I ask you both that you write about the

Radetzky March yourself, and that you induce Otto Zarek, who is writing about me in the *Vossische*, not to "trash" me. I am *so utterly* dependent on the wishes of Mr. Landauer, and *so utterly* revolted by the whole business, the publisher, his wishes, reviews, that I tell you without beating about the bush, simply so as to be able to report back to the publisher that I have done as required. It's disgusting, nauseating! I know you know I'm being utterly straight with you. If I were to think "sensibly," I'd have to say Landauer is right. He means well by me. I don't want to lie to him, or to you.—I hope it doesn't upset *our* relationship. I live off Landauer, I have to write to you, and I write this pukeworthy request, and I hope you understand me . . .

   your old Joseph Roth

160. *To Stefan Zweig*   *Hotel Schwanen*
                                                Rapperswil am Zürichsee
                                                24 September 1932

Dear esteemed Stefan Zweig,
   your kind letter of the 22nd arrived half an hour after I mailed my disgusting one to you. I am not protesting in *an effort to move you*! I am not complaining, believe me! I know I attract misfortune, I have gotten used to it, I don't want you in your serenity to be affected by me. You obey other laws. You are—how many times do I have to tell you!—one of the blessed! Stay that way. *Forget about me!* It pains me that I once tried to attach myself to you. But I didn't know you at that time. Believe me, won't you! I gave you no cause to think I was playacting (not even unconsciously, not even 3 or 4 layers down).—All I know (as far as practical things go) is that I am supposed to read from my novel on the radio in Frankfurt. That's all I know. I live by the practical measures undertaken by Landauer. I can't live like that. I have no more strength. No strength! Possibly I am sinful, because I get through far more money than more deserving persons require. I comfort myself with the (base) thought that I have shorter to live than the deserving ones. I have no plan for the rest

of my life. If the [. . .] Jewish scribblers trash me, then I have no money,
Landauer has no money. I am 20,000 marks in hock to the publisher. The
publisher has done a lot for me. He needs money. He doesn't have any.
Please understand that I can do nothing. I cannot live like this.

Maybe I am pampered. I can't help that.—So far as I know, I'll be
here till 4 November. My postal address remains Englischer Hof, Frankfurt am Main. I cannot appear before you in my present condition. I'm
like run butter, like ghee. At any rate I don't want you to see me like
this.—I'll never forget you!

Cordially,   your old J.R.

161. *To Blanche Gidon*   *Hotel Schwanen*
                                                 Rapperswil am Zürichsee
                                                 25 September 1932

Dear esteemed Mrs. Gidon,
I have no "representatives" in Paris. The person who is responsible for
foreign rights at Kiepenheuer is Dr. Landshoff. He is the only one who
can sell translation rights to my book.[1]

I would be very happy if you were to translate me, and if Kiepenheuer
and Plon were able to come to an agreement.

Very cordially, with many thanks and good wishes,

your old Joseph Roth

1. my book: of course and still refers to *The Radetzky March.*

162. To Friedrich Traugott Gubler   2 October [1932]

Dear friend,

it seems I have to write to you after all, afraid as I am that you haven't heard from me. I feel like someone calling out into the desert, and no echo. I write and write, and I hear nothing from you.

I would like to see a statement again. I have no idea of where I stand with the paper with regard to lines and money.

I'm in urgent need of the latter. I don't even know if I'm allowed to approach you with this silly nonsense. But I need about 100 marks a week—and I'm writing and writing, and I never see a penny. I'm in quite a good way, and not at all drunk.

Cordially   your Joseph Roth

Another article just mailed.

163. To Blanche Gidon   *Hotel Englischer Hof*
Frankfurt am Main
4 October 1932

Dear esteemed Madam,

thank you for all your trouble! If Plon has doubts—whether literary or financial—then he should forget the idea. I am by no means so consumed with ambition as to think my work must be translated. I have far too low an opinion of the public world, of literature, and publishers—in Germany and in France—for me to care about translation or "literary effect." . . .

Thank you too very much for your efforts regarding Mrs. Manga Bell's son (she says hello, and sends her best wishes). But 300 marks a month is out of the question for her. I've managed to find out since that the boy could get a place in the Lycée Janson for 120 a month. But there seems to be some doubt about their taking him. He doesn't speak a word of French! On balance, though, it's better that the son suffers, than the mother. Not merely because I'm involved with the mother; but because I think it's a sin for mothers to lay down their lives for their sons. Mrs. M.B. gets (*entre nous*) nothing at all from her very rich husband. She has to earn everything herself. She is very poorly. She has, moreover, a lung infection. She has a daughter as well. How can she manage all that? The husband is a "sovereign" nobleman, and has the right, even by French law, not to pay alimony or child upkeep.

But don't worry too much about all that! If Plon were to decide against the *RM*, then the only aspect of that I would find regrettable is that *you* wouldn't be able to translate it! I have *zero* literary ambition in this plebeian literary cattle market of Paris (or Berlin).

My regards to your husband!

Ever your old   Joseph Roth

164. To Blanche Gidon   *Hotel Englischer Hof*
                                           Frankfurt am Main
                                           11 October 1932

Dear esteemed Madam,

thank you for your two kind letters. Where the *Radetzky March* is concerned, I've never doubted that publishers of all nationalities are businessmen. What annoys me is that they're *bad* businessmen, and that, particularly in France, foreign books are badly paid for, badly translated, and badly sold. I care too much about words for me to be able to look on while my words are twisted and mutilated—merely because a publisher won't give up the false vanity of continuing to bring out foreign books, nor admit that he doesn't have deep enough pockets to do it with dignity. When I look at the revolting literary "scene": that *une heure avec,*[1] the quasi-Communist *Nouvelle Revue Française,*[2] the stupid "conservative" periodicals in Paris, these snobberies and cliques, prepared to genuflect before each "novelty," the incomprehensible Joyce,[3] the latest postwar epsilon out of Germany, well: *it makes me shudder*! The book trade has become a matter of fashion—it wouldn't surprise me in the least if Coty[4] and Poiret[5] were to be the next editors of the *Nouvelles Littéraires*. I won't participate in that. I won't join in the cult of Gide either. See: in Germany everyone is unliterary. I don't get upset if they make idiots of themselves in literary matters. But I care too much about the grand traditions of France for me to be able to bear the way they now make *une heure avec* with driveling idiots from all over Europe—and on the basis of paid advertisements! I'm used to German barbarity. It's my own. I live off it. But I can't get used to French barbarities. It's enough to make a *boche* out of me, even though, God knows, I have little aptitude for that.

Now, to Mrs. Manga Bell's son:

Thank you so much for your trouble (and Mrs. Manga Bell sends her best). She would write to you herself, only she's bedridden. She's been ill since the beginning of autumn, she can't take the adjustment. But she'll write tomorrow!

It seems to me that Mrs. Tardieu would be very good for the little black boy. The expenses, if I've got this right, are 900 francs all told—150 marks a month, including laundry and sundries.

Well, I'd be in favor of the little fellow's spending the 2 months before entering school in a French household.

But if he does have to go to the Lyceum, then the money question changes:

a. School fees—or is it free?
b. Transport?

So the boy would end up costing Mrs. Manga Bell ca. 1,200–1,500 francs per month.

(My arithmetic has always been poor, but isn't that right?) And pocket money and clothes on top of that. So two months @ 1,500 francs comes to 3,000 francs = 500 marks. Then there is Mrs. Manga Bell's second child, a daughter, in Hamburg. The children's guardian (in financial matters as well) is an uncle of Mrs. Manga Bell's in Hamburg. In my estimation, we'd have to allow 10 days before she learns:

a. Whether the money is there

b. When!

Could Mrs. Tardieu wait that long?

To recapitulate: the children's father is the Count of "Duallo and Bunanjo," and stands under French protection.—He abandoned Mrs. Manga Bell, the mother of his children.—They were born in Paris, therefore have French nationality.—They won't be able to stay in Germany for very long—on account of their race—and also on account of their future! (1) They are Negroes, and therefore dependent on France. (2) They are French Negroes, therefore they are French. (3) They have decent possibilities in France, because their father is a French "Negro chief." They are respectively 12 and 11 years old: the boy 12, the girl 11. There is no suggestion of any childhood illnesses—unpredictable chance aside.

Dear Madam, please forgive the dryness of my tone here! It seems necessary to me, when dealing with practical matters. Incidentally—an instance of the strange hand of destiny in all this "practicality": Mrs. Manga Bell's daughter was born in the Levallois-Perret clinic.

I myself am very much concerned with the fate of the children. I love them as if they were my own.—I would adopt them, if that didn't mean removing them from the protection of their much more powerful natural father.

And now: it's a *terrible* thing to have you doing so much for me—and myself powerless to respond in kind. I can only thank you from the bottom of my heart,

Yours ever   Joseph Roth

1. *une heure avec*: an interview feature in the literary weekly *Les Nouvelles Littéraires*.

2. *NRF:* an imprint of Gallimard, founded by André Gide and Jean Schlumberger.

3. Joyce: James Joyce (1882–1941). As much as he disliked musty intellectualism, so JR also had it in for a sort of games-playing modern trickery.

4. Coty: François Coty, parfumier—and newspaper owner (*Le Matin*).

5. Poiret: François Poiret, a Parisian dressmaker and designer.

165. To Hans Natonek

Englischer Hof
Frankfurt am Main
14 October 1932

Dear Hans Natonek,[1]

your lovely review[2] puts me to shame: firstly because I don't entirely deserve it, and secondly because I was so slow in thanking you for your own book. Excuse my dilatoriness. Yours is a real friendship. It even overlooks flaws in my writing—even though it clearly has eyes with which to see them.

I will try to give you my sense of your book. First its shortcomings:

1. In the conception, already. You take up two intertwining themes, either one of which would have sufficed for a novel:

a. The children of a city[3]
b. The monster disfigured by hatred, and then cured.

This is a truly Shakespearean figure. Beside him, all the others would have had to look as small as they truly are. But if you wanted an antagonist, then you would have had to confront the hellish wickedness of Dovidal with the goodness of a saint. All the time I read your book, my fingers were itching to write in such an antagonist! Partly because of my personal feeling for the author, but more the *latent charm* of the material. Dovidal is bedeviled; Epp would therefore have to be blessed. (And Waisl is redundant. He needs his own story.) Remember, brevity is the soul of etc. You commit a very common German mistake that even great Germans have perpetrated—including, if you ask me, Goethe, in *Faust*—if it weren't heretical to accuse such a one of failing. You packed in too much. Dovidal's story on its own, told in detail, phase by phase, would have been enough. Do you see? Something very *cold*, in the way that my *Job* is something very *warm*. Forgive me for mentioning myself. The mother, the father, the sister, and Dovidal himself: complete story. Instead, you (vainly) tried to squeeze this prince of hell into something ordinary and human. You ended up underestimating your own character. You turned a *metaphysical fable* into a humdrum *realist story*.

2. You still make the huge mistake—have done since you've been writing books—of interpreting, of explaining, of being a know-it-all. You over-egg the pudding, you clue the reader in, you betray what is going on in your brain-cum-workshop. You offer commentaries not only where, for some external reason or other, you haven't been able to show fully, but also where, probably without your knowing it, your construction has been brilliant. You know, I'm a clever dick as well. But I keep it under wraps. Only when you've won the Nobel Prize can you allow yourself to publish your work journals. You have fabulous scenes that speak for themselves. You present them with an extensive commentary. Your best scenes come ivied with commentary.—Your coarsest mistake: the final scene far too obvious. (Your fear, presumably, of lack of understanding on the reader's part.)

3. *The strong points of your novel* are *at the same time its flaws*. Which proves to me that you're a real writer. So I'm not just prejudiced in your favor—a relief to me. Dovidal is UNFORGETTABLE! Unforgettable the scene with the *Rabitzwänden*. Waisl's first appearance. The mother. All of them unforgettable. Waisl's marriage! Unforgettable!

4. The language is superb, but for some highly abstract remarks. A novel is not the place for *abstractions*. Leave that to Thomas Mann! If anything, your natural gift is too concrete at times.

And a few personal *eizes*:[4]

a. Read more of the greats and the immortals: Shakespeare, Balzac, Flaubert!

b. No Gide! No Proust! Nor anything of the sort!

c. The Bible. Homer.

d. *Don't distrust the "reader" too much!*

e. Try to keep yourself clear of journalism at heart.

f. No interest in day-to-day politics. They distort. They distort the human.

g. You have sufficient means—thank God—that there's really no need for you to write para-feuilletons! Fuck them. All they're good for is a hat for the wife and a dress for the girlfriend.

Sorry, forgive the know-it-all tone, the superiority, and anything else that bothers you here. Listen, if you do listen, to the *absolute honesty* of my words.

Always cordially your old   Joseph Roth

1. Hans Natonek (1892 Prague–1963 Tucson), journalist and novelist.
2. your lovely review: of *The Radetzky March*.
3. Natonek's *Kinder einer Stadt*, published in 1932.
4. *eizes*: (Yiddish) tips, advice.

166. To Friedrich Traugott Gubler   *Sunday, 25 October [1932]*

Dear friend,

I'm just over a bad shock. Mrs. M.B. was pretty seriously ill. I felt the chill breath of an operation. And worries, worries, and the need to suddenly honor a bond I'd given my parents-in-law. And a great swarm of little adversities, interrupting my work. Also my articles. And money— needing money! And a remittance from Kiepenheuer lost in the post, inquiries—and only then compensation. And the feeling of being pursued by demons. And doctors and pharmacists, and the smell of camphor again and again, and the bloody shimmer of the Red Cross, before me and behind me. Forgive my silence, all right, I'm going to get back to work tomorrow.

How is your daughter?

Cordially   your very old Joseph Roth

167. To Stefan Zweig   *26 October 1932*
                                                  Casa Bellaria
                                                  Ascona, Ticino

Dear esteemed friend,

read your book[1] in two days of breathless excitement. My friendship
for you can't make me so blind—and if blind, then at least not so excited.
I used to read like that when I was a boy, Karl May, *Robinson Crusoe*.
There was material for a master, and you mastered the material. The
way it tightens and tightens till the end—I got more and more breathless
myself, I played along—that was how Schiller wrote history plays. My
dear clever friend and Stefan Zweig. I am enraptured! You interpreter
and poet! That's really what you are.

Tell me where you are going.

At this stage, I know nothing, except that I'll have to stay on here
another 8–10 days, while Landauer sends money. Then, if sufficient,
maybe Paris?

Always your loyal friend   Joseph Roth

1. your book: *Marie Antoinette*.

168. To Otto Forst-Battaglia   *Caffè Centrale Ascona*
                                                  as of: Englischer Hof
                                                  Frankfurt am Main
                                                  Ascona, 28 October 1932

Dear Doctor,[1]

thank you for your kindly letter. I am the son of an Austrian railway
official (early retirement, died at home) and a Russian-Polish Jewess. I
attended middle school (gymnasium) in Silesia, Galicia, and Vienna, and
then studied German language and literature under Minor and Brecht
(in Vienna). I volunteered for the front in 1916, and from 1917 to 1918

fought on the eastern front. I was made lieutenant and decorated with the Silver Cross, the Merit Cross, and the Karl Truppen Cross. My service was initially with the 21st Jaegers, then the 24th Land Reserve. The most powerful experience of my life was the war and the end of my fatherland, the only one I have ever had: the Dual Monarchy of Austria-Hungary.[2] To this date I am a patriotic Austrian and love what is left of my homeland as a sort of relic.—I spent six months in a Russian prisoner of war camp, fled, and fought for two months in the Red Army, then two months flight and return home. In Vienna I began to write: first in the *Arbeiterzeitung*, then for the *Neuer Tag* (not to be confused with the *Tag* of today), then in the *N. Wiener Journal*; *Flight Without End* is largely autobiographical; thereafter I was a freelance reporter in Berlin, then roving reporter for the feuilleton section of the *Frankfurter Zeitung* [. . .] then for the *Münchener Neueste Nachrichten*. My first book appeared in 1923 or 1924. It was called *Hotel Savoy*. Since 1930, I've lived as a freelance author in Germany and abroad.

I want to thank you for your interest, and on this occasion for the warm notice you wrote about my novel *Job*.

Your humble servant   Joseph Roth

1. Doctor: Otto Forst-Battaglia (1889–1965), publicist, writer, scholar, diplomat. Ended his life as professor of Polish literature at the University of Vienna.

2. This and the following sentences are very often quoted in writing about Roth.

169. To Félix Bertaux   *Hotel Englischer Hof*
                                           Frankfurt am Main
                                           14 November 1932

Dear esteemed friend,

I'm surprised you never got my letter from Ascona. I have been back from Switzerland for just two days. I expect to be in Berlin later this month. Please give me Pierre's address, I'll be only too glad to look him up.

Mrs. Manga Bell won't have money to move her son until December, and so I hope we'll be able to see each other early in January in Paris. Perhaps I'll even enlist the Parisian boulevards to help me forget about the dreary celebration of Christmas. So I might be in Paris as early as the 22nd. Admittedly, I'll be short of money, and living in pretty reduced circumstances. The income from the *Radetzky March* won't come through until next spring.[1]

I'm very glad the book means something to you. I think it's time I thought about people "of today" once more—and I hope, come January, when I'm better, to start on a big novel set in the present. To that end I think I'll be resurrecting my old friend Franz Tunda.[2]

For a week now I've been drinking only wine, no schnapps, because I'm unfortunately getting a cirrhosis, albeit only in the initial stages. It can still be tamed. I've promised to look after myself. I feel I still have something to live for.

Give my best wishes to your wife.

Ever your old and grateful   Joseph Roth

1. In view of what happened then, it never did.
2. Franz Tunda: originally from *Flight Without End.*

170. *To Jenny Reichler*   *5 December 1932*

Dear Mother,

my condolences on grandfather's death. I adored him all his life, he was like a natural grandfather to me. I'm thinking of you and your pain, and hope that Friedl's return to health may comfort us all.

I will write in more detail from Leipzig, where I am going now.

Your loyal son

171. To Stefan Zweig   *Hotel-Pension Savigny*
Berlin
5 December 1932

Dear esteemed Stefan Zweig,

your letter came winging its way to me yesterday—I always see your letters as somehow winged. They are as bright and agile as swallows.[1] I'm not sure I'll be able to come to Munich. You know it's a long way from Berlin—and I'd need to go back as well, to join my girlfriend in Hamburg. Very early in the New Year, I'm bringing her son to Paris—I've probably told you this already. That's a lot of silly to-ing and fro-ing—and I need to be mindful of costs as well. I'm sure you know how much it goes against the grain for me to advance arguments against a suggestion that would allow me to enjoy your dear, good, dear proximity. I will be even coarser now, because I would like to see you for just *one* day, soon: could you see your way to being in Berlin 2 days before the Christmas holidays? I'm sure you could easily, forgive me for putting it like that. Alternatively: do you think you could meet me somewhere in January, any day before the 10th? Again: Hamburg is probably too far and too inclement at this time? Forgive me for being unable to find more diplomatic expressions in my haste. I know you won't mind. You know I want to see you whenever possible. Your great friendship has been lucky for me. And my great fear that it might be unlucky for you turns out not to have been justified. I really was afraid of that! I thought of all sorts of unlikely, partly ridiculous but also serious things between the two of us. Thank God! I'm so relieved! I want to get back to work at the end of January, but need to talk to you first. Three old themes are circulating in my head. My book is selling about 100 copies a day. Everything would be fine, in material terms anyway, so long as the publisher is able to enjoy a bit of success. But none of their other authors are shifting at all, including Arnold Zweig, for whom they paid the most money.[2] Just between you and me, it's a silly book too, internally and for gloomy reasons. The Jews are so stupid. It takes the even stupider anti-Semites to come up with the notion that the Jews are dangerously clever. At the end of 2,000 years, they still managed to be sympathetic—and they're perverse enough to take themselves and their Judaism for the center of the world. Like the *Neue Freie Presse* really. How petty and stupid it all is—and how easily one has slipped all chains, all of them. To my regret, I no longer find myself able to solidarize myself with this form of continually self-abnegating Judaism. Arnold Zweig is a very talented chatterer. Through an aperture of precisely one and a half degrees, he proposes to take in the entire cosmos! There's chutzpah for you! Cosmic chutzpah!—But as far as I'm concerned, I owe the publisher 22,000 marks. He's living entirely off of what I bring in. All I have is a better conscience vis-à-vis accepting advances.—My wife—and the lasting grimness of her illness—that's something I'd rather speak to you about. I'm unable to set it down.

Please write back by return!

Good luck with the Strauss business![3]

Your old true cordial   Joseph Roth

1. See Roth's tremendous story "Stationmaster Fallmerayer," in *Collected Stories*.
2. isn't shifting at all: Arnold Zweig's novel *De Vriendt kehrt heim*.
3. Following the death of Hugo von Hofmannsthal in 1929, Richard Stauss turned to Zweig for the liberetto to his *Die schweigsame Frau*.

172. To Albert Ehrenstein   29 December 1932

Dear Albert Ehrenstein,[1]

as God is my witness (though He is the only one), I've thought of writing to you every day since I left Ascona. But I've given up—had to give up—schnapps, and I spend my days sick as a dog. I have a cirrhosis in its early stages—all I can do is hope to slow its progress. I hope you'll forgive me. 3 of my books—I don't have copies of the others—will be sent to you sometime from the warehouse in Leipzig. I don't have your book either! Lio[2] has become a strong and stubborn critter. Mrs. Manga Bell sends you her gratitude and best wishes. She's (rightly) fonder of the cat than of me. Write, and don't be offended if I don't write back. The address is:

c/o Englischer Hof, Frankfurt am Main. Financially, for all the success of my novel, my situation is lousy, because the publisher can't afford to let me stay in debt. Sick, wretched, old, lonely, pathetic—and somewhere up above strolls my name or fama, which is not at all the same as my real existence. Don't be cross with me.—Best wishes to Mrs. Sommerfeld—

Cordially your   Joseph Roth

Would you please get my coat (plus invoice) sent to me, Jos. Roth, c/o Kiepenheuer Verlag, Kantstrasse 10, Berlin (Charlottenburg), it's getting cold. Thanks again!

1. Albert Ehrenstein (1886 Vienna–1950 New York), poet, novelist, essayist.
2. Lio: Ehrenstein's pet tomcat.

173. Benno Reifenberg to Joseph Roth   29 December 1932

To Mr. Joseph Roth, c/o Kiepenheuer Verlag, Berlin
Dear Mr. Roth,

I don't hear from you. But perhaps you'd like to hear this sentence from a letter of Hausenstein's on the *Radetzky March*: "The book is so lovely, that one has to cry, like Picard, when reading it; so lovely that I don't know what other book of recent times one could set alongside it."

Cordially your old   [Benno Reifenberg]

174. To Stefan Zweig   [Berlin] 12 January 1933

Dear, esteemed friend,

I'm going to Paris round about the 20th, don't know yet where I'll be staying, as the Foyot is closed, and will stay till about the 10th February. Can we meet? Returning to Berlin probably round about the 20th February.

Cordially,   your old friend Joseph Roth

175. To Blanche Gidon   *Berlin, 12 January 1933*

Dear, esteemed Mrs. Gidon,

About the 20th I hope to be in Paris with the little pickaninny, and talk to you and your dear husband. I don't doubt for a second that you have translated my book[1] splendidly. I am very grateful to you.

Till soon! Your humble   Joseph Roth

1. my book: *The Radetzky March*.

176. To Stefan Zweig   *[Hamburg] 18 January 1933*

Very dear and esteemed friend,

so I will be going to Paris on about the 25th, and then Switzerland, and meet you in Munich. I *cannot embark on anything new* without first talking to you. I require your goodness and cleverness. A couple of people on the "right," who have heard about my "left-wing" Jewish origins, are just starting to agitate against me too. In the same right-wing journals where they praised my book, they're now starting to attack me. The Jews and the Leftists are no better, if anything worse. Forgive a friend for blurting out something he just intuits: some of what the Right is saying against you will have been given to them by the Insel Verlag itself; just a hunch, nothing more. Be on your guard. You may be smart, but your humanity blinds you to others' wickedness. You live on goodness and faith. Whereas I have been known to make sometimes startlingly accurate observations about evil.

Warmest best wishes!

Your old   J.R.

Please don't be too "amused" by my meanness[1] here.

1. meanness: JR is alluding to his (terribly discreet) adverting to alleged remarks by Zweig's publisher, Anton Kippenberg, director of the Insel Verlag since 1905 and soon to become a Nazi, that he had to correct the German of his (Jewish) author Zweig.

PART IV

1933–1939

After Hitler: Work, Despair, Diminishing Circles, Work, and Death

JOSEPH ROTH IN THE COMPANY OF DUTCH WRITERS
IN A CAFÉ IN AMSTERDAM IN 1937

On the morning of 30 January 1933, the day Hitler was appointed chancellor, Joseph Roth boarded the Berlin–Paris train, and never set foot in Germany again. The hair-fine precision of the timing might have been an accident; the rigor with which Roth drew his consequences assuredly wasn't. His immediate attention—in the letters, at least—was needed for matters closer to home: what was to become of Andrea Manga Bell's son, and worries about the quality of Blanche Gidon's French translation of *The Radetzky March*. By mid-February, though, events in Germany had fully claimed their place, which they were to keep for the remaining years of Roth's life: "It will have become clear to you now that we are heading for a great catastrophe," he wrote to Stefan Zweig, to whom this may have been far from clear, and who—like many of the most "assimilated" Jews—continued to believe in the intactness, and quite possibly the immunity of his personal arrangements. Roth had no such illusions, and went on, "Quite apart from our personal situations—our literary and material existence has been wrecked—we are headed for a new war. I wouldn't give a heller for our prospects. The barbarians have taken over. Do not deceive yourself. Hell reigns."

The intensely dramatic, complicated correspondence between the two unequal friends takes up most of the latter part of this book. Roth begins writing to Zweig in no. 49; starting at no. 216, some of Zweig's letters are also included. You could say that Zweig picks up where this or that publisher of Roth, or the *Frankfurter Zeitung*, leaves off; he is, so to speak, the one in the blue corner; he is not really an adversary, but—like the publishers, like the *FZ*—he comes to be seen in the role of an adversary. Roth simply carries on as before. His own letters are always uphill. He is always the underdog, always indomitable, always David to the other's Goliath. By same token, he is always the better writer, and he is always in the right. The other is the one with money, power, authority, patronage, prestige. Roth has nothing, is nothing, all he can do is make a noise, and issue threats. He can withdraw his labor, or he can tell the other—tell Zweig—how badly he is doing, how desperate he is for money, medicine, tranquillity, affection, understanding. In the early letters, up until, say, 1928—up until the catastrophe with Friedl—Roth was always reserved, dignified, keeping things back until there was a chance to say them, face to face, in a meeting; keeping them out of letters, where he felt they didn't belong. This gradually is turned on its head. First, they come with apologies ("I come to you with a revolting request"), and by the end, they come anyway. Eventually there is nothing that Roth will not write; a letter, in his hands, is an instrument of necessary terror. The extremity of his situation justifies it. Anything less is the waste of a stamp.

When the calamitous events of 1933 happened, no one was perhaps better prepared for them than Roth. He had been building up his *Feindbild* of Germany and the Germans—of Prussia and the *boches*—for the best part of fifteen years. He knew from repeated bitter experience that life was a catastrophic sequence of losses, betrayals, and disappointments. His birthplace had been ceded to Poland, his country—the supranational Dual Monarchy comprising seventeen nationalities—was a figment of history, and he lived off his wits, out of a couple of suitcases. He expected nothing else. He may have thought he had little left to lose (he was wrong). And conversely, perhaps no one was worse prepared for them—or had more to lose, was more invested in the fiction of a *heile Welt* where not only was there no 1933, there was no sure sign that *1914* had happened—than Stefan Zweig, whose "world of yesterday" had not fallen about his ears, not any part of it: who was born on the Ringstrasse in Vienna, and was free to go back there whenever he liked; who grew up in the bosom of a wealthy and sympathetic Jewish manufacturing family; studied in Berlin; had traveled around the world; was a pacifist and an internationalist during the war; lived, when he cared to, in a fourteenth-century bishop's palace above Salzburg that his lovely and capable wife had found for him; was on close personal terms with a who's who of European intellectuals; and was the mainstay and virtual editor-at-large of a German belletristic publishing firm with extraordinary production values called *Die Insel* (the Island—*sic*), where for the best part of thirty years he had been a best-selling author of error-free books snapped up by an especially devoted and largely female readership. Roth, one might say, was all instinct (albeit the instincts were not always correct); Zweig had none, and duly experienced—at the proper time, so to speak—all those losses and disappointments that Roth had suffered proleptically.

To Roth it will have looked as though Zweig's advantages were such that he would never stop defending them, whatever the moral cost; Zweig will have thought that Roth, shifting and transient, with no real sacrifice to make, had no proper understanding of the painfully slow accrual of property or reputation. The exchange goes through all sorts of phases: sometimes it is a dialogue of the deaf, sometimes we have two competing prophets (or egocentrics); then Roth blusters and wails, Zweig pleads, reasons, extenuates. Zweig evokes his freedom and his good intentions as an individual; Roth assures him that anyone continuing to have dealings with the enemy had no further claim on his friendship. The very quick and fiery and aggressive Roth and the obtuse, decent-minded, and squirming Zweig are a fascinating—and distressing—study in contrary temperaments. Their relationship was further complicated by the fact that Roth was monetarily—one could almost say physically—dependent on Zweig, and handled his dependency predictably badly, with histrionic begging, intermittent gratitude, and shorter and shorter intervals. When Paula Grübel offered to buy her cousin a new set of teeth, Roth straightaway refused: "If she pays for my teeth, she will own a bit of me," he is said to have reasoned. He took Zweig's money, but refused to be bought. On the one hand, his need for more was basically unappeasable; on the other, he maintained his natural dominance in the relationship, in spite of all Zweig's advantages.

Hermann Kesten tells a superb story of the time[1] they were all together in Ostend in 1936, how they would work during the days, and in the

---

1. Related in David Bronsen, *Joseph Roth: Eine Biographie* (Cologne, 1974), p. 471.

evening Zweig would take Roth out to expensive restaurants and bars, Roth in his only pair of, fraying, trousers. One day Zweig took Roth to a tailor, and had him fitted for a new pair of trousers. They turned out to be terribly expensive, because the tailor needed to be bribed to make the trousers the way Roth wanted them, in the style of Austrian cavalry trousers, very narrow below the knee. To Zweig's satisfaction, Roth turned out that evening in his new trousers. The next day, Kesten relates, he came upon Roth sitting with Irmgard Keun at a bar in the market. The waiter brought out three glasses of brightly colored liqueurs. Roth took his, and slowly and deliberately, and to applause from Keun, emptied it over his jacket. Kesten asks Roth, "What are you doing?" "Punishing Stefan Zweig," replies Roth, emptying the next lurid glass over the jacket. Roth explained to Kesten that that evening he would shame Zweig with his stained jacket. "Millionaires are like that! They take us to the tailor, and buy us a new pair of pants, but they forget to buy us a jacket to go with them."

There is a photograph of the time, taken on a café terrace in Ostend: a Great Dane with a terrier. Zweig, big, sleek, friendly, glossy, leans in toward his friend affectionately and indulgently; he looks animated, enthused, warm; he is about to say something kind and perhaps ever so slightly witty. Roth looks like an old boxer or wrestler, a square head on thick shoulders, slumped, pouchy, impervious, a lumpy jack-o-lantern face under a few damp squiggles of hair squeezed out of an icing bag, the eyes between blinking and glowering. No one looking at the picture would guess that Roth is the younger by some thirteen years. Nor could anyone be oblivious to the fact that he is the dominant personality. Soma Morgenstern describes his friend in these terms:

> As he took a sip of cognac to recover from his coughing laugh, I stud-
> ied him closely. The changes to face and form staggered me. He was
> not quite forty-three years old, and—my heart won't forgive me for
> saying so: he looked like a sixty-year-old alcoholic. His face, once so
> animated and alert, with its prominent cheekbones, and short jutting

chin, was now puffy and slack, the nose purple, the corners of his blue eyes rheumy and bloody, his head looking as if someone had started plucking it and given up part way, the mouth completely covered by heavy, dark red, Slovak-style drooping mustaches. But when summoned to the telephone, he slowly hobbled away with the aid of a stick, his thin legs in narrow old-fashioned pants, his sagging little paunch at odds with his birdlike bones, the east Galician Jew made the impression of a distinguished, if somewhat decayed, Austrian aristocrat—in other words, exactly the impression he had striven all his life to give, with every fiber of his body and soul, by means both legitimate and illegitimate.[2]

This understands—as it is important to understand—the balance between tragedy and dignity in Roth, sadness and success.

2. Translated from Bronsen, *Joseph Roth,* where it is quoted on p. 557.

177. To Félix Bertuax   *1 February 1933*
                                                   Hotel Jacob
                                                   44 rue Jacob

Bien cher ami,

I'm here at last, and would love to see you—this week still, if you can manage it.

I need to talk to you about my little pickaninny.

Looking forward to seeing you.

My best regards and those of Mrs. Manga Bell to Mrs. Bertaux.

Your old true   Joseph Roth

178. To Félix Bertaux   *9 February 1933*

My dear friend,

I must burden you with the horrible business of the translation.[1] Here enclosed is Mr. Marcel's letter—a copy—the original is back with Mrs. Gidon—from which it appears that Mrs. Gidon has delivered an excellent translation.—I don't know what to do now. Either Mr. Marcel doesn't know German or French—or else he's lying. I'm tired of all these things, because of the goings-on in Germany I'm incapable of settling the least personal matter, and I feel completely downtrodden. What sort of moral responses are open to me anyway, if the publisher insists on his legal right to proceed with the translation?

Cordial wishes to Mrs. Bertaux and yourself, your desolate old
Joseph Roth

Please don't call, but give me a written rendezvous.

I am never at home, just wander around randomly, I can't stand to be in a room.[2]

1. translation: of *The Radetzky March*.

2. in a room: this note (typically) has interposed another drama, and another crisis, but this remark surely wants to be taken in relation to events in Germany. Even so, however, we have a description from Gustav Kiepenheuer of seeing JR once—unusually—in an apartment in Berlin, ten years previously, "pacing up and down the vast, gloomy drawing room, his hands in his coat-pockets, as though in a station waiting room, waiting for his train to be made ready." He could never stand to be "in a room."

179. *Gabriel Marcel to Blanche Gidon (written in French)*

8 February 1933

Dear Madam,

I have just read the first two chapters of your translation. It seems to me that the only criticisms one might make are trivial, that overall *this is an excellent translation* and I won't even contemplate the idea of giving the rest of the book to anyone else. By all means show this letter to Mr. Roth.

Yours sincerely,

G. Marcel[1]

Director of the Feux Croisés

1. Gabriel Marcel (1889–1973), philosopher, dramatist, critic. Winner of the 1964 Peace Prize of the German Book Trade. At the time an editor at Plon. The Feux Croisés was an imprint at Plon. It is very difficult at this distance in time and language to get a sense of the rights and wrongs of Blanche Gidon's translation of *The Radetzky March*, which came out in 1934. (The fact that it is still in print in France today speaks in its favor.) Roth in any case brought a characteristic energy, confusion, and offense to the matter, which, somewhat surprisingly, his personal and professional relationship with Mrs. Gidon managed to survive.

180. To Félix Bertaux   *11 February 1933*

Dear friend,

I have just written to Gabriel Marcel that I find the translation utterly unusable, and that I consider it my *duty* to appear before the French public in an adequate translation.

At the same time I replied to Mrs. Gidon's letter, which you saw yesterday, as follows:

"The only person, my oldest friend in France, on whom I can depend, is Mr. Bertaux, as you know. He is very stringent and harsh (even with me), and he is familiar with my style. *Without a second's hesitation*, I would give my public approval to any translation he deemed good."

I hope you're not annoyed with me for thus enlisting you, unasked.

The whole business is deeply unpleasant!

1. Gidon is a friend of Reifenberg's;

2. Reifenberg is my friend;

3. it is deeply embarrassing to encounter a piece of sharp practice in France that I would never have thought possible.

4. I am completely wiped out

    a. without a penny, since, between ourselves, Landauer is giving up the publisher.

    b. With debts of 18,000 marks in Germany.

    c. With prospects of having to sleep under the Seine bridges within 4 weeks. (figure of speech?)[1]

Forgive me this trespass into personal affairs. Perhaps—let's hope—it's only a bad dream.

I hope to be more cheerful on Monday.

Please kiss Mrs. Bertaux's hand for me—in Austrian. (Do read Hofmannsthal's posthumous *Andreas*!)

Your old and desolate   Joseph Roth

---

1. See *The Legend of the Holy Drinker*, Roth's last completed work of fiction.

181. *To Félix Bertaux*   *11 February 1933*

My dear friend,

I come to you with a revolting request: I have been sent a banker's draft from Kiepenheuer: 550 marks, roughly 3,300 francs.

I have no bank account here (none at all).

Is it possible for you to cash the check for me, so that, through your bank—assuming you have the appropriate facilities—I might get the money as early as Wednesday?

I'm meeting Pierre on Monday.

I would give him the check if such a transaction is indeed possible. If not, then please don't trouble yourself! I'll try something else.

My antagonism with Sieburg makes it impossible for me to use the offices of the *Frankfurter Zeitung*.

Very cordial wishes to Mrs. Bertaux and yourself, ever your old

Somewhat mad and desolate   J.R.

182. *To Stefan Zweig*   *47 rue Jacob*
                                          Hotel Jacob, Paris 6ᵉ
                                          [mid-February 1933]

Dear esteemed friend,

I've been here for a fortnight trying to find accommodation for a young French pickaninny. It will have become clear to you now that we are heading for a great catastrophe. Quite apart from our personal situations—our literary and material existence has been wrecked—we are headed for a new war. I wouldn't give a heller for our prospects. The barbarians have taken over. Do not deceive yourself. Hell reigns.[1]

Warmly your old   Joseph Roth

1. Hell reigns: aptly, the obtuse and temporizing Zweig is the recipient of JR's first explicitly monitory reaction to the Nazi takeover.

183. To Félix Bertaux   *14 February 1933*

My dear friend,

Mrs. Manga Bell is just back from seeing Mr. Diagne. As I guessed—going by my experience of minorities—Jews and Negroes—Mr. Diagne didn't "daign" to meet Mrs. Manga Bell in person, had her received by a trainee, and merely for the purpose of sending her away again. He was unable apparently to do or promise anything. Meanwhile, a brother-in-law of Mrs. Manga Bell's (her husband's brother) is in Paris, is a member of the "etudiants evangeliques," has a 12,000-franc scholarship, thanks to Mr. Diagne, and Mr. Diagne seems not even to want to lift a finger for any member of the Manga Bell family. *At the most*, Mr. Diagne's trainee—a loathsome white bigot—would agree to confirm that Mr. Diagne knew Mrs. Manga Bell. The only way will be through the Ministry. The little fellow is French by birth. In my opinion, it doesn't matter if he's a black or white Frenchman. In political terms, black is even slightly preferable. If it can be done, a direct petition from Mrs. M.B. to M. de Monzie[1] resolved favorably by Mr. V.,[2] that—from all I know and sense about Negroes—is probably the only way forward. I tell you this, my friend, with the heavy conscience of a friend abusing friendship—but also with the clear conscience of someone who is responsible for the fate of a completely helpless child. It's a given that a black French boy can't stay in Germany. It's almost equally given that France doesn't need to support etudiants evangeliques who also happen to be black. By the way, Mrs. Manga Bell's brother-in-law is no Frenchman by birth. What I'm demanding is an injustice in the name of justice. It's enough that someone be black. He doesn't need to have a set of black feelings.—My dear friend, I wouldn't be so insistent, if Hitler hadn't got in, and robbed me of my livelihood. I'm, as you know, stuffed. Otherwise I could have got together the 150 marks a month for the boy.

Would you speak to Mr. Viénot? If he helps, I'll be very grateful to him—naturally enough. Unfortunately, we don't have much time—I can only keep the boy fed for another 6 weeks. Lousy, isn't it.

Please forgive me, and tell me—tell me *honestly*—if it's not too much
of a burden for you.

Your old   J.R.

1. de Monzie: Anatole de Monzie, author.
2. V.: Jean Viénot, senior civil sevant, subsequently Socialist minister.

184. To Bela Horovitz   *18 February 1933*
                                                          Paris

Dear, esteemed Dr. Horovitz,

thank you for your kind letter. What a question: how am I! Seeing as I can't get the money I need from Kiepenheuer, and the Jews
are ducking behind Hitler's back, and I can't go back to pre-election
Germany—merely because it makes my heart bleed to see German
fraternal quarrels—I'm feeling great. You might think about making
discreet preparations to welcome new German authors. The Jewish publishers in Germany are shutting up shop.

I'm staying here for another 2–3 weeks. I'm between hotels. If you
have something to send me, send it for now to Joseph Roth, c/o Mr. Isaac
Grünberg,[1] Bon Hotel, rue Vaneau 42, Paris.

I have a lot of *zores* and two small favors to you. Can you settle the
Roth account (enclosed), and send 15 schillings to Mrs. Jenny Reichler,
Am Tabor 15? It's a *mizwe*.[2] (If you can't, I won't be angry.)

As far as *Rebellion* goes—it's a stroke of luck for me that you have
the book—but what about the fee? I'm waiting for it—how can I not:
we've both been waiting 3,000 years to be given a role to play in German
literature.

And on top of that, it's taken me a further 12 years to acquire a nice
conservative reputation.

Since you must have paid at least 1,000 marks for *Rebellion*, I'll ask
only another 100 schillings for *Savoy*. Between you and me: *Rebellion* is

still in print. For falling for it, another 20 schillings. Are you now going to spoil the success of all my reactionary works to follow?

What about *Hotel Savoy*?

To live is to outlive.

I mean the Third Reich.

So, no hurry, please. Otherwise I'll have to say *Rebellion* is by my twin brother of the same name.

Nothing against God and Christians, if you please.[3]

Your old   Joseph Roth

1. Isaac Grünberg, writer and friend of Joseph Roth's. He translated Céline's *Voyage au bout de la nuit* into German in 1933.

2. *mizwe*: (Yiddish) kindness, solace.

3. If you please: a wonderful breezy irony—hopelessness in its early stages—pervades this letter.

185. To Félix Bertaux   *Café des 2 Magots, [Paris]*
                                           24 February 1933

My dear friend,

I am now staying at: Le bon Hotel, rue Vaneau 42. I have had some more ill luck in the last few days. The boy was returned to me with high fever and a serious flu. He's in the hotel with me now. Apparently, I can't cure myself of these misfortunes. Quite apart from the fact that with all these terrible and unplanned expenses, I won't have anything left to live on. I am completely crushed.

Still no word from Mr. Gabriel Marcel. Because of the little pickaninny, I couldn't even think about all that. I'll write to Marcel today. In the meantime—before I fire the Big Bertaux—I'm asking you whether you can find out from *Stock*[1] whether Mrs. Gidon was the original [sacked] translator of Kästner.[2] (*Fabian*.) André Thérive[3] is said to have attacked the translation so violently in *Le Temps* that the publisher was forced to withdraw it. If that was Mrs. Gidon, then I really need no further argument, and I don't need to send you off to the front, when I'd rather keep you behind the lines as my general. Could you find that out? Will you? It has to be soon.

Could you also pass my new address to your son Pierre? It's very important to me that I find some accommodation for my little picka-ninny. How much is the Lycée Janson per month? More than 400 francs? And boarding? I may have to go back to Germany, if the thing with the publisher doesn't work out. I have to anchor my existence for at least six months.

Please write back. And let's meet.

Sincerely, your old   Joseph Roth

1. Stock: Librairie Stock, a French publishing house.
2. Kästner: Erich Kästner (1899–1974), novelist, poet, essayist.
3. André Thérive (1891–1967), critic and writer.

---

186. To Félix Bertaux   *1 March 1933*

My dear friend,

I'm seeing Marcel on Saturday morning. He wrote back yesterday, at long last. I'm going to appeal to you. If you can manage, can we meet tomorrow (Thursday) afternoon? I'm free then.

Sincere best wishes to you and Mrs. Bertaux, your humble

Joseph Roth

---

187. To Félix Bertaux   *4 March 1933*

My dear friend,

I'm just back from seeing Mr. M.[1] He is very keen to have my book on his list. He is one of too many figures in the book business with strong aesthetic convictions, and a quick and instinctive grasp of things, but who remain fundamentally unreliable. He completely understood my position. He even said I was right. He is a nimble translator, and is quick to find the right form of words. He wants to send me someone who, he thinks, will match my intentions. He would rework the translation completely. I am to give this gentleman a sample. I can then present that to you for approval. Then we'll see. It appears that Mr. Marcel has several reasons for not offending Mrs. Gidon. I said more than once that I relied entirely on you. He spoke very warmly of you. Almost dismissively of Werfel.[2] All in all, I formed the impression that he doesn't want to lose me, but that he's a little hemmed in by Mrs. Gidon. If I get a good translation from someone else, then I don't really care what happens between Mr. M. and Mrs. G.

I'll phone you on Monday evening. Grim news from Berlin.[3] I'm exhausted. I can't even go on working on the novella. I really am exhausted.

Best wishes to Mrs. Bertaux,

Ever your old   Joseph Roth

1. Mr. M.: Gabriel Marcel.

2. Werfel: Franz Werfel (1890 Prague–1945 Beverly Hills), writer, poet, essayist, one of the most successful and bankable names among German writers between the wars. His best-known novel is *The Song of Bernadette*, completed in the United States in 1942, after he and his wife, Alma Mahler, made a dramatic escape through occupied France. It was also made into an Oscar-winning film during World War II.

3. Grim news from Berlin: a reference to the burning of the Reichstag on 27 February 1933, and the promulgating the next day of an emergency decree that suspended civil liberties and permitted the central government to take over authority in the individual states. This "temporary" decree was never rescinded.

188. To Félix Bertaux (written in French)   *Tuesday 1:30 [no date]*

My dear friend,

I've been making myself try and telephone you for the past hour. It seems the telephone has other ideas.

I hope you're not angry with me. I would like to see you at the end of this week or early next. (Give me a written time and place.) I will come, or be there already.

Mrs. M.B. is doing better, at any rate—thanks be to God—she won't need an operation.

As for me, I'm doing very badly. I can't write any more. I am too weak to endure the crowd of misfortunes that are too small to give one any satisfaction, even the satisfaction of being "unfortunate."

Will I see you soon?

I crave the reassurance of your presence.

Forgive this indiscreet confession from your (old) friend

Joseph Roth

Best wishes to Mrs. Bertaux, and to Pierre. Will I not see him in the time he's "in purdah"?

189. *To Blanche Gidon*   *16 March 1933*

Dear esteemed kind Madam,

thank you for your dear letter. My publisher was here, and kept me from answering you at once. I never accused you of ill will. I have always been grateful to you for going to so much trouble over my book. I never doubted that you took on the translation for no selfish motive. However, I cannot avoid saying to you that your translation is a bad translation, and—in spite of my debt to you for going to so much trouble over the book, and in spite of the friendship I feel for you—it remains a bad translation. I fail to understand how a perfectly objective criticism should strike you in light of a personal grievance. Anyone is free to tell me that such and such a book of mine is no good. I would *never* draw personal conclusions from it. You are free to rework the translation with the help of the party Marcel will suggest, or by yourself, or with whomever else you like. I need to look to my own survival. I cannot—even if my French

were up to it—busy myself with the translation. I have to go to Switzerland now for a week. Please believe me, at least, that I continue to believe
in the unselfishness of your motives. But that has nothing to do with my
conviction that your translation—in the form in which it is in front of
me—is not good. Do you want me to tell you it is good, against my own
convictions, when I am convinced of the opposite?—Maybe I am a *boche*.
But, be it out of politeness or friendship or anything else, you can't expect
me to say something that doesn't accord with my convictions. Is that why
you're angry with me?

Sincerely your   Joseph Roth

Hotel Foyot, 33 rue de Tournon, Paris 6ᵉ.

After 4 p.m. you will always find me in the Foyot. I am writing a
novella,[1] six hours a day, every day, for Ullstein. 6 more days. Every day,
after 4 p.m.

1. novella: "Stationmaster Fallmerayer."

190. To Stefan Zweig   *Hotel Foyot*
                                                         Paris
                                                         17 March 1933

Dear esteemed friend,

I know you understand why I haven't written to you for so long, and
I know you can't hold it against me. Nor do I have any idea what to say
or write now. It's no longer the case—as it was still a year ago—of the
sensible person being driven mad by the world, it's the world that has
gone mad, and there's no point in common sense any more.

To stick to practical matters:

My publisher[1] is being wound up (this between you and me). He is trying to sell me on. I don't know to whom. I have no idea what I am going
to live on. I really don't want to be an émigré.

What will you do?

There is no question of being published in Germany any more. Now do you understand why I always was, and am, presciently sad?

Yours sincerely, your old　　　　Joseph Roth

1. my publisher: Gustav Kiepenheuer, Berlin.

191. To Stefan Zweig　　　　　　　*Paris, Hotel Foyot*
　　　　　　　　　　　　　　　　33 rue de Tournon
　　　　　　　　　　　　　　　　19 March 1933

Dear friend,

I've waited till now to answer your kind letter, because I'd hoped not to have to need your practical generosity. However, even the tiny sum I've been expecting from Poland has failed to come in these 3 weeks. I can't even say any more how much or how little I need to get a little breathing space. If you're kind enough to transfer whatever money you have disposable by *Wednesday* or *Thursday*—because that's a critical date for me—then you will have gained me a deal of breathing space, certainly enough to finish my book. It'll be finished in 6 days.

Please can you help me. It's a dreadful thing for me, to "disgust you"[1] like this.

Ideally, Grasset,[2] who knows my name, wouldn't get to hear about it. Is it really no trouble for you to wire me the money by Wednesday?

I do feel some compunction, I will admit, because I know *how the French think*. I know what Directeur Brun[3] thinks.

Forgive me for saying this to you.

Write soon, and tell me why you are quite so het up.

Your old　　　　Joseph Roth

1. "disgust you": JR, presumably, never got wind of it, but Zweig privately referred to (and thought of?) his friend's financial affairs as "Augean."
2. Grasset: the publishing house of Bernard Grasset, in Paris.
3. Brun: director of Grasset.

192. To Stefan Zweig   *Hotel Foyot*
                                                          Paris
                                                          22 March 1933

Dear esteemed friend,

thank you for your kind letter. The day I next clap eyes on you will
be a red-letter day. I think of you to myself as "The Wise Man of the
Kapuzinerberg." In such times, I have to talk to you, not just correspond.
Never mind that I have to contradict you in many things. Discussions
with a wise man are never without contradiction. You speak for and
from yourself: fate has given you sorrow, happiness, fame, success, and
50 years, a happy youth in peacetime, and a vigorous maturity.[1] Forgive
a friend for pointing out that that's not the universal lot. You know my
lot pretty well, but I'm not talking about myself. I'm speaking, rather,
for a world, a good world, a tried and tested world. Of late, it's not the
majority of writers who have fared well, but rather a minority—and
that, only in relative terms. In a time that had no Woolworth magazines,
Lessing and Wieland fared much better on small incomes than—well,
let's say Arnold Zweig in the time of Tietz.[2] You have in mind a couple
of youngish authors, without worries, without grave private fate before
them, living on relatively high royalties quite frivolously, though (even
they are) not entirely without worries. And, as far as the Jews are concerned, firstly they are facing their dissolution (thanks to Russia), and
will no longer exist in 50 years' time. Secondly, today's Jews, not having
lived in their spiritual home for 200 years, are no longer capable, physi-
ologically speaking, of enduring the torments of their ancestors. Did you
learn the Talmud? Do you pray every day to Jehovah? Do you lay tefil-
lin? No, it's over, and you and I are Germans in the midst of Germans,
with a strange inheritance that other peoples in the civilized world react
to, if not with joy, then at least without a rubber truncheon. And for
your information, however sensible it is of you not to be going out giving lectures at this moment in time: you will understand that there is a
conflict between your legitimate expectations as a European, which you

have always voiced as an important and gifted German author against bestiality, and the spontaneous recognition of your duty to suffer and be silent, which your forebears will certainly have felt, though not yourself, not freely anyway. One can't repudiate a 6,000-year-old Jewish inheritance; but it's almost as hard to repudiate a 2,000-year-old *non-Jewish* inheritance. We come from "emancipation," from humanity, from the humane *tout court*, rather more than we come out of Egypt. Our forefathers are Goethe Lessing Herder as much as they are Abraham Isaac and Jacob. And anyway, we are not being beaten, as our ancestors were, by devout Christians, but rather by godless heathens. The Jews are not the only ones they are out to get. Even though they—as ever—are the ones that raise the most piteous lament. The onslaught this time is against European civilization, against humanity, whose proud champion you are. (And against God.)

And the practicalities:

1. The time has come (*entre nous*)—the Jews Landshoff and Landauer are unable to keep the publisher K.[3] afloat any longer.

2. Landauer is in Vienna, and has spoken to Zsolnay, who doesn't have any money to buy me with.

3. I've cut my advance from 35,000 to 10,000 marks; not all that much really for an author as successful as me. But there are no takers.

4. Aside from 4,000 marks and what I owe you, all my debts have been paid.

5. If Fischer doesn't take me now, I'll be left hanging. And now, for you.

It's not right that you want to stay even if things get dangerous. "It is written," that the man who willingly courts danger is committing a sin. Life is a gift from God. One may risk danger only for the sake of God. Nor may one seek to know in advance where or how danger may choose to strike. One has to flee a burning house, and if a tree should fall on top of you, then that is God's will.

I know you understand what I mean, and how concerned I am for your welfare, physical and other.

My best wishes to your wife.

Your old friend   Joseph Roth

1. See Zweig's autobiography, *The World of Yesterday* (1942).
2. Tietz: Oskar Tietz (1858–1923), founder of the first German supermarket chain.
3. K.: Kiepenheuer.

193. To Stefan Zweig   *Paris*
                                               33 rue de Tourmon
                                               Hotel Foyot
                                               26 March 1933

Dear esteemed friend,

I'm of the view that one should stay in constant contact in these times. Hence the prompt reply.

You should make sure your letters to me go via Switzerland; some go via Germany.

I completely agree with you: we have to wait. For now. Only I'm not quite sure how long for.

The world is stupider now than it was in 1914. The human no longer bestirs himself when humanity is hurt and killed. In 1914, all parties tried to come up with human reasons and pretexts to explain the bestiality.

Whereas today people just offer bestial justification for bestiality that are even more foul than the bestialities themselves.

And nothing stirs in the whole world. I mean, in the world of writing people, aside from the eccentric Gide, who, recently converted to Communism,[1] has held a meeting for snobs and international Communists, without the least success; aside from the Jews of England and America, but they are just disturbed by anti-Semitism, which is a little spoke in the great wheel of bestiality.

You understand, the difference between 1933 and 1914 is roughly that between a sick animal like Goering, and Wilhelm II, who at least kept vestiges of humanity.

Obviously, fools perpetrate folly, and beasts commit bestiality, and madmen commit mad acts: all of them suicidal.

But it is not at all obvious that our equally sick and confused surroundings *discern* stupidity, bestiality, and madness.

That's the difference. And I ask myself whether the time hasn't come where it is our duty to quarantine the world around us, so that it doesn't get infected.

My fear is that it is too late.

I'm afraid I'll be forced into the position of *wishing for* war as soon as possible.

I won't be going to Vienna, for lots of reasons. The past 10 years I've lived 6–8 months a year in France. Why not now? And in particular, why not when those people who hate me will always say I fled anyway. (And why not, when it is plain to see that one really is fleeing.)

In Vienna word would get around even quicker that I've left Germany. There especially, because I'd be returning to a place I once lived.

In a French gutter magazine, your name is listed among those who have fled to Switzerland, while I appear as *Ernst* Roth—no doubt, because they left Toller off their list.

I can't take the initiative with Zsolnay myself, because Landauer is my friend, and I want him to take what advantage of the situation he can—by selling me. He's not in an easy position either.

But I'll go to Salzburg to see you, even if it's just for a couple of days, as soon as I have a new contract and a little money and security.

As far as the Jewishness in us is concerned, I agree that one mustn't give the impression one is concerned for the Jews, and no one else.

But we must remember that being a Jew absolves no man from the duty to go to the front line, along with any conscientious non-Jew.

There is a certain point where noblesse is disobliging, and doesn't help anyone. Because for the beasts over there, a filthy yid is what one remains.

You opposed the war as a Jew, and I fought in it as a Jew. We each have many comrades. We didn't hang around behind the lines.

On the battlefield of humanity, you could say, there are such people as behind-the-lines Jews.[2]

We mustn't be like that.

I have never overestimated the tragic destiny of Jews, least of all now, when it is a tragedy to be a decent human being.

It's the nastiness of the others to see only Jews. It's not fitting that we, by hanging back, should reinforce the argumentation of those foolish animals.

As a soldier and an officer I wasn't a Jew. As a German author I'm not a Jew either. (Not in the way we're talking about.)

I'm afraid there will be a moment when Jewish reserve will be nothing more than a reaction of the discreet Jew against the chutzpah of the indiscreet Jews.

The one is as damaging and foolish as the other.

As I said already we owe a duty as much to Voltaire, Herder, Goethe, and Nietzsche, as to Moses and his Jewish fathers.

From there may be derived the duty:

To save one's life and one's writing, if they are threatened by the animals.

No premature surrender to what we are pleased to call fate.

And to "take a hand," to fight when the moment has come. The question is whether it might not be sooner rather than later.

As ever, sincerely yours   Joseph Roth

1. Communism: on his return from Russia in 1931, Gide remarked that Russia was the land where the future was being born, only to repudiate his belief in Communism five years later.

2. behind-the-lines Jews: this will have nettled (and is clearly meant to nettle) SZ, who tried to keep his pacifism and humanism together.

194. To Stefan Zweig

Hotel Foyot
Paris
6 April 1933

Dear esteemed friend,

I hope you've recovered your calm somewhat. What happened to you is of course bitter. But you must get a grip, and understand that you are atoning for the sins of all Jews, and not just those of your namesakes. Do you think Mr. Goebbels cares if he's got you confused with someone else? As far as he's concerned, you're no better and no different than those he currently has it in for. What I wrote to you before is true: our books are impossible for the Third Reich. They won't even advertise us. Not even in the *Börsenblatt*.[1] The booksellers will turn us away. The SA storm troopers will smash the display windows. The racial theorist Günther will use your photograph for his typical Semite. There is no compromising with these people. Watch yourself! I'm telling you! You won't be safe in Salzburg (remember the story of the Rotters[2] in Liechtenstein) if you chance your arm. See no one. Get used to the fact that the 40 million who listen to Goebbels are remote from making any distinctions between you and Thomas Mann and Arnold Zweig, Tucholsky, and me. Our life's work—in the terrestrial sense—has been for nothing. They confuse you, not because your name is Zweig, but because you're a Jew, a cultural Bolshevist, a pacifist, a cosmopolite, a liberal. It is pointless to hope. This "national renewal" will go to the extremes of madness. It takes exactly the same form as what the psychiatrists term manic depression. That's this people. All one can do is wait. Don't for God's sake imagine you can address these people in any form. You can do it later. There are no manners when dealing with these apes. Don't issue any pieces of paper! Don't protest! Shut up—or fight: whichever you think is advisable.

Sincerely,   your old Joseph Roth

1. *Börsenblatt*: the magazine of the German book trade.
2. Alfred and Fritz Rotter, from 1914 to 1932 theatrical impresarios in Berlin, till their theater business failed.

195. To Stefan Zweig   *Paris*
                                                   28 April 1933

Dear esteemed friend,

You probably won't get this letter till your return.

I have your happy postcard.

I hope you get home feeling calmer and stronger.

I can't get away.

I need a new publisher and promise of new earnings.

Things are grim—both in the world at large, and for us as individuals.

We all overestimated the world: even me, an absolute pessimist.

The world is very, very stupid, and bestial. There are more brains in a cowshed.

Everything: humanity, civilization, Europe, even Catholicism: the cowshed is cleverer.

I have been asked whether you'd care to offer a "Balzac" to a new publisher in Zurich, where I too am to appear (with one book).

Not a lefty outfit. Nothing oppositional. Lots of solid untouchable things. I vouch for it.

Please reply ASAP. One of these days it may turn out to be very important for you. We can't drown out the madness in Germany. Your books were burned in Breslau. You probably read about the demonstration of German students.

It will be good for you to publish something somewhere else—and in a house that doesn't stink of opposition.

So far as I'm concerned:

I see myself compelled to follow my instincts and conviction, and become an absolute monarchist.

In 6 or 8 weeks, I will publish a short book about the Habsburgs.[1]

I am an old Austrian officer. I love Austria. I view it as cowardice not to use this moment to say the Habsburgs must return.

I want the monarchy back, and I will say so.

Several thinking persons are of the same view.

I hope I succeed.

I don't dare ask whether you are of the party.

I assume, though, that you will take me for a "romantic."

If, counter to expectation, you *are* able to join me, then you will know already how happy that will make me.

Sincerely   your old Joseph Roth

1. short book about the Habsburgs: not known—as the time frame perhaps suggests.

196. To Stefan Zweig   *9 May 1933*
                                                   Hotel Foyot
                                                   33 rue de Tournon
                                                   Paris 6ᵉ

Dear highly esteemed friend,

thank you for your letter. I love your idea of a joint manifesto, in exactly the way you describe. It's the only thing one could with dignity bequeath to posterity. I am not quite clear yet whether only Jewish authors should sign, or their origin should be pointed out. If I understand it in its whole solemnity, it is intended to be our *monument*. And for all my skepticism vis-à-vis posterity I know that a hundred years from now people won't understand the word "Jew" in the sense it has today. That's why I think we would do well to recruit the best of the other victims. And quickly too. The acute interest in our singularity will wane very quickly. In two or three months we'll just be a few obscure individuals. In ten years the generation that knew us will be over. A monument will only stand if carried into the future by the passion and commitment of the generation in which it was built. I can think of no one better than you to collect and distribute this manifesto. You have friends all over God's earth, cleverness, calm, and acuity. Do it now. Choose the names you want yourself.

As far as your work is concerned, it's my feeling that quite soon—and who knows for how long, if Hitlerism persists—the Insel Verlag will renounce it. You must not think in any part of you that you are still viable in Germany as the author whose reputation even your enemies were unable to deny. It's my sense that you exaggerate the moral qualities of the Insel Verlag. Have you still not heard enough stories about his treachery? Still not? If you were physically within reach, the son-in-law of Insel would hand you over to the SA. I urge you: quit Insel. A few of your books will be republished in other houses, and contribute to your wealth and fame.

(Did you get a letter from Amsterdam [from Praag][1] as well?—There is some thought here as well, of Grasset's bringing out a new list.)

Remember that you will need money; and that you will be called on to help other deserving parties with the luster of your name, who need a publisher if they are to live.

I don't think you should write the article about children now. The people it would appeal to don't need you. The rest won't understand it. The charges you lay against the Hitler beasts are mistaken too: they're not pursuing the Jews because they've done something wrong, but because they're Jews. In that respect, the "children" are every bit as "guilty" as the fathers.

It occurred to me too that one might write the Habsburg pamphlet anonymously. Against that there is the desire of my political friends. They are convinced the statement of a "leftist" author—you know how little I was ever that—would have some propaganda value. Plus: *this is a time when the Jews are needed.* In all discretion, the Christian Socialists (the Vaugoin[2] group) are with us right now. Starhemberg[3] very strongly, Dollfuss[4] and Winkler[5] are wavering. But in the army and the civil service, anything is possible. I need Prince Polignac[6] Do you know him? Are you able to get me an *introduction* to him?

It's good for us now to have the Jews on board. Even if the Nazis yell. We have enough anti-Semites and Catholics.

So far as I'm concerned, I stood in the field for nine months for the Habsburgs. No swastika merchant can claim that. I have a right to my fatherland.

Please write soon.

I can only come and see you when I am in possession of a new contract. Maybe 6–8 weeks.

Sincerely,   your old and loyal Joseph Roth

1. Praag: Siegfried Emanuel van Praag (1899–2002), profilic Dutch writer and essayist. He sought to woo exiled German writers to the Dutch publisher Allert de Lange.

2. Vaugoin: Karl Vaugoin (1873–1949), Austrian politician.

3. Starhemberg: Ernst von Starhemberg (1899–1956), leader of the Fascist home guard, from 1934 to 1936, Austrian deputy chancellor.

4. Dollfuss: Engelbert Dollfuss (1892–1934), from 1932 to 1934 Christian Socialist Austrian chancellor, establishing a "Christian state" (aka a Catholic dictatorship) in 1934. Shot by the Nazis.

5. Winkler: Franz Winkler, Austrian politician, deputy chancellor in Dollfuss's cabinet from 1932 to 1933.

6. Prince Polignac: the nephew of Prince Edmond de Polignac and his wife, Winaretta, née Singer.

---

197. To Klaus Mann

19 May 1933
Hotel Foyot
Paris 6ᵉ

Dear Mr. Klaus Mann,[1]

of course I should like to get the money[2] as quickly as possible. The sooner the better. First serial rights are 600 francs. Emigré prices. Second serial 300.

If I'm still in Paris, I should like to see you both[3] again—For now, all the best!

Sincerely   Joseph Roth

1. Klaus Mann (1906 Munich–1949 Cannes), journalist, writer, essayist. Edited the exile magazine *Die Sammlung* from 1933 to 1935.

2. money: for a contribution to *Die Sammlung*.

3. Presumably Klaus and his sister Erika Mann, sometimes known as "the terrible twins."

198. To Stefan Zweig   *[Paris] 22 May 1933*
                                                    Hotel Foyot

Dear esteemed friend,

in three or four days Dr. Landshoff will be with you.

He will bring with him, as others have already, a new publishing project.

Of all that I have heard so far, it's the only proper and trustworthy one.[1]

If it comes about—and one should be a little careful, because Dr. L. went to Berlin yesterday for a couple of days—then I'll write my next novel[2] in 3 months, for the first time in my life. Wonderful material, remote from Germany, though with obvious application to it. Plays in the eastern borderlands. Par discretion:

St. Julian the Hospitaller, modern version, instead of animals, Jews, and at the end the removal. Very Catholic.

I stumbled upon it in a Ukrainian newspaper. Fully formed.

You don't write me. Mrs. Van Praag conveyed me your best wishes, nothing more.

I am afraid, I fear for your immortal soul. You don't mind if I'm open with you?—I am afraid you don't quite see events straight. You're pondering your alternatives. You're making up your mind.

Here's my view:

a. It'll last for 4 years;

b. Hitler will end in disaster, or in monarchy,

c. We will have nothing whatever to do with the 3rd Reich;

d. Within 5 months, there will be no publisher, no bookseller, no author of our kind;

e. We must give up all hope, irrevocably, and be as strong and braced as we have to be. There is war between him and us. Any thought for the enemy is punishable by death. All authors of repute who stay will suffer their own literary death.

f. As long as we are banished, no common cause with the "Left": Feuchtwanger, A. Zweig, the *Weltbühne*. They are partly to blame for our plight. They are the party of the fools with chutzpah.

Please come and be on my side. Ditch the Insel Verlag. For the last 4 years his behavior toward you has been scandalous. His recently published denial on the subject of your German was, frankly, disgusting.

These are not temperamental reactions on my part. I go to meet these people with a riding crop. You in your high-mindedness don't grasp the instincts of the janitor. You don't know the Prussians, the way I do. I know them from the field. It's true, everything they say about atrocities in Belgium. All true! The Prussians are representatives of the *chemical* inferno, of the industrialized inferno, in the world. I hope lightning strikes them. I know they will be destroyed far sooner than people think.

You won't take anything I say amiss, will you?

Sincere and loyal regards   your Joseph Roth

1. Publishing project: the Querido Verlag, a principal publisher of exiled German writers, with Fritz Landshoff's participation, in Amsterdam.

2. novel: *Tarabas*, published by Querido in 1934.

199. *To Stefan Zweig*   *Hotel Foyot*
                                                Paris 6ᵉ
                                                Saturday [24 June 1933]

Dear esteemed friend,
in haste:

Your telegram yesterday. My letter was pretty important. Its loss indicates that Nazi cells have been at work.

Whether I make it to Zurich or not depends on many factors, of which more later.

I don't know of a single one here that's important.

Expecting your letter with impatience.

Please confirm safe arrival of this one.

Sincerely   Joseph Roth

200. To Stefan Zweig   *[Paris] 26 June [1933]*

Dear esteemed friend,

please consider my material situation, as much as my yearning for you. I *can't* go to Basel. Come here! No one will know. I have to see you! For me a great deal depends on it. I cannot leave. But you can come here. Please show yourself to be the way I know you are. Come, even for 2 hours.

Sincerely   J.R.

And wire, please, on Monday!

201. To Hermann Kesten[1]   *Hotel Foyot*
                                              Paris 6ᵉ
                                              29 June 1933

Dear friend,

I am awaiting the check with impatience.[2] I suggest you send it express. Landshoff is coming tonight.

There is no gossip. We're looking—according to Mehring[3]—for a cheap room for Hugenberg.[4]

I am writing, very badly, very unhappily, no money.

Jakob Hegner,[5] whose letter I will forward to you, is starting a publishing company in Zurich.

I'll give Tuke your instructions. Mrs. Manga Bell asks to be remembered to you both. We're positively longing for you.

God help us. Dr. Bermann was here. Wants to copublish Landshoff's authors in the 3rd Reich in the Fischer Verlag. As a proud Austrian, I declined to be a yid.

Write soon, Hermann!   Best wishes J.R.

1. Hermann Kesten (1900–1996), author and editor (for Kiepenheuer); JR's friend from 1927 to his death, he probably did more for the retrieval of his reputation following World War II than any other individual. Brought out a three-volume edition of JR's fiction, and assembled and edited the 1970 selection of his letters on which the present book is based.

2. For "Stationmaster Fallmerayer," which appeared in an anthology of exiled German writers brought out by Kesten.

3. Mehring: Walter Mehring (1896–1981), poet, essayist. Went into exile in Paris in 1933.

4. Hugenberg: Alfred Hugenberg (1865–1951), media proprietor and film entrepreneur, in 1928 leader of the German Nationalist People's Party. In 1933, after strongly supporting Hitler, became a minister in his cabinet. In June of that year, he abruptly resigned and withdrew from politics, realizing that he had no control of the direction of the party.

5. Jakob Hegner (1865–1962), printer, publisher, and translator.

202. To Stefan Zweig   *Hotel Foyot*
                                                                            Paris 6ᵉ
                                                                            13 July 1933

Dear esteemed friend,

forgive me, since I left you, I've thanked you neither for the day you sacrificed to me, nor for the letters you've written since. These days have brought one misfortune after another. My father-in-law underwent an operation, the operation failed, and he is blind. God, I have nothing! I can't go on. Eight people are depending on me. No one helps me. I am already in the circle (perhaps I'm feeling it too quickly) of the scroungers. Huebsch's behavior is inexplicable! I've just written him a very forthright letter. If he's angry with me, I can't help it. I work 10 hours a day, have another 7,000 francs (700 gulden) coming to me from Landshoff, and am 3,000 in debt. Dear friend, Mr. Alexander¹ doesn't write back to me; perhaps not to you either. My last happy day was my day with you. Black clouds have closed in.

I want to know that you got this letter. Please, send a card to confirm arrival.

How can I live, even if I get the strength to finish the novel in 8 days? Can you invoice Mr. Alexander?

Sincerely,   your old Joseph Roth

I was just given the news—I'm writing in a café—that a telegram from Mr. Alexander has come for me, but it's in English and the porter can't translate it. I'll send it along ASAP. If it's positive, then disregard these lamentations.

1. Kurt Alexander, a literary agent in London. Roth will have been trying to get money owing to him out of America, either for *Job* or for *The Radetzky March*, only to be foiled by the Nazi laws, and a plethora of middlemen.

203. *To Stefan Zweig*   *Hotel Foyot*
                                                Paris 6ᵉ
                                                33 rue de Tournon
                                                14 July 1933

My dear friend,
    here is the telegram, my reply, and Mr. Alexander's reply to me.—I refuse to believe it. I refuse to believe there's a chance that I'll survive all this.

Please confirm receipt of both letters.

Yours sincerely, your old   Joseph Roth

204. To Klaus Mann   *Hotel Foyot*
                                               Paris 6ᵉ
                                               33 rue de Tournon
                                               18 July 1933

Dear Klaus Mann,
    the novella isn't finished after all. I'll give it to you next week, here.
That seems better to me. Don't panic!
    Sincerely,   your old Joseph Roth

205. To Stefan Zweig   *Hotel Foyot*
                                               Paris 6ᵉ
                                               19 July 1933

Dear esteemed friend,
    here is Mr. Alexander's latest telegram. I don't understand your last
kind letter at all. Even if you believed I could be so thoughtless on my
own account, do you think me capable of exposing or embarrassing *you*,
discrediting you in some way, I don't know?—I asked for the money all
at once, because the pound is falling. I've been stung before. Mr. Alexander first wires his authors, and only then, armed with their replies, does
he approach their publishers. It's not at all—as you seem to think—that
Mr. Alexander makes an offer to an author, *having first* discussed it with
a publisher.—But, irrespective of that: do you take me for a fool?—The
only thing that will help me in my position is if I get the sum of 80,000
francs at one fell swoop—and since you said so yourself, I can tell you
that if I ever believed I might have good fortune on such a scale, my first
action would have been to send you half of it, and ask you, you in person, to keep it safe for me. But this is all hypothetical! People don't come
to me offering miracles.—And our friend Huebsch—such a friend!—
stood me up, treated me positively sadistically. I would tell you what he
did, only physical disgust prevents me.

My dear friend, I have often been foolish in the course of my life. I still am. But don't think I don't see the vileness perpetrated by others. *You*, however, don't see it. You would go rigid with pain and dread if I told you how I lived, and how Huebsch and others have let me down. I refuse to do it in writing. Please drop me a line to let me know you've got this, and I don't have to wire.

Sincerely and faithfully,   your old Joseph Roth

206. *To Stefan Zweig*   *Hotel Foyot*
                                                       Paris 6ᵉ
                                                       20 July 1933

Dear esteemed friend,

would you happen to have a copy of my novel *Zipper and His Father*? Or can you manage to get hold of one? If so, then please send it to A. Corticelli, Viale Abruzzi 19, Milano.

He wants to publish it, and will pay me for it. It's shocking, I have no copies of any of my books.

Sincerely,   your old Joseph Roth

207. *To Stefan Zweig*   *Hotel Foyot*
                                                       Paris 6ᵉ
                                                       33 rue de Tournon
                                                       24 July 1933

Dear friend,

misunderstandings should be cleared up as soon as they occur. So I'm writing you back straightaway.

1. You write and say they've agreed to pay 800 pounds. But it wasn't *my* idea to ask for 1,000. *It was Mr. Alexander who offered me that*, in his first telegram. Should I have written back to say, no no, too much?

2. Maybe Pinker[1] is behind Alexander. But what I don't understand is that carry-on of making an offer, and only when the author has replied, start to negotiate a deal. I've heard from three separate publishers that Mr. Alexander isn't among the ones who are taken seriously.

3. I hope to see Mr. Huebsch here tomorrow. I'll write to you. For now, here's this: (a) Huebsch sends 1,000 dollars to Kiepenheuer *after* Hitler's arrival, and only 100 to me, even though I've wired him that Kiepenheuer is broke and he should just hang on to all moneys for the time being; (b) Mr. Huebsch sells film rights to *Job*: a 3,000-dollar advance is paid to the publisher by the film company: 2,000 are still outstanding: Huebsch writes that they'll be paid as soon as Kiepenheuer confirms that he is giving up my film and foreign rights: I get Mr. Landshoff to put up the 5,000 marks the Kiepenheuer Verlag, or its liquidators, want for the surrender of my foreign rights; Landshoff pays the money: whereupon Huebsch writes that the film company is unsure what to do: I owe Landshoff 5,000 marks; furthermore, Huebsch should have paid another 500 dollars for the *Radetzky March* in April: they haven't reached me yet. Meanwhile, the dollar falls.

All this to Huebsch.—I don't think he's a bad man. He's just a so-called businessman. He's even a decent man—except where dollars are at stake. I have no comprehension for that kind of thing. I know only comradeliness, including in business.

4. More important: the fact that you say advances are a consequence of the inflation. Maybe so. But the world has changed. Taking myself for an example, without an advance I couldn't have written *Job* or the *Radetzky March*. Between the old writers and me there is the war. If Austria-Hungary had survived, then I'd be a major in Witkovitz, and could write without an advance. And irrespective of that: why seek to abolish advances, if the inflation that gave rise to them remains a factor? Why do you suggest that the weakest people, authors, return to solid bourgeois conditions, while all around the colossuses are crumbling? Where's the logic in that, my dear fellow! In Kipling's time, capitalists were still decent people. The world was in order. But in today's world,

you want *us* to be the solid and respectable ones?—It's not possible for us to live and work without an advance, any more than it is possible for capitalists to get by without bank credits and state subventions. Do you think Roosevelt isn't a swindler? The dollar inflation no wheeze? And you want me to live like Kipling? Without advances?

I'm not just being polemical here for the hell of it, but because you seem to me to have "romantic" opinions on several matters. You're so much wiser than I am, you know life and people better than I do. The way you *behave* in the world is infinitely wiser than me. But strangely you're less realistic than I am. And even though I'm younger and more foolish than you, I come to bring you enlightenment. I am your friend, and that's my right.

(Excuse these stains!)

5. You say, may God free me from money. Not so, dear friend! May God *give me* money, a shed load of money! Because in today's world money is no curse any more, and poverty no blessing. To put it bluntly, *that's* "romantic." (Quite apart from the fact that I'm not poor, but something that's grim and in-between.) I need money! I write with money, I help six or seven people to get by with my money, which isn't "gold" any more, and so isn't a curse! It's a figment! What's real is my work, and the lives of those dear to me. I've never earned as much as a Wassermann,[2] but I've never lived like him either. And the people who live at my side— apart from my poor wife—they're already living like "proles." And I can't even afford to keep them like that. I can't eat decently. Show me the prole who lives as badly as I do!—And above all, where did you see a prole doing such important work as we do?—Even our nearest and dearest, our friends, our families: haven't they got the right to live better than donkeys? Who works in the night for the light of the world? Doesn't my work entitle me to look after a few people whom I love, as much as it entitles me to drink schnapps? Looking after people is a legitimate spur, every bit as much as alcohol.

6. As far as the "chance" circumstance that we're the victims now, that has nothing at all to do with what has gone before. It's a misfortune,

a calamity. But firstly: I'm convinced we'll get through it; and second, while the world hasn't forgotten me, am I to tighten my belt till Hitler tightens it for me!?—*You* live and write like a *romantic*. That would be OK if the president of the United States was a straight-up guy. But he's a cheat. A big cheat, like Krueger![3] Bigger! Worse.—If a gangster's in charge of America, you can't be Kipling!

I had to tell you that. Please reply right away. I'm hoping I can be with you in 3–4 weeks.

Your very old and faithful   Joseph Roth

1. Pinker: J. Ralph Pinker, son of a literary agent, and himself a noted literary agent in London.

2. Wassermann: Jakob Wassermann (1873–1934), highly successful German novelist and essayist who lived on a lavish scale. Author of *Caspar Hauser* and many other titles.

3. Kreuger: Ivar Kreuger (1880–1932) owned a match factory in Sweden. When it suddenly went broke, he committed suicide in Paris.

208. To Stefan Zweig   *Hotel Foyot*
                                          Paris
                                          2 August 1933

My very dear friend,

I'm dripping with heat and work, burdened, strained, oppressed, but I'm working. I think I can be with you in about 3 weeks.

You should speak on 2 September, which is Sedan Day, and also my birthday, nebbish.

Your old and faithful   J.R.

209. *To Max von Hohenlohe-Langenburg*[1] Hotel Stein
Salzburg
24 August 1933

Dear friend,

thanks for your sad letter. You tell me nothing new. You're right about almost all the general things. But everything personal is completely wrong. Neither Landauer, nor me, nor Ludwig Bauer[2] have the feeling that we're "Jews," in the sense in which the Nazis are "Aryans." To a Catholic like myself, my Jewishness is more or less what it would be to a Hasidic wonder-rabbi: a metaphysical affair, high above everything to do with "Jews" on this earth. It certainly has nothing to do with the fact that I can't, for example, send you money. The true reason for that is this: I'm a beggar. I don't have money for the next fortnight, nothing for me, and nothing for the 8 people whom I support, who are dependent on me. Of course, like you, I know that Jews are detested everywhere. That's the way God wants it to be, and so it can't be any other way. It won't be the Jews who will overcome Hitler, it will be God. Our individual fates have nothing to do with that.—Incidentally, I never spoke badly of you to Mrs. Kiepenheuer,[3] definitely not.—Nor should you get general and individual things mixed up. Don't seek general reasons for the private behavior of your friends. That way madness lies. It seems to me you think about Jews more than I do. I simply cannot give you any money. I live off alms. I have to write articles to live. I feed off my name, which I gained in the course of writing 14 books. I am not familiar with any Jewish support group. And the Jews that are, get given 5 francs a day. I understand and feel sorry for your plight. You don't need to explain it to me. Bear it, believe in God, be devout, as I try to be. If you are a "worldly" type, you can hardly complain if we are ground up between Bolshevism and National Socialism.

Landauer will write to you.

Sincerely your old   Joseph Roth

1. Max von Hohenlohe-Langenburg: Prince Max Karl Joseph Maria zu Hohenlohe-Langenburg (1901–1943 in concentration camp, in Stuttgart), went into exile in 1933. Wrote articles against the Nazi regime. Had already offered his memoirs to Kiepenheuer before 1933.

2. Ludwig Bauer: a Viennese journalist.

3. Mrs. Kiepenheuer: Noa Kiepenheuer, wife of the publisher Gustav Kiepenheuer, and a regular visitor to Paris.

210. To Stefan Zweig   *Hotel Schwanen*
                                          Rapperswil am Zürichsee
                                          31 August 1933

My dear friend,

thank you so much for the days you gave me.

I sometimes worry if my attitude doesn't alienate you from me.

I also have a distinct feeling that you're not seeing straight, where our respective political views are concerned; and our reaction to one another.

There is something else too: I can't quite grasp that you are not content to be an Austrian pure and simple.

Yours is a conservative and respectful character. All you have in terms of literary and human qualities is old Austria.

Impossible to imagine you as the son of a Prussian Jew.

It is imperative that you must love Austria, it will love you back. It is not the same as Prussia.

I came to know the Austrians and Prussians in the war, when I was seconded to a Prussian division. My *active* Austrian patriotism dates from that moment.

I do not expect you to become an outspoken monarchist; that would be too much.

But you grasp it as well as I do: that's the only possible salvation for Austria.

Each one of us is tethered to his past. But you can help us with your precious gifts.

I was sorry you didn't want to meet Mr. W.[1] I know you avoided sitting at the same table as him. From ethical wisdom, so to speak. But it would certainly have gladdened your heart to see how esteemed you were in that quarter. And when you saw me off, you stood so to speak between Mr. Fuchs,[2] the not actual but symbolic representative of the "Left," and me, the actual representative of the "Right."

Or perhaps I'm mistaken. Tell me if I am.

And what you said about Thomas Mann.[3] It can't be right. We are human. I have never cared for Thomas Mann's way of walking on water. He isn't Goethe. He isn't entitled to such pronouncements. And only the words of one who is entitled can be right.

Thomas Mann has somehow usurped "objectivity." Between you and me, he is perfectly capable of coming to an accommodation with Hitler. Only for the time being, it's been made impossible for him. He is one of those persons who will countenance everything, under the pretext of understanding everything.

As far as I am concerned, I can't be objective any more. A man like Mr. Rieger[4] is worth a million Thomas Manns. Merely by being, Rieger achieves more than Mann with all his writings. And his Nobel Prize too. I've always jibbed at the name "Mann." I always thought he was more of an "it" myself. Whereas someone like Mr. Rieger is a man. And that's more than an "author."

Please, write to confirm arrival.

Something went missing from a *registered* letter to me in Salzburg. It can only have been a postal official. I'm complaining to the authorities concerned.

Sincerely,   your old J.R.

1. Mr. W.: Von Wiesner, ministerial councillor, leader of the Austrian legitimists, and a friend of JR's.

2. Fuchs: Martin Fuchs (1903–1969), press attaché to the Austrian embassy in Paris, and a friend of JR's. Following the Anschluss in 1938, he edited a Habsburg journal in Paris, to which Roth contributed. In his last years, he was Austrian ambassador in Paris.

3. Thomas Mann (1875–1955), German novelist and essayist. Went into exile in Switzerland in 1933, then the USA. For a variety of reasons—class, politics, nationality, self-complacency?—Roth never liked him.

4. Rieger: Erwin Rieger (born 1889; died 1940 in Tunis), essayist and writer, friend of Stefan Zweig's.

211. To Stefan Zweig   *Hotel Schwanen*
                                          Rapperswil am Zürichsee
                                          5 September 1933

Dear esteemed friend,

in haste, thank you for your kind letter.

So Mrs. Thompson[1] is going to try and meet you. I'm seeing her tomorrow in Zurich. I would ask you to make her welcome. There are many things she can do in America.

I'm never sorry to get any of your letters. I just can't reply to everything you say. I dread any chance of a misunderstanding.

Please write and let me know where you're going. My regards to your dear wife.

Sincerely   your Joseph Roth

1. Mrs. Thompson: Dorothy Thompson (1906–1961), political journalist. Evicted from Germany on Hitler's orders. Married to the writer Sinclair Lewis from 1928 to 1942. She translated JR's novel *Job*. President of the New York PEN Club for a time. See no. 457.

212. To Carl Seelig   *Hotel Schwanen*
                                          Rapperswil am Zürichsee
                                          5 September 1933

Esteemed Mr. Seelig,[1]

thank you so much for your kind letter of the 30th last, and for asking me to read in Zurich. Unfortunately I suffer from so-called psychological barriers, I am unable to read aloud in front of an audience, and have thus lost many opportunities of earning money over many years.

It was very kind of you, however, to make me such an offer, and I would be glad of the chance to thank you personally, if you cared to write me when I could meet you.

Yours humbly and thankfully   Joseph Roth

1. Carl Seelig (1894–1962), Swiss critic, and editor of the works of his friend Robert Walser.

213. To Blanche Gidon   *Rapperswil am Zürichsee*
                                           20 September 1933
                                           Hotel Schwanen

Dear esteemed Madam,

please excuse the dictation. I am hard at work, and I find it difficult to write detailed letters by hand.

Thank you for your friendly postcard. I am very sorry we didn't meet. I hope you and Mr. Gidon recuperated very well in the holidays. Are you and your colleague making good headway with the translation of my novel? I am very disturbed that the book is not yet ready to appear. Please send me news here, and also how your dear husband is faring.

I was very glad to meet Mr. Poupet in Austria. I hope he likes my poor fatherland.

In loyal and sincere devotion, and with best regards to your husband
Your Joseph Roth

214. *To Stefan Zweig*   *Rapperswil am Zürichsee*
                                          20 September 1933
                                          Hotel Schwanen

Esteemed and dear friend,

please excuse the dictation.—I have a great favor to ask of you. A good friend of mine over many years, a wonderful human being and a doctor, Dr. Walter Neubauer, has been forced to leave his hometown of Hamburg and his family very suddenly, and is going—which I find quite admirable—to Shanghai. I doubt if I could find anyone else who had connections there, with the sole exception of you. I imagine you know people there, Chinese professors or people in public life there, that sort of thing. Do you in fact know such people, and please will you not take it amiss if I ask you to furnish Dr. Neubauer with two or three introductions? I am very serious. He is an utterly reliable and wonderful person. Compelled to leave Hamburg by the idiotic Aryan laws, even though he is a Christian son of Christian parents.

Everything else I will write by hand, as soon as I've got a bit further with my misbegotten book.

In loyal friendship your old   [Joseph Roth]

215. *To Blanche Gidon*   *Rapperswil am Zürichsee,*
                                          27 September 1933
                                          Hotel Schwanen

Dear esteemed Madam,

thank you for your kind letter of the 23rd. I am delighted you liked Austria so much. Please give my regards to Mr. Poupet. And, inasmuch as it's in your power, try and do something for the country to rescue it from Nazi barbarism.

Dear Madam, I beg you once more, please see to it that my book appears quite soon and in a decent form. I am faring very badly—in financial terms too—and I am utterly reliant on a success in France.

I am sorry the Reifenberg family are doing badly. On the other hand, it is impossible for me to have any sort of fellow feeling with my friend Reifenberg. Persons who neglect their honor cannot remain my friends. Whoever enters into a relation with the Third Reich, and a public one at that, like my poor friend Reifenberg,[1] is struck out of the book of my friends.—Please give my best regards to Professor Gidon.

I am your humble   Joseph Roth

1. my poor friend Reifenberg: JR, as will have been seen, was often impatient with his gentle, sanguine editor, who said of him in turn that "he did not care to understand when it was possible to judge." Reifenberg, a half-Jew married to a Polish wife, politically left of center, and personally devoted to JR and his memory, was no one's idea of a Nazi. He attempted, though, with others, to keep the *FZ* going through the Nazi period as a liberal paper, steering his habitually gentle course, and hoping for change from within, until the *FZ* was finally shut down in August 1943. Some years after the war, Reifenberg thought to put out a collection of articles from the Nazi period, only to come to the dispiriting conclusion that the opposition supposedly encoded in them was so faint and obscure as not to exist in any real sense.

216. Stefan Zweig to Joseph Roth[1]   *[postmarked: London,
                                                 30 September 1933]*

Dear friend,

we feel extraordinarily well here, I have rented a nice apartment, work all morning until 3 o'clock in the library, and then at home; the people are pleasant and considerate, the climate positively helpful to one's work, I am sure you would feel much better here than in Paris, or in your solitude. I haven't smoked now for four weeks, it helps me no end, and what makes me breathe even more easily is that I hear no news of home.[2]

Sincerely your   Stefan Z.

11, Portland Place

1. At this point in the collection, some of Stefan Zweig's letters to Joseph Roth are also included.

2. Really a bizarrely, almost provocatively insouciant note to go from someone in Zweig's position to someone in Roth's.

217. To Stefan Zweig   *Rapperswil*
                                          2 October 1933
                                          Hotel Schwanen

Dear, esteemed friend,

congratulations on your cure. I well know how hard it is for you, and I know too that part of you is thinking not just of you, but also of me. I am not so strong as you. I don't write. I can't write. I am indifferent. All my friends in the business have dropped me.

Excuse the harshness and brevity. I'm sad that you didn't go to Paris. You could have done a lot for Austria. But perhaps you could still do that in Paris, behind the scenes. A few days ago, I met Mr. von Wiesner. He came directly from the emperor.[1] The empress is in Italy. Foolishly, she is trying to prevent a marriage with an Italian princess, which the Italians are apparently trying to bring about. I tried to prove the foolishness of her endeavors. But in Austria, the situation is that Mr. Dollfuss is tacitly ready to acknowledge the monarchy. As soon as the fait accompli has been created, he will agree to it. Our plan is to convey the dead emperor[2] from Lequeto to Austria, and with him the live emperor. We need 30,000 schillings, which for the time being we don't have. Austria is in the bag. There is no cause to worry about National Socialism there.

My dear friend, you must commit the entire weight of your public person to Austria. Believe me, I know, I can feel that it is of great importance for you to appear as an Austrian. At a stroke you will set aside everything you have suffered and continue to suffer in Germany. We need a Romain Rolland[3] for Austria. You know I've never been one for glib phrases. And you know I don't need to reach for them when talking to you. On the contrary. My friendship for you is such that I would rather say disagreeable things to you, than agreeable things.

Yours sincerely   your Joseph Roth

1. emperor: the pretendant Otto von Habsburg.

2. dead emperor: Karl I (1887–1922), emperor from 1916 to 1918, when he was forced to abdicate.

3. Romain Rolland (1866–1944), writer and essayist, pacifist, later Communist. Was awarded the Nobel Prize in 1915, which he made over to the Red Cross. A close friend of Stefan Zweig's, who very much admired him. By a species of triangulation Roth is trying to recruit Zweig for the monarchist cause.

218. To Stefan Zweig   *[Rapperswill]*
                                                  9 October 1933

Dear esteemed friend,

in haste, and in an effort to calm you down: how can you overestimate the importance of that printed bullshit! In this world it's a matter of absolute indifference—unfortunately—what is written about us or by us. There's a handful who know, and they know everything. All the others are blind or deaf. Haven't you got that yet? The word has died, men bark like dogs. The word has no importance any more, none in the current state of things. I had an interview in the *Mois*[1] where they said I was an anti-Semite. Do you suppose I cared? In the space of three days, even a true word is dissipated. And a lie is even quicker. There is no "public arena" any more. Everything is shit.

More soon!   Your old Joseph Roth

1. the *Mois*: *Le Mois*, a monthly magazine for French publishers and booksellers.

219. *To Carl Seelig*   *Rapperswil*
                                             16 October 1933
                                             Hotel Schwanen

Dear Mr. Seelig,

thank you for your kind letter, and your Basel address. I am insufficiently musical to offer a one hundred percent guarantee. But I like what I heard of the work. I'm a layman, but I trust that my ear won't be absolutely wrong about something.

Just come along on any day you fancy, even if I'm working you won't bother me. At the most, good company like yours will spur me on,

Sincerely   Your J.R.

220. *To Félix Bertaux*   *Hotel Schwanen*
                                             Rapperswil am Zürichsee
                                             22 October 1933

Dear, esteemed friend,

I haven't heard from you in weeks, and had no reply from you to my letter from Salzburg to Lescun. I expect you'll be back in Paris by now. Perhaps you'll be kind enough to drop me a line here—I'm always eager to hear news of you and your wife and Pierre.

I am working hard on my novel, which I should have delivered long ago, but can't seem to finish.

Please give my regards to Mrs. Bertaux, say hello to Pierre, and be assured of my long friendship.

Your loyal and grateful   Joseph Roth

221. Stefan Zweig to Joseph Roth   *[postmarked: London,*
                                                        3 November 1933]

Dear friend,

after some wonderful days, some *very* painful ones. Just imagine:
from some attacks on me in Vienna and elsewhere, three weeks after
the event, I learn that Insel took the letter I had written at their request
to spare them unpleasantness in the matter of Klaus Mann's magazine,
and published it, *without asking me, without telling me at any stage, so that
to this day I haven't had sight of it*, in the *Börsenblatt*[1] (apparently—I don't
know—without even saying it was *written to them*). Now the decision
I was agonizing over for so long has been made for me. I sent a correction to the *AZ*[2] which has to appear tomorrow, and I would ask you to
inform anyone you happen to see, and also to send me any attacks on
me, so that I can energetically and promptly put them right. And I was
working so well when it happened! Another week now, and maybe see
you in December.

Your St. Z.

1. *Börsenblatt*: The *Buchhändler Börsenblatt*, magazine of the German book trade.
What happened was that Zweig had written at Insel's request (rather as previously
Thomas Mann, Döblin, and Schickele had at Bermann Fischer's) a letter distancing
himself from Klaus Mann's—politically inflected—magazine of German exile writing, *Die Sammlung*, thereby rather leaving Klaus Mann high and dry. He, it has to be
said, had proceeded to use their names either without having asked at all or having
offered only a misleading prospectus for the magazine. Basically, the middle-of-the-
road-to-right-wing exiles were embarrassed to appear under leftist colors, or in some
cases (Thomas Mann, Döblin under special circumstances) to be outed as exiles at all.
2. *AZ*: *Arbeiter Zeitung*, an (in)appropriately left-wing newspaper in Vienna to
launch such a correction.

222. *To Stefan Zweig*   *Hotel Schwanen*
                                          Rapperswil am Zürichsee
                                          5 November 1933

Dear, esteemed friend,

let me congratulate you, me, and all your friends, on your decision!
Robert Neumann[1] passed through here yesterday, and talked about you.
I am very glad—you should be too. You have remained Stefan Zweig,
and I have remained your friend, without any reservations. Please don't
think this is "youthfulness" speaking from me, or that it's youth that
made me suspicious of Thomas Mann. Suspicion accompanied me when
I was younger—suspicion of the young. Simply because most of them
were and are not real writers. They are not real people either. The absolutely *comme il faut* Professor Thomas Mann is simply naïve. He has the
gift of writing better than he can think.[2] Intellectually, he is not on the
level of his own talent. With Schickele you get spasms of cowardice, with
Döblin the occasionally irritating infantilism that shapes two-thirds of
his literary production, and three-thirds of his personal life.

Shit on the *Neue Deutsche Blätter*.[3] It's a bought-and-paid-for Soviet
affair. Werfel, Döblin, and I, were all attacked in the same number. It's
the Communist pendant to the *Gartenlaube*. Boring. Jakob Wassermann,
whom I saw as a German patriot not long ago in Zurich, has just published parts of his very boring novel there.

If you have ex-friends who are now out to hurt you, then you should
be pleased. You always had too many friends for my liking. The worst
of it was they came from all over the spectrum. I never cared for that. If
you shed a few friends, that can only do you good.

I don't know any lawyer for you. It seems better to me that you take
someone in England, not a Swiss or a Dutchman.

Stay strong, calm, and happy.

Thank your dear wife for the greeting on the envelope, and kiss her
hand for me.

Greet Schalom Asch for me, the Homeric Jew. I think of him often, for no reason I can think of. He could have taken part in the Trojan Wars.

Your old   Joseph Roth

1. Robert Neumann (1897–1975), novelist, satirist, and parodist. Went into exile in London in 1934.

2. Mann, Döblin, Schickele—see my note on no. 221.

3. *Neue Deutsche Blätter*, a monthly magazine for German life and letters, produced in Prague between 1933 and 1935.

223. To Stefan Zweig   *Rapperswil*
                                          Tuesday, 7 November 1933

Dear, esteemed friend,

I was happy to get your postcard. I'll be honest with you, and say I wouldn't have known what to say. I saw the *Börsenblatt* and the *Arbeiter Zeitung*; or rather, I was shown them with a great display of mockery. Of course I made the pathetic attempt to deny everything. You can imagine with what feelings. You don't know that I was about to lay into Thomas Mann, Döblin, and Schickele for their similar statements. When I heard about you, I felt I'd been slapped. At least with those three you could argue that they were too dependent on [. . .] Bermann Fischer. You are not dependent on Insel. At the time you wrote your letter, I'm thinking you must have known the resounding comment which the ministry slapped on the loyalty declaration of the three valiant little tailors: that they still didn't approve of the intellectual position of the loyal writers.

Well, I'm glad of what separates you from that trio: they write to their publisher, knowing it will be published—they even wired him. Whereas your letter to Insel was private. What I'm not glad of is the fact that you saw fit to write at all. Sure, many things separate me from Feuchtwanger. But only things that divide human beings. But what divides me from everyone, *without a single exception*, who is today active in Germany, with Germany, for Germany, is precisely what divides a human from an animal. Compared to stinking hyenas, compared to the spawn of hell, even my old foe Tucholsky is a comrade in arms. And even if the *Sammlung* were wrong a thousand times over: they would be right about Goebbels, about the violators of Germany and the German language, about those stinking Luther farts. I think Klaus Mann, with whom, God knows I don't have much in common, still gave the most dignified reply to your letters to German publishers: the appeal of Romain Rolland in the latest issue of the *Sammlung*.

Rolland is right. An upright man should have no cause to fear "politics." We have outstanding examples in literature. It is *hubris* to want to be more Olympian than Hugo and Zola. But I admit it's a question of temperament, whether one seeks to intervene or not. However, to swear fealty to that band of killers and cackers, of liars and morons, of madmen and illiterates and rapists and robbers and mountebanks: that I don't understand. Drop your misguided respect for "power," for numbers, for 60 millions,[1] leave it to the stupid Hendersons[2] and Macdonalds,[3] the Socialists, the politicians of bankruptcy. If *we* don't see the truth, and quake at those jumped-up farts: who's going to see the truth?

Ah, I can hear you say, but we're Jews. Well, even though my head is too precious for me to waste it by running against a brick wall, I don't see why my blood should absolve me from fighting in the front line, and condemn me to clerkdom. Only beasts like those yonder mention my blood to me. I'm staying in my trench. I daren't ask what others think of me. I am human, and I'm fighting for man, and against animals. Numbskulls can say what they like. The just cause is stronger than the appeal to my Judaism.

Then comes your second objection: I'm underestimating the enemy. Oh dear, I'm afraid you're overestimating him. However stupid the world is: in the long run they won't fall in with the shower that's running Germany just now. There is a fight to the death between European civilization and Prussia. Or hadn't you noticed?

All right, avoid joining sides publicly. Maintain that—to me, incredible—respect for everything you term the "elemental-national" or whatever you want to call it. But I tell you, stop trying to build bridges to Germany. Stuff the Insel. Anyone who has a public function in Germany today, no matter who he is or what he once did, is a BEAST.

It used to be that you were happy to deny that you were Arnold Zweig. What you're doing today, with the least association with Germany, is denying that you're *Stefan Zweig*. (A reader of yours came up with that.)

You have so much to lose: not just your personal dignity, but your literary—and world-renowned—bearing. To thousands who think of Germany the way I do, *not you*, you were a prop, a pillar of faith. In the war you stood at the side of Romain Rolland. And now, now that things are at a worse pass than they ever were then, you're writing anxious little letters to the Insel. It's as if, during the war, you'd written letters to a captain in headquarters—merely because his reputation might have suffered on account of his old friendship with you: to say that you weren't opposed to the war at all, "not really."

Everything is the fault of your shilly-shallying. All the badness. All the ambiguity. All the stupid newspaper comments on you. You are in danger of losing your moral credit vis-à-vis the world, and not winning anything in the Third Reich either. Put practically. And in moral terms: you're repudiating your personal principles of 30 years. And why? For whom? For a business partner. A decent, narrow-minded person, that's about the most that could be said about him, who's made a fortune from publishing you. Whose son-in-law is [. . .]. Who, merely by remaining in Germany himself, has undone all the good he may have done to you and others. (Though that too was business.)

Dear friend, you know I belong more to those who want to be fair than the implacable ones. I am revolted by narrow-mindedness and sectarianism. But now the hour of decision is at hand. More than in the war. Now, confronted by this hellish hour in which a beast gets itself crowned and anointed, not even a Goethe would have remained quiet. (At least he wouldn't have denied involvement with the enemies of the Third Reich.) This is no longer the time to speak of Jews and non-Jews either. Why didn't you think of it then, when you were in Switzerland, in the war, that you mustn't do anything to strengthen the disgraceful calumny that Jews were sabotaging the fatherland? You were a Jew then, as much as now.

I can't approve of your position. I'm a better friend to you than the Insel. If only for my sake you should never have written that letter. Not without asking me. Even if you didn't know it, you will still have sensed that I would not have approved of such a letter.

It's the hour of decision, not just in the sense that it's time to take the side of mankind against Germany, but also in that it's time to tell every friend the truth. So I say to you—and believe me, haste forces me to a ceremonial tone that is rather embarrassing to me—there will be an abyss between the two of us, unless and until you have finally and innerly broken with Germany. I would prefer it if you were fighting against it with all the power of your name. If you are unable to do that, then at least keep quiet. Don't go writing letters to Insel, or to some other Tom, Dick, and Harries. To spare the addressee from any "unpleasantnesses." You'll only incur worse ones yourself. You're smart enough to realize that in Germany nowadays the proprietor of the Insel is just as much a state-appointed functionary as a minister of state. You should have known all by yourself that your letter would never remain private. Any ordinary German citizen is an ass-kissing employee of the state; never mind the publishers of Insel, or Fischer. (They should all be packed off to a concentration camp.)

(Please send the *Tagebuch*[4] a copy of your reply to the *Arbeiter Zeitung*. Mr. Schwarzschild mentioned your letter to Insel to me as well. I think it's important that he knows where you stand.)

One more time: you will have to finish with the Third Reich, or with me. You cannot simultaneously have relationships with representatives of the Third Reich—which includes every single publisher—and with me. I won't stand for it. I can't justify it, not to you, not to myself.

Reply, please, as soon as possible. Kiss Mrs. Zweig's hand for me.

Your old friend   Joseph Roth

Wednesday [8 November 1933]

Dear friend,

I've just read over the letter I wrote you yesterday. Lest you be in any doubt: I did not write it while intoxicated. I drink almost nothing but white wine these days. I am stone sober. Please be in no doubt about that.

And be in no doubt either that I am your friend. Even if you don't answer my plea, and don't end your commerce with Germany, I remain your friend, and will defend you wherever possible.

I am, further, quite clear about the fact that it constitutes an act of crass presumption to approach you with rules for conduct. I apologize. I have probably made a mess of my own life. But I still think I can see the life of one dear to me perfectly. I think I am right where you are concerned.

Stay true to the picture I have of you. I have painted you as you are.

You yourself will know that best (and your wife knows it too).

If it's even necessary to say this, and even though it sounds offensive: I can see straight through your worldly wisdom, and into your poetic heart.

Don't repudiate it! Remain true to it. It's worth it.

Don't betray the "emigration" any more! Leave that to the bastards and the idiots.

I appeal to you once more: keep your DIGNITY!

Your old   Joseph Roth

1. 60 millions: the number of Germans at the time, and hence the number of Stefan Zweig's potential readership.

2. Henderson: Arthur Henderson (1863–1935), leader of the British Labour Party. Foreign secretary from 1929 to 1931, Nobel Peace Prize in 1934.

3. Macdonald: James Ramsay Macdonald (1866–1937), co-founder of the Labour Party in 1900, prime minister in 1924 and again from 1929 to 1935.

4. *Tagebuch*: *Das neue Tagebuch*, weekly magazine in German, edited by Leopold Schwarzschild. It existed from July 1933 to May 1940, and was based in Paris and Amsterdam. Roth wrote many magnificent and wrenching pieces for it.

224. *Stefan Zweig to Joseph Roth* [*November 1933*]

Dear friend,

forgive me for giving such a rushed reply to a letter whose human content I sense so profoundly. But I am exhausted, this affair has put me into a quite unparalleled situation—all brought about by the remissness of friends, the complete silence on the part of my publishers, by my own change of address (which probably no one will believe). I have communicated the enclosed explanation to the world press via the Jewish Telegrafic Agency (you can show it to anyone not yet familiar with it), and set other necessary steps in train. I have still no idea of the legal position, even a year ago my work was a vast object of speculation for the Insel, its standing today is impossible for me to ascertain, I must consult an expert (Swiss or Dutch) as to how to conduct the affair, in the event that—and this is why I exercised self-restraint—it is not amicably resolved. You, you young people, who have been involved with the German publishing scene for no more than 3–5 years, and are able to move with your houses, you can have no idea of the fact that Thomas Mann and I are involved in ties that cannot be undone overnight (for instance, Fischer demands 200,000 marks for the release of Wassermann's rights), this just so that you get some idea of how things look after thirty years of ties to the damned material world. Not that I am out for money, I shit on it, but I must clarify the situation (do you happen to know, by the way, some expert from whom I could get advice, and who might ultimately represent me, not a Jew, nor a German?); I don't think it will prove necessary, because things are moving my way through the planned *Zwangsschriftstellergesetz*,[1] and then I would have the advantage that I wouldn't have to negotiate my freedom, but would be offered it on a plate. Please don't think I'm such a fool or weakling as to seek to be "tolerated" in Germany, or be boycotted silently instead of openly: what I am concerned about is getting control of my own work again and not (my nerves wouldn't be up to it) having to go to court over it. But it couldn't be done violently, the way you imagine it. Why won't you give someone you've known for many years a few weeks' grace, and not shout "Treason!" right away where you don't understand something (as with Thomas Mann too, a highly principled man, who as an Aryan has no need to share the fate of Jews). You can't rub out the seventy million Germans with your outcry, and I'm afraid the Jews abroad are in for more disappointment, it's quite possible that a pact may be concluded over their heads, diplomacy is capable of any sort of dastardliness, and politics of the wildest leaps, we will have to bear a lot of disappointment in the time to come: how crazy to rage against each other now! If only the meeting I suggested had come about, then our joint position would have had enormous strength, whereas today, to the glee of the Nazis, we are tearing strips off one another.

More soon   your St. Z.

1. *Zwangsschriftstellergesetz*: a recent law required all writers and journalists to become members of one of several chambers (for literature, press, theater, etc.). Eligibility for membership was controlled by Goebbels's Reich Chamber of Culture (established in September 1933).

225. *Stefan Zweig to Joseph Roth*   *[postmarked: London, 13 November 1933]*

Dear friend,

I have *finally* heard from Professor Kippenberg.[1] He was undergoing a cure all this time, everything transpired in his absence. Now, that won't do for me as an explanation, I have already written to say that following this abuse I have (regretfully) decided to leave the Insel, my life is there, but honor is more important. I don't know where I'm going to take my new book, but I don't care either. At any rate, I am now in a state of inner freedom. And if my books disappear for a few years, that doesn't matter, I don't care for them that much. What I am shaken by, though, is what is done to me on both sides by *friends*, in the next issue of the *Neue Deutsche Blätter*, you will find an incendiary article about me, again by a friend.

Well, one will have to learn to live in solitude and in hatred, I'm not about to hate back. I'm looking forward to your book.

Sincerely St. Z.

1. Kippenberg: Professor Anton Kippenberg, director of the Insel Verlag, with whom Zweig had published since 1905.

---

226. To Carl Seelig
Rapperswil
23 November 1933

Dear Mr. Seelig,

I would very much like to see you, and if it's all one to you, then Saturday rather than Sunday, because there's a chance that another visitor might come, and we wouldn't be alone. I would like to be able to talk to you undisturbed.

I would be particularly grateful if you were able to bring along a couple of Balzac novels, either very cheap paper editions, or for me to return, in German or French. If it's not too much trouble!

Sincerely   Your Joseph Roth

---

227. To Stefan Zweig
Hotel Schwanen
Rapperswil am Zürichsee
24 November 1933

Dear esteemed friend,

please don't forget to give me your address when you leave London. I don't yet know myself when I'm leaving here, but will certainly write and tell you first. I'm working very hard, feeling ill and staring into a grim and empty space.

I expect you saw, in yesterday's *Temps* that a law has been passed in the Third Reich invalidating contracts between Jewish authors and Aryan publishers. So they've beaten you to it. I'd be surprised if the Insel expected you to remain. You will be spared no disappointment. The Insel will be happy if you go. Today you are a burden on it. Jews nowadays are something to be ashamed of. The fatter the Jew, the greater the "shame" for those madmen.

I am no agitator. But if you have something on your conscience, write it down. It will do you good. Your friends will be pleased. And no doubt you will write it very cleverly and place it effectively.

Sincere friendly greetings from your   Joseph Roth

228. To Franz Schoenberner   *28 November 1933*
                                                Rapperswil am Zürichsee
                                                Hotel zum Schwanen

Dear esteemed Mr. Schoenberner,[1]
your kind letter finds me here, where I've been living these past three months. I am unable therefore to tell you anything about what Mrs. Luchaire[2] has achieved. I fear: nothing.

I am here working on my novel. Ten pages are still to be written. Then I will have to go to Paris and Amsterdam. I may be able to get hold of some money for the next couple of months. My advance is spent. It's a wretched life.

I'll have them send you my novel from Amsterdam. Thank you kindly. You are very dear.

I've heard nothing from my friend Kesten for months now. Do you see him?

Sincerely your   Joseph Roth

1. Schoenberner: Franz Schoenberner (1892–1970), journalist, essayist, editor. Exiled to France in 1933, and then New York in 1941.
2. Mrs. Luchaire: Antonina Vallentin.

229. *To Stefan Zweig*   *Hotel Schwanen*
                                          Rapperswil am Zürichsee
                                          29 November 1933

Very dear and esteemed friend,

thank you so much for yours of the 27th. I think I can promise you
that I'll be in Paris on 10 December, admittedly only for two days; I have
to go to Amsterdam to see my new publisher and assure myself of the
immediate future. I think we have the same journey. Perhaps we could
meet somewhere. Yes, let's meet. (Please, *drop me a line to confirm arrival.*)

I fear you are overestimating the whole literary kerfuffle about the
Insel *once again*. To begin with, it is a matter of complete indifference to
the Third Reich whether you write that you want nothing more to do
with Germany, or with Germany today. You must understand that Germany today is just as indistinguishable from the Third Reich as, say, you
are, in Goering's eyes, from Feuchtwanger and Arnold Zweig.

Further, I don't believe there are any *legal* obstacles, even though I
have no way of assessing the whole business legally and financially. If you
haven't heard back from Insel yet, then there are other reasons for that:
perhaps Mr. K's[1] conscience is paining him, belatedly. Your separation
from Insel will go very smoothly, much more smoothly and easily than
you believe today.

Of the three possibilities of expressing your views, the public exchange
with Romain Rolland seems the most effective to me. The prominence of
your names is a guarantee of effectiveness. Furthermore, the reproaches
that have been hurled at you will be defused by the authority of Rolland.
If it's in your hands, I would choose that form.

Don't get so worked up about those left-wing shits! It's too late to tell
you that that little Fischer[2] (I ordered a couple of articles of his in the *AZ*
specially) is a narrow-minded bourgeois numbskull, a dilettante. [. . .] Let
him print what he likes. (I think his sponsor is Davidl Bach.) You are on
a different level, and the judgment of people who matter to you has noth-

ing to do with the writers and readers of the *AZ* or the *Neue Deutsche Blätter*. Forget about those people already!

"Germany" isn't about to do Mr. Fischer's bidding. Somehow, you still fail to see it: for Germany, you (or me), and Arnold Zweig, Fischer, the *AZ* in Vienna, Feuchtwanger, Thomas, Heinrich, and Klaus Mann are all absolutely the identical same Jewish shit. That's the way of it.

Bonsels[3] was here. He asked me via intermediaries if I was angry with him. I told him by the same method he can take a flying ——

Germany is dead. For us it's dead. It's not possible to take account of it any more. Neither its unscrupulousness, nor its magnanimity. It was a dream. Please see that, won't you!

Your old   Joseph Roth

1. Mr. K.: Anton Kippenberg.
2. Fischer: Ernst Fischer (1899–1972), Communist journalist in Vienna.
3. Bonsels: Waldemar Bonsels (1880–1952), author of a celebrated German children's book; in 1933 he was a Nazi.

230. To Stefan Zweig   *Rapperswil*
                                          30 November 1933
                                          Hotel zum Schwanen

Dear esteemed friend,
about two hours ago, I finished my novel. Its final title is: *Tarabas, a Guest on This Earth*. When you see the book, you'll understand why. I have no idea yet how it's turned out.

Yesterday I ordered a copy of the *Neue Deutsche Blätter*. Even though I don't care for your ex-friend Fischer, I have to say that he didn't publish your private letter out of low-mindedness, but from the feeling of having to "absolve" you. Further, it was an editorial note that specified that it was *Hitler*-Germany and not "Germany" that you were finished with. But as I wrote you yesterday, the Third Reich couldn't give a shit whether you say Germany or Hitler-Germany, the editorial note made it clear that you meant Hitler's Germany. You needn't worry any more about that.

I dislike your friend Fischer, because for me he reeks of socialism. About three years ago, I was startled to note that little [. . .] Ebermayer[1] was your friend. Well, frankly, he could never have been mine. No more than the Marxist Fischer. Just by the by. I just mean to say that the scurrilousness of printing a private letter wasn't in any way scurrilous where Mr. Fischer was concerned, quite the opposite: he wanted to "see you in the clear." He's a plebeian (just like his wife, whom I met once. She looks huge, but only sitting down. A stumpy-legged plebeian.)

(You know my intentions with all this stuff are not personal.)

I read further, in my *Neue Deutsche Blätter*, that you are supposed to have told Mr. Fischer that it hardly matters whether a Stefan Zweig writes any more or not, when one considers that the Communists are transforming an entire continent.

Well, for myself, I'd rather that you and I wrote, than that Russia be changed or "improved." If you really imagine "Communism" is any better than "National Socialism" then your letter to Insel is perfectly all right. If you told Fischer the Soviets have right on their side, then you will have to say the Nazis have right on their side as well.

Modest as I am, a single invention from the likes of us is worth more than all the proletariat garbage that you get over the airwaves. Wherever they oppress us, in Russia, Italy, Germany, is a TOILET. It stinks there. It's not true to say that Communism has "transformed an entire continent." Like fuck it has. It spawned Fascism and Nazism and hatred for intellectual freedom. Whoever endorses Russia has *eo ipso* endorsed the Third Reich.

All of which is to say: if you decide to raise your pen against Hitler's Germany, then you must not repeat or repeat approximately the sentence you are supposed to have said to Fischer, or to Gerhart Hauptmann.

It is more important that a Stefan Zweig writes, than that a hundred thousand plebeians learn to read and write, as now supposedly in Russia.

As soon as my book is typed up, in another 2–3 days, I'm going to Amsterdam.

Sincerely,   your old Joseph Roth

1. Ebermayer: Erich Ebermayer (1900–1970), lawyer, novelist, playwright, scenarist.

231. To Félix Bertaux   *Rapperswil*
                                               1 December 1933

My dear good friend,

I've made you wait a long time for a reply, but this time too I regret to have to say, there were many reasons which will make you take a lenient view of my silence. I had to finish my novel at a great rate, after urgent warnings and even threats from the publishers, Querido of Amsterdam. So I worked like a madman, whole nights through sometimes with temperature of 99 degrees. I finally finished it last night. I hope the book will be able to come out before Christmas, because the first part was typeset even before I'd written the middle. I'm afraid it will be my last book. I used up the whole of the advance. I have just enough money to see me through to 15 December. I need to go to Amsterdam, and try to find a rich man who will help me out for a couple of months. If I don't, my end is certain. Please, dear friend, forgive me these explanations. You understand that I am in desperation and thinking of nothing else than keeping alive, day and night. It's absurd to be in this situation, at the end of 14 books, 3,500 newspaper articles, having made a name for myself, and lived through so much personal unhappiness! It's not even tragic any more! In almost every country I have publishers, readers, buyers. No one knows I'm dying, at the end of twelve years that were stuffed with paper, paper, paper!

Do you know if my *Radetzky March* is on sale in Paris yet? I don't hear a squeak from Plon. I expect the translation is god-awful. But what does it matter to me, in my position?

Please give Mrs. Bertaux and Pierre my warm regards.

Maybe we'll see each other in Paris.

Sincerely,   your old Joseph Roth

232. To Stefan Zweig   *Hotel Foyot*
                                          Paris
                                          22 December 1933

Dear friend,

thank you for your letter. I congratulate you on the *Erasmus.*[1]

I have asked for new and proper proofs in Amsterdam. They're due at the very beginning of January. I'll send them to you.

I have the keen sense that my book is bad. But my indifference towards "literary" questions has become such that my shame at showing you the book has become rather slight.

I wasn't able to see the publisher Querido.[2] He had the flu. Instead, I saw the publisher de Lange.

I told him that I am unable to let him have the book: "Jews and Anti-Semites" by 31 January. You remember: we spoke about it in Zurich, about the extensive changes I would make, changes from the ground up. Now I must have it ready by 31 March instead. Mr. de Lange said promptly then he would pay me another 3 installments. That means 3 x 750 marks, at the moment (and at other moments) a great deal of money for me. Even more, seeing as I quite literally have nothing at all right now. I got to Amsterdam by borrowing 100 francs. I sat in the American Hotel for 3 days, without eating anything. Mr. Querido was, for the first time in his life, confined to bed.—Little tricks of the devil, things I'm pretty much used to by now. In the end I was able to secure 1,000 francs from Mr. Landshoff. Then I began to drink. I had a supper invitation from Mr. de Lange, for which I turned up completely drunk. Now, Mr. de Lange is a mighty drinker, and he wasn't sober either. But something happened that I thought would never happen to me. For the first time in my life I experienced a complete blackout. My recollection of the evening is *absolutely nonexistent*. It's possible I've wrecked my chances with de Lange. You know, he's a sort of Junker type really. He knows from somewhere that writers drink, but in his imagination or experience it doesn't stretch to their actually being drunk. He can only have had a very approximate sense of me. I was a "literary name" to him, little more. He was very nice, but I'm afraid I've messed up my chances. For the first time I felt a real sense of weakness. My dear friend, it's possible that my "self-destructive instinct" put in a major appearance; even though, in *physiological* terms it's easy enough to explain how a man can get very drunk if he hasn't had anything to eat. I'm still rather shocked at myself. For the first time. In the field and after, I sometimes had an awful lot to drink, as you know. But I never had the feeling afterwards that I had been completely awol. Maybe it's a sign to me to stop. But believe me: however much I believe that my muse is the muse of desperation, I know perfectly clearly that she is driving me to suicide. I can't live any more with five francs in my pocket. I can't imagine that I'll get through this time. Bear in mind that I've spent 20 years of my life starving, was in the war for four more, and was "desperately up against it" for another six. It's only in the past three years that I can be said to have lived at all. And now these global events. And before that the business with my wife. I know that all this is part of me, that it's what I consist of. But with all that, I *remain a private individual*, who eats, sleeps, fucks, and so forth. I can't historicize myself. But nor can I continue to convert this intrusion of private grief into my "true," unliterary life into literature. It's killing me. And believe me, never did an alcoholic "enjoy" his alcohol less than I did. Does an epileptic enjoy his fits? Does a madman enjoy his episodes?

But to turn to the intended topic: Mr. de Lange sends you his best regards. He has infinite respect for you. He sees me principally as your friend. And I have the wretched feeling that it is your friend upon whom I have brought discredit, through my lack of moderation. Please forgive me!

If you felt able to write him a kind word about me under some business pretext, then I wish you would. (He intimated that he was involved in some sort of business correspondence with you.)

Indeed—and now I'm not writing, as I'm sure you will suppose, for myself—I'm ashamed to say so, even though the next 6 months or even a whole year could be assured by you: if you were to give just some trifle to de Lange, he would, as they say, kiss your feet. You can write your own terms. All foreign rights free. Any sum—I know it doesn't matter to you. You can hardly imagine the degree to which this basically unintellectual man is *devoted* to you.

Well, it won't matter much—to you. For me, a book of yours with de Lange[3] means staying alive another year. Not that I'm trying to tell you to underwrite my life for a year. I'm afraid I'll live another year anyway (as a beggar, a down-and-out). But I certainly wouldn't be writing you all this if I didn't seriously think that you would have all possible freedom here, with him. De Lange would agree to any conditions of yours. And now: you surely won't believe I'm writing this on my own behalf. You can't think that, my dear friend! All I've said to you is that I depend on you—perhaps I've even exaggerated a little—because, to you, I want to say everything. I don't want you ever to get a letter from me in which I keep silent about something, or in which I hide or keep back anything from you.

I am very, very unhappy. Please reply, right away.

All the best! Kiss Mrs. Zweig's hand for me.

Your old J.R.

*-----

* I wanted to put: alias Beierle. But I'm not so strong. And I'm not so forlorn either—I think, at the last moment.

1. *Erasmus*: Zweig's book *Triumph and Tragedy of Erasmus of Rotterdam*, English edition with Cassell in 1934, German edition from Reichner in Vienna in 1935.

2. publisher Querido: Emanuel Querido, owner of the Querido Verlag in Amsterdam. He was deported and gassed by the Germans.

3. a book of yours with de Lange: no book of Zweig's appeared with de Lange until long after Gerard de Lange's death in 1935. (His novel *Ungeduld des Herzens/Beware of Pity* did in 1939—too late to do JR any good.)

233. To Stefan Zweig   *[Paris] 27 December 1933*

Dear, esteemed friend,

I'm just reading the beginning of your fine Erasmus in the *Freie Presse*.[1] I want to alert you to a few irritating trifles right at the beginning: the *most indisputable* fame; the *form* shaded by others' *profiles*; to *procure* one's own biography; "just like us": unnecessary and weakening; "the *contrary spirit* of common sense"; the *unilaterally beating* whip; war *the most violent* form . . . is pleonastic; "truly in no country" is dubious; to refer to Latin as "artificial Esperanto" is probably more than dubious.—Such little things—perhaps they wouldn't bother anyone else— and more like them. There is a pleasing momentum to the whole, and a few deft phrases. Its bearing on the present time is distinct and abundant.

All for now, and for today.

Happy New Year

Sincerely your   Joseph Roth

1. JR means the *Neue Freie Presse*, a Vienna paper.

234. To Klaus Mann   *Paris 6ᵉ*
                                           33 rue de Tournon
                                           28 December 1933

Dear Klaus Mann,

I hear to my consternation from Mr. Landshoff that you and other acquaintances of mine are of the opinion that people have been collecting money for me in Switzerland. Unfortunately, this is not the case. I want you to know that this is not the case. Not because I would be ashamed; but because it would be harmful in the event of there one day actually being a collection. People would say, "oh, they're always collecting for him." I would be very grateful to you, therefore, if you could inform all persons within earshot, and *write* to Miss Schwarzenbach[1] and Mr.

Schickele, *that it is not true.* Will you do so? Whether you do or not, I look to you, please, to reply.

Furthermore, I am sending you a novella by Isaac Grünberg, whom you know from the Deux Magots. I am surprised myself: it's a good novella. And the man's name is Isaac. In the emigration that seems even more appropriate. Even in the Second Reich, we should all have been called Isaac.

Furthermore: Prince Hohenlohe (to balance out the Isaacs) would like to know *when* his contribution is to appear. He is very poorly.

If you should have happened to let fall something in front of Erika Mann[2] and your parents about any "collection for me," then kindly let them too know that that was a misunderstanding.

To you and all others a good New Year! It just occurs to me that it was three years ago today that I had the pleasure of meeting you for the very first time. It was in the Hotel Foyot. There was a lady present too, with a dog.

Yours sincerely   Joseph Roth

1. Miss Schwarzenbach: Annemarie Schwarzenbach (1908–1942), writer, journalist, socialite, and friend of Erika Mann's. Coming from a Swiss industrialist family, she supported *Die Sammlung* financially.

2. Erika Mann (1905–1969), eldest child of Thomas Mann, actor, writer, reporter. Was briefly married to the Nazi actor Gustav Gründgens, and later, in a(nother) marriage of convenience, to W. H. Auden. Ran the famous anti-Fascist Peppermill cabaret in Zurich from 1933 to 1936; was later an English war correspondent, and edited the letters of her father, and the works of her brother Klaus.

235. *To René Schickele*   *Monday [end of 1933 or early 1934]*

Dear esteemed Mr. René Schickele,

how can you think I might be angry with you? What a peculiar notion. If every debate would lead to such serious consequences, where would that get us? Once everything has been said, my heart harbors nothing, therefore I tend always to say everything. I hold nothing back. If I'd been angry with you, then I would have said, I'm angry with you. Therefore, I have nothing to say on your sticking up for Reifenberg that I would not have said to you previously. Otherwise I wouldn't have said anything. I'm not stupid enough just to be "angry" with someone.

"Mess spirit" I took to be the splendid training of young officers (at least in Austria) to respond to an insult with an insult back, and to prefer death to disgrace. That is a clear human quality. Only God or his holy saints are allowed to suffer an insult without immediately punishing it, God because He is exalted, and the saint because his life is worth nothing in his eyes anyway. And I am not a saint.

Nor am I a judge. But where would it get us, if we drew different, sensitive, wavering lines between good and bad, depending on the state of our sympathies for the parties?[1] If, 30 years ago, someone who claimed to be a man of honor had said that he would allow himself in this instance to be spat at, because he and his family had to live, well, he would have been despised for it. Since when is it the case that a writer can say: I must lie, so that my wife can continue to live and wear hats? And since when is it the custom to approve of that? Since when is honor cheapened beyond life, and the lie a ready means to save life? Above all, let us avoid making appeals to Christianity here, at an instant when to do so makes one an associate of the Antichrist. I am a feeble man, but the one thing that God has given me to help me comport myself in His image is the ability to identify evil. After I have identified evil, which is to say Germany, I have no choice but to hate His editorialists, the editorialists of the Antichrist—and, if possible, to try and root them out. Yes, in that respect, and in all humility, I am a *gladius dei*. I say so without conceit. A proper Christian, a true Christian, a dime-a-dozen Christian has the duty to fight with pitch and sulfur against hell and its minions. Grace is with God alone. *I am too humble to grant forgiveness to the Antichrist and his minions, who have become his minions to save their skins.* It's not for you, my dear René Schickele, to say: good deeds last forever. No man is lost before the moment of his death. To do so is to arrogate to yourself the role of God. You speak in the manner of Christ, when all you are is a mortal writer of books. Your job is to distinguish good from evil, following *earthly* measures. You may forgive and you may love. You are even instructed to do so. But you may not move the absolute line between good and evil because it suits you. A vile act is a vile act—there's no more to be said about it. To lie *in order to* keep your family safe is a vile act. If you take the fact that you are no "judge" to its logical conclusion, you would have to say: hm, I don't actually know what's vile and what isn't. And you do know—how can you deny it? You don't commit any such acts yourself? Or at least not consciously?

In fact what you say resembles the heathenism to which you are opposed. Be careful not to support barbarian heathenism with your Christian indulgence. Leave the Church's errors out of it. It's not for us to criticize the Church. Least of all when we know the Vatican less well than Reifenberg, whom you allow to get away with almost as much as you accuse the Church of. You cannot in one breath pardon an editorialist or editor of the Antichrist—only God may do that—and attack the politics of the Church, which is certainly less familiar to you than those of the *FZ. That way lies Protestantism*. Perhaps you are—a Protestant. I don't know your declared religion. You've always struck me as "Catholic" in the old sense of "inclusive." As you know. So why do you fight it?

Anyway, there is no "anger" between you and me. I have the habit of speaking my mind. Embarrassing, I know. But I will speak it only in front of people I like and am fond of, as I like and am fond of you and your wife. Otherwise I keep silent.

Yours sincerely   Joseph Roth

1. sympathies for the parties: JR's tremendous tirade against all ethical relativism. It reminds me a little in its rigor of the Polish poet Zbigniew Herbert's poem "A Knocker" with its "yes—yes / no—no."

236. To Klaus Mann   *Hotel Foyot, Paris 6ᵉ*
                                              33 rue de Tournon
                                              12 January 1934

Dear Mr. Klaus Mann,

I have a bone to pick with you—several, in fact—and I want to do it right away.

In the latest issue of *Die Sammlung*, you print a rather long (and rather clever) essay by Golo Mann[1] on Ernst Jünger.[2] I find that extremely *tactless*. There is, so to speak, a *politics* of the literary emigration. Let's not even get into the question of the importance or otherwise of Jünger. Even given that he has some—though in my view, he's a fool, and a barbarian, and a muddlehead—one would either have to ignore him altogether, or have done with him in a couple of dismissive sentences. A magazine— in these times—isn't there to serve the book business. You showed that you understood that in your clever book review. Have we left Germany just to alert the world beyond to "interesting" new literary products of the barbarian heathens? Is that what we're for? And another thing: your magazine addresses itself to emigrants, to writers, to tastemakers for a wider public, to people who are absolutely opposed to Jünger and everything he stands for. You don't just alienate such people—you offend them. Because each one of them has his own conceit, and he will ask himself: hm, why not six pages on me?—(I need hardly tell you that I am not among these people.) So you make yourself enemies, quite needlessly.

Another thing: you take George[3] for a great poet. I take him for a great con artist. It's not the time—whatever one thinks of George—to show respect to a guy, a great guy if you like, who has landed us in some of this shit we're in, some of the loftier or deeper parts of it. Factually, too, it is not true to say that George wanted to die far away from Germany. He was very keen on life, and very keen on death, period. Not far from the "hurly-burly"—which I can understand. But in the hurly-burly of clouds, because he preferred clouds to people. Goebbels and Sieburg are among his disciples. Your disciples say something about the kind of person you are.

It's a good thing that *Die Sammlung* isn't too "long-term" in its orientation. But if you continue to edit it outside with that "objectivity" that you did for us inside Germany, then you will soon find yourself hated.

I wanted to warn you of that danger.

Yours sincerely   Joseph Roth

1. Golo Mann (1909–1994), second son of Thomas Mann, historian and biographer.

2. Ernst Jünger (1895–1998), essayist, militarist, diarist. Fought in World War I, 1919–1923 in the Reichswehr, from 1941 to 1944 and his dismissal in the German occupying army in Paris.

3. George: Stefan George (1868–1933), cultish poet and translator. He resisted Goebbels's overtures to him in 1933, and died—this is at issue here between KM and JR—on Swiss soil.

237. *To Stefan Zweig*   *Hotel Foyot, Paris 6ᵉ*
                                          33 rue de Tournon
                                          14 January 1934

Dear friend,

this is my belated answer to yours of the 27th last. I beg your pardon.

I cannot reply to you, not to what you wrote me.

I no longer understand what happened. Don't you understand what I tell you in the simplest terms?

You have gone to the trouble to write to me by hand. At one and the same time, you simplify and complicate the things I tell you.

The simplest things—I should like to say—but I'm afraid I can't.

There's no question of "drinking out of despair" or "Russification." I would be stupid to be doing that. Please understand, *I don't lose my clarity for a moment.*

No, I don't want to go on either. Forgive me. I can't. Writing only makes it worse.

I am perfectly sober.

I embrace you   your J.R.

238. *To Klaus Mann*   *Hotel Foyot*
                                              Paris, 16 January 1934

To the editorial board of the *Sammlung*,

Querido Verlag,

Amsterdam, Keizersgracht 33

  Dear Mr. Klaus Mann,

  thank you for yours of the 14th. When you refer to the Communists—
"radical émigrés," as you are pleased to call them—who tell you it's your
duty to portray the most interesting minds on the other side, that (*at
least to me*) constitutes no defense. For me the Communist minds among
the Germans—the Germans, NB—are just like the National Socialists.
Apart from that, I think you're making a mistake when you suppose
Jünger has any influence in Germany. With all that one might say about
him from my point of view, he remains sufficiently decent as a human
being for the people in Germany to be profoundly suspicious of him. So
he's not at all as "interesting" in current political terms as the Communists suppose. In every other respect, be it as an author, or "thinker" or
anything else you want to call him, he's a bonehead. All right, perhaps
there is a difference within the Third Reich between his personal decency
and the absolute indecency (personal as well) of the Third Reich: but for
me and many others, standing outside, there is a straightforward equa-
tion between Jünger and Goebbels. If out of woolly-mindedness or bone-
headedness or stupidity he has supported or prepared the ground for the
bestial ideology of National Socialism—and apart from that remained
a decent human being—it's completely ridiculous, in an émigré journal,

a journal of his direct or indirect victims, to give him six pages of space, even if it finally comes down against him.

This isn't the time or place for a proper discussion of the case of Stefan George. Perhaps we'll talk about it together sometime.

I understand of course how you "intended" it to come across.

Overall, if advice from me is acceptable and useful to you: your personal "literariness" (George is just one example) may turn out to be utterly detrimental to the magazine you are bringing out. To attempt to put it at its briefest: you will not manage to be fair to *all* of those for whom the magazine is intended.

As far as my own contribution is concerned, I won't have it ready for another 3–4 weeks. There are a couple of chapters in my new book that would be suitable for separate publication. What do you offer in the way of royalties, and how much could I expect for 5 or 6 pages?

Yours sincerely   Joseph Roth

239. To Stefan Zweig   *Paris, 20 January 1934*

To Dr. Stefan Zweig, Salzburg, Kapuzinerberg 5

Dear esteemed friend,

forgive the typed letter, and dictation. I just wanted to thank you quickly for your kind letter. I hear terrible news from Austria. In spite of that, I continue to believe in its independence. I'll write you in a week. Mr. de Lange is due here, and I'm impatient to see him—you'll understand. Give my best regards to Mrs. Zweig. I can't force myself to make the corrections. Querido has sold the serial rights to my book[1] to an émigré newspaper for a tiny sum of money, which has only increased my reluctance to going through the book and making changes. Please write.

Yours sincerely   Joseph Roth

1. my book: *Tarabas.*

240. To Stefan Zweig   *Joseph Roth*
                                                Hotel Foyot, Paris 6ᵉ
                                                33 rue de Tournon
                                                28 January 1934

My dear friend,

It's sweet of you to send me Mondadori's[1] letter. I do beg you to forgive me for continuing to bother you, on top of everything else. I sent the letter on to Querido right away. You see, my dear friend, I'm not always the one to blame for the frittering away of my strength and books. (Don't sigh with relief just yet.) I have some pretty bad news here.

Sincerely,   your old [Joseph Roth]

1. Mondadori: Alberto Mondadori, celebrated publisher in Milan.

241. René Schickele to Joseph Roth   *Sanary-sur-Mer (Var)*
                                                "Le Chêne"
                                                28 January 1934

Dear Joseph Roth,

it seems to me you could hardly have paid my book[1] a greater compliment than allowing it to eclipse your long and great rage. In a bid to retain your renewed friendship, for such time as the delights of *Widow Bosca* may have lost some of their freshness, I would like to seize this opportunity to make my position clear, and it is certainly no accident that *you* are the designated recipient of my clarification.

I don't like to think back to the telegram. Particularly with reference to Klaus Mann, who was left exposed by it. I was working at the time, and in the all-consuming, volcanic manner of my working, I am at times not fully aware of what I am doing (which isn't intended as an excuse, but may partly explain my folly in disregarding Annette Kolb's and Meier-Graefe's warnings concerning the *Sammlung*). For, while Klaus Mann may not have behaved absolutely correctly when, without asking me, he put my name on a list of contributors to a magazine that was not in line with my own views, even so I should not have snubbed him. The fact that it was a snub only dawned on me later, just like the other matter, that the "use" the Fischer Verlag reserved the right to make of the telegram "in an extreme emergency" might have as a consequence its publication. I'm sure I will have an early opportunity to make it up to Kl.M., and I will certainly take it. I say that in the knowledge that you don't especially like Kl.M. I, for my part, do. I have a strong liking for him.

Now the telegram.

In my form of words, I went further than Thomas Mann (which I would ask you to note!), who merely stated a fact, namely that when he had given his consent, he had had a different notion of the character of the *Sammlung*. The telegram was not addressed to any "Ministry" but *to the S. Fischer Verlag*, to which, surely rightly, I felt obligated in many ways. (Here the prehistory. After a protracted exchange of letters, Professor Saenger[2] came to see us, and told us in some considerable detail about the state of the Fischer family, and of the publishing firm. Among many other things, not all of them strictly necessary, he told me that Fischer was physically threatened. He said old Sami,[3] to whom I am utterly devoted, would rather be clubbed to death than leave Germany. He spoke for many hours over the course of two full days. He himself made such a pitiable impression that his appearance was more eloquent than all his words. Whether I did right or not, I gave the statement. I felt obliged to give it, and in exactly the form in which the publisher wanted it given. Other factors were involved, too. (1) we were of the view[4] that whoever among us *could* still appear in Germany should do so, as long as it was done decently, every non-approved, non-*gleichgeschaltet* word mattered more than all the bluster that no one in Germany would ever get to hear anyway. (2) I was resolved not to go political, because I know that the politically engaged émigré is forced onto one or other extreme of the debate, and winds up either with the CP or else with the (French) Nationalists. (3) If Fischer had dropped me, I would have found myself penniless. This last point is important enough on its own, because I have no aptitude for financial rescue plans where my own person is involved. I suppose I could have gone to Meier-Graefe, who is a close personal friend, and who has some savings, and he wouldn't have turned me down. I mention this, so that point (3) doesn't get more weight than it should have.)

What I regretted soon after sending the telegram (and regret to this day) is the form of words, in which I followed too closely the wishes of the publishers and that (this is not insignificant here) was criticized mildly but distinctly by Thomas Mann. Whereas Heinrich Mann, long before I had decided to send the telegram, said to me, and these are his very words: "Deny it in the crudest possible terms." It was clear to me that his vehemence was out of friendship for me, because he thought it was principally his own essay that had caused the ruckus.

Dear Roth, in your letter you talk about comradeship—but how does the friend differ from the enemy, if he condemns his comrade without even giving him a hearing? Neither Annette Kolb nor anyone else led me to suppose you were baying with the wolves against me, which, quite apart from our friendship, is not your style at all. Your letter hit me unprepared. It is a painful experience, the most painful of all of those I have undergone in this matter. If you, Joseph Roth, committed a murder, and the whole world arose against you, then I would be blindly on your side and seek illumination from *you*, and not join a band of pathetic but for all that no less malign dervishes.

On 28 August 1932 we were all sitting together on our terrace in Badenweiler . . . You remember the occasion, don't you? We were very harmonious. At a time when the leaders of today's emigration were successively hailing Brüning,[5] Papen,[6] and Schleicher[7] as "the lesser of two evils," and were ready to take all sorts of kicking, so long as the government left them the possibility of receiving them at home . . . I, though not personally affected, was physically ill at the sight of this charade, but at no time did it cross my mind to break with old friends over this . . . I rebuked them when they were with me, and able to defend themselves, and basically my pity only heightened my fellow feeling for them. How could I ever have guessed you in the chorus of those who would defame a man who voluntarily, facing no threat, *left Germany together with them*, who *resigned from the Academy*[8] (and not, like the others, whose names feature in all the émigré publications, not over the matter of the declaration of loyalty), and condemned him, of whom even his enemies said, they "would never have expected it of him," without even taking the trouble to inquire how this uncharacteristic and unexpected action had come about?

The first to approach me over the telegram was someone who had come to me during the war when I was in Berlin editing the *Weisse Blätter* and brought me a "heroic" war novella asking me to publish it. I returned it to him, and talked to him long and patiently, and since he was a Jew, told him about the role of Judaism in the world that did not consist of putting on the beard of Father Jahn[9] when the hour seemed to call for it. Unfortunately, I was unable to convince him. When the war was over, and pacifism was the "order of the day" the man rewrote his novella in the new spirit, and dedicated it to me. It's in one of his books, dedication and all. So this man was the first who approached me in Sanary. And in what manner? *Bursting with malignity*, like a whore catching a previously respectable woman in flagrante. I swear, his voice cracked with malice! At home I had the manuscript of his latest book, with a foreword where he explained how certain regards compelled him to publish anonymously. (In the meantime, the need for these regards has fallen away, and his book will shortly come out, with his own name bravely on the spine.) This was the emigrant who, powerless in the face of real violence and oppression, plays his one sorry trump against a "comrade"—a goy who "won't live in Germany, but doesn't want to lose out on the German market"! (What a foolish reproach, by the way! As if the deepest desire of all emigrants throughout history were not precisely to be heard in the land from which they had been expelled: from Marx and Heine and Victor Hugo to Lenin and Trotsky.) I say "goy," because it struck me that in the course of what I suppose I may call his tirade, that he only ever spoke of Thomas Mann and me, and never of Döblin . . .

I always had the deepest suspicion of émigrés—for their noted senti-mentality (it was Victor Hugo's *friends* who accused him of continuing to see France the way he saw it in 1851, the year he left), and this wave of emigration in particular, *whose leading members I know all too well*. With few exceptions, they have all swallowed shit, until the Nazis put an end to it, and they had to leave. If Hitler hadn't been such a rabid anti-Semite, they would be hailing *him* today as the "lesser evil" and reserv-ing their fire for Bolshevism and the Nuremberger Streicher.[10] And now they feel like big heroes, which is always how the people behind the lines felt. Which of them seriously thinks about the poor devils standing in the front line of indignity and abuse, *unable* to flee, and having to gulp down their own shit every day? I would excuse all those in Germany who betray themselves with each action decreed by those in power, and who with each new day sink further into self-contempt. Those are the ones whom God will forgive first, their sufferings are possibly even greater than those others, gifted with physical courage, who are simply beaten to death or strangled.

Curious how readily the victims take on the habits of the jailers! Whoever takes revenge is not just evil, but also stupid. If the victims don't yet rule the world, it can only be because of that. Cometh the hour, cometh the hour of vengeance, and the intellectual victim happily turns hangman. There is no end to cycles of grief and revenge. The empire of Christ has barely even begun. No sooner was he dead than a general took over the enterprise. His name was Paul. He was a stupid and ambitious fellow, another general who dabbled in politics.

The true horseman of the Apocalypse is Stupidity, the others just trot along after.

You speak of the Antichrist, dear Joseph Roth. But you're underesti-mating him if you think he wears just the one uniform. He is in every camp. And that's what makes him so powerful. He forces his enemies into a fighting style that turns them inevitably into his creatures. To go back to my starting point: something of that is what I wanted to show in my Widow Bosca—she forces her daughter to kill her lover, she even forces her husband to strangle her. Burguburu[11] doesn't want revenge—

which is why I allow the mechanical clock of the seasons to play a soft little "Gerettet"[12] at the end. It's just a windup clock. But I hope it sounds pure. I don't have the strength for amplification. But how I'd love to stun and change the whole world with that same tune!

Excuse the long letter. And now: not another word! I don't demand an answer, and I don't need one. Whatever you might say by way of reply, I couldn't say anything back to you that I haven't said here. Even more than your judgment, I want your friendship, even if you won't agree with me over this matter here, ephemeral though I think you will agree it is,

Yours sincerely   René Schickele

1. my book: the novel *Die Witwe Bosca*.

2. Professor Saenger: Samuel Saenger (1864–1944), editor of the S. Fischer house magazine, *Die Neue Rundschau*. Went into exile in France in 1939, to the USA in 1941.

3. Sami: as S. Fischer was known to intimates and unqualified persons alike.

4. we were of the view: the counterargument to Roth's intransigence and inflexibility-leading-sooner-or-later-to-war—the importance of going on talking, going on trading, going on dealing with an opponent.

5. Brüning: Heinrich Brüning (1885–1970), chancellor between 1930 and 1932. From 1934 to 1951 in exile in the United States.

6. Papen: Franz von Papen (1879–1969), 1932 chancellor, 1933 deputy chancellor under Hitler, then personal envoy and ambassador in Vienna and Ankara till 1945.

7. Schleicher: Kurt von Schleicher (1882–1934), chancellor from December 1932 through January 1933. Murdered by the SS in June 1934 during the Night of the Long Knives, on direct orders of Hitler.

8. the Academy: *recte*, the Preussische Akademie der Künste: Sektion für Dichtkunst, founded in 1926, and taken over in 1933 by the Nazis. (The poet Gottfried Benn, for a brief, unhappy, and regrettable period, allowed himself to be used as their cat's-paw.) Schickele is pleading for more sympathy for the likes of himself, Heinrich (who was elected its new chairman in 1931) and Thomas Mann, Ricarda Huch, Käthe Kollwitz, and others, who lost prestige and living, and in some cases went into exile, though (!) not themselves Jews.

9. Friedrich Ludwig Jahn (1778–1852), who gave German nationalism a gymnastic and Prussian inflection.

10. Streicher: executed for war crimes in 1946, Julius Streicher (born 1885) was a racial theorist and founder and editor of *Der Stürmer*.

11. Burguburu: a character in Schickele's *Die Witwe Bosca*.

12. "Gerettet": "rescued" or "saved." Cf. the quartet in Beethoven's *Fidelio*, act 2.

242. To René Schickele   *Hotel Foyot, Paris 6ᵉ*
                                             33 rue de Tournon
                                             31 January 1934

Dear esteemed René Schickele,

your desire for no reply won't prevent me from telling you two things. Firstly, my thanks and a friendly greeting to you.

Secondly, the book I am working on now is called *The Antichrist*.[1] It will contain all his manifestations. Precisely that is my subject: the Antichrist as enemy and friend. By the end, a fragment of him will be in me.

You could say we are the last Christians. That's the result of these times: it's not Christ we see and recognize—he's too distant—but his enemy.

Regards to your dear wife!

Good luck to your *Bosca*! I remain enraptured.

Your old   Joseph Roth

I reread these lines and see that they do not say how very fond of you I am. Let me tell you so, then, *expressis verbis*: I am very fond of you.

And forgive me: one other thing I am unable to bite back:

When I ran into Döblin, I told him I would not sit down with him unless and until he had explained the telegram: well, at that time his two eldest sons were in Germany. Saenger talked about concentration camp. That's fairly easily understood. Even I understand it. Forgive me my strictness! It's the old tribe of Jehovah, from which I am descended.

Forgive me!

1. *The Antichrist*: *Der Antichrist*. A polemic, published by Allert de Lange, Amsterdam, 1934. It was translated into English in 2010, and published by Peter Owen.

243. To Stefan Zweig *Hotel Foyot, Paris 6ᵉ*
33 rue de Tournon
9 February 1934

Dear friend,

on 4 February I wrote to you at the Hotel Louvois, because I'd heard you were in Paris to give a lecture on Austrian literature at the Sorbonne. I didn't understand why you didn't meet me, or alternatively, didn't tell me why you wouldn't meet me. Well, were you here or not? Today I got a card dated 7th inst. about the novella.[1] But I don't have the novellas yet. Did you send them registered mail? Then they'll be sure to come a day late.

I've spent the last 6 days in bed with flu. But I will read the novella right away, and tell you what I think about it.

Most sincerely your Joseph Roth

1. the novella: (Zweig's) *Angst* (Fear), 1925.

244. To Blanche Gidon (written in French) *Hotel Foyot*
Paris 6ᵉ
16 February 1934

Dear Madam Gidon,
here are some facts:
Born on 2 September 1894
in Szvaby,[1] a German settlement
close to the Austrian frontier,
to a Russian Jewish mother
and an Austrian father (state employee, painter, alcoholic, went mad shortly before my birth)[2]
school: lycée (humanist gymnasium)
very poor, gave lessons to very rich people

university: Vienna, "German language and literature"

1916 war

volunteered

eastern front

1917 promoted to second lieutenant, 2 months in Russian detention

1918 revolution

1919 journalist in Vienna

1920 journalist in Berlin

many foreign trips (Russia. Africa, Albania, Balkans)

1922 France – la lumière, la liberté PERSONELLE

(not a figure of speech!)

Cordially, all yours   Joseph Roth

1. Szvaby: actually one of the villages outlying Brody, Roth's actual birthplace, and hence part of his systematic mystification regarding his birth. Swaby (to German ears evoking "Schwaben," Swabia, from where German emigrants settled parts of south-eastern Europe, in some cases many hundreds of years ago) has the effect of making Roth appear thoroughly and ancestrally German. Brody, a known center for Jews since the eighteenth century, if not a particularly miserable center for particularly miserable Jews (as witness the saying *"verfallen wie in Brody,"* desperate or wretched as in Brody), has and had a very different resonance, which Roth for much of his life sought to avoid.

2. His father (Nahum) was the most mythologized person in Roth's life, possibly including himself. Roth's biographer David Bronsen reckoned up seventeen versions of his identity. The "painter" and "alcoholic" here suggests an identification with the character of Moser in *The Radetzky March*.

---

245. *To Stefan Zweig*   *Paris, 18 February 1934*

Dear friend,

I am pleased to have your letter. I was getting a little nervous.

The causes and consequences of the catastrophe in Austria[1] don't seem quite so plain to me. Both sides, all three sides, if you like, seem to have made one mistake after another. A good party line is hard to evolve at a time when the party has no power. A child could have worked out that

the Social Democrats were doomed. They could not look to their enemies for fear or respect. A year ago they might still have won. This time,
whether provoked or not, it was a glorious suicide. I don't myself believe
in the wholesale switch of Socialist workers to the Nazis. If it can even be
expressed in figures at all, then I see about one-third Nazis, mainly those
Socialists who were closer to Communists. For all the tragedy and catastrophe, I don't yet see the Anschluss or the end of Austria. Hitler's situation was never so bad as now. The foreign powers are watching him like
a hawk, and he's almost lost his only friend, which was Italy. If Dollfuss
cuts a sorry figure in the world, then Hitler cuts a worse one, because he's
frightening into the bargain. Besides, you know how quickly the world
forgets and forgives violence. Objectively it's not right to speak of a war
debt. Certainly, the elemental moment was important here. But I am cast
down, and at my wits' end. It's made me even sicker than I was before.
I'm still spending half my days in bed, unable to write a line. Please forgive me for dictating now. In particular, forgive me for dictating what I
have to say on the novella.[2] I'm returning it by the same post.

Of course you know that your novella is another masterpiece. Whoever manages such clever construction, and heightens the tension almost
to the very last line, knows a thing or two about literary artistry. I have
nothing to teach you about craft, my own artisanal soul delights in those
tiny solder seams invisible to the layman, those tiny, concealed, and silent
hinges and joints, and those lights, each one brighter than the one before,
or rather all continuing to cast their light however far one goes. It's like
a walk along a beautiful, gently climbing path where you have the feeling right from the start that you're going uphill, and that affords a score
of surprises at every bend. Then, when you reach the end, you have the
unaccountable feeling that the path has been perfectly straight. I have to
ask myself whether I've been had. I don't think so. I'm certain my craft
conscience wouldn't allow itself to be bribed.

Keeping pace with this mastery of craft is your psychology, and what
I would term the ethical component of your writing. It's splendid how
the narrator's psychology identifies ever more strongly with the psychol-

ogy of the subject, and how therefore simultaneously, even those who
disapprove of the subject have their ethics refined. The most original
way of defending a murderer is when the being with the most developed
conscience, namely the writer, identifies with the criminal. You get a
poet pleading. And a clever poet like you deploys his nobility so deftly,
not only knowing his own psychology and that of the criminal, but also
that of the ordinary reader. How easily someone else might have become
irritating, in the name of conventional morality!

Now I have a bone to pick with you. The last page and a half or two
pages, it seems to me, should be either shortened or lengthened. I might
be tempted to leave out the conclusion. There is no need to indemnify
the criminal for his fear. Here a personal—and hence, in a literary sense,
implausible nobility—mingles with the previous, legitimate, plausible
form. Right at the end, something personal is shared with us. It becomes
a confession, which diminishes the necessary distance between your per-
sona and the reader. Moreover, it's inconceivable that the man out there is
still afraid. He must have that much human understanding, and indeed
he does, as you've told us yourself. I don't know how to improve it. But I
think the ending has to change. I have complaints about the beginning as
well. I see no justified connections between the special character of that
day, and the subsequent events. I would make cuts. And also shorten the
address to Paris. It's all too "somptueux" for me. Both the introduction,
and that address. Style and use of metaphor are a little careless. I would
cite the word "capricious" for April showers, I don't like the notion of
a spring that leaves a calling card, because that's more than an urbane
spring, that's a positively genteel one; you wreck the planned irruption of
the elemental into the urbane by stressing the capricious qualities of the
elemental. Nor do I want to associate the damp and streaming season
with the crisp dry edge of the visiting card. Nor yet the regiments of
water, when to keep faith with a military metaphor, they should be pro-
jectiles, which indeed you go on to say in the same sentence, and thereby
confuse your metaphors. The capitulating locomotive I find a little precious. Then how do you come to associate sunbeams with tridents? I
wouldn't use the word "biped." It's a little facile. Day of curiosity seems

like a private usage. Other pages too have some slapdash expressions, too many to list. You will see them yourself. There are some rather worn adjectives.[3]

Thank you so much, my friend, for the novella. Please write and let me know when you're coming. I hope to be able to start work tomorrow or the day after. I have many private woes in addition to my illness, but I am reluctant to dictate them to you.

Sincerely, your old   Joseph Roth

1. the catastrophe in Austria: 12 February saw the beginning of an uprising by the Social Democrats in Austria in Linz. A countrywide general strike followed. Fighting in Vienna and Graz led to the dissolution of the SPÖ (Socialist Party of Austria) and to the Dollfuss dictatorship on 1 May.

2. novella: *Angst* (Fear).

3. some rather worn adjectives: Zweig and Roth were both (rightly) of the view that Zweig was not a tenth the writer that Roth was. Zweig—to do him credit—was quite open about it, and would say as much to anyone who cared to hear. In JR it takes the rather tortuous form of combining (as here) excessive praise of the whole with copious criticism of details to appease his—unappeasable—literary conscience. Or he could be (alas!) straightforwardly duplicitous, talking behind Zweig's back. Roth would explain to friends that he was a friend of Zweig's, and they would therefore have to forgive him for having to read his books; Zweig's *Beware of Pity* was as little a great novel as its author a great writer. And so on, and so on. It seems to me that Roth—always needy, always manipulative—plays Zweig like a big fish he's not quite sure he wants. Several decades later, strange to say, there is a creeping inability to distinguish between Zweig and Roth, which is basically illiterate and unpardonable.

246. To Stefan Zweig   *Paris 6ᵉ*
                                          33 rue de Tournon
                                          Hotel Foyot
                                          6 March 1934

Dear esteemed friend,

I think you're being a little unfair on Matveev.[1] Remember, he's forty, and a painter, and he won't straightaway understand some of the technical points. Also, I think—it happens to me sometimes—that one is slow to find something tragic because it's too personally upsetting. Then, when you take a second look, you come to see that the upsetting doesn't preclude the tragic. I am saying, I suppose, that we always react personally and humanly, in spite of our line of work. At any rate, I've gotten to know Matveev, and have spoken to him. It seems to me he's invented more things than he's actually experienced, which of course speaks for him, in literary terms. Don't you think Huebsch could be interested?

Write me something of what's happening to you personally. I'm appending a few handwritten lines. Also, albeit a little reluctantly, the final galleys of *Tarabas*, and what appears to me a rather nasty review from London.

Tell me if I'm mistaken.

Sincerely   Your Joseph Roth

8 March. Dear friend, my life is still more complicated than you think, even though you seem to have a lot of understanding for me. I think it's my foe, the Antichrist, hatching little plots to cripple me. And I can, following your advice, retire all I like, he keeps running the doors down. Let me be a little less cryptic. I have an old friend, one Konstantin Leites,[2] a 56-year-old Russian, an important person (he was a financial counselor under the tsar). Some 8 months ago, his wife lost her mind. Of late, she was doing better. I advised him against taking her out of the asylum. The doctor was in favor. He followed the doctor and his own sentiment. He rented an apartment for her, and spent many hours there with her. Well now, a couple of days ago she threw herself out of the window. Terrible hours with my friend. A terrible funeral. I spent two whole days in bed, unable to do a stroke.

But lest this tragedy lack also the most banal awfulness: my friend many times offered to lend me money—I always refused. The tragedy happened on the day that for the first time, I had to accept. I called him to that end—and caught the tragedy instead.

I am completely done in. I have to live somewhere, eat something.

I owe you, my dear friend, the following sum—but I could be wrong about that:

2,000 marks

4,000 francs.

Would you be able to lend me more? Do you have it handy? Things with de Lange are serious. I have to deliver on the 30th.[3]

This is, putting it crudely, so crude that I remind myself of Beierle, but what am I to do? Lack of funds makes one crude. And no amount of stylistic finesse can prettify that ugly reality. Promise me you'll tear up this letter. *Don't hold it against me.* (Even the most decent of men can make mistakes.) Write back.

Your old   J.R.

1. Matveev: Michel Matveev, painter and Yiddish writer, a friend of Roth's then living in Paris.

2. Leites: Konstantin Leites, a Russian financier and publisher of Russian writing. Went to Paris in 1933.

3. deliver on the 30th: i.e., *The Antichrist*.

247. *To Félix Bertaux (written in French)*   *Hotel Foyot*
                                                    Paris 6ᵉ
                                                    33 rue de Tournon
                                                    8 March 1934

My very dear friend,

I just read in *1934*[1] the preface you wrote for the excerpt from my novel. I thank you from the bottom of my heart. You know—and this isn't a figure of speech—you demonstrate more than an "understanding" of me—it's already more like a divination. Friendship has taught you much about me. And it's friendship too that is the basis of my deep gratitude.

I am sad not to have heard from you for many months. I was sick then, and I'm sick now. I can't make myself understood on the telephone. And, as before, I am very unhappy, and very impoverished. I can't describe it to you.

What about you, though? And Mme Bertaux? And Pierre?

I am writing *The Antichrist*. And having to write 10 pages a day, so as to be finished on the 25th. Feverish and impoverished.

I remain   your old and sad Joseph Roth

1. *1934*: a weekly publication, in Paris.

248. To Blanche Gidon (written in French)   *Hotel Foyot*
                                                     Paris 6ᵉ
                                                     33 rue de Tournon
                                                     8 March 1934

Dear Madam Gidon,

I have just read the preface.[1] I want to thank you with all my heart for the deep understanding you have of my work, and of my still poorer life. I found the quotations particularly well chosen. I want to say: how did you know?

And how is Mr. Gidon? How is he doing? Do you want to see me? I am writing *The Antichrist*, and must be finished by the 25th. Would it be possible to meet sometime after that?

Your ever grateful   Joseph Roth

1. The foreword (by Mrs. Gidon, and using the materials in no. 244, ones assumes) to the French edition of *The Radetzky March*.

249. To Carl Seelig

Joseph Roth
Paris 6ᵉ
33 rue de Tournon
Hotel Foyot
12 March 1934

Dear Mr. Seelig,

thank you for thinking of me. I go to the cinema so infrequently that I am afraid I could embarrass myself with the accompanying statement.

I am very poorly. I've been sick for a couple of weeks. I have no money at all, and "spiritually" I am no better off. I heard from Polgar[1] via the Austrian embassy. I haven't heard from Max Picard for a long time now. My book, which I finished in Rapperswil,[2] I no longer have any feeling for. I am writing a new one. It is called *The Antichrist*. Nevertheless, I will send you *Tarabas* as soon as it comes out. I am afraid to look at the proofs, which is delaying publication. Mrs. Manga Bell is at present not in Paris. She thinks of you sincerely. And that I do, you won't need me to tell you.

Very sincerely,   your humble Joseph Roth

Please excuse the pencil. I am in bed, very ill, with a bad throat.

1. Polgar: Alfred Polgar (1875–1955), Austrian novelist, translator, reviewer, and, above all, author of feuilletons, where he was probably the most admired in the business. Roth liked to call himself a pupil of Polgar, who, in fact, published some of his early pieces in Vienna. Fled to the United States in 1941.
2. in Rapperswil: *The Radetzky March?*

250. To Stefan Zweig

Hotel Foyot
Paris 6ᵉ
26 March 1934

Dear friend,

Thank you so much. Mr. Alzir Hella[1] brought me the money, I gave him a receipt for it.

a. I finished *The Antichrist* an hour ago. At last, for the first time in my life, I'm satisfied with a book.

You too, I'm sure, will be satisfied with it. It's a thousand times better than *Tarabas*. I spent 10–12 hours on it every day, 8 on the writing, 2–4 *preparing* it.

I'm at the end of my tether, but very happy.

b. Forgive me for talking about myself first.

The embassy isn't claiming that you publicly spoke out against Austria.

But a few weeks ago—or it could have been longer—you may have said something negative about the current state of Austria to a French journalist.

It's nothing to worry about, in any way.

Nothing happens here concerning you, without my being consulted.

I think that what you say about your criticisms being broadcast through all the embassies is an exaggeration.

c. More important, to me much more important, is that there is a rumor going the rounds that you are reluctant to sign a new publishing contract, because you are still counting on Insel and on Germany.

Please write and tell me that isn't so.

d. Just as important to me is our relationship. Or to put it another way: my fear that you may view me in a different way because I owe you money.

I know money can have that effect: it corrodes the noblest of relationships.

But I can't help it. I'm living in abject poverty. (Some of it through my fault, if you like.)

You haven't written to me about it—thus far—even though you must sense how awful it feels to me that you haven't mentioned it to me. If it doesn't suit you, though, to mention it, *then please don't.*

I'll send you the manuscript of *The Antichrist*, if you like.

Sincerely,   your old friend Joseph Roth

1. Mr. Alzir Hella, the French translator of Remarque's novel *All Quiet on the Western Front*.

251. *To Blanche Gidon (written in French)*

Hotel Foyot
Paris 6ᵉ
Monday
[postmarked:
26 March 1934]

Dear Madam Gidon,

thank you for your kind letter. Rest assured, there is not a single cloud in our sky. I'm not sure if I'll be able to see you before you leave. I am in the Deux Magots almost every day, and write there at night.

(There we are, I've just been summoned to the telephone)

So it seems we'll meet tonight!

All yours!

Greetings to Mr. Gidon.

Your Joseph Roth

252. *Stefan Zweig to Joseph Roth*   *[London] 27 March 1934*

Dear friend,

thank you for your letter. You can imagine how furious I was when it was bandied about that I had made some political utterances in Paris that were directed against Austria—I gave an interview in *Paris-Soir* or in *L'Intransigeant*,[1] I don't remember, it was *three months ago* with the stipulation: *not one word of politics*, and I wanted to see it before it appeared, and it duly came out without a single word of politics. Every other account is a barefaced lie. You know yourself I was only there for a very short time, and that was taken up by publishing business (and one day, if you remember, at Fontainebleau for work).

As for the lecture, I had promised Radio Paris a talk when I was in Salzburg, and wrote it, and had it translated into French at my own expense (I still have it)—proof of my best intentions. Then it turned out that some two years ago I had promised some learned society a talk on a different subject, and I didn't want to deliver two lectures in Paris at the same time, because—as you know—I like to guard my anonymity when I'm there, and don't want to be drawn into the social whirl. I asked the government councillor Hofman-Montanus whether someone else couldn't be found to speak on my behalf, and was all set to give him the lecture—my intentions were the *best*, and of course I was giving my services *for nothing, not even expenses*.

The lecture that I canceled—to be honest, because of Germany—was a year ago in Strasbourg, shortly after Hitler's coming to power. I would have made myself liable to attack if I, a German author, had spoken in *French* in *Strasbourg* of all places, where everyone understands German; Strasbourg friends of mine had told me under the then prevailing tensions it would cause embarrassment. I understood, as any sensible person would have understood it in my place.

This is all perfectly straightforward. But on the basis of it, and reports from Paris that were circulated against me in Vienna, I was made subject to a sort of inquiry, the newspapers were banned from publishing anything of mine, and there was tittle-tattle, as though I had been abroad, giving talks against Austria, about the latest developments. You will hardly believe that people can proceed in such fashion against someone who, as you know, both at home and abroad, has always been the most reticent of men, and discreet to the point of hysteria: but that is indeed the case, and it's no fabrication of mine and no exaggeration. Surely to God, they must understand in official places in Paris, where they know about the spread of my books, and my position there, the lengths I've gone to avoid every public utterance since the political poisoning of the world, and what *feats* I perform to prevent a single word of mine coming to light that was capable of being politically exploited. Here in London, the papers leave me alone, but you know yourself how I have to hide myself in Paris.

Sincere regards from   Stefan Zweig

Please for God's sake tell no one about this matter, otherwise it's certain to end up in the French and émigré newspapers.

If you were to go to the embassy in person, and offer a vigorous explanation, you would be doing me a service, because the situation is serious.

1. *Paris-Soir* or *L'Intransigeant*: both popular Parisian newspapers.

253. *Friderike and Stefan Zweig to Joseph Roth*   *[London]*
                                                            28 March 1934

Dear Joseph Roth,

Stefan says you've finished your book, and are pleased with it. I am very glad to hear it. Now you must reward yourself, and look to your health. If you are satisfied with your work you no longer have any excuse not to.

I send you my fond regards and all good wishes. There is so much we might talk about: I think you would understand how I view the situation, but there is too much of it, so I just send you my warmest good wishes

Yours, Friderike Z.

Dear friend, I didn't reply to your question yesterday. I never think of money matters when I think of you[1]—that's a complex of yours that you must shrug off. I am happy that you are for once satisfied with a piece of work, how good it must be for you, your own archenemy, to be proud of it!

You're not seeing my situation in the correct light. It is very serious. I am the subject of an investigation in Vienna, none of my friends will tell me what's going on, and the only cause is an accusation from Paris official channels concerning alleged talks, or public utterances given by me. Luckily I can prove that I haven't given any lectures, and only one interview, with no political content, three months ago, I haven't spoken to journalists, otherwise they would have fabricated an interview out of it, but how do you defend yourself against something when you don't even know what it is, or whom it's coming from. You'll remember that I told you, one of my closest friends (you remember, I said: because you're a drinker) that there are certain things of a personal or political nature that I just don't want to talk about, and you laughed—but that shows you how circumspect I, by nature so open and candid, have become. The denunciation that forms the basis of the Vienna investigation (of course my absence from Austria is accounted "suspicious" too, though it's to do with *Mary Stuart*[2] and America), has come from Paris, that's all I was able to find out about it; here too I have an official questionnaire to deal with, but evidently, because they know how I live and the manner of work that I do, they don't think it's worth accusing me in such a way. Oh, I'm so fed up with these torments, they always disturb my work, which is the only thing that matters to me.

1. when I think of you: not quite, and hard to see how he couldn't. For instance, when the writer Joseph Breitbach told SZ in 1935 that he was lending money to JR, Zweig warned him that it would cost him his friendship with Roth.

2. *Mary Stuart*: *Maria Stuart*, published in 1935; Zweig researched it in the British Museum in London.

254. *To Carl Seelig*   *Paris 6ᵉ*
                                               33 rue de Tournon
                                               Hotel Foyot
                                               28 March 1934

Dear Mr. Seelig,

things are so bad, I have decided to ask you for help.

Perhaps you could advance me some or all of the fee the newspaper is to pay me for my answers to the questionnaire?

I don't want to go into particulars. Awful things have happened. I am running around like a trapped mouse, there are no chinks between the bars, no way out.

I was sick for a long time. Even so I managed to finish a book, a new one. It's called *The Antichrist*. It's not a novel, but a sort of "wanted" poster of the Antichrist.

I'll send you a typescript in a week. Please, if you will, be very discreet, and tell me what you think of it.

I wish I didn't have to turn to you. I know you're a mensch. But I don't know if our relationship is ready for something like this. I don't know anything any more. I can no longer look after myself. Don't be angry with me, please!

Sincerely, your   Joseph Roth

I need the loan of Picard's book,[1] just for a fortnight. Can you help me?

1. Probably *Das Menschengesicht* (The Human Face), 1930.

255. *To Carl Seelig*

Paris 6ᵉ
33 rue de Tournon
Hotel Foyot
24 April 1934

Dear Mr. Carl Seelig,

awful things have kept me from writing to you straightaway. Thank you so much for all your kindness and affection. I will write you in more detail by hand soon. Please be patient with me. Things are very bad.

I send you my sincere gratitude.

I am very unhappy. I will write soon.

Yours, Joseph Roth

256. Stefan Zweig to Joseph Roth   *[April or May 1934]*

Courage, dear friend. I must have your novel SOON. Huebsch will be here at the beginning of June, and the film person, I will HAVE to have it then. Get on to Landauer!

Your Hollywood-style *Job* is said to be, well, exquisite. They've turned Mendel Singer into a Tyrolean peasant. Menuchim yodels. I simply have to see it. I will roll in the aisles on your behalf.

You must work. I am working too, on that novella, which is more of a Jewish legend,[1] built up by me from a very slender foundation. I think it will turn out well, though I'm not given to optimistic prognoses. I'm not yet convinced of the style. For that I need your once-over. But all in all, it's looking good. I can write only things that are in some relation to the time, and that have something comforting about them, in spite of their tragic philosophy. Before long, you'll have my Castellio to read.

I'm glad the money has got to you. Please don't send or give any of it away. Pay your hotel bill for three weeks *in advance*, so you can work undisturbed. You must have some tranquillity.

My wife is in Salzburg. Since she's gone I'm quiet and clear in my head, and working smoothly and peacefully. Really all we need is peace and quiet, and a little solitude. In a fortnight at the latest, I'll have the legend finished. Then I'll take a deep breath, and write another couple of decisive moments (for my *Collected Novellas*, a selection from thirty years, old and new, which Reichner will be bringing out in two volumes in the fall). Then South America for a couple of months.

Warmly,   your Stefan Z.

1. more of a Jewish legend: this sounds like Zweig's novella *The Buried Candelabrum* (1936).

257. *To Carl Seelig* *Paris, 6 May 1934*

Dear Mr. Carl Seelig,

you really do have superhuman patience where I am concerned. Thank you so much. Now, if you will just wait a little, I will write in more detail, and in the way I wish I could write to you today. I'm getting *Tarabas* sent to you today. Unfortunately, I have no copies here, and everything has to go via Amsterdam.

There are many reasons for my unhappiness. Please be patient a little longer.

With sincere gratitude, your Joseph Roth

258. *To Blanche Gidon* *Hotel Foyot*
Paris
9 May 1934

Dear Madam,

what I have to say to you I am unable to say in French. Please therefore allow me to write in German.

I was quite shaken when I left your house last night. Shaken by the proofs of your kindness and humanity toward me. *I didn't deserve them. I didn't deserve them.*

It's something I'm cursed with, that I sometimes hurt people who are dear to me. I know I have hurt you. I beg you please to forgive me.

I am shaken too by Mr. Gidon's goodness. It's quite extraordinary that an important man should undertake something so difficult for my sake. I will never forget that. Please give him my warmest regards.

I used to think I was smart, and had graduated from the school of life.

In the last few weeks, I have learned that I am stupid, a fool, and an idiot.

I have learned it with you too.

Please forgive me all the ill I have done to you.

Your faithful   Joseph Roth

259. *To Hermann Hesse*   *Paris 6ᵉ*
                                                 Hotel Foyot
                                                 33 rue de Tournon
                                                 18 May 1934

Most esteemed Mr. Hermann Hesse,[1]

I happened to read in the 6 May edition of the *Basler National Zeitung* the flattering lines you wrote on my book. Allow me, the younger man, who when still a boy worshipped your books, to thank you profoundly, and to tell you what an honor it is to be praised by your pen.

I beg you to excuse me that I don't have a copy to hand, to send you with an inscription. There are irksome customs barriers between Amsterdam and Paris, that won't permit me to send for personal copies from Holland without high penalties.

In long-standing veneration, I remain your humble   Joseph Roth

1. Hermann Hesse (1877–1962), Swiss author of *Steppenwolf* and many other books. Won the Nobel Prize for Literature in 1946.

260. *To René Schickele*   *Saturday [1934]*

Dear Mr. René Schickele,

since you will best know where a letter will find Annette Kolb at this moment, I ask you kindly to forward the enclosed to her. Her book is MAGNIFICENT,[1] and I want her to know it right away.

And one other favor, if you will: I want to exploit your "unpatriotic mastery of foreign tongues." I would like to send my *Antichrist* to Thérive and Praz,[2] with inscriptions that will indicate that I am aware of what their good opinion might mean. "Hommages" is too general. What can I say that would be short, pithy, and not too groveling in French?

Please don't mind that I'm availing myself of your helpfulness! Thank you!

Yours sincerely   Joseph Roth

And please, if you will, just a word back to tell me the letter to Annette is safely on its way.

1. her book: *Die Schaukel* (The Swing).

2. Praz: Mario Praz (1896–1982), the noted critic and writer on the Romantics (*The Romantic Agony*, 1930).

261. *To Blanche Gidon (written in French)*   Hotel Foyot

Paris

[postmarked: 20 May 1934]

Thank you, dear Madam Gidon!

Please, I beg you, don't believe all the "scuttlebutt" people tell you—as Miss Kolb was wont to say to me.

I hope to see you again one day.

My obeisances to Mr. Gidon.

Yours devotedly,   Joseph Roth

262. *To Fritz Helmut Landshoff*   Hotel Foyot

Paris, 26 May 1934

Dear Mr. Landshoff,

thank you for your thoroughness. Let's stick to the numbered headings, it'll be easier to follow.

1. The Englishman[1] will send the contract for me to Mrs. Vallentin

today or tomorrow. Probably he will have agreed to my demands. (But I don't *know* that he will.) The novellas[2] are included in the contract, also my two following books.

2. If I agree to give you the novellas before the novel is ready for de Lange, then I run two risks: (a) I may risk Walter[3] far too early; it would have the same effect as concluding an "entire" deal with Querido right away. (b) I risk losing the Englishman; in which case Querido, as the only contractual partner, would give me less than he does at present.

From which follows (a) that it seems impossible to me to have the novellas announced or published before I deliver the novel to L.[4] (b) that I get from you the absolute certainty—even if the English interest disappears—of getting everything *he* offers me; otherwise I would be missing out on a good opportunity.

3. It seems to me I will *have* to leave L. The only impediment is Walter. But then I don't have as much time as he does. My only choice is between you and the English. And I have to make up my mind before I leave.

4. You probably see Walter all the time. He must know whether he can still work with L., or not. If he still doesn't know, and doesn't tell me either way today or tomorrow, then I will have to decide before I leave here—whether it's you or the Englishman. I can't sell my fate to a madman. If I decide in favor of Querido, then it would be better if you tried—with Walter's support—to buy back my next book from L. It's a surefire success, on account of its theme.

I have no time. I am provided for for the next 4 weeks. After that I will be in Marseille, starving. I don't have time to wait for the whims of a lunatic.

Please write me straightaway whether Querido is ready to match the English conditions. Or better still, wire! (I might be leaving as early as Monday.)

In general, the English will be giving me about the same as L. (This is the basis) 80% foreign rights, 40% set off against advance, 40% payable immediately to me, 850 marks per month.

If L. really hasn't spoken to Walter yet, then I won't believe in L's interest in German literature any more.

5. The personal dedications have gone out.

6. *Rischon le Zion* is the destination, Palestine will do. (Erna Steiner.)

7. So far as the *Sammlung* is concerned, I enclose this letter to Dr. Wasserbäck, the secretary at the embassy. Would you please send it, along with your own, registered, to the addressee, at the Austrian embassy, Paris. I'll give you a rough draft—only rough, mind. KM can refine it. Esteemed Dr. Wasserbäck, we turn to you at the suggestion of Joseph Roth, the Austrian writer. Mr. Roth, who, as you know, is a patriotic Austrian, is working with us on our magazine. His collaboration, if nothing else, would tend to rule out a radical left-wing orientation for our magazine, which is in any case an unpartisan literary journal. The unhappy article about Austria came to be in our magazine through a mistake on the part of a Dutch editor (or publisher), whose German was not good enough. The editors of the *Sammlung*[5] are prepared at any time to publish an official rebuttal from an official Austrian source. Many conservative Austrian authors write for us. They surely deserve to be read in Austria. The character of our *Sammlung* is purely literary. A single error surely cannot lead to the banning of the journal. We beseech you to mediate . . . etc.

8. At the same time, you can write a little more freely—because he's a Jew—to *Dr. Martin Fuchs*, also at the Austrian embassy, Paris. You might suggest to him that he compose an official reply.

9. In general: don't bother appealing to rigid official-line people. *I* could have written you a fairer and less damaging article about Austria than that.

10. I'm meeting your wife tomorrow. My personal and family life is ghastly.

Sincerely,   your old Joseph Roth

Herewith the letter to Wasserbäck (Dr. Erwin): put it in a separate *sealed* envelope.

1. the Englishman: Roth was in negotiations with a Mr. Reece at the Albatross Press (*sic*!), an English reprint publisher, about the financing of some of his books.

2. the novellas: probably *The Coral Seller*, first printed in *Das neue Tagebuch*, in

Paris, in December 1934. It appeared in book form as *The Leviathan* with Querido, Amsterdam, in 1940.

3. Walter: Walter Landauer.

4. L.: de Lange.

5. the *Sammlung*: Klaus Mann's magazine *Die Sammlung* had been banned in Austria because it had carried an anti-Austrian article—a heavy blow for the exile magazine. Much of what follows here is the attempt to restore its credit.

263. To Erwin Wasserbäck   *Hotel Foyot*
                                                  33 rue de Tournon
                                                  Paris 6ᵉ
                                                  26 May 1934

Dear and highly esteemed friend,

I approach you with a heartfelt request: the *Sammlung*, a purely *literary* and if anything rather *conservative* periodical, for which I *personally write*, has fallen victim to a stupid article by our stupid old compatriot Stefan Grossmann[1] about Austria, and has therefore been banned in that country.

As I say, I'm a contributor. There are other conservative Austrian writers whose work this periodical helps to disseminate.

It's perverse that, for instance, the Communist, Moscow-bankrolled *Neue Deutsche Blätter*, published in Prague, and where Mr. Ehrenburg[2] unleashes savage screeds against Austria, is *not* banned at home.

What can be done? The *Sammlung* would be happy to redress the balance by publishing an "official" article on Austria.

It's unjust to ban it, and to permit the Muscovite *Neue Deutsche Blätter* to continue to appear.

Can you help?

The *Sammlung* has quite rightly asked me to represent them. I do so with the clear conscience of one who—as you know—is a *passionate* Austrian.

I send you salutations in old dear friendship,

your old Joseph Roth

1. Grossmann: Stefan Grossman (1875–1935), an Austrian journalist, co-founder of the weekly *Das Tagebuch* with Leopold Schwarzschild, which the latter went on to edit alone.

2. Ehrenburg: Ilya Ehrenburg (1891–1967), novelist, essayist, a ubiquitous figure in those days, working now for the Bolshevik regime, and now as an exile against it.

264. Stefan Zweig to Joseph Roth [May 1934?]

[. . .]

representations, and reverted to my erstwhile student nature. I have begun to learn again, like a high school kid. I am once again uncertain, and full of curiosity. Now, at age fifty-three, I am enjoying the love of a young woman![1] A book like yours is perhaps a lesson to me not to forget the bitterness of this world. My political pessimism is boundless. I believe in the coming war, the way others believe in God. But merely *because* I believe in it, I am living more intensely now. I hang on to the last shred of freedom we still enjoy. Every morning I thank the Lord that I am free, and in England. Picture my happiness, in such a lunatic age, I feel strong enough to lend moral support to others. That's why I am so sorry that you are not here with me, who knows how long my strength may endure, strength that comes, I repeat, not from ignorance, but from a lucid sense of the brittleness of our existence. "In spite of" and "for all that" need to become our watch words in life: "to understand people and still to love them," as Rolland unforgettably said.

I embrace you, dear friend. I suffer from the fact that you're so far away. The last time, in the teeth of my difficulties—I didn't tell you: they had searched our house in Salzburg two days before, and looked through my sock drawers for weapons of the Schutzbund,[2] and I had the strength to keep quiet about this flagrant show of disrespect from a city where I have been living for 15 years, and thank God it didn't get into the papers, they persecute me with reports from spies as if I was a criminal—all that was weighing me down, when I spoke with you in Paris I was quite beside myself with my own silence and shame (or rather, the shame of those others). But how I should like to see you now, when I am myself again, and almost cheerful.

You should have my *Erasmus*[3] in a fortnight. I think it's a decent book (written for the small readership of those who understand halftones.)

Once again, then: love and gratitude.

I'll probably be in Austria in August, straightening out one or two things. But Salzburg is over for me, in the fall I'm going to lecture in North or South America. I have an appetite for distant places again, and the desire to see this world in the round once more, before it burns.

1. the love of a young woman: Zweig had started an affair with his secretary, Lotte Altmann, later to be his second wife. Roth, one feels, disapproved (personal happiness would not have struck him as possible or even permissible at such a juncture), and was in any case bound also by his affectionate relationship with Friderike Zweig.

2. Schutzbund: (literally, protective union), an organization founded by members of the SPÖ.

3. my *Erasmus*: *Triumph und Tragik des Erasmus von Rotterdam*.

265. To Blanche Gidon (written in French)   [no date]

Dear friend,

this is a lady[1] I recommend to you; she could work for you or your friends. She is Polish, persecuted by Hitler, and very unhappy. She will tell you about it, if you care to listen to her. Could you help her make 200 francs a month, for her poor children (two of them, about 5 years old)?

Thank you very much, my friend.

Entirely yours   Joseph Roth

She needs addresses. She is very hardworking.

I've known her for a long time.

1. lady: a Mrs. Kokotek, conveyor of this card to Blanche Gidon. JR's generosity and willingness to help strangers and unfortunates—while often in desperate straits himself—is wonderful and extraordinary.

266. To Blanche Gidon (written in French)   *Marseille*
     4 rue Beauvau
     1 June 1934

Dear Madam and friend (if I may presume to address you like this!).
I'm pretty well set up here. This afternoon, I'm going to start working.
I'll write to you again in a week, and maybe I'll even be able to send
you the story for the *NL* (20 pages?).[1]
Entirely yours (and Mr. Gidon's)
Your old Joseph Roth

1. The story for the *Nouvelles Littéraires* was *Triomphe de la Beauté* (The Triumph
of Beauty), first published in 1934, in Blanche Gidon's translation.

267. To Blanche Gidon (written in French)   *Grand Café Glacier*
     La Canebière
     Marseille
     4 June 1934

Dear Madam and Friend,
thank you for the article! I've corrected a few words in it. The sentence
on the Austrian officer, etc.[1] made me laugh. It seems to me the aristocratic genius of the French language is opposed to personal professions of
faith—just as the genius of German seems to call for them. In French it
comes across as "too personal." Ah, how I wish I could write in French!
Now, at almost forty, I'm at last beginning to understand that writing in
just one language is like having only one arm. Having two fatherlands,
I ought to be able to master two mother tongues. But I am old! And the
language of a country is still more difficult to know than its inhabitants!
This is all too difficult for me to say—I am shaping the expressions in
German in my mind.

Once again: thank you for your goodness to little Manga![2]

You are good, good, good. I will always be put to shame.

Your old Joseph Roth

1. In the series *une heure avec*, the journalist Frederic Lefèvre had conducted an interview with JR, to which he had given somewhat fantastical replies. See no. 244.

2. Manga: Manga Bell's son went by that name.

268. *To Blanche Gidon (written in French)*   Hotel Beauvau

                                                      Marseille, 7 June 1934

Madam and dear friend,

thank you for your letter and please excuse the typed reply. I spend all day writing, and am simply too tired to take pen in hand.

Yesterday I finished my story for the *Nouvelles Littéraires*. Tomorrow I'm getting it typed, and you'll have it the day after. I hope it'll be of interest to your readers. Myself, I think it's good enough to go in my next collection of novellas that is now under discussion.

It will contain three novellas, and I make so bold as to ask you, madam, to translate two of them; half of the third was translated some time ago by an old friend of mine, Madam Vallentin. I will also ask you to show the letter here enclosed to Monsieur Lefèvre. I hadn't read the interview with him. Thank you for having sent it.

It seems to me he took me for a Trebitsch-Lincoln type,[1] rather than a Joseph Roth. As far as the public is concerned, he's probably right. (All this between us, please.)

Madam and dear friend, you are very dear to me, but I won't be able to write to you again for a fortnight, not before I've finished my three novellas, the first of which you'll have in your hands tomorrow or the day after. But please write to me yourself, in the meantime, if you're not angry with me.

If the novella seems too long, please tell me right away. I have the feeling it's all right as it is.

My sincere and heartfelt greetings to Mr. Gidon.

Your already aged friend and more   Joseph Roth

1. a Trebitsch-Lincoln type: Ignaz Tebitsch-Lincoln (1879–1943), a rather adventurous journalist, Buddhist monk, and political agent. If Lefèvre came to such a conclusion, it will no doubt have been with the encouragement if not the connivance of JR.

269. *To Blanche Gidon (written in French)*   *Hotel Beauvau*
Marseille
14 June 1934

Madam and friend,

thank you with all my heart for your letter. If women were to think my novella[1] is directed against them, I would be sorry. It's not informed by misogyny—it's simply my conviction that a woman finding a man incapable of loving her as she would like to be loved will one day become a plaything of the devil's. That would be a possible title for my poor little tale: "The Devil in Miss Gwendoline." Of course, not a serious possibility. I hope it's not too long to be published.

I will write to you once I've finished my third story, and am in possession of a contract. Forgive me for not writing you a longer letter today—and forgive me too for turning to you for *practical advice*.

I would like to enroll Mrs. Manga Bell's son in a military academy. Since he was born in Paris—and hence France—the son of a French protégé from Cameroon, it ought to be easy. I don't have any more money to keep him, nor does Mrs. Manga Bell. I don't have the feeling he's any more [*sic*] gifted than I am, and I made it to officer.

It's all rather urgent. The little fellow has finished the year at school, and I can't pay his fees any more. He must be in the military academy 4 weeks from now, or 8 at the outside.

I know I'm allowed to abuse your kindness, madam. But if I am presuming too much, perhaps Mr. Poupet could assist?

As for Mr. Breitbach,[2] he has, as we say, made his bed and must lie in it. It's a typical literary feud. Mr. Breitbach discussed his article with Mr. Kesten. Mr. Kesten discussed it with the (Communist) Mr. Weiskopf in Prague. And so it comes about that the Communist—they are in a hurry, because the World Revolution keeps not happening—has dashed off an article in response to an article that has yet to appear.

I am sad about this. I wanted to write a reply myself—and can't because that would be making common cause with the Communistic Weiskopf. (I haven't read his article.) At any rate, I would have written a different sort of reply, and I would first have shown it to Mr. Breitbach.

If you see him, tell him this. Apart from that, it wasn't exactly noble of him to write an article like his at precisely this moment. Certainly, I am more "reactionary" than Mr. Breitbach. But anyway, it's in poor taste to go singing German songs now. I have never associated with left-wing Jews like Mr. Breitbach. And now he denounces them to the French public for being "not German"! It's so childish. And not at all noble. [. . .] And then if someone like Breitbach claims to know "real Germans" [. . .] and begins in the manner of his literary heroes, by loving his dim "blond Gretchens"—well, between ourselves . . .

Excuse me, dear friend, for talking to you thus frankly.

Greet Mr. Gidon for me.

I remain your loyal and appreciative friend   Joseph Roth

Mrs. Manga Bell sends you her very sincere regards.

1. my novella: *The Triumph of Beauty*, whose leading female character, Gwendoline, is a relentless flirt.

2. Mr. Breitbach: Joseph Breitbach (1903–1980), playwright, novelist, journalist.

270. *To Stefan Zweig*

Hotel Beauvau
Marseille
14 June 1934

Dear friend,

your letter made me as happy as it is possible for me to be in the circumstances in which I have now been living for many months. I believe
my *Antichrist* is an honest outcry, not a book, I know how bitter my life
is becoming for universal reasons—and unfortunately also for personal
reasons—but it's basically all one; I wrote my *Antichrist* out of private
need. Very private.

Film is not just a contemporary phenomenon. It may make people
happy, but the devil sometimes does that. I am unalterably persuaded
that the devil shows himself, so to speak, in living shadow play. The
shadow that speaks and acts is what *Satan* is. The cinema marks the
beginning of the twentieth century. It ushers in the end of the world.
Please don't underestimate that. Telephone, radio, aeroplane, are nothing in comparison to it: the separation of the shadow from the man.
It's a turning point in human history, more significant than the Russian
Revolution with its so-called liberation of the "proletariat." (If only it had
freed people instead! But of course it couldn't do that.)

You're right: I didn't plan the *Antichrist*, but simply wrote it out, and
for the first time in my life, I felt detached from this world. I got a sense
of what a saint might feel, if such a one ever sat down to write. I was
simultaneously furious and ecstatic. I'm sure a few trivial and irrelevant
things will have made it into the book. But I still have the feeling that
it's not a book of mine, rather as though someone had dictated it to me. I
don't have the right to do more than correct the misprints.

I read what you told me about Salzburg[1] with astonishment and indignation. If it hadn't been you telling me these things, I wouldn't have believed
them. If we pooled our imaginations, we still couldn't come up with such
vileness. What was it? The revenge of jealous people? There was certainly
no simple-minded credulity involved. It was malice, insane malice.

I understand why you can never go back to Salzburg.

For purely selfish reasons I am very unhappy that you are going so far away. Of course I am pleased for you as well, but let me tell you straight: here you are my most influential friend and—even if that's not what I like you for—I do find your power pleasant and soothing. You don't know, you have no idea how I live. Your great and shining cleverness doesn't recognize me, *can't see me*, even though I'm one of your most honest friends. Between us too the Antichrist has cast his shadow.

I beseech you now—and don't make me mention it again—it costs you so little to get me an advance from an English publisher. They will listen to you. I beg you, I implore you to take this trouble upon yourself! Take the rope off my neck that's on the point of choking me! Please, please understand. I'm going down, I'm already wallowing in filth. All sorts of ugly private painful humiliating things on top of that. I cannot WRITE to you about them. In spite of that, I've completed 2 novellas, each of 40 pages. I'm working like a pack-ass. I have worries, such worries, and I'm so UNHAPPY. Please, please secure a little freedom for me. I can't live like this any more, it's killing me. Absolutely. Is that what you want? Do you think I'm blackmailing you? I'm writing to you in desperate need. Please will you talk to the publishers.

Please. And let's meet BEFORE you go. Definitely.

I embrace you,   your old J.R.

1. about Salzburg: i.e., the searching of SZ's house for weapons. Soon after, Zweig moved to London.

271. *To Stefan Zweig*   *Marseille*
                                                          Hotel Beauvau
                                                          22 June 1934

Dear true friend,

I know I ask too much of you. I am writing to you again today, even though I wrote to you only yesterday. I want to thank you first for your letter about Gollancz.[1] I have *no* agent, Landauer and de Lange didn't try to sell the *Antichrist* in England. It might not be easy for you—or pleasant—to hear all the acts of folly I perpetrated since you left Paris—all under the pressure of repulsive experiences. I know how difficult it is even for a great understanding to cope with a small derangement. But I still beg you to continue to think of me as a sensible person subject to occasional fits of madness but broadly in control, and as a conscientious friend who only writes like this in hours of clarity. I have debased and humiliated myself. I have borrowed money from the most impossible places, despising and cursing myself as I did so. And it was all because never in my life have I had anything like a secure financial base, never a bank account or savings. Nothing, nothing, just advances—expenditure, expenditure, advances, and until the Third Reich, I had publishers. (And I've paid all my debts in Germany.) When you were in Paris, I only had 2,000 francs of debts. Since then it's risen to 11,000 urgent, pressing, terrible debts. I feel obliged to come before you quite naked, my dear friend. Whatever you do, you cannot judge me more harshly than I do myself. I abuse you too, with the desperate selfishness of someone putting the life of his friend in danger by clinging to him like a drowning man clinging to his rescuer. I can think of no other image! If anything is able to exculpate me in your eyes and in my own—which are probably more indulgent—then it will be this: that I am working every day, that here in Marseille I've written 3 half-decent novellas, each of 35–40 pages. At the beginning of October I need to hand in my novel, which is just one-third written. I can't go out any more. I've felt the rope around my neck for months now—and if I haven't been throttled, it's purely because every now and then some good-natured individual comes along and allows me to push a finger in between my neck and the rope. And straight after, the rope draws tight again. With the rope around my neck like that, I work for 6–8 hours a day. If you knew what commitments I'd incurred, you would laugh. But my dear friend, I must be free, just once, the relaxing of the noose isn't enough, it has to be taken off. Oh, please, I need 12,000 francs by the end of August. Maybe an English publisher will provide them. Maybe, maybe! I am working, it's all I can do, I can't do more! Please, please don't forsake me! Don't take anything here amiss! Picture me lying flat out on my deathbed. Forgive me. I have drunk nothing while writing this to you. I am stone-cold sober.

I embrace you fervently,   your J.R.

1. Victor Gollancz (1893–1967) was a British publisher, who gave his name to his imprint.

272. *To Blanche Gidon (written in French)*   *Hotel Beauvau*
                                                            30 June 1934
                                                            Marseille

Madam and dear friend,

forgive me for interrupting your painstaking labor, but it's to do with the article about Breitbach. Hermann Hesse *is Swiss*, and I would certainly not have written that he *has become Swiss*. He wrote to me very kindly about my book, and I would risk losing a friend who is very proud of his nationality just as, in fact, Switzerland is very proud of him. I risk losing other Swiss friends. Mr. Breitbach can hardly say he is "of Swabian extraction." *All* German Swiss are of Swabian extraction. Just as all the Swiss from the canton of Geneva are of French extraction. The Swiss from the Ticino are of Italian extraction. We, the Austrians, are of Bavarian extraction. No, it's impossible to claim that Hesse has become Swiss. One might as well say that Mr. Gidon was of "Norman" or Germanic extraction. Or that Rilke "was Czech" and "had become Austrian." [. . .] It's the desire to conquer the whole world on account of its Germanic roots, as far as the Italians of Milano, who are of "Vandal extraction." No, Hesse is Swiss, just as Rilke, Kafka, and I are Austrians—for the whole world, except [. . .] and Breitbach.

I'm sorry. But if he gets threatening letters I have to say he himself writes letters to all and sundry, foolish, imprudent letters. [. . .] I know that at bottom he's a good boy. [. . .] He's one of those people who will always have "contacts" and "acquaintances," but never any friends [. . .]

Enough. It's not worth the trouble. Forgive me, my dear friend. Each time I write to you, I congratulate myself on having found you. And as I have already once had the unhappy experience of showing you my fatal propensity for shamelessness, believe me equally when I say how fond I am of you and of Mr. Gidon.

Your loyal friend, Joseph Roth

273. *To Carl Seelig*   *Marseille*
                             Hotel Beauvau
                             7 July 1934
                             (*good as an address,* even though I'm leaving)

My dear, dear Mr. Seelig,

one day, *in case* we should ever meet again, I may be able to say to you how wretched I am. No—I'm still no better.

Thank you very much for your good opinion of my *Tarabas*. It's a *bad* book.

The *Antichrist*—which I think is *good*—is going out to you in uncorrected galleys. (Lacking the quotations from Picard's book, which need to be added.)

I am very fond of you, the longer since I last saw you, the fonder I become.

Write soon!   Your Joseph Roth

274. Stefan Zweig to Joseph Roth   *11 Portland Place*
                                                  London, 10 July [1934]

Dear friend,

now the whole thing is fucked again, and it's not my fault. I asked
you expressly whether you had the rights to your book, and it turns out
that you're contracted to Heinemann[1] for the next two. I now need to
conciliate, so that Viking doesn't take your doings amiss, and I will talk
to Ginzburg,[2] who is here at the moment, tomorrow, I hope. It's such a
pity, my dear fellow! If only you'd informed me correctly! I did my best
for you, and was quite close to gaining my objective!

Your Stefan Zweig

   1. Heinemann: William Heinemann Ltd., a London publishing house.
   2. Ginzburg: Harold Ginzburg, co-owner and (with Ben Huebsch) director of
Viking Press, the New York publisher.

275. To Stefan Zweig   *Dégustation Cintra*
                                                  Marseille
                                                  11 July 1934

My dear friend,

thank you for your telegram and letter. Of course I wrote to Gollancz
straightaway. It's a great coup, only unfortunately my foolish publishers—
how often you wisely warned me against my friends L. and L.![1]—force
me to pay 60% to de Lange. Of the 2,000 dollars that Huebsch was
paid—for film rights to *Job*—Landshoff gets 1,600 gulden, and I barely
3,500 francs. You have no idea how furious I am with myself; much less
how the others, taking advantage of my craziness and helplessness, are
furious with me. It's the story of Aladdin and the 40 thieves, only with
a bad ending.

I'm leaving in two hours. My chum Hermann Kesten has invited me, because he's seen how wretchedly off I am. His address will be the one, until further notice: *119, Promenade des Anglais (for J.R.).* I won't be able to stick it with him for long. He has his wife and mother with him. After two days I'll have to move into a hotel. I can't share a toilet with acquaintances, and be seen in pajamas[2] and see others so dressed. Grisly! Sooner be completely destitute, as once before. No other possibility. I'm too sick.

Please give Mr. Gollancz my address sometime. At the time I wrote to him, I wasn't sure when I was leaving.

Should I thank you? In what form? It would be so much easier for me to think up an entire novel, than a warm and yet dignified way of expressing my gratitude to you. When did I ever have a friend like you? As good? As noble? As natural? Since the time I got your first letter to me—here in Marseille—five or 6 years ago, I've had a sense of being happier (the feeling of a barge at sea, when it encounters a steamer, I imagine, naumorphically) and unfortunately also the feeling that I'm bringing you bad luck. And believe me, this friendship is very difficult to bear.

And I still have something more to beg of you, harder than everything I've sought from you so far: will you give me 10 lines or so from your latest book, *Erasmus*—unpublished, to set at the head of it, or to conclude the book with—that might fit (or fit by association) with my *Antichrist*. I am asking for quotations from friends, to proof it—call it superstitious of me—against hell.

Yes, you strike me as very cheerful, and it makes me glad. Your words are full of cheer.

If only you knew how I felt! How ringed with darkness! For days at a time, I fear for my reason, and presentiments come back that I haven't had since boyhood: that I will go mad at the same age as my father. My dear friend, my sufferings are appalling! Work is flight, for me. I have written 3 novellas and 6 articles, and many private jottings for myself. I am horribly beset with mortal and immortal darknesses. Write to me right away, at Kesten's address. As soon as I've found a cheap hotel, I'll give you that address.—I wish I could throw my arms around you. The business with Gollancz made good sense, I am so, so fond of you. Rescue me please, believe in me, believe in my reason not least!

Your old J.R.

1. L. and L.: Landauer and Landshoff.
2. pajamas: A slightly frivolous-sounding but inalienable principle of the self-styled "hotel-patriot" Joseph Roth.

276. *To Blanche Gidon (written in French)*   *Grand Café Glacier*
                                                           Marseille
                                                           11 July 1934

Madam, dear friend,

you can't have known how much I would panic on learning that you lent me 500 francs in 1934. How will I ever get out of my debts! At least write and tell me how much the *Weekly Review* is paying you! This is awful! Write to me—quickly! Urgent!

The address of Mr. Moreaux is Vauxvain [?], Oise, près Gisors, Eure, 75 km from Paris.

But he's already written, Mrs. Manga Bell will write to you. I am leaving, to stay with my friend *Hermann Kesten*, 199 Promenade des Anglais, Nice.

Here, I've completed 3 novellas and 6 articles, I must write another 6 articles and a novella before I can get on to my novel. Write to me! And remember to look up my friend Fuchs at the Austrian embassy, *well in advance* of your departure for Austria. If practical, take Mr. Poupet with you. He is a good friend, a good politician, a good sort—but he won't write to me. You always have to *go and see him and speak to him*. He is "concrete" like a good many of my compatriots: they're not good at physical distance.

[Joseph Roth]

277. *To Walter Landauer*
Hotel Nordzee, Zandvoort [*Nice, no date*]

Wire right away what to do stop Zweig is writing Gollancz heard from Heinemann that contract exists between Heinemann and Huebsch for Antichrist as Huebsch has rights to next two books stop wire Zweig 11 Portland Place London my innocence stop check contracts send Zweig and me copies address Kesten Nice

Roth

278. *To Stefan Zweig*
11 Portland Place, London [*Nice, no date*]

Inform Gollancz immediately that according to information from Kiepenheuer and Landshoff Antichrist rights free stop wire him also stop preserve my honesty at all costs stop Huebsch subcontract with Heinemann only applies to novels am in despair wire me address Kesten 119 promenade des anglais Nice

Roth

279. *To Victor Gollancz*
London (written in English) [*Nice, no date*]

Assure by my honor that conforming to informations of my German publisher Antichrist free and agreement Viking and Heinemann does not apply Antichrist stop near explanations follow

Joseph Roth

280. To Stefan Zweig   *Nice*
                                                    13 July 1934

Dear friend,

I am writing to you in high excitement, half an hour after wiring you and Gollancz.

I enclose a letter from my publisher Landauer—proof that I couldn't have known of the agreement between Huebsch and Heinemann about *Antichrist.*

I implore you, *please explain this to Messrs. Gollancz and Huebsch and Ginzburg.* I am an innocent victim—I'm terrified that I'll be seen as a swindler.

I am writing to you in high excitement, I am washed up. 40% of 100 pounds does not represent salvation.

I am finished.

I've telegraphed away the last of my money, including to Gollancz, in wretched English. Please, I care desperately about preserving my *honor.* Help me! It's all I can do to keep stammering those words.

Please believe me. You know me. Landshoff and Landauer told me *Tarabas* was the last book that I had under contract to Viking.

[. . .]

I am beside myself, at the end of my tether, finished, I am feeling close to suicide, for the first time in my life.

I beg you, my dear friend, your   J.R.

1. *Orcovente*[1]

You remember this exotically named company set up by my friends: Landauer, Landshoff, and Schottländer (garment dealer in Berlin) after Hitler's accession, and on my behalf, as Landauer told me at the time.

Apparently, this company shelled out 6,000 Swiss francs to Kiepenheuer Verlag, to free up my foreign rights.

So all the moneys for my foreign rights were paid in to "Orcovente."

In the meantime, Viking had sent 2,000 dollars to Kiepenheuer [. . .]

In the meantime, as you will recall, little Rosner[2] became a fixture in my house, and—voluntarily, as I believed at the time—my secretary.

He had also become—by my agency—because I took him to be poor and honest—Landauer's secretary.

He lied to me, he couldn't even type—and Mrs. Manga Bell did all his typing for him.

One day Kesten became aware of some inconsistencies,[3] and threw him out.

(I paid half his tab at the Hotel Foyot—750 francs.)

[. . .]

Kindly note, from the top part of my letter, which I have drawn up with all my available papers, to the best of my ability, and with the assistance of the very conscientious Mr. Kesten, that I am not so stupid as I might sometimes appear.

2. Kindly note, further, that, for all the friendly feeling between us, you would do well to avoid looking at your best friend in too predictable and summary a fashion: I am not just a Jew inclined to "lostness" but also a savvy Jew; I am not just a disinherited lieutenant of the old army, used to shelling out 60% of everything, but also one of those used to lending money to officers of my type; it's not Huebsch on the one side (caricature version thereof) and me (caricature version thereof) on the other.

3. Straining myself to the utmost, in feverish agitation, tormented by the thought *to whom* and *why* I have to pay money in 8 days' time—terrible, terrible—*you have no idea how terrible!*—I am writing to you with colored crayons, and in the hope you might break free of the iced-over notions of me that you have formed. (This isn't a game, you know.)

4. I have always told you the truth. What I didn't like about you, what I did. But desperation and torment and what has offended and hurt and upset and destroyed me was never so strong as now, in all the time I've been fond of you. And I tell you now, with the justification of the condemned friend that you are unfair to me, *unfair*, UNFAIR!!—You do

NOT have the right to judge me from your privileged knowledge of my person in the way one (*you too, alas*) judges other people whose external situation may resemble mine.

5. Even if I'm pissed, I'm still sufficiently sober to understand who's trying to diddle me and who isn't.

6. You're smart. I'm not. But I see things you can't, because your smartness blinds you to them. You have the grace of reason, and I of unhappiness. Don't give me any more advice—help me, act for me. I'm going under.

Is it possible you have so much brilliant insight into dead figures—and none for your living friend? Or am I dead to you? Listen, I am still alive, I am a human being, I can see for instance that Gollancz shows solidarity with Heinemann, and is therefore withdrawing his offer.

And you have no right to distrust my insight as if it were some grocer's.

Oh, what do I care! Just tell me you don't like getting letters from me.

I know the process:

Gollancz doesn't want to antagonize Heinemann.

The *Antichrist could* be a success!

They don't want to step on each other's toes. Solidarity! You withdraw your offer and call a man of honor a cheat.

Not with me you don't!

I DON'T WANT YOU going through my affairs with a publisher.

Believe me or don't believe me. See for yourself! And while you're going through my affairs, just set aside for a while your preconceptions regarding my character.

Don't you worry, I'm as clever as your Huebsches, your Gollanczes, your Heinemanns and your Landauers!

I was just lazy, and easily deceived.

I've had it anyway.

In my will I will write down the names of all those I mistrust.

(I'll send you a copy.)

None of my tormentors will take any pleasure in my end.

Gollancz has offended me—I am going to challenge him. What do I

care about his "bond" with Heinemann. Heinemann gave bad information. Landauer and Landshoff never gave me any statements.[4] I destroy
all my manuscripts. I'm making a will. It won't be any good for anyone
if I die. But before that, I'm going to kill at least 2 grocers who have the
cheek to accuse me of cheating. No apologies! And that's called "solidarity." It's the Antichrist. Mr. Reece is in the picture. I've lost because I
was careless—lost my life. Well, *soit*. The war was no fun either. I was
doomed 15 years ago.—Write to me straightaway, and tell me you wash
your hands of me. Go with God. I am very fond of you. I embrace you.
Believe me,

    your J.R.

1. Orcovente: The laws governing foreign exchange, and the efforts of the Third
Reich to seize the funds of exiled German writers, made the arrangements of such
companies as Orcovente too complicated for their beneficiaries and authors to follow.

2. Rosner was a young Communist and protégé of Egon Erwin Kisch; he fell on
the Republican side in the Spanish Civil War.

3. inconsistencies: Hermann Kesten writes, "I do not recollect any 'inconsistencies'
on Rosner's part, and I certainly didn't throw him out, being neither his employer nor
his hotelier."

4. L. and L. never gave me any statements: Here, Kesten—a onetime publisher as
well as author—writes, "Like many authors, Roth was sometimes subjectively right
and objectively wrong in his remarks about his publishers, sometimes objectively right
and subjectively wrong, often plain right, and often plain wrong. In conversation, one
could listen to his polemics against his publishers, and either agree or disagree with
him. So far as Landshoff and Landauer were concerned, there were not many publishers who were so close to their authors, and there was no author for whom they took
more trouble and expense than Joseph Roth."

281. Stefan Zweig to Joseph Roth   *[July 1934]*

    [. . .]

I implore you, don't[1] do anything in your present state, don't post letters without showing them to a friend first, you are *overstrained*. Don't
send any telegrams at all, pretend the telegraph has been disinvented. It

won't make the desired impression, it will *do you harm*. It will disadvantage you, because others will feel your impatience, your inability to wait. I beg you: please calm down! Don't drink. *Alcohol* is the Antichrist and money, not the wretched cinema. They're not stealing your shadow, it's you making yourself into a shadow, a pale shadow of yourself, by your drinking—please, my friend, take my offer, take a cure for a month, and under strict supervision. . . .

1. don't: Zweig might as well have written to Don Quixote, asking him to desist. The expression "dialog of the deaf" comes to mind. At the bottom, at the root of everything is temperament.

282. To Carl Seelig   *Nice*
                                              c/o Hermann Kesten
                                              119 Promenade des Anglais
                                              17 July 1934

Dear Mr. Carl Seelig,
    thank you! My friend, Hermann Kesten, invited me here; how long I'll be able to stick it out, I've no idea. I'm feeling so wretched, I've no alternative but to endure everything. I'm penniless, otherwise I'd be back in Rapperswil. The *Antichrist* is paid for. I'm not getting anything more out of it. I'm *morally* washed up too—so people tell me.
    Oh, I'm so wretched! I can't write it all down.
    Allert de Lange will send you the *Antichrist*.
    Sincerely,   your old Joseph Roth

283. To Stefan Zweig   *[Summer 1934]*

    [. . .]
    my friend Kesten, as a suitable representative in my business affairs. Only, Kesten is a *close friend of Landshoff's as well*. In addition, he's a writer himself, who rates me—as a writer, not as a human being—much

lower than he does himself. Part envy, part inferiority. You know human beings are not straightforward, nor do they want to be. And all that's easily squared with friendship. I can SEE it.

So he can't be my representative.

None of which matters.

What matters is this:

What matters, and *this is all that matters*, is that I have a guaranteed income between 1 August 1934 and 1 August 1935.

Only that will allow me to draw a deep breath, and begin to think.

What if Huebsch together with one of those English publishers were to leave *you* a sum of money to last me a year, and you send me a fixed amount each month—I'd be happy with that!

End of October I'm to deliver my novel.[1] It's terrific material. I won't tell you about it just yet. I was really into it. When that shit happened, I completely lost the thread.

It's done, I haven't written a line for 3 weeks!

You're leaving Europe, and you're my only real friend!

You will leave, and I must have a secure income for a year, and with you not there, and your authority vis-à-vis others, and toward me, I'll be up against it.

Will you promise me the following:

That you leave me 12,000 marks for one year, before you go.

It's the only thing that matters. Oh God, I can't write a line without some security.

And then I'll promise you in return *that I won't put myself out for strangers any more.*

I will lock myself away. But I need to have that security.

Surely I can have 1,000 marks, if I'm responsible for 8 people?

If you like, I can make do on less, *but I have to be able to rely on it.*

The "whip" is very bad. It's at the point where it's no longer driving me on, but killing me instead. How would you like to write my obituary?

I'm through anyway, I'm too serious, you know, I wouldn't be able to say something like that glibly.

Give me your exact address for the near future. I'll send you my will.

You decide what's to be done with it if you're not there either. Will you be so kind? Please. Tell me, honestly.

I beg you sincerely not to go away before I've got a year ahead of me. I can't deal with Landshoff and Landauer any more. I'm finished. And I can't write a line, unless I have some security.

The most pressing debts are important! Please tell that to Huebsch!

I embrace you sincerely   Your J.R.

I'd like to write a big novella before this next novel. It's a lovely thing, and it's been preoccupying me.[2]

Please believe me, I've been so maltreated by Kiepenheuer.

1. my novel: presumably *The Hundred Days*, published by Allert de Lange in 1935.
2. preoccupying me: possibly *The Leviathan*.

284. Stefan Zweig to Joseph Roth   [July 1934]

Dear friend,

as your friend I'm going to be honest with you—for the first time, I'm really afraid for you. You're overwrought, it's alcohol or it's something else, I can see it in your (senseless) letter to Gollancz, in your whole being. I must beg you, please not to be so *impatient* always. Those wires going out every which way were a sign of it. A letter would have had the same effect—no, it would have settled the matter much more calmly and clearly. You can't write to Gollancz like that. He never made a contract with you, he just declared himself in principle willing to pay you a certain amount, and then, when he learned that future books of yours are going to be with Heinemann, he took a step back. No contracts were signed; he never made an offer for your book, it was offered to him, and he tried to do the best he could. And then you write him an idiotic letter which is the *first thing that could really harm you in this whole affair*. I'm sure Kesten never saw that letter. A *plea* to him might have been a different matter, asking him to stick to his original position, but instead in the second part of the letter *you start to threaten him*! Left to ourselves, Huebsch and

I could have come up with a compromise solution—but come on, you're an examiner of souls, you must see that your wires and express letters are *symptoms*. You wanted everything quicker and more excitably than the natural course of things allows. You sought to force time, as you seek to force money. Just think how much energy you've wasted in this continual haggling and back-and-forth; I've been imploring you for years, *adjust to the reality that as a German Jewish author nowadays* you'll only be lucky enough in certain exceptional circumstances to earn money, and that the writer's life is historically a pretty unprofitable one. Don't try to force an income for yourself that's impossible, that'll only get you into warped contracts, tangles, and these unceasing difficulties! *For God's sake, man, get a grip on yourself*, since that Gollancz letter I've begun to really fear for you. You've got to stop boozing. You'll have to go on a proper cure for a month and get dried out—please believe me. I wouldn't say it otherwise. You know I've been urging you to do it for a year, only that can help you, nothing else.

And calm down, my dear fellow! It's your haste and panic and nervousness that makes everything so difficult. I can't go back to Gollancz after your latest letter, but I will talk everything through with Huebsch, and think of what's best to do as soon as he's here.

Sincerely,   your St. Z.

Please *take it easy*. Stay in bed if you must, but don't drink.

285. *Stefan Zweig to Joseph Roth*   *[postmarked: London, 18 July 1934]*

Dear Roth,

I hope you've calmed down again. You take a wrong view of everything—there is a thousand times more punctilio among publishers here than in Germany, it's viewed as a gross breach of decorum to snatch an author away from someone else, and Gollancz's interest in the book was first and foremost a way of getting you all to himself. You really need to suppress all those telegrams and express letters (that stem from your inner unrest)—the more calmly you negotiate, the better it is. Huebsch will be here soon, and I want to talk everything through with him. But please stay calm, you must save yourself for your work, nothing is more important than that, in every sense.

Sincerely,   your St. Z.

I am leaving here as soon as I have seen Huebsch. Regards to Kesten, and thank him for his letter.

286. Stefan Zweig to Joseph Roth   *11 Portland Place*
                                                       London W 1
                                                       [July 1934]

Dear friend,

got your express letter (but why express, Huebsch won't be here for another 6 days!) plus contents. Dear *dear* Roth: clarity, common sense! Please! Won't you see that no one wants to offend you or cheat you, not Landauer, not Gollancz, not Heinemann—the two last-named are enormous enterprises where some clerk passes a memo to an undermanager: as a realist or man of imagination, you need to see it in the correct proportions. But the idea that Gollancz or Heinemann (basically not actual persons, but concerns) wanted to "*offend*" you, is completely *bizarre*!!!

I know you are *extraordinarily* clever. But cleverness has never been enough to save someone from stupidities that stem from some inflammable part of his emotions. My dear friend, can't you feel me suffering because of the compulsive way—even at times you earned a lot—you were always thinking about money, WITHOUT *really* EVEN BEING GREEDY. If you were a miser, a Harpagon, I would see it as lust, for you it's a *torment*, only *partly* created by circumstances, partly by you yourself, and from which I fear it won't be possible to free you in this life. Believe me, I rack my brains over how to help you, and when I say you can't be helped by money alone, you have to give up these self-destructive self-lacerating urges! Allow me, your true friend, to tell you one symptom. I have letters from you over many years. They were often full of bitterness.

But never full of hatred. Now all of a sudden, I see in your letters hate and vengefulness against individuals, threats to denounce them even in your last will—Roth, I implore you, you're a kindly, helpful, understanding soul: don't you feel the evil in them, an evil that isn't in you, but that comes from outside? THAT's what alarms me for you now, the fact that you see evil, and feel evil intentions everywhere around you, and that evil is already inside you. Yes, initially as a fantasy and resistance, but to be forever thinking of the evil coming from others means to hoist it into you, to let it nest in you and grow like a cancer, like a tumor. No, Roth, I don't *want* that, it's not you, it's—though you may deny it till you're blue in the face—alcohol, which has made you more irritable and choleric than you are by nature, which has falsified your true being. I don't *want* the author of *Job* to go writing books and letters fueled by resentment: the *Antichrist* was a yell, magnificent, but now you must defend yourself against yourself! As before, I remain convinced you should take a cure, just to be taking steps against yourself, and especially because the moment is not yet at hand when you *need* to withdraw, but merely *should* and *ought* and not *have* to, and that would be the best moment.

I will only discuss the publishing questions with Huebsch. Perhaps he'll still be able to turn everything round. Don't despair. You know that I will help you financially if need be, but I am loath to do it in such a way that it melts in your hands (or in your mouth). I would rather have helped you once and for all, with the month's cure that would mend your health.

Sincerely, in haste   your S.

A copy of my *Erasmus* has gone from Vienna to Paris. An idiotic misprint drove me wild: on page 224 it should of course say Machiavelli's *a*moral politics, not moral.

287. *To Stefan Zweig*   [Marseille] *19 July 1934*

Dear friend,

read the enclosed, the copy of a letter I wrote to a friend,[1] an old Russian aristocrat, a consul in tsarist times (has money—between ourselves:

he wanted to give it to me once, but I thought L. could use it—then through my agency lent it to Landauer—strictly between ourselves.) You'll see from it the sort of things that befall me. I fear you're overestimating Gollancz, just as you overestimate my dipsomania.

You can give or show it to Huebsch too. I want him to be in the picture.

I can see the time coming when you won't want any more letters from me.

I am doomed, that much is clear.

You think I'm mad, when I'm rational. I'm not imperiled either.

I'm just furious when my honor is impugned. Mr. Gollancz did that. He owes me an apology.

Since you're not sitting facing me, eye to eye, you of course jump to the conclusion that I'm self-destructive. The enclosed is a little supplemental proof of what it is that's actually destroying my life.

It's too late, I'm sick of this world.

I embrace you warmly, your old   J. Roth

I can't show dear Kesten everything, for instance not the enclosed letter. He is close to Landshoff, and I mustn't destroy their thing. I see everything, Kesten only sees some things, albeit more clearly than I do at times.

1. friend: Konstantin Leites.

288. Stefan Zweig to Joseph Roth   *[July 1934]*

Dear friend,

you're getting too excited. Gollancz already knows you weren't ill-intentioned, but that you were the victim of a misunderstanding. But English publishers insist on fair dealing among themselves, and G. hopes that Heinemann will publish the book, and then all the others as well. His principal interest in the *Antichrist* was that it would have given him on option on your subsequent work, and precisely that is ruled out by your contract with H.

My dear fellow, I *implore* you: (I have been imploring you for years) don't always try and market yourself to six people at once. It's Huebsch, it's Landauer, it's Alexander, it's yourself, it's Albatross, it's de Lange, and Tal—confusions are bound to result. What you're doing is crazy, negotiating with firms on three unwritten books at once, and making deals that resemble the IOUs of officers (madness giving away 60% of your foreign rights). You need to draw up a schedule with a friend like Kesten. Put everything on it exactly as it is, a list of all your obligations to various publishers, and tabulate it, so that it can be taken in *at a glance*, and then Huebsch and I can look it over[1]—what the position is with de Lange, with Querido, to whom have you offered, sold, part-sold future books of yours. My dear fellow, you must make clarity, get Kesten to help you, and sign off on the paper. Then I'll go through it all with Huebsch.

And as regards the future. Don't scare away publishers by putting money front and center. You will *harm* yourself if you are too urgent and insistent about money (remember your psychology). It scared me in your letter to Gollancz that, even before the contract was signed, you were asking him to *wire* you the money. Of course something like that is *bound* to set a publisher's alarm bells ringing, he won't have much faith in an author who's so desperate.

So don't worry! No one thinks badly of you. I'll straighten out the *Antichrist* business with Huebsch. But please—*a clear statement of your obligations*, in graph or table form, and Huebsch and I will look at it.

Ginzburg must be somewhere in your vicinity, in the south of France, only I don't know where   Sincerely, S.

In haste

---

1. look it over: absolutely well-meant, utterly demeaning, and completely impossible.

289. Stefan Zweig to Joseph Roth   *[July 1934]*

Dear friend,

don't let's argue about morality! *That's* not immoral, what's immoral
is you proposing to write a novel by October, when you sat over your
Radetzky March for two years! You, Joseph Roth, will face your ultimate
judge alone, not the 8 persons you always mention. Let them wreck your
life if they must, but not your art.

Second, I can sense your rising fury. You are beginning to see people
like Landshoff, Landauer, and Kesten as your enemies. One day you will
see me as your enemy. It won't break my friendship for you. Only add to
my regret that the Antichrist has you in his claws. It's a dangerous thing,
to sup with the devil.

Huebsch has been chasing around like a mad thing. I'm meeting
him tomorrow, Saturday. There's no question of income for a year, but
I hope to be able to secure something. The book trade over there is in
terrible shape. The numbers of 1931 are a distant dream, just as they are
in Germany.

Erasmus set off on his way from Vienna to Paris long ago. I have no
idea where he's gotten stuck.

I enclose a little something. Just to make sure you have no anxieties, if
Huebsch's money gets delayed.

In haste, your S.

No, I won't enclose it, I'm going to send it to Kesten instead, with the
request that he buy you the needful.[1]

---

1. the needful: at this point, the demeaning takes over.

290. To Stefan Zweig   *Nice, 20 July 1934*

Dear dear friend,

every day you are kind enough to write me a few words, and every day
I repay you with some *bêtise* or wickedness. Please try to understand how

much this Gollancz business has thrown me off-kilter, after your telegram and your letter with the hundred pounds made me dance with joy.—You must understand that I'm getting horrible demands by mail every day. I have borrowed money in a really foolish way, from a waiter, from my translator—and worst of all, on behalf of a poor crippled painter at the Austrian consulate, where they wouldn't have given him any themselves. So I borrowed 1,000 francs against my good name (with tricksterish self-confidence), and again at table, again sinfully, another 1,000 from a little man by the name of Grünberg who called on you in London, with my recommendation. Dear friend, you're the only one I can tell all this to, and may God forgive me for doing so, because you are so unmoving in your incomprehension of me (no doubt therapeutic, because at heart you must know what's going on with me). If anyone finds himself in urgent need, I go into a panic, God forgive me for saying so—and even writing it down—maybe 50% of my debts are incurred for others, just as half of my life belongs to others.[1] You reproach me with being a professional expert on the human soul and committing mistakes—and you are an expert, and an expert in particular on my soul—and the mistakes that you make are also considerable.—You see, I can't go somewhere and say: help so-and-so! Instead I say: help me! His pregnant wife is my pregnant wife, and at that moment I'm not really lying. But the outcome is that I get into spectacular difficulties, because I don't calculate for myself either. And since I'm not a true saint, but a human being with ideas of being decent, I become furious and unreasonable. And it seems unfair to me that Gollancz can plead solidarity, and I think it's unfair too that you, my friend, make common cause with the clever people. Be clever, be as clever as you like, but leave me out of it—I'm past repairing. I work like an ox, I live badly, I feed 8 people dear to me, and sometimes as many as a dozen strangers, I am honest, neither Mr. Gollancz nor anyone else has any right to say otherwise. I shit on his solidarity with Heinemann, he knew I was Heinemann's author *before* he wanted to buy *Antichrist*, he has no moral or legal right to retract his offer *subsequently*. I don't like it—not for my sake—but out of principle. It can't be right that I write an *Antichrist* for the public, and suffer from anti-Christian wheezes in private. So I'm going to fight it, using all the means of worldliness, the duel, the court case, the insult, I don't know what else. This "solidarity" among messrs publishers in London is a work of the Antichrist, just like the lack of solidarity among publishers in Germany. And—unless my ear trained from Russian descent and Austrian birth deceives me—then a gentleman by the name of Gollancz is going to be a Jew from Budapest, or Keeskemet, or Pressburg.[2] Just by the by. When old Fischer once asked me where I was from, and I replied: Radziwillow, he confided: "Between you and me—I wasn't born in Germany either!"[3]—I have the feeling that this Mr. Gollancz is Hungarian. It's not the *cz* in his name. It's the tone of his letters. But I know: this too is hubris. Without the grace of God, one may not be a prophet. Anyway what does it matter, perhaps Gollancz is English, and Chamberlain[4] is a Magyar. What's important is not doing the Antichrist's bidding, not in England and not in Hungary. To return to the case in question: I can see the devil's grimace in the way that Gollancz, in spite of knowing that I was Heinemann's author, begins by taking the book; then—later—thinks to himself he is being uncollegiate against Heinemann; thereupon asks him, and without so much as checking the *veracity* of his information, suddenly allows "solidarity" to obtain. It's more honorable to give 100 pounds to the author of *Antichrist* than to believe a colleague who was manifestly telling an untruth. I don't have the least respect for the good morals of these Magyar Englishmen—who could be bona fide Englishmen for all I care (my business is not geography, but moral geography)—who are capable of insulting a man of honor, but incapable of apologizing to him. No! I must say I can't see any distinction between the sell-you-down-the-river Germans and the my-word-is-my-bond English. It's not a nice thing to call an author a cheat, because you prefer to believe your lying brother publisher. And [you my] friend and comrade, fourth estate like me, we have no cause to acknowledge these worldly values, which do not even obey the world's laws. Maybe I am not behaving "sensibly." But I behave the way I write. And what sort of inconsequence do you expect from a man who has written the *Antichrist*? I will not allow a lie to stand—and then not because it happens to be directed against me, but because it's a lie, and because tomorrow it may be directed against others. And it's an even worse lie if it makes appeal to solidarity or morality or British royal family la-di-dah. And money—I know—is the Antichrist (just like the cinema, which you take under your wing)—but I have never spent more on myself than a bookkeeper. And I work more than ten bookkeepers, and need money for others. That's the law of my life, and it's the only way I know.

In practical terms, this Gollancz business has wrecked a year of my life. Mr. Reece was all set to pay me for a year. Maybe the solidarity craze will take hold of him now as well. And for the rest of my life I'll be tied to a certain publisher whom I don't like any more—purely because his colleagues showed solidarity. I don't know what you find to admire in it. It's legally and morally reprehensible.

You're going away, and who knows if we'll ever see each other.

Please try and see that Huebsch pays me for the *Antichrist* right away—preferably before the first. I'm dying. And—what's worse—others are dying too. And I'm not at all too proud to ask a second time for the money to be wired. At least with Huebsch that wouldn't be a psychological error. He should be with you soon. Please, don't waste a moment, you will really be helping me. (And that's the only way you have of helping me.) I embrace you, and beg your pardon!

Your Joseph Roth (very sober and very desperate)

1. to others: Hermann Kesten writes, "I was witness on dozens of occasions when Roth gave—for him—considerable sums of money to some needy individual."

2. from Pressburg: Victor Gollancz was born in London. *Ceteris paribus*, Roth tends to have it in for Czechs and Hungarians most of all—see his later outburst against Budapest in no. 378—because he blames them for the breakup of the Dual Monarchy. Villains in his books are very often Hungarians.

3. Fischer—S. Fischer the publisher—was born in Lipto Szent Miklos, in present-day Slovakia. Joseph Roth was not born in Radziwillow.

4. Neville Chamberlain (1869–1940)—or Czamberlain?!—was the prime minister of Great Britain from 1937 to 1940.

291. Stefan Zweig to Joseph Roth   *11 Portland Place*
                                                      London W 1
                                                      21 July 1934

Dear friend,

of course the setting up of the company[1] was a specious business. [. . .]
It's not possible to judge these things from outside. In general, I see only
two alternatives: either you don't go into business with friends, or you
only do business with friends you can trust implicitly, like Huebsch.

You chose something like the middle way, which will always be the
worst. [. . .] You're magnanimous and suspicious at one and the same
time, which is a bad mixture.

You're going to have to steer one course or the other, either purely
commercial or purely on trust, and the best thing would be if you didn't
take personal charge, but had someone like Kesten work on your behalf.
I know how clever you are, but your cleverness is forever being crossed
by emotional complexes and points of honor. That's why you ought to
keep everything to do with money separate from yourself, and leave it in
the reliable hands of someone you trust. Of course it was idiotic to wire
Viking when you knew Huebsch was going to be here in 6 days. [. . .]

I'll be in touch again when Huebsch is here. I have a lot to get through
in my last days in London. From the beginning of August my address
will be Salzburg again for a while, even though I won't be there in person.

Sincerely,   your St. Z.

1. the company: Orcovente.

292. To Stefan Zweig   *Nice, 2 August 1934*

Dear friend,

I beseech you urgently, because the publisher is pressing, please give
me a few apt lines from your work for my *Antichrist*. I don't have your
books to hand. Or kindly write me something new.

Kesten got the 10 pounds. He gave me none of it. I am torn, so to speak, between shirts and a suit. I'm thinking a shroud would be a useful acquisition.

Unless Huebsch gives me something, I won't get through September. He's offering 250 dollars for the American rights, 500 for English and American.

I'm left with 40% of that, i.e., 1,500 or 3,300 French francs, respectively. Huebsch deducts another 20% from the English rights.

(Gollancz would have given me 100 pounds for the English rights, as you know, but for the Huebsch-Heinemann mess-up. Please don't call me a complainer again now.)

I'm reconciled to it now, by the way, I'm happy to atone for the mistakes of others—if only I knew how I'm supposed to write the novel. Of course you're right, I mustn't write so quickly, especially not now, when I'm so exhausted.

But what else can I do?

I have another 6,000 francs to come from de Lange.

Even without a family, I couldn't possibly stretch such a sum so that I could write a novel on it, in the requisite peace and quiet.

Reece has been frightened off, and he wanted to pay me for a year. He has gone to Berlin, by the way, and doesn't write me from there, only briefly, to say that he begs your pardon. He had had to leave suddenly, and hadn't been able to visit you.

Well, what do I do?

You're right in everything you say about me.

But that applies to my general errors, and not my specific plight during these hours. Even if we assume I could correct my general errors constitutionally, so to speak, then I can't do it now, not when I don't know what next week will bring: bread or dead.

There's no sense in thinking about generalities when the particular situation is as acute as mine is now.

You're thinking strategically, like a general, I'm thinking tactically, like a lieutenant. You're right, like a good general. And, like any good general, you don't pay any attention to the tactical details, any one of which could make the difference between life and death for me.

I hope this letter still reaches you in London. You won't be going to S.[1] now.

I implore you urgently for a reply. (NB please note first sentence.)
Sincerely,   your Joseph Roth

1. S.: Salzburg.

293. Stefan Zweig to Joseph Roth   [postmarked: London, 4 August 1934]

Dear friend,

just got your letter. Please inquire, *Erasmus* should have arrived at the Foyot long ago, everyone else has gotten it and confirmed. Huebsch will do his best for you, I can only repeat that the prospects in America are not so good as they were two years ago. Today I am leaving for Switzerland, where I will see if I'll have to go to Salzburg for a day or two at most, I'm engaged in breaking up the household. I have another three months' work on a book. Huebsch will visit you in Nice! Or meet him in Sanary![1] I'm off in half an hour. Greetings from your fully packed
St. Z.

Write to Salzburg—everything will be forwarded from there.

1. Sanary-sur-Mer, a fishing village near Bandol and Toulon in the south of France, was to become the headquarters, so to speak, of the German literary exiles, who remained a riven bunch. W. H. Auden, the son-in-law of one of them, Thomas Mann, speaks of "'the malicious village of exile.'"

294. To Stefan Zweig   10 August 1934

Dear friend,

excuse the paper, I'm writing in a boutique.

The *Erasmus* finally came, and I read it right away.

It's the noblest book you've ever written. It's the biography of your mirror image—and I must congratulate you on your mirror image. It's wonderful when I think that one and the same person has written on Fouché and Erasmus!

Very noble. The style "sobre," as simply and precisely as you've ever written.

Very clever and deft, your opposition of Luther and Erasmus.

Clever the way the bulk of history is left in the background, and so to speak the aroma of events alone is described.

Spiritualized history.

Very moving, the ending quite shattering, the handling of the last 3 pages exemplary.

When I saw that you wouldn't get my letter in London any more, I copied out a few quotations from Erasmus for my *Antichrist*.

If you want to give me more lines besides, please send them directly to de Lange.

It's very urgent.

(Damrak 62, Amsterdam.)

No sign of Mr. Huebsch.

He's no good to me anyway. I won't be able to finish the novel.

I'll say no more at this point.

Please confirm safe arrival of letter.

God knows whether it'll get to you.

Warm embrace and congratulations.

Your old J.R.

295. To Carl Seelig   *c/o Hermann Kesten*
                                               119 Promenade des Anglais
                                               Nice
                                               11 August 1934

Dear Mr. Carl Seelig,

I'm very late in replying to your letter, please excuse me! I don't even
have any particular grounds: it's just that having been one of the most
punctual of men, I have become dilatory. I'm in a bad phase, demoral-
ized by poverty, I have no strength left, I am rebelling against myself, my
skepticism is stronger than my faith, I'm, so to speak, in no good skin.
You wrote far too kindly about my *Tarabas*. Thank you. Any praise I
get is more like an advance to me than a royalty. And following ancient
habits, I rate advances more than I do royalty payers.

Did you get my *Antichrist* yet?

Your rather reduced, but very grateful   Joseph Roth

296. To Blanche Gidon (written in French)   *Nice*
                                                     20 August 1934

Madam and dear friend,

thank you for your postcard! I have no news, just the perceived impossibility of writing. Austria is deeply worrying to me. I am now *brouillé*[1]
with the Austrian monarchists. They are happy to let time go by, keep
the emperor at a distance—me, I am his only subject. You must recall
the poor young man in *King in Exile* by Daudet?[2]—And apart from
that? My finances are going from bad to worse. Those Kiepenheuer fellows have tricked me and fleeced me. I can't burden you with these difficult and disgusting things. In a word: they've cost me almost 18,000
francs. They bought up my rights from Kiepenheuer for 5,000 marks.
My American publisher paid them directly. I have no say whatever. Then
there were the other publishers: the English, the Hungarian, the Italian,

etc. In the end I decided there's no point in hopeless court actions. At least I am free at the present moment. But how do I finish a book by the 1 October? I'm in need of a miracle. And I'm too much a believer not to know there are no miracles in these matters. Write to me, my dear, Mr. Kesten is leaving, and I'm not sure how much longer I'll be able to stay here. How is Mr. Gidon? Is he with you? Have you seen Mr. Poupet? Mr. Zweig has written to tell me he saw a full account of *Radetzky* in the *Matin*, did you know that? And the *Antichrist*? Did you get a proof copy?

Your friend, the old   Joseph Roth

Give me the dates of your return to Paris, if you will.

c/o Kesten, 119 Promenade des Anglais.

1. *brouillé*: (French) literally "scrambled"—*oeufs brouillés* are "scrambled eggs"— but here used in the sense of "through" or "on the outs with."

2. Daudet: Alphonse Daudet (1840–1897).

297. *Stefan Zweig to Joseph Roth*   *[end of August 1934?]*

Dear friend,

yes, *friend*, thank you so much! It was a clever essay and not malicious in its technical observations, but what happens to these things is best shown by the enclosed: the local Nazi rag grinning under its ban, and *endlessly* happy at the way that in 1934 the Jews are still beating each other up. If only the émigré press would finally understand that if it hails the Reichswehr as a potential savior (two months ago), it kills it as a real factor. If it so much as suggests Schleicher as successor, it murders him. If it attacks an intellectual ally, even from the highest or deepest standpoint, it paves the way for *Blut und Boden*[1] literature. But it was ever thus. I personally have reached my personal limit: to be attacked from left and right at once, just like Erasmus. Don't believe I was so stupid as not to realize that in advance: that's precisely where the courage of such a book lies. I'm not surprised, just irked. I understand Marcuse[2] completely, just from the *tactical* point of view, I wish he hadn't.

Did you read the wonderful story about the police chief of Berlin con-fiscating the "Burning Secret" (apparently by Stefan Zweig)? Of course not my novella,[3] but some Communist leaflet that was sold under the same title.

I have a lot to report to you, but as soon as I have a hand to write with, I'll be off to Salzburg tomorrow, we're expecting Toscanini,[4] and then on. On 10 September I'll be in London.

Sincerely your   St. Z.

Till soon!

1. *Blut und Boden*: literally "blood and soil"—the sort of violently patriotic writing that was acceptable to the Nazis.

2. Ludwig Marcuse had reviewed Zweig's *Erasmus* on 18 August in the *Neues Tage-buch*, and accused Zweig of urging the exiles to remain neutral in their writings.

3. my novella: *Burning Secret*, an old story by Zweig, published as *Erstes Erlebnis*, 1914.

4. Toscanini: Arturo Toscanini (1867–1957), the Italian conductor, who was vehe-ment in his opposition to Fascism, chose exile in London and New York, in contrast to other prominent Italian musicians, like Victor de Sabata, the conductor of La Scala, who chose to remain in Italy despite being half Jewish.

298. To Stefan Zweig   [Nice] 26 August 1934

Dear friend,

from my enclosed reply to M.[1] you will glean more or less what he replied to my first letter.

Oh, I know the whole thing isn't that important! But there are times when I take it seriously, and think it may even prove decisive.

Maybe those times are right.

Then I can get rather beastly—and I'm *not* sorry for instance that Ossietzky is in a concentration camp. Think of the damage he would do if he were still at large!

I hate those types. And if I have some feelings for the odd one among them, as with Marcuse, I *never* trust them.

My grandfather—and every other Jew—used to say: if a fool throws a stone into a garden, a thousand wise men will be unable to remove it.

Be careful, my dear friend, in friendly conversations. It might be good to be a little standoffish, just out of caution—next time. As an individual, Marcuse is fine. As a *type* he's unbearable. As an individual, he has a thousand virtues, as a type: jealousy, [. . .] etc.

Write soon! Huebsch hasn't written, I don't know where to reach him, I'm desperate.

Sincerely,   your old loyal Joseph Roth

I kiss your wife's hand. (It may be she is very unhappy herself—she appears so to me.) Forgive me.

1. M.: Marcuse.

---

299. *To Ludwig Marcuse*   *26 August 1934*

Dear Marcuse,

here in black and white are the consequences of your cleverness: the Austrian press is having a field day with your article on Zweig. I quote, under the title *"A Traitor"* the following: "Stephan Zweig is an epicure——The Jewish émigrés take no pleasure in Zweig's Erasmus. *Their spokesman is Ludwig Marcuse*, who in the latest number of the *Tagebuch, lays into Zweig*——It's possible to understand the émigrés' rancor against Zweig——perhaps Marcuse and his party are even prepared to believe the rumor according to which Zweig *shows his manuscripts to a professor, and has him improve his German for him* . . . Sic transit Gloria mundi."

I'm just quoting a couple of sentences. Now, think of the damage you're doing! What it means for Zweig, to have that appear in *Austria*, in cozy little Salzburg, where he has so many enemies among the German Aryans! Think of what you've done to yourself! The spokesman for the Jewish émigrés. Querido is mentioned in the German article. Imagine

Landshoff's embarrassment! Imagine the harm to yourself! Then tell me again that I'm just sensitive, and write pretty sentences, and I'm the one who's doing the damage. Come on, Marcuse, admit it, in this world, you'd have done better to listen to me. In the other, you could be right, if God is as intransigent as you are. There's no disgrace in being stupid now and again. You know how often I am. You know a lot about me. Now admit that in these matters, I'm cleverer than you!

In your article, which I have in front of me, I read: ". . . just as Christianity averts its gaze from the world . . ." and you write to me: "Where did I say that Christianity averts its gaze from the world?" Have you lost your marbles? Can you no longer remember today what you wrote yesterday?

Are you a writer or aren't you?—If you tell me I write "pretty sentences" and am a stickler for good grammar, then you must know that these qualities are a *direct* expression of reason, perhaps the only reason in the world!

Dear Marcuse, I know you have accumulated much wisdom, and you have a lot of character, but you direct your gifts against the world, and against yourself, like weapons. They bring you no profit. I tell you again you are the eternal Protestant, just as there is an eternal Jew. You refuse to bow to the laws of the world, you are like a guest behaving badly in the house of his host. You are subject to bad influences, without knowing it. Believe me, I can feel it.

The fact that Strauss's operetta[1] was banned you take as proof that Zweig couldn't have been published by Insel. And you even say "even." What use to you is all your philosophy if you can't get your head around simple logic: Strauss is the president of the Musikkammer. His operetta therefore has *official* status in the Third Reich—a *book* by Zweig is not "official." And you say: how can Zweig appear in the Insel when EVEN Strauss isn't performed! Oh, the logic of it!

(Furthermore, I know that Strauss personally struck Goebbels as suspiciously Jewish. He is said to have Jewish relations.)[2]

What to do now, I mean, in practical terms? Will you write to the *Tage-buch*, to tell them I will write a reply to your article? Is it right to expose Zweig to attack from the nationalist press? Undefended? Betrayed? Do I reply to you in another paper, and thus give the Nats even more ammunition? Are we to fall out over this? Zweig's house, family, descent, and passport, are all Austrian. Am I to abandon him to his vilifiers there? Or do you want to take issue with these anti-Semitic attacks? Then you will have to say clearly that you have been *misunderstood*. I don't know which is most sensible:

a. either I defend you and Zweig together against the Aryans. Or

b. you admit your words lent themselves to misinterpretation. All I want is for our enemies to have least occasion to crow.

Don't underestimate them. They are concerned with everything that happens in our camp:

Only we, unfortunately, underestimate our camp.

Write me a reply—or else come here!

Your old   Joseph Roth

1. Strauss's operetta: Richard Strauss's *Die schweigsame Frau*, libretto by Stefan Zweig.

2. In fact, Strauss was not Jewish, but he did have a Jewish daughter-in-law, whose family he was instrumental in saving during World War II. Toscanini questioned Strauss's principles, remarking in 1933, "To Strauss the composer I take off my hat, to Strauss the man I put it back on again."

300. *To René Schickele*   *[September 1934?]*

Dear esteemed René Schickele,

we always see each other in the company of many others, and so there are things I'm unable to tell you that I think would interest you. This table where we sit together so often is like an orchestra, in which every musician plays a different tune, or seeks to play, or MUST play. (Perhaps we could meet at quieter times, if it suited you. Mornings in the Monod,[1] perhaps.)

What I have to say to you is that the Habsburgs will be coming to Vienna soon, and that the Wittelsbachs are closely involved with them. The Catholic clergy in Germany, at least in Bavaria, is informed. The Protestants in Austria have swung around from supporting the National Socialists to supporting Austria. Evangelical pastors in Austria have even switched sides. Perhaps our pessimism is premature, Germany can still be saved by Christ—almost directly—a new wonder for another 1,000 years. Marcu[2] is mistaken, like many students of history. A further war is not inevitable.   Sincerely,

Wednesday   Your J.R.

1. Monod: The Café Monnot on the Place Masséna in Nice.
2. Marcu: Valeriu Marcu (1899 Bucharest–1942 New York), Jewish Communist writer.

301. To René Schickele   *8 September 1934*

Dear René Schickele,

thank you.

"Old Germania" was evidently a hope. Not even Heine was free of that optimism.

In the latest issue of the *Sammlung* another scandalous piece on the majesty of Russia. Criminal stupidity!

It makes me sick with fury.

Sincerely   Joseph Roth

302. To Stefan Zweig *Nice, 9 September 1934*

Dear friend,

not a squeak from Huebsch. He swore he wasn't going to drop me.
Now he has dropped me. As of 15 September, I will be without means.
He didn't reply to my registered letter.

The *Antichrist* has appeared. With *crude misprints*.

I don't know, I don't know what to do.

You are not such a *complete* friend either, my friend. I have to tell you
that.

I have nothing terrestrial left to accomplish on this earth, except to
complain.

You all drop me, you are so worldly, and so canny, and I am guilty of
so much "foolishness." I have helped so many people, I am left so alone.
I was so nice to people, they are so mean. I am so much your friend, in
spite of all, I remain

Your Joseph Roth

303. To Stefan Zweig *[Nice] 11 September 1934*

Dear friend,

even though you forbade its use, I had to telegraph Huebsch today.
I must beg your pardon too for bothering you again with my wretched
affairs, and to ask you to write to Huebsch to ask him to do what he said
he would do. Kesten is leaving Nice on the 15th and I will have to move
next door, and pay at least 2 weeks in advance. I was expecting another
400 dollars from Huebsch (de Lange agreed to Huebsch's conditions),
but I hear *nothing from him*. My address, for the time being, will be *121
Promenade des Anglais, Nice, Jos. Roth.*

Please write to me, and write to Huebsch as well. Begging your pardon once more, your old   Joseph Roth

304. To Stefan Zweig   *New address:*
                                          121 Promenade des Anglais
                                          Nice
                                          18 September 1934

Dear friend,

I wouldn't have written to you so soon, but am compelled to, by a letter
from de Lange, which I am faithfully passing on to you. Well, the situation is that de Lange is prepared, and with pleasure—so he says—to
offer you an EXCEPTIONALLY large sum for ONE book. Between
the lines I can discern that de Lange might agree to get rid of disagreeable authors whom he might be harboring for your sake. Yes, they would
try hard to publish you as something outside, so to speak, the normal run
of things. Between the lines I can further discern the familiar expansive
gesture that, if they'd had an author like You, then I might have found
myself, so to speak, underwritten for the whole of next year. No point
in telling you that I am reporting these things to you, purely and simply
so as to be able to report with clear conscience that I have discharged
my duty properly. I don't want to have to lie, so I say everything. (For no
other reason.) Nor may I allow myself a lie. For on 1 October my advance
stops, but my novel[1] is not yet concluded. I have no hope, but may not
pretend to be indifferent to the interests of de Lange. I am incapable of
addressing you "officially," so I have to degrade you to my accomplice.
Forgive me, you who have already forgiven me so much. I don't have a
"personal" opinion—in this case—except in the event that you should
happen to *need* said exceptionally large sum. In that case, I would urge
you to take the money, the only reality that allows us to *survive*. That's
all that matters.

With me, terrible things are happening on top of terrible things. *My
parents-in-law are emigrating to Palestine*. It was for the sake of those old
people that I undertook so much for my wife, now the mother is leaving
her daughter, and I alone will be the mother. But the Steinhof[2] is paid
only till the end of October. It's about 150 schillings a month, which I

don't have. What shall I do? Does Mrs. Zweig know anyone at the Stein-hof? I hardly dare burden her with that. At least I would like to know that I won't have to bother myself with the Steinhof for half a year. What shall I do? Time is ticking, I can't do anything, I work, I work 10–12 hours a day, very well, VERY well. With all my worries. It's like suicide. I think it's more respectable to drown in the sea of work than in the actual sea, and I have hit upon a method to cheat my faith, which forbids suicide. So I will die with my pen in my hand. Soon, soon, I won't see you again, my dear friend. Have you received my *Antichrist* yet? I don't know if my novel will be completed, or when or where or why! I have nothing, nothing at all. I can calculate nothing. I know nothing. I find myself far, far outside the realm of calculation.

Write to me soon, you're leaving me so soon.

Sincerely, your old   J.R.

1. my novel: *The Hundred Days*.

2. the Steinhof: sanatorium, into which Friederike Roth was admitted through the agency of the writer Franz Theodor Csokor; it is also where the farsighted Count Chojnicki winds up—see *The Radetzky March*, pp. 356 ff.

305. To Carl Seelig   *Nice*

Till October: 121 Promenade des Anglais
20 September 1934

Dear Carl Seelig,

I would be very grateful to you if you could put in a good word for my friend Dr. Ludwig Marcuse with the Zurich Stadtbibliothek.—I think you won't mind either if I encourage him to apply to you directly.

Have you gotten my *Antichrist* yet?

Max Picard won't write to me any more. I am very sad.

Best wishes,   from your old Joseph Roth

306. To Stefan Zweig   *Nice, 23 September 1934*
                                          121 Promenade des Anglais

Dear friend,

I'm missing a reply to my last letters. Not from impatience, no, but because the post is functioning so badly. I've had one or two unfortunate experiences in these last weeks.

I've persuaded Marcuse to come here. He will write another article for the *Tagebuch* about your *Erasmus*.

I think it's in your interest. I sometimes get the impression that you underestimate the effect of criticism, and of the so-called émigré press. It's avidly read by French, English, and American journalists, and then not quoted, but *used*, which is better.

If you happen to see Huebsch again, tell him not to forget me. In two weeks, I will be left destitute. I can't write so quickly. I'll be finished with my novel[1] in December, not before. I am very pleased with it. But I'm too old now to be able to write with just two weeks' security.

(I've been boring you with this for a year now, my dear friend.)

Tell me precisely *when* you're leaving Europe.[2] I can already feel you've detached yourself from it. I hope not from me. Have you gotten the *Antichrist* yet? Ever since Hitler, the Austrian newspapers treat me as if I didn't exist. I have no friends left in the editors' offices either. Do you know anyone who would give a mention to my *Antichrist*?[3] Not on my account, you know, but on de Lange's. For his naïveté it's important that his books don't sink without trace.

The world has seemed very dark to me ever since Germany went off on its own. People are assuming that Hitler will stay, and they *want* a war—in the world outside now, as in Germany previously. He has no option either. What will Austria do, and I, her poor lieutenant?[4]

1. my novel: *The Hundred Days*.
2. *when* you're leaving Europe: Stefan Zweig went to the United States on a short lecture tour (with Arturo Toscanini and Schalom Asch, the renowned Yiddish novelist); he didn't go to South America until August/September 1936.

3. Antichrist: *The Antichrist* was published on 9 September 1934 by Allert de Lange.

4. her poor lieutenant: words from a song.

307. To Stefan Zweig   *28 September 1934*
                                          Nice, 121 Promenade des Anglais

Dear friend,

one of your letters must have gotten lost. I got the cheerful postcard.
I am not straightaway discouraged, I am not overly vain, but you must
see that it takes colossal courage to write a novel when you have precisely
3 weeks to live. "Just concentrate on it, everything else will take care of
itself"—but even to concentrate like that and write is beyond me. You
know that I am incapable of giving in anything unfinished, it's physically
impossible for me to hand in half a book, I mean, I can't hack off one arm,
and mail that either! I am a very honest man, I have never once cheated
a publisher, at the most I have handed in manuscripts a month or two
in arrears—how do I come to have a reputation for being unreliable?—
I can't possibly give in half a novel—and anyway what is that: half a
novel? It doesn't exist! Those are dreadful offers from pathetic writers:
"I can show you the first 3 chapters" and so forth. What does that mean:
3 chapters? a half?—No, please, tell me, not that. You know it as well as
I do. Your great and kind friendship forever leads you to deal with me
pedagogically. Why when it's between us? You know how awful my life
is? How much courage I have?—Ach, let's not talk about it.

After this novel, I will need to have at least 4 months of absolute peace.
I repeat what I have written since Hitler's accession, 8 hours a day on
average, day after day: a novel (botched, but still a finished book); 3 novellas, highly successful,[1] the *Antichrist*; ½ a novel (new); 34 articles. Inter-
spersed with sickness, poverty, betrayal. What do you expect from me,
my dear friend? Am I a god?—The betrayals of friends, being conned,
looking after 6 others—what more should I do?—court cases, lawyers,
letters, negotiations, and writing, writing, writing.—Of course you can

tell me everything. But explain it to yourself, not me. I'm not an author, I'm a fakir! Won't you at least see that?—I'm dying. You'll be sorry. Why force me to so much self-praise and vanity?

Thank you for the translator! Important! Yesterday in *Le Temps* a big review, the translation wretchedly reviewed—and where they're attacking my book, I see the fault of the translator. Even the malicious Thérive can see my quality shine through the translation.

Who knows whether it's just one letter of yours that's been lost. That's why I'm sending this registered. I'm sorry.

When is the new date for the *Erasmus*?[2] I need to know.

Hugs, sincerely, your old friend

1. Three novellas: *The Coral Seller* (*The Leviathan*), *The Bust of the Emperor, The Triumph of Beauty*.
2. the new date for the *Erasmus*: Stefan Zweig's *Triumph und Tragik des Erasmus von Rotterdam* originally appeared in August 1934. The first printing had to be pulped by Zweig's new publisher, Herbert Reichner of Vienna, because it had so many misprints.

308. *To Annette Kolb*   *[postmarked: Nice, 30 September 1934]*
                                          Saturday

Truly loved Annette Kolb,

here is confirmation of your great talent, and my great devotion to you as well. If I could ever have thought your charm led me to rate your work higher than my cruel authorial conscience permits: well now, thanks to your divine *Schaukel*,[1] I can turn to myself in triumph, and say: you know, you were right about her all along. She is beguiling IN EVERY WAY! Annette, I want to say—no Kolb—but don't worry, I'm only intrusive like this in my initial rapture! I have just finished reading your *Swing*, interrupting work on my own book, thinking I can read ten pages—and now you've cost me a day and a half of work. Blissful vacation! How rotten I feel, confronting my own book again! You write like a bird, and I like an elephant. You are the only woman who has God's leave to exercise this masculine calling. Every sentence is a pearl, every scene a life, every thought a truth, every observation a gem of wisdom. Charming priestess, darling of the small old gods, and the great Lord God—and of connoisseurs, of connoisseurs! You can do everything: rush to maturity, dance with wisdom, overcome gravity, you wonderful acrobat! And Germany is no longer there to hear you, and I am no longer able to hail you even in the *Frankfurter Zeitung*! Worse times are coming, now that I have read your book. I would like to give you now beautiful flowers from the gardener's old garden. I am just checking, to make sure I am not exaggerating—I detest untruth, and fear I may have fallen into it—but no, no. By God, I'm right.—Come soon, before I'm all done in.

I kiss your hand, authoress, woman,

your old Joseph Roth

1. *Schaukel*: *Die Schaukel*, novel (The Swing).

309. To Klaus Mann *Nice, 6 October 1934*

Dear Mr. Klaus Mann,

thank you for your letter and for what you say about the *Antichrist*. You're probably right: it's not religion that lives in Austria, but the *negative* effects of wars. You may have heard that I have broken off all ties to the Heimwehr, following the killings of the workers in February. I wasn't the only one of the "Conservatives" to have done so.

I have just read your article on Moscow, and felt an itch to write a reply. In your notes, more of your ambivalence comes out than you'll admit, and probably more than you're even aware of. One day—when I have the time—I'd like to write a piece on Potemkin and the West. I will demonstrate that a western European, going east of Warsaw for the first time, becomes an utter child. It happened to the most brilliant European, Napoleon, and also to Balzac. Other examples abound. But first I'd like to draw *your* attention to that fact, not the shriveled arena[1] that's all we're still allowed to address in our language.

I think of you as a scrupulous person: so you would have to admit that you don't know a syllable of Russian. You've seen how men and women go to the congress in "work clothes" and heard them speak there with surprising freedom. What you don't know is what platitudes, really offensive platitudes, these good people mouthed. It would have been better for them to stick to their normal tasks, and not to venture into the literary arena. (Cobblers and engineers get no *eizes*[2] from me either.)— But it's worse than that. As I know Russia, they will have been disguised Jews, and not workers at all, not representatives of the people, but semi-intellectuals, ambitious inadequates.

Second, you should understand that for the average Russian, a subway and a book and a phonograph are all equally great miracles. Earlier, it was the sight of a governor, a general, a tsar. It's nothing to do with Communism. Only a naïve and genuinely rustic people like the Russians is capable of such enthusiasm. The precursors of the subway and the book, just as public, were the parade and the procession.—For western European eyes (Catherine the Great was a German) the Russians don't *paint* their villages any more, they *build* them. That's why they remain Potemkin villages.—The notion of all these things turns the heads of the West. In the consciousness of the Westerner, who hasn't clapped eyes on Russia before, the astonishment at Russia merges with that at Bolshevism. What so impresses you isn't BOLSHEVISM, IT'S RUSSIA.

Third, you don't seem to understand that thanks to Bolshevism Russia isn't on the way to becoming some new West, but that Bolshevism is merely the route by which our repulsive Western civilization is leaking into Russia. No new world is being readied, but our repulsive old one is moving eastward. (The League of Nations marked the beginning.) In 1927 I wrote an article for the *Frankfurter Zeitung*, called "Russia Goes to America." That's it, that's what's happening. You are young enough, you'll live to see it.

Fourth, you mentioned tradition. What you don't know is that the editions of Tolstoy and Dostoyevsky are "purged." You don't know Asia.

Fifth, you make comparisons with Germany. Don't make comparisons with Germany. Only hell is comparable. Everything, everything evil in the world, becomes noble by comparison with Germany. Germany is accursed, you have to learn to get out of the habit of comparing anything at all to this German shit.[3]

Sincerely,   your Joseph Roth

1. the shriveled arena: wonderful and terrible phrase for the German readership of these writers in exile—on average, 5 percent of their previous editions.

2. *eizes*: (Yiddish) advice.

3. German shit: worth noting that this was written well before the establishment of the concentration camps.

310. Stefan Zweig to Joseph Roth   *11 Portland Place*
                                                      London W 1
                                                      9 October 1934

Dear friend,

I'm sorry to hear about your sciatica. I had a bout of it myself just a year ago, but then did the needful immediately, namely diathermia, which almost always helps, and I also went to Baden near Zurich, which I can recommend, a small, quiet, inexpensive place with the best baths, and from where, if you have to, you can be in Zurich in twenty minutes. What you mustn't do is let it establish itself, because then it'll eat its way into your bones, and you'll have the unflattering sense of being an old Jew.

I haven't seen the Vienna papers for weeks, and so I don't know if they carried anything on the *Antichrist* or not. If they didn't, I'm sure it wasn't malice but another equally noble quality, which is to say cowardice. The so-called Christian course is steered by the Jews there with almost religious devotion. It's been a long time since I published anything at all in that country.

Erasmus comes out ca. 20 October, and is encountering the usual difficulties in Germany. The official policy is much stricter now, since someone from Eher[1] has taken over the booksellers. It's very clear that the publishers are to be slowly choked off on the Russian model, and the Eher-Verlag will be made the state publisher. That will give them control

of the few Aryan German authors who have hitherto been independent.
It's the same method everywhere.

You should fight to get your health back, first and foremost. The body
has more importance than we are usually willing to allow, and if there's
something wrong there, the brain will sense it. You need to concentrate
hard for your novel, it's all-important.

The *Antichrist* translation is coming along well, so I hear, and I can
imagine the book will be a success here as well, although the English
have a tendency to shy away from anything too impassioned or vehement.
Then again, they do have a feeling for biblical and prophetic writing, so
let's hope for the best, and anyway I promise to do what I can for the
book myself. Don't worry about the other things, and continue to rely on

Your St. Z.

1. Eher: Franz Eher, Hitler's publisher, the press czar of the Third Reich, and publisher of the *Völkischer Beobachter*, the official newspaper of the Nazi party.

311. To Carl Seelig   *Nice*
                                           c/o Kesten
                                           121 Promenade des Anglais
                                           21 October 1934

Dear esteemed Mr. Seelig,

it's three weeks since I sent you a signed copy of my *Antichrist*. I should
like to know if it's gotten to you safely. Lots of things are getting lost in
the present climate. I have the feeling the secret police have their men in
all the sorting offices.—The *Antichrist* is a great success, with 5,000 sold
in 4 weeks—how I wish I hadn't taken an advance, then I might stand
to get some money now—but what else could I have done then? I never
hear anything from Max Picard. Do you?

Sincerely, ever   Your Joseph Roth

312. To Ernst Křenek   *temporarily in Nice*
                                                       121 Promenade des Anglais
                                                       c/o Kesten
                                                       24 October 1934

Dear esteemed Mr. Křenek,

I only saw your review in the *Wiener Zeitung* rather late, hence my thanks to you are also rather late. In the meantime, I hope you may have received a copy of my *Antichrist*.

It was very noble of you to write about me as you did. Yes, the kingdom of the fathers, I fear for it *again*, a different fear now, will it be realized? Drop me a comforting line, if you have a moment. I fear for the following reasons: (a) it was destroyed by that repulsive National Socialism = Nazism, whose fathers were Social Democrats, whose grandfathers were Liberal Jews. (b) These latter two are both still alive, they have outlived their sons—the shard outlives the pot, as the Eastern Jews like to say. (c) Socialism was only destroyed by force of arms—therefore it still exists! (d) The new governors have too much "soil" about them for my liking, too much Alpenland, not the breadth therefore but the narrowness of the physiognomy of our forebears' kingdom. Is it possible that a geographically diminished Austria can give rise to our geographically boundless one (as an idea?). I sometimes hear that the chancellor[1] admires a well-known poet[2] as "Austrian"—when we all know that if the world was as it ought to be, he would just about have been famous for the length and breadth of Brünn. Is that true? And does the chancellor believe that that's the way to create a balance between the Alpine narrows and the "breadth of the horizon"? Between Andreas Hofer and Moritz Benedikt[3]—Catholic now? Is that timely? What do you think about it?

Sincerely,   your old and grateful Joseph Roth

1. chancellor: Kurt von Schuschnigg (1897–1977), leader of the Christian Socialist Party, and successor as chancellor to Dollfuss, whom the Nazis had murdered in July

1934. In 1938 he yielded before the march of Hitler's armies. Interned in a concentration camp until 1945, then went to the United States.

   2. a well-known poet: the Jewish (but in JR's view unimpressive) Franz Werfel.

   3. Moritz Benedikt: then editor of the Viennese paper the *Neue Freie Presse*.

313. To Félix Bertaux (written in French)　　　*121 Promenade des Anglais*
　　　　　　　　　　　　　　　　　　　　　　　Nice
　　　　　　　　　　　　　　　　　　　　　　　25 October 1934

My dear friend,

I'll be here another 4–5 weeks, to finish my novel. Almost all of literature is here, the good and the bad, even the wicked. I am staying in
the same house as Heinrich Mann and Hermann Kesten. I see a lot of
Schickele, and the Jewish author Schalom Asch . . . They are all doing
much better than I am. They have much more money, and much less
sense. The only one I really admire is Heinrich Mann, and I'm not quite
happy about that. Just now he's in Prague. He's gotten very old and seedy.
A proper Professor Unrat[1] with his amour, a very blond and very deceitful woman, a tart to be frank, who is costing this great writer even more
in terms of worries and run-ins with the police. He's quite fallen from
grace. I don't quite understand it.

I am waiting for a few hundred francs from my editor to help me
finish the book.[2] I left Marseille, because it was too expensive. When the
book's finished, I'll go back there and try to find Mr. Lasne.

It's strange! Only you—and besides you a couple of Jesuits—recognized
me in my *Antichrist*. One wrote: "Excellent, excellent! I can smell heresy
here!" But the others! The people on the left think I'm a "reactionary."
Those on the right think I'm with the others. Apart from that, it's a great
"success." They're declaiming it from lecterns in Amsterdam. It's selling
well. That's why I hope to get a few more francs to help me finish this
book. What a world! What a world! The most rational people have been
driven mad! And Félix Bertaux—in the company of Jesuits!

Greetings to Mrs. Bertaux, and to Pierre.

And, as ever, for you too, from your faithful friend   Joseph Roth

1. Professor Unrat: title character in the early novel by Heinrich Mann. It's true that the novelist, with his goatee and his ungovernable blond wife, Nelly Kröger, came to resemble more and more the familiar hero of the film version of the book, *The Blue Angel* (1930), played with unforgettable pathos by the great Emil Jannings.

2. book: *The Hundred Days*.

314. *To Blanche Gidon (written in French)*   *1 November*
                                                                121 Promenade des Anglais
                                                                Nice

Dear Madam and friend,

once again, forgive me for the brevity of my letters. Right now I need to know when the *Antichrist* is due to come out in France.

My English publisher needs to know. The English translation is ready to come out. Did you have any more doubts, or questions? Don't be afraid of interrupting me, please.

I will write you a longer letter once I've finished the novel. For today, all friendly greetings from your old and (still) unhappy

Joseph Roth

315. *To Carl Seelig*   *Nice*
                                        121 Promenade des Anglais
                                        11 November 1934

Dear Mr. Carl Seelig,

I make haste to reply to you, even though I have no time, and my reply must needs be very short—or at least not sufficiently detailed. But I don't want you to remain uncertain a moment longer than necessary, as to how I took your letter. How little we know of one another, even when we are close! It's touching to imagine that I wouldn't care to hear a negative response from my friends. Where else other than in candor is the decent relationship of one person to another to be found?—Of course I know that you are unfair to me, like various other friends of mine—and I can't change your mind, I can only hope that you will later change it by yourself. I made a silly mistake by padding the book[1] with journalistic work. It should have been half the length. But I wanted to be unambiguous. The cause I was fighting for seems to me to permit an address to the psyche of the common man. But how to persuade him? Purposeful simplicity, of the sort you'll find in many religious works, is a means to an end, and it was only the end I had in mind. But that's by the by!—More important to me than being in the right is that none of those who are dear to me should think me vain. Vain I am not, I swear. Vanity is the attribute of the common and the dilettante. It's regrettable but true that vulgarity and dilettantism today are included in the makeup of the true master; hence your misunderstanding, as I sought to account for it to myself.

Until I've finished the novel,[2] I will be in a bad way, spiritually and materially. It's far worse than it was a year ago. I don't know what to do—for all my self-imposed limits. It's my first attempt at a historical novel—certainly not because I want a "success"—do I still need to say that? But because I've found in the material a way of expressing myself *directly*. And I'm in the worst pickle: I despise the low modes of the historical novelist, and become lyrical, in the way of the novelist. It's difficult, but it tempts me, perhaps in the same way it seemed tempting once to write a *Salammbô*. Only "balladesque" rather than "Homeric." Please excuse these hasty obliquities.

Sincerely,   your old Joseph Roth

And give my best regards to Mr. Polgar.

1. the book: *The Antichrist*.
2. the novel: *The Hundred Days*.

316. To Blanche Gidon (written in French)   *[postmarked: Nice,*
                                                     17 November 1934]

Dear Madam and friend,

the mountain still looms as tall as ever, thank you. The novel: it's sad, I don't want to give it away, but I'll let you into the secret: the hundred days. He interests me, your poor Napoleon—I want to *transform* him: he's a god who went back to being a man—the only time in his life when he was a "man" and unhappy. The only time in history that you see an "unbeliever" visibly SHRINK. That's what draws me to him. I wanted to make a "humble" man out of a "great" one. It's all too clearly DIVINE PUNISHMENT, for the first time in modern history. Napoleon humbled: a thoroughly terrestrial soul lowering and raising itself at the same time. That's what you can tell Gabriel Marcel, if you like.

Don't apologize, my dear! And don't always say you want nothing for yourself. That I know. But I am loyal, an old soldier who firmly believes that loyalty is the greatest human virtue.

Greetings to Mr. Gidon, and LOYAL regards to you, from your old Joseph Roth

317. To René Schickele   *[Nice] 17 November 1934*

Dear Mr. René Schickele,

thank you very much for the Lawrence.[1] The subject is foreign to me, but you are dear. Yes, I don't think any subject has ever been further from me, and the sender so near. I am delighted you have the same views on Lenin's mausoleum and Marx's opium as I do. The chapter on the revolution is superb. I am utterly remote from Lawrence, so I can't understand why he has to be the peg for you to hang all those things that do concern me so much. Never mind! I am struck by the book, and in what you say I see a clear reinforcement of the position I try to take up.

Kiss your wife's hand for me

Sincerely,   your old Joseph Roth

The part about the Jews is outstanding as well. Even though I don't think you have any Jewish friends who are so typical. You must have intuited it from the falsified conversations of your Jewish friends.

Lovely style! Wonderful style: my deepest artistic pleasure.

1. the Lawrence: Schickele's essay on Lawrence, *Liebe und Ärgernis des D. H. Lawrence* (Love and Irritation in D. H. Lawrence), Amsterdam, 1934.

318. *To Carl Seelig*   *Nice*
                                                 121 Promenade des Anglais
                                                 19 November 1934

Dear Mr. Carl Seelig,

excuse this letter (and please confirm its receipt). It's about something important, namely a human being. The German writer David Luschnat,[1] no Communist, not even a Jew, a perfectly harmless fellow with strange original ideas, is being extradited from Switzerland.

He has no "name," no money, he can't even pay his way to the border. In this labyrinthine world, there is no way of helping him and his ilk. So we have to help in the individual case, wherever we can. And here I appeal to you. You are a Swiss citizen, and a journalist, perhaps you can assist Mr. Luschnat in some way. He lives in Ronco, with Signora de Marcos. I don't know what he can have done in his eccentricity that would attract the ire of the Swiss authorities. He is a good person, a frail person too, he has strange ideas, not a Communist, not a Jew, his name David probably drew suspicion to him. It's too bad that things happen in that way. If you can't help him officially, perhaps you'll know someone who will at least shell out a few francs to get him to the border. There is no time to waste in his case. I blush at the thought of my own helplessness, and also that the world is so wicked, so unfathomably mean. David Luschnat has done nothing more than Thomas Mann: both have left

Germany. Both are writers. It's not for the police to judge their respective literary merits. I know you, dear Mr. Seelig, hence my appeal to you. Please, surely it must be possible to take on such a case. Tomorrow, because your name is Seelig, you will be extradited from Austria. What a world! What a country, where such things are possible! Mr. Luschnat hasn't won the Nobel Prize. That's why he is being extradited! At the latest on 4 December, he must have left. And he and his wife were starving long before Hitler came to power. I know him from Paris. (He is a straightforward man, mediocre, and slightly comical.) He has appealed for leave to stay, but he won't be given that, because Mr. Luschnat doesn't have a "name." I am furious, I should like to throw bombs. Please forgive me this letter. Don't leave yourself in peace, we all have to do what we can, privately, we can't do it publicly any more, we missed our chance.

Sincerely,   your old Joseph Roth

1. David Luschnat (1895–1984) was a German writer who went into exile in 1933.

319. To Blanche Gidon (written in French)   *27 December 1934*

Dear Madam and friend,

thank you so much for your letter. I still need another two or three weeks to finish my book.[1] After that, I shall go to Amsterdam, but probably not to stay, just to get my contract extended till early March at least. Mrs. Manga Bell sends you her best. Her brother has sent his children to her. She is very happy. But me, I don't know how to send them back again. It'll have to happen, anyway. There are miracles in my life, poor little miracles, but miracles just the same—only fair for a poor little believer like myself.

My book seems atrocious to me. It can't be helped! I have no time. My literary conscience is my worst enemy.

There are many things I should like to tell you—but not before the book is finished. And then over a small cognac at your house.

Please give my warmest best wishes to Mr. Gidon. I wish you both a very good new year.

Your faithful old   Joseph Roth

Nice,

121 Promenade des Anglais

1. my book: *The Hundred Days.*

320. *To René Schickele*   *[no date]*

Dear esteemed Mr. René Schickele,

since yesterday I've been staying at the Hotel Imperator, Boulevard Gambetta, as befits a café habitué, next to the France.[1]

Please come by, I am relieved to hear you are better.

Kiss Mrs. Schickele's hand. Sincerely

your old Joseph Roth

1. the France: i.e., the Café de France, in Nice.

321. *To Stefan Zweig*   *Café de France*
                                                   Nice
                                                   4 January 1934 [1935]
                                                   Friday

Dear friend,

I think I must tell you quickly, because otherwise you will do something precipitate. I don't like the little man[1] at all—what I will say now is based on pure instinct, consciously without other basis, spoken to you, purely the way my nose speaks to me. He is the type of Jew who has a subscription to Karl Kraus[2] lectures and the *Weltbühne*. ("*Weltbühne* readers forgather in the Café Augarten.") You can have no idea what you confer upon a little twerp when you suddenly make him your publisher. *Your* publisher! Think it through, purely on a financial level. And even if he was a good, devout, little Jew! But this! He is a cheeky Lefty, who CAN'T possibly relate to your work! He's a pocket-sized Tucholsky, a mini Marcuse—it's wrong, it's unseemly. You can't have a gnat like Tucholsky for your publisher. It's unworthy. Even a murderous goy would be an improvement.

It almost shocks me when I see something more clearly than you do, because we both know you're so much cleverer than I am. I do crazy things, but I'm at least *sighted*. You (with "blind" holy credulity) surround yourself with lots of *little* people—you know, it's possible to sin through too much holiness. Please, dear, dearest friend, stop scattering your credit all over the place. A little analphabetical cacker, a *Weltbühne* yid, can't be your literary representative! How incomparably bigger is the Hungarian jester Brug!—Please give up your divine indifference! You're laying claim to a sort of British fair play, and you're only human. There is a point at which forgiveness becomes a sin.

A so-called Austrian publisher! If you have to have an Austrian, then a good Catholic, not, not, not please a *Weltbühne* yid. Please be careful! Don't put yourself in the hands of someone who THROUGH YOU can suddenly acquire prosperity and influence, and who at the same time will go on shamelessly badmouthing you in his shitty intimate circle of "Jewish-aware" and "Progressive" illiterates. (That's what I feel.)

Please understand, I'm talking freely, as though to myself, I lay no claims to objectivity or fairness. It's my instinct that's writing to you. I hate sawn-off Jews with that sort of haircut. It's a *Weltbühne* readership haircut. It's absolutely not the place for you.

Forgive all this, and don't suppose I'm drunk. (If anything, alcohol makes me even more clear-sighted than I have the misfortune of being when sober.) I've drunk one beer while writing this. And I say again: I know I am being "unfair." I don't like the fellow with his *woollen*—don't laugh: it's a sign!—mittens. I don't like it. It doesn't go with you.—Now, tear this up please. I'm going to leave it with the hotel porter tonight.

1. the little man: Zweig's new publisher, the Viennese Herbert Reichner.
2. Karl Kraus (1874–1936), Viennese satirist, polemicist, and playwright, author of *The Last Days of Mankind*. His emphasis on purity and correctnesss of language should have made him more attractive to JR than it did.

322. *To Blanche Gidon (written in French)*   [*Nice*] *9 January 1935*

Madam and dear friend,

I allow myself to send you 1,500 francs, of which I ask you to keep 900 initially for yourself, and the other 600 for me. Unless I instruct you otherwise by the 15th, would you be so kind as to then pay the 600 to the little Manga Bell girl's school, Lycée Victor Duray, Boulevard des Invalides?—Dear, dear friend, I'm so sorry to put you to trouble like this. But to explain these proceedings psychologically: I have received by chance 1,500 francs from England. I had cause to fear my own weakness and poverty, so I decided to send you the money. I am asking a lot, even from a friend as good as you. But—if not you—who else? Whom to trust?

I am unhappy with my work. I will have finished by the end of January. At that time I'll be coming through Paris, on my way to Amsterdam.

Work is difficult. There are many things I could say.

I kiss your hand, and send sincere greetings to Mr. Gidon,

your old Joseph Roth

323. To Stefan Zweig

Monnot
Café Restaurant
Tuesday
[Nice]

Dear friend,

you must forgive me for writing instead of telling you the following. But it's not easy to say, and those are further grounds for recriminations with myself.

It seems to me that sometimes in your dealings with people, with colleagues in particular, you adopt a stance that is capable of harming you. Innocent, without side, and magnanimous as you are, you make yourself too accessible, you are on too relaxed a footing with the world. I know that none of us is able to see himself at his or her true worth. You, though, underestimate yourself, and I am for absolute hierarchy, externally as well as privately. It's not good that you are on too intimate terms with shits. In Germany, you almost criminally squandered intimacy and trust. Outside Germany, you seem to me to display the same inclinations. *You* are wholly unable to deny credit—not me. I allow myself to be rough with people at times. At certain moments, I can be quite brutal, and let the person concerned see how much separates me from him. I don't stop short of insults. You are incapable of that. That doesn't mean that you should be *familiar* with certain people, or allow them to gain the impression of your being familiar with them. You are a *prince ès letters*—as the French so beautifully put it—and they are little skivvies. I rule out any imputation that I may be speaking to you thus out of personal devotion to you, and from a sort of possessiveness. I have gone into myself. If there was the least possibility of that being the case, I would never have been able to write to you in this way.

Don't, please, say: well, it's no skin off my nose. It *is* skin off your nose. You don't hear it, but I hear it, what little shits say about you, their envy, their foolishness—and I watch them lying, how honored they are to be on brotherly terms with you, and how they then have to get their own back on you, for the feeling of having been honored. My indulgence works differently. I remain suspicious. I don't scruple to slap faces either, metaphorically, or—sometimes—actually. But not you. Please, I beg you, be aloof, as you ought to be, and not too democratic.

Now forgive me,   your Joseph Roth
Please destroy this letter.

324. *To Blanche Gidon (written in French)*   *Nice, Alpes-Maritimes*
                                                      Hotel Imperator
                                                      Boulevard Gambetta
                                                      15 February 35

Madam and dear friend,

thank you for your kind letter. I venture to enclose these hasty lines to Plon, with the request that you translate them for me. It seems to me that cowardice and fear of going against current politics are hindering them from publishing my *Antichrist*.

As for my novel, I don't know what to do. I am working in real panic and anguish. I haven't had any money from the publisher for two months now. My unhappiness is too great for me to be able to describe it, and I beg you, my dear, also to excuse the typewriter. Mrs. Manga Bell sends you her best wishes. She is terribly unhappy. I don't know how all this is going to end.

Your old faithful   Joseph Roth
Kindly greetings, please, to Mr. Gidon.

325. *To the publishing house of Plon*   *[Nice, 15 February 1935]*

Gentlemen,

the translator of my *Antichrist* informs me that she has not yet heard from you when you are planning to publish my *Antichrist*. Since this work has just appeared in the United States and is shortly to appear in England, I ask you to tell me when it will appear in France. My American publisher asks that I inform him of the date.

Respectfully, your humble   [Joseph Roth]

326. To Stefan Zweig   *[Nice] 15 February 1935*
                                          Hotel IMPERATOR (NB: not Imperial)

Dear friend,

I just received your postcard. I've moved, after various complications, without Huebsch's money it would have been impossible. You were quite right, I'm not cut out for apartment life. It's the last time I'm going to let myself be drawn into foolish experiments like that.

I can't write you a detailed letter, of the sort you request, without bursting into tears, in a way you abhor.

My novel is advancing every bit as slowly as I thought it would. It can't be helped. I am not able to cheat and deceive myself. I tried to in *Tarabas*, the book failed in literary terms, and didn't succeed in other ways either. A simple infantryman like me can't expect to pull off cavalry stunts. The *Antichrist* was a failure—except in Holland. Both were rushed—counter to my literary rhythm. Now I can't run the risk a third time, of being slapdash. That would be literary—and physical—suicide. If I remain scrupulous, at least it will only be physical.

And it will be physical, because Mr. de Lange—legally speaking, he has a point—claims he has already paid out too much. It was my fault, for concluding a cheap contract over seven months. All my fault. I acted in the panic that governs most of my life, and from ill-advised affection for the two striplings from the Kurfürstendamm.[1] Mea culpa.

Out of panic I have written hurriedly and badly since your departure. It's worth nothing. Behind each sentence I write, I can already see the sentences of the begging letter I will have to write to de Lange. My pathetic "business correspondence" betrays itself in my prose.

The hotel has given me a little alleviation. Today I rented a small study, to have the illusion of a cell, and so as not to have to sit in the café any more. It even comes out cheaper: ten francs a day, undisturbed by friends checking up on me, and with a bottle of marc thrown in. Tonight I'll start the second part over again. I have the courage of desperation. (I have only the courage of desperation.)

Still, it means: in spite of my hopeless and panic-stricken position, I am relieved. It's like having a very high fever, and getting up to go to the toilet. Is that a feeling you know?

I owe you so much, as I always do, in every crisis. You give me confidence, and rescue me from (practically) desperate situations. If Huebsch hadn't sent me the money, I would have cut my throat in that wretched flat.

I thank you, but what does it mean to thank you? What meaning do thanks have in a situation like this?

I wrote to Huebsch to send me another 100 dollars. It's no telegraphophilia on my part if I ask you to wire *him* to send them to me. He only does what you tell him. Not me. (I got the American reviews of *Tarabas* today. Lots of savagings, with lots of respect.)

I need to know that I will certainly be able to stay alive for another 3–4 weeks, to be able to write. This horrible book—I wish I'd never embarked on that wretched story—must be brought to an end quickly. And I'm so slow! And on top of my slowness, there's my crippling fear, slowing me down.

If you wire Huebsch, he'll send me 100 dollars, before the *Antichrist* flops.

Because it will, in America—and then Huebsch will be grumpy, and not send me any more money.

What should I do? I beg of you. I can be finished in 4 weeks, so long as I know those 4 weeks are in the bag, promise, promise.

Please write back immediately, sincerely,   your old Joseph Roth

1. two striplings from the Kurfürstendamm: Roth's moody, bitter, and anti-Semitic (anti-Western Jews) description of Landauer and Landshoff.

327. Stefan Zweig to Joseph Roth   *Salzburg*
Kapuzinerberg 5
16 February 1935

Dear friend,

I'm back, and wanted to get in touch with you right away. Tell me first whether you've finished your book, and whether you got my postcard from New York. It made me so happy to see how good your *Antichrist* looked in its U.S. edition. *Mary Stuart* is being printed even now, and I can't wait to have that book behind me (instead of always in front of me), and be able to embark on something new.

Now my dear friend, I have a discreet request to put to you, but please not a word to anyone. You remember how at the time I wrote several letters to Strauss, but—sign of the times—he didn't get them all. There was one in particular which I sent him registered from Nice, and I would be very thankful if you could apply to retrieve this letter for me from the post office. They're sure to have the other part of the form in case it did reach him; otherwise, they would have to pay damages. Since I think a public dispute is likely in the affair sooner or later, it's very important to me (you will understand this) that I have proof of postage. The letter, like the others, will have been intercepted en route. Once again, please be absolutely discreet; I don't want to have to read about it in the newspaper, which would certainly happen if you were to tell anyone at all about it.

As of the day after tomorrow, I'll be in Vienna. Sincerely, your loyal
Stefan Zweig
Post receipts enclosed.

328. Albert Einstein[1] to B. W. Huebsch   Princeton, N.J., 24 February 1935

To Mr. B. W. Hübsch, The Viking Press Inc., 18 East 48th St., New York City

Esteemed Mr. Hübsch,

I am truly grateful to you for sending me this consoling book[2] by a real mensch and great writer. As I read it, I was able to share the pain of a clear and kindly human soul, inflicted upon it by the callousness and spiritual blindness of the present age, and felt myself strangely shriven by the sort of objective invention of which only an artistic genius is capable.

Friendly greetings from your   [A. Einstein]

P.S. Please forward this note to the respected author. You have my permission to use it to publicize the book in any way you see fit.

1. Albert Einstein (1879–1955), physicist.
2. this consoling book: JR's novel *Job*, translated by Dorothy Thompson. No American journalist in the 1930s was more steadfast in her opposition to Hitler and her support of the German Jews than Thompson.

329. To Blanche Gidon (written in French)   *27 February 1935*
                                                      Nice
                                                      Hotel Imperator

Madam and dear friend,

thank you for your kind letter. Mr. Gidon's condition[1] makes me very sad. So it's true what people write about suffering being the badge of noble men and great souls! It's sad, so very sad. I fear that Mr. Gidon may not have enough "faith" to appreciate any "religious" sentiments, otherwise I should have written to him already. But I imagine he is probably very fixed and certain, and I would find myself in the state (give or take) of an abbé chased off by an invalid. Tricky, even, or especially for a friend. At least, my dear, tell Mr. Gidon that I am very devoted to him, and feel very much for him in his suffering. Thank you!

My story will reach you one of these days. Perhaps it's too long. If so, I'll send you another one tomorrow, a better one, it seems to me, written in Marseille. That one is short enough to go in the *Nouvelles Littéraires*. Since my agent hasn't paid me any money yet, I'm in a truly desperate situation. I can't wait for things to improve! If M. Lefèvre will publish one of the stories, and pay for it in advance, he can have it. Because—in truth—I'm at the end of my rope. I don't want to go into details, not at the moment.

I hope Plon really does owe me 3–400 francs. I beg you, my dear, for you and Mr. Poupet to go and cash them.

I'm working 8–10 hours a day. This will be my Waterloo. I'm "finished, finished," a writer who promised more than he could keep. Such is "a Russian soul."

I don't know the story of Wetzlar.

As to the anti-Semitism in those right-wing papers: believe me, my dear, Mr. Blum's[2] brand of it is more dangerous. It's the Jews—you know I have the right to speak frankly about the Jews—who have introduced Socialism and catastrophe into European culture. "novarum rerum cupidissimi": that's the Jews for you. They are the real cradle of Hitler and the reign of the janitors. One shouldn't always believe that "the Left" is good and "the Right" is wicked. If I was in your shoes, I would talk to Mr. Bailby,[3] and show him that blind and vulgar anti-Semitism is not of the "Right." The Jews have unleashed the plebs. There's progress! But I'm "philosophizing" too much.

Warm greetings, my dear friend, and thank you, thank you!

Your old and wretched　　　Joseph Roth

1. Mr. Gidon's condition: the radiologist Ferdinand Gidon underwent several finger amputations; he eventually died in 1954, a victim of his research.

2. Mr. Blum: Léon Blum (1872–1950), leader of the French Socialist Party. He was several times elected minister president, and was in Dachau between 1943 and 1945.

3. Mr. Bailby: Léon Bailby, an extreme right-wing journalist.

330. To Stefan Zweig   *[March 1935]*

Dear friend,

while seeing to your business with the post (Strauss) I had occasion to be in your hotel, and there this letter was given back to me; no one had picked it up.

As for S. (whether he ever got your letter or not) I will know more in a few days. The German post hasn't written back yet, in 8 days. Perhaps it is censorship.

I embrace you,   your Joseph R.

331. To Blanche Gidon   *Hotel Imperator*
                                                        Nice
                                                        4 March 1935

Madam and dear friend,

I don't want to wait for your promised letter to come because I am in the middle of the third section of my book,[1] and I have absolutely got to finish it tomorrow or the day after.—Thank you so much for the 650 francs, it's a real lifesaver, but I need to know for which story I am being paid. Write and tell me, please. Tell me, too, my dear, how *Mr. Gidon* is faring. Is he calmer in himself? Give him my warmest regards, please.

Yours sincerely (and longing to see you again soon),

Your old Joseph Roth

1. my book: *The Hundred Days.*

332. To Stefan Zweig   Hotel Imperator
                                                          Nice, Alpes-Maritimes
                                                          Boulevard Gambetta
                                                          6 March 1935

Dear friend,

thank you for your lines, and please excuse the fact that I'm dictating these to you now. It dawned on me that I was being perhaps too demanding of you with my affairs. You probably have lots of other things that need your attention in Vienna. Please tell me whether your mother's condition is as grave as it seemed to you before.

Please, my dear friend, don't push me with the novel. I can only write at my own speed. An inadequate book would mean literary and physical suicide for me. A slow book that refuses to be finished is merely physical. I am very industrious these days, and mindful of you.

Don't be upset if my letters are full of impatience and even irritations. It so happens I live and write in a continual state of confusion.

I send you lots of kind and fond wishes—please write me before you leave for Salzburg.

Yours sincerely   [Joseph Roth]

333. Stefan Zweig to Joseph Roth   *[Vienna, March 1935]*

Dear friend,

this will have to be brief, I have the final proofs to correct,[1] no secretary, and forty phone calls to make, I am frantically busy. You'll have a letter from me next week, I can't do anything now, I need to supervise the typesetters at their work.

I'm sorry I can't help as I'd like to. It's like this: as long as I'm in Austria, I'm obliged to adhere to the (unusually pedantic) currency regulations, i.e., can't send funds abroad beyond a certain minimum, and have no funds with Hella at the moment. You must understand, you know I insist on obeying all regulations absolutely to the letter, especially here, so that I can't have any accusation leveled against me that would mask the earlier injustice done to me. In April, though, it looks as though I'll be in Italy, and will be better able to act from there.

Dear friend, I don't have the peace of mind to go through this all with you, the telephone is ringing off the hook—you can have no idea, by the way, how badly off authors are here, how much even small sums mean to them, nor again how *many* of them get in touch, including a few I would never have expected. It's ghastly, and I'll be glad when the book is printed, and I can leave. The arrangement with your wife will be extended with good old Csokor's[2] help, but it will become doubly acute in two or three months; but the only thing that matters *now* is that you finish the novel, and that's it. Everything else can be sorted out more easily after that.

One thing, Roth, don't name figures to *anyone* but me. You have no idea on what tiny amounts people get by here, and how much resentment it causes when (to them) fantastic amounts are referred to deprecatingly. The newspapers pay 20 schillings for a feuilleton, and people come to blows over royalties. More anon. I am frantic in a way I haven't been for years, please forgive me.

Sincerely, Z.

Don't worry about the R.S.[3] affair any more. I've found what I wanted to know.

1. the proofs: of Zweig's *Maria Stuart* (Vienna: Reichner, 1935).
2. Csokor: Franz Theodor Csokor (1885–1968), Austrian playwright and essayist, friend of JR's.
3. R.S.: Richard Strauss.

334. To Stefan Zweig *15 March 1935*

Dear friend,

thank you for your letter. The R.S. business is in the hands of the post now, I can't do anything about it. I'll get an answer in a day or two. It's no extra trouble for me, the wheels are turning.

Forgive me for burdening you with financial stuff. Not because it matters, but to clarify things let me tell you that of course I name sums only to my closest friends, and secondly, that if compelled to by some necessity, I would not scruple to say how much money I need or think I need, even in front of other needy persons or beggars. I myself allow Rothschild to tell me he's short of a million to develop his goldfields, for instance. Neither in my personal nor my public life is there *anything* I have to hide, if occasion should demand that I say everything. The consideration that more wretched individuals than I might view my particular wretchedness with envy is not one that I will permit myself to indulge. Even if I had to assume the presence of envy, or resentment, or something of the kind, I would of course still have to speak the truth. (And so would you!) I have written bad books, but never lying books. I can't and mustn't, not even in personal life, pay false regard. It's foolish—however "prudent" it might appear. Besides, even on an objective look and closer inspection, I don't believe I am any less miserable than others are. My "helpfulness" and my "comradeliness"—horrible words by the way, that need to be encased in quotation marks—you yourself are so familiar with that you would never suspect me of not having such virtues. They are all as natural to me as breathing: giving, needing, and being open about needing.

All this is said for reasons of principle—*lest any misunderstandings occur.* AT LEAST not between the two of us.

I am working hard, at night, by candlelight, this letter too. Candles are rather stimulating. (The ceiling light is poor here.)

Please, write me something personal to you, that's what matters.

I embrace you, your old   J.R.

335. To Stefan Zweig   *Café de France*
                                                21 March 1935
                                                Hotel Imperator
                                                Nice

Dear friend,

here is the R.S. bumf for you. I can't understand why you don't write. I
am going under, and haven't the strength any more to explain everything
to you. Bad things have happened, Mr. de Lange is ill, I can't have any
more money, I have become Beierle, only without Beierle's penchant for
naughtiness.

Sincerely your   J.R.

Please observe that the receipt is the property of the post office, and
you are merely permitted to keep it, but are not allowed, much less
obliged to return it. Madness!

336. Stefan Zweig to Joseph Roth   *Hotel Regina*
                                                Vienna, 29 March 1935

Dear friend,

thank you very much for sending me the receipt. I'm unable to write
proper letters, because I had to finish correcting the proofs, and do many
other things in between. Pretty much everything has now been seen to.
The book[1] will be a very handsome object, and in no way inferior to the
"Insel" in terms of production standards. I do feel very happy with the
choice of Reichner, because he publishes good things, Lernet-Holenia's[2]
poems and a lecture by Bruno Walter[3] on "the moral force of music."
Someone told me de Lange isn't as happy with his house as he once was,
but perhaps that's just tittle-tattle, and your new book[4] will re-enthuse
him. (If only it was finished!) Curiosity is making me impatient, and also
for your sake. I so want you to clear your decks again. I'm staying here

another week or two, then Budapest for a couple of days, and then away from Austria, either to Italy, or else London, and the next book. We have to work now. If you pay attention to the world, it makes you very melancholy, here too every conversation automatically turns to politics . . . Well, you'll have my book in a fortnight, and by that time I'll be able to write you a proper letter, wherever I end up going.

This just as a sign of life, so you don't go demented at

your Stefan Zweig

1. the book: *Maria Stuart*.

2. Lernet-Holenia: Alexander Lernet-Holenia (1897–1976), Austrian writer.

3. Bruno Walter (1876–1962), the noted conductor and friend of the Mann family, who emigrated to the United States in 1939.

4. your new book: *The Hundred Days*.

337. To Blanche Gidon (written in French)   *Café de France*
                                               Nice
                                               [postmarked: 11 April 1935]

Madam and dear friend,

I'm interrupting my work to make you the following offer: Mr. Schalom Asch (whom you will surely have heard of, as *the greatest Jewish writer* of our day) would like to be translated into French. He suggests that you translate him (his book *Trost des Volkes*, published in German in 1934, with Zsolnay), and he will pay you *2,000 francs for the translation*. But you must also try and find him a publisher, Plon for example. Schalom Asch is the "classic" among contemporary Jewish authors, the successor to PEREZ,[1] "the grandfather" of non-Hebrew Jewish literature. Schalom Asch—who is my friend, and is not at all Left—is looking for a French publisher. Do you think Plon would do it, my dear? (And how is Mr. Gidon? I am very worried about him.) Why have you not written me in such a long time? WHY? Please write back straightaway, and let me know if you would like to translate SCHALOM ASCH for 2,000 francs!

Always your loyal   Joseph Roth

As for me, I will write you properly soon.

Mr. Schalom Asch's address is:

Lanterne, Nice, Villa Schalom

1. Perez: Itzhak Leib Perez (1851–1915), Yiddish writer and dramatist.

338. To René Schickele   *[undated]*

Dear dear Mr. René Schickele,

I'd like to see you, but I am horribly busy and even weighed down with my stupid book. This is the first and last time I'll ever tackle anything "historical." Devil take it—in fact, I think it was the Antichrist in person who got me into it. It's improper, simply improper to want to form existing, historical events all over again—and it's disrespectful too. There is something godless about it—only I can't quite say what.

Please, come soon. And, for "practical reasons," before S.Z. goes to America.

Thank you so much for the beautiful Klopstock.

Sincerely your   Joseph Roth

339. To Erika Mann[1]   *[Spring 1935]*

Dear Madam,

I want to thank you for the wonderful evening in your theater.[2] I feel I should tell you that you do ten times as much against the barbarians as all we writers put together. I am a little ashamed, but also powerfully encouraged. I thank you, and kiss your hand. Your humble

Joseph Roth

1. Erika Mann (1905–1969), actor, writer, rally driver, daughter and later amanu-ensis of Thomas Mann.

2. evening in your theater: from 1933 to 1936, Erika Mann ran the anti-Fascist Pep-permill cabaret in Zurich, in which she appeared, with Therese Giehse, Klaus Mann, Sibylle Schloss, and others. For a vivid description of the troupe and its ambience, see Wolfgang Koeppen's novel *A Sad Affair*, first published in English in 2003.

340. To Blanche Gidon

Hotel Bristol
Vienna
26 May 1935

Madam and dear friend,

don't be surprised you haven't heard from me of late. I suddenly had to leave Amsterdam for Paris,[1] on account of my wife. I am having awful days here. I am very, very unhappy. It's an awful thing the way the calam-ity keeps overtaking me.

Sincerely, your old   Joseph Roth

Please remember me fondly to Mr. Gidon

1. Paris: *recte*, Vienna.

341. To René Schickele

13 June 1935

Dear, esteemed Mr. Schickele,

now I "really" am leaving, and I'm sorry we didn't see each other first.

You were wrong: my chance meeting with your son an hour after my return doesn't "prove" at all that I wasn't going to call on you.

The fact that you are capable of believing something of the sort "proves" rather that you harbor suspicion of me "in the depths of your soul," which is something I deeply regret.

It probably was unmannerly of me to leave Nice without saying good-bye to you. But I had to leave in a hurry, and I knew that I would be back.

It is NOT TRUE to say that I was ever indifferent to you, not even for a moment.

I am too conceited, and too clever, to bother with lying. I would be really sorry if you still thought otherwise after this letter. I like you very much, the writer especially, "the human being" I wasn't able to "get to know," possibly through my own fault, possibly through yours as well. Kiss your lovely wife's hand for me,

Sincerely, your   Joseph Roth

I am going to Marseille, then to Paris.

342. To Blanche Gidon (written in French)   *Dégustation Cintra*
                                                Marseille
                                                17 June 1935
                                                Hotel Beauvau

Dear friend,

as I didn't think I'd be back in the south again, I had my mail forwarded to Paris. But I didn't get your letter at the Hotel Foyot. Was your second letter mailed to the Foyot as well? If it's anything urgent, then please write to me here at the Beauvau, express. *I will be in Paris at the end of the week*. Unfortunately, I have to go to Amsterdam again. It's a difficult thing to explain in a letter. I have a ghastly thing going on in Vienna, over my wife. I have taken steps to start to divorce her, which is horribly difficult, like everything in that area. Mrs. Kolb probably heard of my return from Mr. Schickele. It's barely a week ago now. Between you and me, it's starting to bother me. It's like a hornet's nest, this agitation among the "émigrés," these letters, this noise, this tittle-tattle. Mr. Schickele has adopted an attitude toward me that's simply incomprehensible—that's the kindest way I can put it. Mr. Kesten too. All these gents are starting to view me with something approaching hatred. And I've done my best for them. It's not my fault that Schickele sent Fischer a telegram after Hitler's takeover—nor am I responsible for the lack of success of his books. Even

Annette Kolb has something against me. I know I'm "uncomfortable" because I have no truck with "compromises" with Germany. And I mean to do all I can to remain just as unyielding as hitherto, and to fight those others who want to "understand everything," basically because they're cowards, JUST COWARDS, with their "profound humanity." In fact, it's profound cowardice.

But we'll talk before long.

All yours, loyally,   Joseph Roth

343. To Blanche Gidon (begun in French)   *Hotel Beauvau*
    Marseille
    20 June 1935

Dear friend,

forgive me for writing to you in German, it's too difficult to explain otherwise:

First of all, I want you not to think for a moment that I'm angry with you. I'm just sad. Because while it takes me a very long time to get used to a human being, once I have, it's equally impossible for me to detach myself from him. After I had done so much that was disagreeable to you, and you continued to give me proof of your friendship, I felt doubly beholden to you. You knew that, and you would also have known that thenceforth, come what may, I was bound to remain loyal to you, and that there was between us something resembling a comradeship-in-arms. Allow me to tell you that you tried to sacrifice your sensitivity to this comradeship a little too quickly. Mr. Gabriel Marcel, to whom I spoke quite openly about your mistakes in the translation of the *Radetzky March*, would have understood quite clearly that you couldn't have given up the translation of my *Antichrist* without my agreement. Mr. Gabriel Marcel is sensitive and clever, he would have understood. You, though— as the Germans say—threw your rifle in the corn, and to some extent it was my rifle too. Why the haste, when the book has been waiting for long enough? I am responsible to my French readership. And I would have revised the translation with you, with Marcel, and perhaps with some other writer. As it is now, I am open to chance. All this I tell you as your friend, and as your true friend. On Saturday I'll be in Paris. Can I see you and Mr. Marcel? I'll be staying at the Foyot, for 2 days.

Give my best to Mr. Gidon.

I kiss your hand,   your old Joseph Roth

344. *To Blanche Gidon (begun in French)*   *[July 1935]*

The very unhappy Joseph Roth

greets you, Madam and dear friend, with all his heart, and asks you please to come and see him.

I am very unhappy. Please don't let it show, my dear friend!

My best to Mr. Gidon

345. *To Blanche Gidon*   *[postmarked: Paris, 13 July 1935]*

Dear friend,

you probably won't have understood why I was so sad yesterday. Something terrible had transpired shortly before, and I wasn't able to cancel our meeting.

Please tell Mr. Gidon for me.

Sincerely, and till soon. I'll tell you about it.

Your old J.R.

I'm writing away from home, and have only envelopes[1] with me.

1. This note was scribbled on a Hotel Foyot envelope.

346. To Félix Bertaux Hotel Foyot
Paris
15 July [1935]

Dear friend,

I've been here for two weeks. You haven't replied to two letters of mine from Marseille and Nice. Would you at least care to *see* me?

Ever your old friend Joseph Roth

347. To Stefan Zweig *24 July 1935*
Hotel Foyot
Paris 6ᵉ

My dear friend,

your dear letter, which confirms you almost as much as it shakes me, will not be put off. I am therefore replying to it straightaway, I'd be grateful if you did the same with a couple of lines to confirm arrival of this one. Of late, lots of mail seems to be getting lost in Germany.—Maybe you're right in saying that you were unable to take the steep fall that Romain Rolland did.[1] It's a plunge into darkness. But you're not right when you describe my defensive fury as an aggressive hatred. That's not well thought out by you, who are supposed to know me well. That I, Yossl Roth from Radziwillow, am defending Germany with all its past glories is perfectly clear to me. My Jewishness never appeared as anything else to me but an accidental quality, like, say, my blond mustache (which could equally well have been brown). I never suffered from it, I was never proud of it. Nor is it the fact that I think and write in German that bothers me now—but the fact that 40 million people in the middle of Europe are barbarians. I share this sorrow with quite a lot of other people, including most of the remaining 20 million Germans, inasmuch as these things can be quantified. I believe in a Catholic empire, German and Roman, and I am near to becoming an orthodox, even a militant

Catholic. I don't believe in "humankind"—I never did—but in God, and in the fact that mankind, to whom He shows no mercy, is a piece of shit. (Though of course, I *hope* for his mercy.) "Palestine" and "humankind" have been repulsive to me for a long time. All that matters to me is God—and, for now, on earth, in the area where I am permitted to labor and discharge my duty, a German Catholic Empire. I will do all in my feeble powers to bring about a Habsburg return. I don't want to "convert" you to my persuasion, because I have too much respect for you. But I don't want you to go imputing hatred and aggression to me, as you do to the *Weltbühne* of miserable memory, and the "émigrés." Mine is not hatred, but righteous fury. And I will be proved right, because Hitler won't last more than another year and a half, and then, slowly but surely, we shall have a new German Empire.

You see, my dear friend, you believed in "humankind," and, had you been as foolish as your "maitre" Rolland, you'd still be a Bolshevik now. But you're more sensible than that, you can't be a Communist. But nor do you wholly and firmly believe in God. Therefore you are in despair. Only God can help you. And free you from the errors of your ways, some of which you even see yourself.

(I don't know what to do with my two novels. I am completely exhausted, in terms of writing. My two books: I don't know, I'm fiddling around with the first of them, it's a scandal, not a work of literature. I'll write you about it under a separate cover.)

You're not right when you say we've all been driven mad. There is a balance in the world between madness and logic. At any rate, we, who have been given the sword of reason, have noright to throw it away.

The Habsburgs will return. Please don't deny what's all too evident! You see I've been right thus far. Austria will be a monarchy. I'm right. I foresaw the madness and excess of Prussia. Because I believe in God. And you, you didn't see it, because you believe in "humankind," a concept so unclear that by contrast with it, you could think to meet God on the nearest street corner.

Of course friendship is our true home. And you may be sure I will observe it more faithfully than anyone else.

Sincerely,   your old Joseph Roth

1. the steep fall that Romain Rolland did: (Stefan Zweig's admired friend) Rolland went to Moscow in 1935, visiting Gorki, and publicly approved Stalin's show trials of Zinoviev and Radek, etc. By pointing this out in such a way, JR hopes to keep his friend from becoming a Soviet sympathizer—even once removed.

348. To Blanche Gidon   [Paris] 7 August 1935

Dear friend, dearest friend,

I am full of anxieties and very unhappy. I cannot write. One catastrophe after another befalls me.

But I love you dearly, and Mr. Gidon too. Believe me!

Your old Joseph Roth

349. To Stefan Zweig   Paris
                                           Hotel Foyot
                                           14 August 1935

Dear friend,

thank you for your kind letter. Of course your plan[1] is completely right. But you should bear in mind the following: (a) there are various efforts in hand to bring together Hitler's enemies. The spectrum goes from the Catholics to the Communists, in Paris alone I have had communications from 3 different sides. A few "Leftists" would like to use me as a "bridge" to the Catholics. Even though all these attempts remain purely political, they would disrupt the much more measured campaign which you have in mind, through *simultaneity*, if nothing else; (b) this campaign must not be restricted to the circle that decks itself in the following adjectives:

liberal, freethinking, Jewish, cosmopolitan, or socialist. These people
have been quiet for too long, some of them have even thrown in the
towel. For the last 2 months it has been clear to the world that Catholicism alone is taking the fight to the Third Reich—I don't know if this
view is correct, but there it is. You were surely right not to indulge in
petty polemics. That's not at issue here. Where you were wrong was in
the matter of *restraint*. With the *vae victis* that *you* blurted out, with the
resignation, in other words, that you showed all too clearly. You were not
alone there, since Thomas Mann and others of your stamp have adopted
the same position, resignation has infected most thinking people, who
had pinned their hopes on you (plural). Since then, the Communists have
taken up the fight, admittedly in their familiarly stupid way; and, more
cleverly, of course, the Catholics. Bear in mind the not unjustified view in
those affected, that all those listed above, the liberals et al., are themselves
partly to blame for Hitler, then you will see that an appeal, however well
prepared, exclusively from these, *now*, after their long silence, is likely
to provoke a certain muteness of response. They have been kept waiting for too long. Too long those who embodied the "world's conscience"
were themselves mute and expectant. When they now, finally, find their
voices, the others will be silent. Quite apart from the fact that I personally don't have much time for the so-called world's conscience. The world
never had a conscience, if you ask me. The world had phases of clemency
and inclemency. (You know my believing skepticism.) (c) So far as Mr.
Weizmann[2] goes, he is certainly one of the most genial men of our day.
(Once, when the *FZ* wanted to send me off to meet him, on the occasion
of his visit to Frankfurt, and I was standing in for the feuilleton editor, I
sent Mr. Kracauer instead. I didn't want to expose myself, journalistically,
to such an inspired nationalist.) (Personally, I'd have done it happily.) A
Zionist is a National Socialist, a National Socialist is a Zionist. I willingly
believe, I'd even assert that Mr. Weizmann is "more than just a Jew."
But his role locks him into Judaism, and into its national form. I'm sure
he is large-hearted and generous enough that he shouldn't be confused
with a "Nationalist." I know: he's not merely a Jew. But his name bears

the association: Jewish nationalist. Clever Weizmann himself suggests: foolish Einstein.[3] (I mean of course: *politically* foolish Einstein.) I am of course aware of W's organizational genius. But for the thing that you're planning, his organization is useful only if he remains *anonymous*. Don't forget that the Jewish boycott has collapsed; that the Zionists—unlike all the other Jews—are in some proximity to the Nazis; that there are relationships between them of all kinds; that even sympathies between them exist, as might be expected among nationalists of various stripe; but that the most powerful urge of the Nazis is anti-Semitism, because Jews are not liked anywhere, and, if there were to be a world conscience anywhere it wouldn't be roused by Jews; if a goy is a friend to Zionists, then it will be out of anti-Semitism. Whereas if we, you and I and the likes of us, support Zionism, it's because we're human beings, not Jews or non-Jews. In this point there is no understanding between Mr. Weizmann and me. (To be concrete, if we were to meet, I would be in his eyes—magnanimity here or there—I would be a "defector.") I am delighted to be a defector, from Germans and Jews. I am proud of it. *As a consequence* I am *not* a defector from the lists of Christians and human beings.

(d) Therefore I fail to understand why you would turn to a brother of the National Socialists, namely a Zionist, never mind how clever he is, in the fight against Hitler, who himself remains just a *stupid* brother of the Zionists. Maybe he'll help you protect Judaism. But what I want to do is protect Europe and humanity, both from the Nazis and from the Hitler-Zionists. I don't care about protecting the Jews, except as the most imperiled advance guard of mankind. If *that's* what Mr. Weizmann has in mind, then I will agree to participate, with my feeble strength—which isn't a manner of speaking.

(e) I am convinced that nothing will have any effect, *today*, that is drawn up and signed only by the so-called liberals. They have failed, been silent, grubbed for compromises, failed to find them, and lost all credit. The Jewish boycott was another failure. The Social Democracy of the intellectuals has played out, like that of the politicians before them. The only thing that will have any effect is this: an appeal of the kind you are planning, *closely worked on* with conservatives of all faiths. To be "symbolic": from Weizmann to Faulhaber.[4] The symbolic name of Thomas Mann doesn't do much any more. From both flanks, the attitude he incorporates, is, if not despised, then at least ignored.—It's too late! Under certain circumstances, even reflection can be suicide.

(f) Even though I'm in full agreement with you about the absurdity of scattered and improvised polemics in silly and unworthy journals, one mustn't underestimate the importance of drain-cleaning labors. Hundreds of foreign newspapers take denunciatory material against Hitler from them. Thousands of journalists writing against Germany help themselves from that crap. It's good, it's very good. (I myself haven't been averse to clearing the odd drain.) And I am ready to go on doing it, *pro nomine Dei*. What's important—but that will have occurred to you too—is that some foreign names (example: Toscanini) join in from time to time.

(g) Personal: any journey I undertake will have to be thoroughly planned in advance. I've got my adopted children[5] in Normandy, I'll have to send my wife there, there's a whole crazy tangle of complications, but I'll tell you about it sometime.

I don't want to interrupt your enthusiasm (so pleasing to me) any more. How long will you stay in Marienbad? Please let me know, right away!

I embrace you sincerely, and kiss the hand of your dear wife.

Your old J.R.

1. your plan: Stefan Zweig had been going to lend his name to a declaration, but later withdrew it. As ever, Roth—see no. 347—wanted to steer his influential and somehow will-less friend.

2. Weizmann: Chaim Weizmann (1874–1952), chemist by profession. Zionist leader, and the first president of Israel, in 1949.

3. Einstein: Albert Einstein.

4. Faulhaber: Michael von Faulhaber (1869–1952), cardinal of Munich from 1921.

5. adopted children: Manga and Tüke Manga Bell.

350. To Stefan Zweig   *Hotel Foyot*
                                                         Paris 6ᵉ
                                                         19 August 1935

My dear friend,

I am delighted by your splendid élan. (At the same time, I permit myself to send you the most recent number of the *Christliche Ständestaat*,[1] and ask that you read the article about Jews in it; apart from my piece in it, and the note on the Olympics,[2] which I also wrote.) Your sensibility may be appalled to see a lousy Jew like me, printed straight after His Holiness the Pope. But please bear in mind that I am very, very much in earnest about all this. I see no other way than the ascent of Calvary, and no greater Jew. I may even go further, if I have the strength, and join an order. Call it a type of suicide if you like. I can see nothing other than the Christian faith (no literature). I don't believe in this world, and I don't believe we can achieve anything in it. If God wills, you can shoot with a broomstick, and if He doesn't not even a cannon will fire.

Of course I'm always at your disposal. But we can do what we like, it will always remain a "manifesto" and I don't think anyone in the League of Nations (say) has any time for our style or our precision. It will just be another manifesto. And even if the League of Nations—which has never yet stopped a war—were to acknowledge us, will they do anything to hinder a pogrom?—The only practical thing we might achieve would be passports, Nansen passports for the poor refugees I often meet, because I work in the committee here—and the papers are always the worst of it! We'll protest: fine! Another protest. A good protest! And people will sit up and take note. And then what? What is it we want to achieve?

You underestimate or ignore a couple of major things:

1. the urge to humiliate Jews didn't begin yesterday or today; it's been part of the platform of the Third Reich *from the very start*. Everyone knows that. Streicher is no different from Hitler, and you didn't need to wait for Streicher to make his way from Nuremberg to Berlin! The founding principle, so to speak, of National Socialism, is none other than

contempt for the Jewish race! Why did it take you this long to grasp that? How come you didn't get it 2 years ago? 2¾ years ago? That bestiality was there from the start. It didn't suddenly set in a couple of months ago, the vilification of Jews. We were insulted and humiliated from Hitler's very first day! Why is this protest so tardy?

2. I don't believe in politicians and their parties, but I see there the last vestiges of *power*. And if I should succeed in bringing Catholics and Communists together in a campaign within Germany, and outside, I will have done a great deal to combat that hell. Why not? Why not try?

I think, my dear friend, that your enthusiasm is just as abrupt as your previous resignation was baffling, to me anyway. We were insulted and dishonored from the first day of Hitler. Why does it take you this long to wax indignant? But let it go. Better late than never.—But do you really think a manifesto can do something *so late in the day*? Which of the affected parties would believe us, even if the League of Nations should— which no longer exists, any more than the world conscience? It's late, it's all so late. We were insulted and dishonored immediately—do we wait 2¾ years to react to a slap? What were you thinking when Hitler took over? When the Third Reich was proclaimed? Was your sense of honor not just as offended as mine was? Yes, it was!—But you were an optimist, and I wasn't. That's why I swallowed hard and took on disagreeable allies.—But there's no sense in going over all that old stuff. (Whatever you want to undertake, I stand at your disposal.)

Nor should you underestimate the technical difficulties: it will take you 8 days—not 3! It's terribly hard to draw up a document like that.

Please be careful not to lose weight too fast! That can be very dangerous.

Tell your dear wife, please, that I didn't get her letter. (Another one lost.) And that I kiss her hand.

Greetings and embraces,   your old J.R.

1. the *Christliche Ständestaat*: an Austrian monarchist publication, edited by Professor Franz von Hildebrandt and Klaus Dohrn.

2. the note on the Olympics: unsurprisingly, JR opposed the holding of the Olympic Games in Berlin.

351. To Stefan Zweig Hotel Foyot
Paris 6ᵉ
21 August 1935

Dear friend,

I want to set out my personal predicament to you—as so often before.
I am compelled to by an alarmingly vulgar letter I've received from Mr.
L.[1] I want to ask you for an effective remedy, namely whether I might not
become an author of the Reichner-Verlag.[2] Since the sudden death of Mr.
de Lange,[3] the situation is completely transformed. I owe the de Lange
Verlag: (a) the 100 days, which are finished, (b) the "regular"[4] which still
needs a fortnight's work or so. Thereafter I am free, and I want to start
work on the great "Strawberries" novel[5] that I told you about in Nice
once—you remember, in the little bistro—which will take me at least a
year, it's the novel about my childhood. Well, for the two books I'm getting paid 4,225 French francs per month till the end of 1935 (*all* rights are
with the publisher). At the end of September I hand in the second book.
Thereafter I'm free. But I see my material end looming even before that,
because I will have to draw on my advance to pay for hotels, children,
schools, and so on. Well, after that coarse letter from L., I will not be able
to work with him again, after the present contract has run its course.
Following Mr. de Lange's sudden death, L. is now playing the publisher
with me—and it was I who got him the job in the first place; remember,
he came to Amsterdam holding a signed promise from me that he had
the exclusive rights to my next book. Thereupon Mr. L. got his job, and
his salary of 1,000 marks a month. And I got advances. Not to mention
the "Orcovente" business that I told you all about in Nice. I enclose his
letter with this. Please return it to me. A callow Kurfürstendamm Jew
who has done nothing makes so bold as to write to me, who gave him his
start in life, in that tone. It's of a piece with those Jewesses with lacquered
nails you see in Marienbad. Please read the letter. The chutzpah of it!
Exacerbated by the circumstance that L. let it lie for a long time, before
sending it off, and forgot to change the date. The chutzpah was stronger
than he was.

So I am facing my end. I don't want to have anything more to do with those shits from the Kurfürstendamm. My question is this: can you help me secure a home and a contract for my "Strawberries"?

Please answer as soon as possible.

Sincerely,   your old Joseph Roth

1. Mr. L.: Walter Landauer.
2. The Reichner-Verlag: but see no. 321 . . . !
3. Gerard de Lange died on 25 June 1935 of a heart attack; he was just 41.
4. the "regular": JR's working title for the book that became *Confession of a Murderer*.
5. the great "Strawberries" novel: one of Roth's long-standing novel plans, which he had talked about with Kiepenheuer, etc. See the exquisite fragment in *Collected Shorter Fiction*. Other material for it found its way into *Weights and Measures* and *The Leviathan*.

352. *To Stefan Zweig*   *Paris, 27 August 1935*

Dear friend,

thank you for your letter of the 23rd inst. I am not in a tizzy about the letter from [. . .]. In view of the approaching end of the world, it's no big deal. But even then, in the trenches, staring death in the face 10 minutes before going over the top, I was capable of beating up a son of a bitch for claiming he was out of cigarettes when he wasn't. The end of the world is one thing, the son of a bitch is another. You can't put the son of a bitch down to the general condition of things. He's separate.[1]

My obligations to Huebsch are not of a contractual nature, but I feel myself bound to them, because we have an agreement: out of gratitude I will give him everything I write that he can use for the rest of my life.

Aside from that, I have no ties that affect the novel "Strawberries, Part I."[2]

On 1 December my funds dry up. That's why I asked you about Reichner. But I'm not asking you to give me any weighty recommendation.

Write and tell me when we can meet!

Your faithful old   Joseph Roth

1. he's separate: this too gets to the core of JR's predicament in the 1930s: where to begin!?

2. "Strawberries, Part 1": is JR teasing Zweig here? Or is he leaving options open for another round of contractual backsliding?

353. To Stefan Zweig   *Paris, 1 September 1935*
                                                          Hotel Foyot

Dear friend,

thank you for having a word with Mr. Reichner. In theory you're quite right that I should seek to reserve all foreign rights. But if I don't achieve a certain minimum for German rights that would enable me to live, then what choice do I have but to sell the foreign rights! And how are the German rights ever going to add up to that minimum! I never earn anything above and beyond my advances anyway. I can work out roughly what I would earn from German rights: maybe 1,000 to 1,500 francs per month. And I have a wife and two children. (My legal wife is currently being put up free of charge at an institution in Baden. But the sanatorium [. . .] is asking for 7,000 schillings.) The children can't live on fresh air. Nor can I stick the whole caboodle in a pokey 1½-room flat either. Even though I'm perfectly sure that none of them will ever thank me for all I have done for them, I can't abandon them now. In my case, love goes through the conscience, the way with others it goes through their stomachs. What do you mean by "sensible separation"? I can see that my inclination to be swayed by passion—and how rarely does that happen—I mean, my private passion to give in, and not to think about it—isn't sensible. (A couple of months later, I bump into reality, it feels like an old bruise.) But separation? I don't separate, I give. And if I don't do that, I'd have to live alone. In other words, I violate my conscience and abandon the 3 poor people who live off me. I could do it. But it would take me a year to get over such an act, just as it took me two years to get over my wife's illness, for which I still feel responsible. What else is there I could cut myself adrift from? Is it possible to live more cheaply than I do, 600 francs for two people, at the Foyot? Should I have a house key in my pocket? Live in fear of the taxman? Have dealings with concierges? Cooking smells and "family life"? I have to be free, but I don't want to be a bad man. I can't give up either humanity or freedom. In theory you're completely right, in practice it's all rubbish. But perhaps you're right in suggesting that to keep freedom, one has to jettison humanity. (It's not possible to reserve "a portion" of it, it's indivisible.)—So what to do?—I would draw it to your attention, my dear friend, that you are able to speak to me from a certain comfort; you may be very clever, very faithful, very friendly, but you have never experienced my sort of collision with reality. You keep forgetting what a light-headed person I am, and you allow yourself to be misled by my experience to suppose that I was sensible. I'm not, not at all, and you persist in thinking I am, and so you write to me accordingly.

I will ask you to bear in mind my practical circumstances:

a. I must and want to leave [. . .];[1]

b. I still need to be able to live;

how can these two be combined?

Should I start looking around for other publishers?

[. . .]

I don't want to take any steps until both my books have been handed in. I'll write to you again, as and when.

My 100 days look as bad in print as they did in manuscript.

The other novel will take me another fortnight.

Sincerely,   your old Joseph Roth

1. [. . .]: de Lange.

354. *To Stefan Zweig*   *12 October 1935*

Dear friend,

thank you for your kind letter. I will have finished my other novel on or around the 25th. (*The Regular.*) Then I will have to go to Amsterdam for at least a fortnight, so that I can "impress" my Dutch friends and the press.—My novel *The Hundred Days* came out yesterday. I'm sending you a copy today. If you would, please confirm arrival of both book and letter.

I've put the girl with the nuns for 300 francs a month. The boy in a school (where his Negro uncle works) also for 300 francs. But, as per contract, I am only getting money from de Lange till 1 November. I refuse to enter into a new contract with him. So I don't know what to do.

I want to and I have to go to Amsterdam after finishing the second book. After that I should like to be alone somewhere for a week, and rest. I don't know what to do. If I were a hysteric, I would take refuge in illness.

What shall I do? I have nothing to eat—not even anything to drink. Please give me an answer.

I beg you sincerely, VERY earnestly, please reply immediately to your old Joseph Roth

355. To Stefan Zweig   *Paris*
18 October 1935

Please, the stories referred to in this letter will follow immediately.
Dear friend,

do I need to tell you that your telegram and dear letter made me blissfully happy? I have no sense of the novel at all, I couldn't even bring myself to read the proofs, I've hardly opened it since, every word and comma reeks to me of ghastly torments, bills presented by porters and waiters, and sundry other ritual humiliations. I have no idea, perhaps you overestimate it, or I underestimate it, everything's possible. On top of which, I'm busy with the next book,[1] completely engrossed in it. As for sales, etc., I'm not optimistic. The only place I have readers is Holland. In Switzerland I've been so far ignored by the leading newspapers. In Austria, I'm between two stools, the reactionaries taking me for a left-wing Jew, and the Lefties for a "renegade." For German refugees, Heinrich

Mann, Feuchtwanger, and Arnold Zweig are all important writers. It would take a miracle, I think, for the book to be a success. In film terms, Mussolini snuck in ahead of me. You don't film the same stuff twice in two years. So much for my "prospects."

For the umpteenth time I want to take advantage of your friendship, and ask you to write to your French publishers about the book. I broke with Gabriel Marcel, the editor at Plon, for not publishing *Antichrist* after he had contracted to do so. It would also help if you could draw the attention of various Swiss and Austrians to the *Hundred Days*; and write Huebsch about your impressions.

I know I'm taking advantage of you. But I need you too, and I can't go on living without your help. Literally: can't go on living. I'll explain my life to you, shall I? You will believe me that I write with a clear conscience—not even disturbed by alcohol—now that you've seen that I have a literary conscience. My dear friend, you surely won't suppose I'm any more unclear in my personal speech than I am in what I write. I beg you therefore to give this letter the same credence as you would any book of mine. I give you my word of honor that I write letters no less conscientiously than books. *And letters to you* at that!

That's why I beg you, my dear friend, to attend to this letter with good will and utter confidence; at least as much as you brought to my book: (I will write numbered headings, for the sake of clarity, and invite you to answer me point by point.)

1. I am not purposing my destruction. Only it so happens that in my case, self-destruction is the same as (my admittedly feeble efforts at) self-preservation. (More of which later.)

2. My material situation is as follows:

a. On 1 November I will be getting my *last* and final installment from Allert de Lange;

b. I have already borrowed 2,000 francs against this installment; [. . .]

---

1. the next book: i.e., *Confession of a Murderer*.

356. To Stefan Zweig   *[end of October 1935]*

My dear friend,

I thank you from the bottom of my heart. There is no other way of saying this in my vocabulary. Admittedly, 2,000 francs are not enough to save me, but even so, it's like a convict getting his chains not taken off him, but at least loosened. If they are loosened for two weeks, to me that feels like a scent of freedom, and I can at least look out my cell window. Would you be able to write to Mr. Hella sometime before the 1st?— Tomorrow I'm seeing Mr. Sabatier.[1] Thank you for that too, with all my heart.—We'll see. *I have yet to hear anything!* I am very much afraid you will be one of just 3 stray individuals who admire my book.[2] You will have made a mistake, I fear.

Whether it is a good book or not, I now have enough strength in me to finish the *Regular* and to go on to "Strawberries." I could have "Strawberries" finished within a year. What matters to me isn't so much being able to rest, as being allowed to work in complete peace and quiet. Work under such circumstances is better for me than sanatorium and vacation. Above all I need to be free of the exploitative contracts and humiliating bossiness of Landauer. It was so stupid of me to sign all those émigré contracts, and so sensible of you to steer clear of them. Everybody now resents me for my big advances,[3] and they hate me and will ruin my book with their hatred. Hate is even more magically powerful than love.

Why do you think I don't want to make any promises to you? *As your friend and as I believe in God and in your friendship*, I promise to stop killing myself if I can have the certainty of being left alive for another 3 months following 15 November. That's what I drink to forget! Only for that reason, and because instead of 6 or 8 I have to write 15 or 20 pages a day. I have found places for the children costing, all told, 650 francs per month. Perhaps that could be reduced eventually to 300 or so, by special dispensation. My room costs 700 francs per month. I beg you, I beg you, please rescue me. I am doomed, I can't go on selling myself *tout compris*, with all subsidiary rights, I can't wake up night after night from dread of what the morning will bring, the hotel manager, the mail, don't think when you see me that I live the way I appear, my life is atrocious, atrocious. I slink around like a wanted man, my hands shake and my feet shake, I only calm down a little once I have had a drink. Free me from my trembling and apprehension, if you can, and I will need only beer and wine to write with, not schnapps.—I have another fortnight clear in front of me, and then nothing, nothing thereafter, and I don't believe my book will be a success, but I still would like to go on living.

I am so sick, forgive me for begging you to confirm that you've received this letter. I no longer believe that letters arrive. I am inconsolable if I don't get word from you, my true, my one true friend! Are you upset with me for some reason? Have you had enough of me?

I embrace you sincerely,   your old J.R.

1. Mr. Sabatier: an editor at Grasset.
2. my book: *The Hundred Days*.

357. *To Stefan Zweig*   *Paris, 7 November 1935*
                                          Hotel Foyot

My dear best friend,
thank you for your dear letter, and for Mr. Hella's visit. You have no idea how oppressive I find small and tiny improvements; especially as I am only able to secure them from such a good and noble friend as you are, and nowhere else. I know, for instance, as a member of the German Hilfskommittee, who among the writers gets money, and how much. You would be surprised at the names, and the sums, too. These men of thought and imagination don't have the imagination to picture the hundreds of simple but very valuable people queuing every day for a work card, a piece of paper, a free meal, a paltry sum to appease the hotelkeeper—only for a short time. Perhaps I wouldn't have the imagination either if I didn't go over there from time to time myself, even

though I can do so little to help. I admit I always go on days when I feel particularly wretched, and then I sinfully gorge myself on the sight of someone skipping out because I've slipped him a carnet of bus tickets. They are so hard there with those poor wretches that I need to pull myself together if I am not to burst out crying—and they have to be hard, otherwise there wouldn't be something for everyone. The office is run by one Mr. Fritz Wolff,[1] he's a hard and kindly man, everybody hates him, I happen to know that he needs pills to help him sleep at night, because otherwise his conscience would keep him up. Thus far, I am almost the only one of the impecunious "artists" who hasn't accepted support from him. And how could I, even if I wanted to? How could I sit there like that, and receive beggars? One author, who lives in the south of France, got a sizable sum—not knowing I'm on the committee. Then he told me his wife had come into some money, and she went back to Germany, and the net result was the purchase of an automobile on the installment plan. That was a heavy blow to me. I can't get my head around that.

Well, enough cursing! You won't strengthen but perhaps lengthen our friendship if you try to order my life for the next 1–1½ years so that I don't have to fear the next decade. Another 6 months like the last, and I'm certain to be in hospital. I can't manage it any more, not physically. I can finish my next book by mid-December, and it would be nice if we could be together for once, without one or the other of us working on a book. Well, please be sure to come then, my dear friend.

Your dear wife spoke to the Humanitas Verlag in Zurich[2] for me. It so happened my good friend Leites went there too, and he came back with the following terms:

a. 18% royalty
b. 2,000 Swiss francs (in installments)

for a book of stories. I am to answer the Humanitas person[3]—he seems to be genuinely humane (and well-off) this week still. The only contracts I have outstanding are for the *Regular* with de Lange, and for 3 stories (with *conditional* acceptance) with Reece. I have a choice, I can either give him 3 stories or 6,000 francs. I have about 8, and when I'm done with the *Regular*, another two already sketched out. So, I'm not short of material.—For the reply to Humanitas I only need to know whether there's any prospect of your getting me publication in England—and what I then do about Huebsch, to whom I feel at least a *moral* obligation?

He hasn't written to me yet. Nothing on my book, except a long article in the *Basler Nationalzeitung*, and a very laudatory advance notice, with excerpt, in the *Prager Presse*. Not a squeak from the publisher, who hasn't even started selling. After chivvying me with about 100 letters to finish, it turns out it's the others who aren't ready, and he wants to put the whole print run on the market at once. But that of course allows the good publicity to wear off.

Please reply soon, I need to hear that you haven't forgotten me. How horribly lost I'd be without you.

Thank you, my friend, embraces,

your old J.R.

1. Fritz Wolff: an exiled lawyer, a friend of Roth's.
2. The Humanitas Verlag was founded in 1934.
3. the Humanitas person: Simon Menzel, who founded the publishing house.

358. To Stefan Zweig   *Hotel Foyot*
                                                   Paris
                                                   12 November 1935

Dear friend,

Mr. Paul Frischauer was passing through town yesterday. He promised me to talk to you very soon. He will have told you my idea about Moses Montefiore.[1] He is full of optimism, but I have to say I don't believe in it, at least not in the possibility of my getting hold of money to survive the next couple of weeks.

Also I'd like to ask you to tell me whether you think Heinemann would raise any objections, though of course he doesn't have an option as such.

You're quite right about the stories. I'll try and negotiate accordingly with the gentleman from Humanitas. But whether he agrees is debatable. I would have to pay out Mr. Reece immediately.

Nothing from Huebsch still. Even if he's contractually bound to de Lange, couldn't he pay me a little money toward the next novel, he must know by now that I'm industrious and diligent, if not always punctual?

It seems I don't have much alternative to Humanitas. I can't stay in the same horrible association with Landauer and Landshoff as hitherto. Please say hello to Joachim Maass,[2] if he's still in London.

I don't think I can do business with Bermann Fischer. I dislike him personally, because he tried pointlessly and for far too long to compromise with the Third Reich. It's the same reason I broke off relations with the *Frankfurter Zeitung*. I don't see why I should judge Bermann Fischer's behavior any differently than, say, Heinrich Simon's.

Dear friend, today's date is 12 November. If you tell me that we should have a detailed and practicable plan by December or January, please don't forget that there are 6 or 8 weeks till then. It's a long time to be writing, in such a pickle. I don't know how I can get through such an interval without taking the Humanitas offer. I'd rather sell a couple of stories and live, than sign a contract that may be more beneficial to my reputation—but only once I'm dead.

Don't worry about my drinking, please. It's much more likely to preserve me than destroy me. I mean to say, yes, alcohol has the effect of shortening one's life, but it staves off *immediate death*. And it's the *staving off of immediate death* that concerns me, not the *lengthening of my life*. I can't reckon on many more years ahead of me. I am as it were cashing in the last 20 years of my life with alcohol, in order to gain a week or two. Admittedly, to keep the metaphor going, there will come a time when the bailiffs turn up unexpectedly, and too early. That, more or less, is the situation.

What you say about the attempt to replace the planned manifesto makes me sad. Even at the time I thought the manifesto was pointless. Even more pointless is replacing it with something else. Basically, the Jews are small and petty. Only the great reflection of Jehovah sometimes lets them appear generous and magnanimous. At the decisive moment, their courage fails, and they run away. I don't blame them for it, you understand, my dear friend, weaklings are always *bound* to run away at the decisive moment. I am just trying to save you from an undertaking that could end up as a bitter disappointment to you. I have completely stopped believing that any undertaking involving more than two like-minded individuals could be the least use anyway. The collectivism of the few isn't going to cut much ice against the collectivism of the many. A couple of individuals have as much chance as anyone against the madness that results from the collectivism of the world today. One would have to organize a sort of guerrilla war of decent people. You wrote perhaps truer than you knew when you said: "If only it would come off, more or less." That's a form of words. It's very apparent that you have nothing beyond a vague hope. Things don't come off, "more or less," they come unstuck.

It's too late is all it is. Back then when the great shit started, a great and united front of decency might have achieved an extraordinary turnaround in no time. But intellectual forces fail, for instance the Vatican. It would have made a decisive impression on Europe, and on the League of Nations, if the Holy Father had said openly and courageously, as befits a pope, that he forbade all support for an Italian war of conquest. But today's pope is to Christians what Thomas Mann is to Nobel laureates, and Bermann Fischer is to publishers, and Gottfried Benn[3] to doctors, and Rothschild to rich Jews.

I would beg you, my dear friend, not to fritter away your strength in some collective; it only has a value when it is alone.

Forgive me these rather lengthy disquisitions. But I had to tell you, and I would have written in far greater detail, had I written by hand. It costs me too much time.

Please answer as soon as you are able.

Sincere embraces

[Joseph Roth]

1. Moses Montefiore (1784–1885), English philanthropist, whose early support of Palestine is considered influential in the founding of Zionism. Roth was thinking of writing an essay or book on him.

2. Joachim Maass (1901–72), German writer, went into exile in the United States in 1939, became professor at Mount Holyoke College, biographer of Kleist.

3. Gottfried Benn (1886–1956), doctor, essayist, and poet.

359. To Stefan Zweig   *16 November 1935*

Dear friend,

you're probably right with your doubts about the Montefiore. If I get only 100 pounds as advance, there's no point. According to Frischauer's account, that was "salvation."

No, it's not your tone that's "harsh," but your argumentation— generally correct and even faultless—but here not fitting the case. You can use any tone you want with me, whatever tone happens to suit you, *any one*; it's almost absurd to think that I might misunderstand your tone. All I sense there is a pedagogy that won't quite fit me, an attempt to influence me in a way that's all too "logical" and inflexible.

I can't come to London. I couldn't stand London. I detest the maritime and Protestant world. I hate the stiff collars and that deceitful "Gentlemen!" I would get sick there inside 3 days. There wouldn't be any point. I wouldn't be able to work there.

Since I've begun to write, I haven't been able to work without an advance. It's a great sin, but an even greater one is the suicide of writing *nothing at all*. I am now 41 years old. For 15 years I ate dry bread. Then I ate bread and butter. Then there was the war. Then ten more years of bread. Then there were the advances. Journalism. Revolting work. Humiliation. 16 books. "Success" only in the last 5 years—associated with personal unhappiness, and therefore invalidated. Loans and being swindled. Hitler. All the time looking after other people.

I can't live on dry bread any longer. (I eat almost nothing as it is.) I can't live in a village. People who order their lives by their income, at least *have* an income. The least of my income was always my advances. And then I fail to see why they had to be so small. Humility has nothing to do with economizing myself to death, which is a false economy. No one lives as economically as I do. A man in a cell is hardly as lonely as I am, sitting in a café to write. I don't need seclusion. *I am secluded.* Go tell a snail to get itself a house in the country.

What use is it to me if I run away with a guilty conscience? With my work? I'm always working, everywhere I go, so long as my conscience is clear. I can't work if I'm on the run.

How am I to live without an advance? Should I go to the baker, and ask him for an advance, instead of the publisher? Is it better, or more moral, if the cheese seller sends me threatening letters, instead of de Lange? Where exactly do you think I should economize? Most people who don't drink spend their money on food. What's the difference. Or on women; or gambling. That's right: "this is what I *have*, and I'll cut my cloth to fit." But I don't *have* anything. What cloth am I going to cut?

If I had ever had anything, it would never have occurred to me to cut my cloth according to what I *need*. But as it is I don't have anything, I never had anything.

I am not resisting, I see everything perfectly clearly. Everyone has his mistakes. I want to live in such a way that I can still bear my mistakes. They are a part of me. With all my mistakes, I still need 5,000 francs per month, and *security* for 2 years. Without my mistakes, I can't call my life my own. As little as I could without my virtues. I need security still more than money. I can't live in a continual state of *panic*. But I do live in a state of panic. Have done for years. As long as I've lived in my state of panic, I can't even see the correctness of a bit of advice. And I can't help it either if my reaction to it is wrong.—I SIMPLY DON'T KNOW. You can't tell a man sitting in a burning house to be a good fellow and fetch his coat before he jumps. It's pointless; even if he wanted to obey, he couldn't hear you.

I sense how many worries you have. Don't go worrying about me as well, to the extent that I become a burden for you. That would be a sin I couldn't bear.

My novel *will not* sell. I am sure of that.

I embrace you sincerely, never think that I don't hear your voice, and your splendid heart,

your old J.R.

---

360. To Stefan Zweig   *17 November 1935*

Dear friend,

I am chasing my last letter with another, because I fear I haven't been clear enough. If you think a "harsh" tone on your part might hurt me in some way, then I counter by being afraid you will still misunderstand me when I'm pretty clear with you.

Of course there can be no possibility—I'm not that cheap—of my ever supposing you had things easy, giving me cheap advice—or dear—from a position of security. The one who thinks like that is a scrounger. I never see you "in the box seat" but always in the tragic fog that shrouds us as writers, and I never see your bourgeois existence. (If I did, I would tell you.)

The way in which you seek to connect God to my writing is inadmissible. Writing is a terrestrial thing, and, from a "metaphysical" vantage point, is in no way different from shoemaking. Say.

If I want to do nothing but serve God, then I must become a monk. (I hope to end my days like that.) As long as I do terrestrial things like write novels, then I don't see why I should live any worse than a bad shoemaker who makes useless boots. Only when you write something like the *Imitation of Christ* do you refuse an advance.

It's unpractical to accept advances. But you can't avoid the unpractical on the grounds that it's also *impious*. All those shit writers I see around about me live more practical lives than I do, and get bigger advances, and, perfectly literally, are less shat upon than I am.

If twenty bad shoemakers live splendidly, then a twenty-first will surely scrape a living too. The shoes he makes aren't any worse because he happens to be a fool in his personal life as well.

I have far too low an opinion of writing for your appeal to my faith to have any weight with me. Writing isn't a question of election or selection. That would be hubris. There are no "artists" and no "genius" in the whole Bible; none in the New Testament; none in the long line of the saints. What *we* do, my dear friend, is worth little or nothing, in God's eyes.

One ought not to confuse—this seems to me a very grave sin—the practical advance with the heavenly "advance" that God also gives the shoemaker. In His eyes, shoemakers and writers are of equal worth.

Tell me this: if a poor shoemaker accepts a sum of money from a customer to go and buy leather to make the customer a pair of boots, is that not perfectly natural? And "unpractical"?

I do exactly the same thing. (Quite apart from the fact that I was one of those rare unworldly shoemakers, who is cheated by his customers all his life.)

I can't live like that. You can't be a saint, and at the same time make profane things. You may say to me that it's my duty to serve literature. I don't *serve* literature. Literature is a terrestrial matter; it's my job. A marriage: worth such and such, or such and such, like a wife. A terrestrial matter. You need God's grace even for a tuppenny fuck. (Excuse pencil, my pen's run out.)

I don't want to live a profane life any more. I've had enough of it. Profane and miserable: It's too much. The profane, which is miserable, is killing me. That's suicide. I am NOT being modest and devout here. An author is a worldly figure. He has, if he has my qualities, to live at least as well as the least of his colleagues. It isn't absolutely necessary, but in an earthly sense it would be justified.

I embrace you,

your Joseph Roth

361. To Stefan Zweig   *Paris, 26 November 1935*

Dear friend,

Mr. Sabatier has just written to tell me Grasset will take my novel, so long as de Lange's conditions aren't too steep.—Now I hear that Sabatier is leaving Grasset, and going to Albin Michel.

Thank you very much for interceding in the thing just now coming about. Probably you're thinking of a type of publisher that could help me. Please God I'll be saved.

Dear friend, if you don't come till January, I fear you'll only find me half alive. The Christmas holidays in particular I will NOT be able to survive. You can have no idea how much I dread them. My whole tribe of Negroes is descending on me, perversely and needlessly decked out with German Christmas trees and Aryan sentiments. There is nothing I hate so much as the smell of pine sap on an empty wallet, when I don't even have small change with which to take myself to a restaurant. It's physically impossible for me to survive that without being autonomous. Even surviving until then, without money, is impossible. I have 200 francs a week for myself till 23 December. I suffer the plagues of Egypt if my wife cannot go to the cinema. *I must be free* in the evening, I must be *alone*, and alone with a clear conscience. In that woman—as in all of them—there is the deadly and perfectly natural urge to constrain me, to make me into a sort of family pet, and the only way I can protect myself from that *with a clear conscience* is if I provide for her in some sort. Without a clear conscience, I cannot go and be free. My sufferings would be redoubled.

There's no point, my dear friend, all my strength is frittered away in this pettiness. I spend three-quarters of my day on foolish things, ridiculous worries, there is no one, far and wide, who could free me of so much as a telephone conversation. Nor do I even want my wife to do it. Everything would then be presented to me one day as "work," "deserving," and so forth. I do not want someone to cook, or type or phone for me; save me from services. They will all come home to roost one day. I must be as autonomous as a pasha in his harem. I don't pay with sex, or by the acceptance of so-called services. I don't care.

I wish a higher force would free me, so that . . .

362. To Stefan Zweig   *Paris 6ᵉ*
                                                 Hotel Foyot
                                                 33 rue de Tournon
                                                 6 December 1935

Dear friend,

I've had piles these past three days, and am unable to sit at a table and write. Forgive the dictation, therefore. Grasset bought the book. According to my contract, Mr. Brun had to deal with de Lange directly, and not with me. I would like to look him up, but can't find a plausible pretext for a visit.

I understand that you can be here on or about 14 December, and that you have no more than 3 or 4 hours to spare for me. I don't think that it is possible to gain a true picture in so short a time. At any rate, I should like to ask you to set aside at least one of these hours for my friend, who will give you exact information, better and more clearly than I can.

Thank you very much as well for your comforting postcard. My state is much too bad for me to get anything out of Döblin, thanks all the same. He was always a shouter, and belongs for me with those deeply detested "activist writers" that Germany was crawling with in those years. He knows this, too.

I embrace you warmly,

Your faithful old Joseph Roth

I beg you to please come and help me.

I want to live, but I can't go on. I am getting sicker, and I have no one. My loneliness is such that I will cling to anyone at all, so as not to sleep, or rather not to lie in bed, not sleeping. Poverty would be happy [. . . illegible] and no guilt. And no material obligations. I am humiliated every day, and my self-contempt takes the form of physical illnesses of all sorts. Who am I to call to, if not you? You know that God answers very late, generally after death. I don't want to die, although I have no fear of death.

Your J.R.

As a curiosity, I enclose a cutting from the *Vienna Journal* where it says that the gangster Schulze had tried to read Shakespeare and you. Gangsters evidently have a better taste in books than American millionaires. You should send the cutting to Huebsch.

363. To Stefan Zweig   *Hotel Foyot*
                                                               Paris
                                                               [December 1935?]

Dear friend,

thank you so much for your help and your letter. Why do you call me not very good? You left me for 3 weeks without a line or an address, and I might have gained the impression you were as anxious to avoid me as success itself. You don't know how much a letter means to me, and how little I deserve only to be found good, once I have been measured against others. You don't know—and will never learn—how darkness, strife, ugliness, and hatefulness are destroying my life, or how impenetrable the [. . . illegible] of futility is. All work, and no success at all. I yearn for it with something like homesickness. You are the only one with the

strength to tear me away from where I am—if you even want to, that is.
I can't write as I would speak. If your mind isn't set on my rescue, I am
certainly doomed.

I don't know what misfortune befell Jacob,[1] but I don't care for him,
and I don't understand, frankly, why you do. There's a sort of ambivalent
halo around his personal and literary life. The death of Alban Berg[2]
is certainly more tragic than the bad luck of Jacob. I hear that he got
involved in changing money. There's bound to be resentment in those
accounts, but what does a writer have to do with exchange rates or per-
centages and those things? Why does he get involved in things like that?
But I'm only talking off the top of my head, and you're sure to know some
justification for it. So I'll expect you, yes? I'll be finished with the new
novel on the 20th. I am working regularly, but badly. I'll await you. Others are as well, I know, and I'm confused and depressed that you want
to lump me with them in your cauldron of worries and embarrassments.

Your old Joseph Roth

Please will you give the accompanying letter to Mrs. Zweig.

1. Jacob: Heinrich Eduard Jacob.
2. Alban Berg (1885–1935), the composer of *Wozzeck* and *Lulu*, died impoverished
and unable to afford treatment for an insect bite.

364. To Thea Sternheim[1]   *4 January 1936*

Dear, esteemed Madam,

I'm sending you the Tolstoy with the same post, and I beg your pardon
for my dilatoriness.

It wasn't so much distraction, as sadness, which led to casualness.

Belatedly, but sincerely, I wish you a happy new year, and kiss your
hand as your devoted   Joseph Roth

1. Thea Sternheim: ex-wife of the author Carl Sternheim.

365. To Stefan Zweig   *20 January 1936*

Dear friend,

please forgive me, another registered letter. Thank you for your most recent letter, and for the regards that your dear wife conveyed to me. She hinted to me why you won't be able to stay in Paris beyond the end of January. If your mind weren't already made up, I would ask you myself to stay away from any disgusting manifestation. But I am unable to absolve you of the friendly duty of rescuing me. You will learn from the accompanying letter that the end is nigh, if not already at hand. Please take me absolutely at my word. The letter will fill you in. It is impossible that I go on living and writing, after 5 books in 3 years. This letter here makes it impossible for me to go on working on my current book. I was 5 days from finishing it. It's possible that here and there a person may still like me, but you are the only one who is yoked to me. You are the only one who can actually help me. Only with you can I change and save my life. Please come to me. I beg you earnestly, de profundis. I don't want a shabby death. I implore you, answer me right away. Don't go interpreting my words, don't analyze me please, and don't make me still unhappier than I already am. Don't write to me, talk to me. I have experienced myself how with the writer's pen, the primary feelings of the human being and friend tend to "overformulation."

Please write back right away, and help me, and save me really. Your
Joseph Roth

366. Stefan Zweig to Joseph Roth   *Hotel Westminster*
Nice [no date but 1936]

Dear friend,

our letters crossed in the post. What Landauer wrote was what I was always afraid might happen—I've known for a long time that the next movement in your royalties wasn't going to be up, but down. That's what made me so anxious when I saw you failing to get by on relatively high sums. With the grim foresight that I have, I *knew* that the next trend for the émigrés was down (it will go up again when there is no fresh blood, when the overcrowding has stopped, and people like you appear at your true worth).

But as I say—we need a plan for the next few months. You've got to get over the dead point. I fear you will once again have incurred obligations. Couldn't Dr. Wolff[1] or Leites send me a full list, so that we can make a plan together in Paris? I don't know to what extent the agreement with Huebsch has panned out, how much you have sold or compromised in advance, whether you are able to count on anything at all in the months ahead, or whether *everything* has been paid out already. *You'll* have to help too. Your daily alcohol consumption will have to be reduced. I can see it in myself—nicotine is as indispensable to me as schnapps is to you—that will power gets you partway there. Then (in *your* interest) we will have to *force* alcoholic reductions upon you. You will curse us and call us names, but for your sake we'll have to do it. We can't prevent your collapse by ourselves. You're going to have to help. You'll have to consent to a plan, you mustn't (quite apart from your health) exceed a certain sum for alcohol—simply because it's immoral to spend more on booze than a normal family spends on living. My dear good fellow, don't forever be arraigning the times and the wickedness of other people, admit that you bear some responsibility for your state, and help us to help you. Don't come up with new sophistries to the effect that schnapps makes you noble, lucid, productive—*il avilit*, it debases. As you *want* to live (thank goodness for that) you will have to put your shoulder to the wheel. I'm just looking back on an *awful* week from not-smoking (normally I get through a dozen big cigars a day!)—at last the pressure is finally reducing, I feel as light and relieved as after a colonic irrigation. *My own chastening gives me the right to demand that you stop, or at least reduce your intake of alcohol.* And above all, finish the novel, so that you can rest.

I was here yesterday with Jules Romains:[2] I think his novel is the best of recent years. Today I'm seeing Schickele—Heinrich Mann appears not to be around.

Sincerely, your Stefan Zweig

1. Dr. Wolff: Fritz Wolff.

2. Jules Romains (1885–1972), poet and novelist. Zweig's reference is to the novel cycle *Les hommes de bonne volonté* (1932–56, 28 vols.).

367. To Stefan Zweig [January? 1936]

Dear friend,

I don't understand why you don't reply to my last letter. If you're angry with me, then our close old friendship demands that you tell me. If you don't, then, for the first time, I don't understand you.

But that isn't the reason why I'm writing. I'm worried something might have happened to you.

This worries me. Why don't you answer? You could just tell me: I've had enough of you, leave me alone. Why don't you say anything?

Another thing: the dubious *Lampel*[1] *is staying in your hotel. Please, don't say a word to him!*

I don't give a damn about Marcu (or Schickele either). I know exactly what you're worth, and the way you like to cast your nobility before swine. I can explain the difficulty and the wailing of Schickele. Please don't be led up the garden path by your sense of justice. And don't listen to Marcu's lies.

But maybe it's too late. I have no other explanation for your not-replying than your uncertainty whether to tell me now or later that our friendship is over. I'd rather you told me now. In my condition, the pain and uncertainty of waiting for word from you is worse than the knowledge itself. You don't care for my friendship? Tell me, then! I've known for a long time that my friendship must become burdensome, one day.

That it would become burdensome *to you* I still can't bring myself to believe.—Why the silence? Why don't you answer? Has something happened to you? What? And why not tell me about it? Please, tell me the truth, all of it right away. I am waiting for every mail delivery. You make me terribly unhappy. I can't stand it. Your silence is unaccountable to me. I can't go on living like that, with you, with the knowledge that you are supposed to be my friend, my silent friend. What do you want? Say! And say it right away,

Your Joseph Roth

1. Lampel: Peter Martin Lampel (1894–1965), the leftist homosexual playwright and screenwriter, was described as "one of those curious characters who came very close to the Nazis before being arrested by them." JR accuses him of involvement in Vehmic murder, a Nazi reinstatement of an old Westphalian custom from the Middle Ages, involving the collective "lawful" killing of an outlaw.

368. Stefan Zweig to Joseph Roth   *[Nice, no date]*

Dear friend,

well, things are a little clearer now—I will be in Paris next week, around the 7th, stay for a couple of days, and am looking forward very much to seeing you. I hope your advisers have worked out a plan, then I will do my best to see that you get at least a *little* quiet. Rely on me!

Aside from you, the only German I want to see is Ernst Weiss. What an awful schism there is right now—the campaign against Thomas Mann, Hesse, Kolb, mostly conducted by people who, if they'd been able to borrow a foreskin from somewhere, would still be sitting in Germany, quietly or otherwise. Why the internecine venom of the other Germany—like Kerr and Kraus just the other day. Imagine Goebbels chuckling over it. It's such a pity, and so *un*political!

Here I'm spending time (a privilege) with Jules Romains and Roger Martin du Gard.[1] Clever minds, especially when unembittered, are always a tonic.

Till soon, my dear fellow!   your St. Z.

I am VERY proud that I, the most fanatical chain-smoker, a veritable Joseph Roth of nicotine, have been completely *off* smoking the last 14 days. It *can* be done, if you want! And you've got to want, and you've even got to got to want, my dear friend, this time (since my struggle with the angel of nicotine) I'm demanding action from you.

1. Roger Martin du Gard (1881–1958), French historical novelist, who won the Nobel Prize in 1937, was at André Gide's bedside when he died. Today, he languishes in obscurity in the English-speaking world.

369. To Stefan Zweig   *Sunday [2 or 9 February 1936]*

Dear friend,

at last your good letter arrived, I really thought you had had enough of my bitterness. I am a great burden on you, but who else can I go to, who am I to confide in, all around me are traitors and worms. What did I ever do to anyone? I always helped people. Now I see a letter from Schickele to de Lange, where he writes that other authors get nothing, because Roth gets such enormous advances.[1] How can he do such a thing? I am vehement at times, but never behind backs, I am capable of hate, but never hateful. Marcu wrote to Kesten in the same way. What's going on? All the work I did in the committee for my poor colleagues. I even collected money for them, and they're all sore at me, from Heinrich Mann to Soma Morgenstern.

The quarrel about Bermann[2] is a bad business. Now we have one publisher less, and have provoked the anti-Semitic instincts of Korrodi.[3] But Bermann bears a lot of responsibility. Firstly, the journalistic émigrés have their spies too, someone from the Sureté générale is even a member of the journalists' union, and Bernhard[4] is organized in France, and is a power in the land. [. . .] Secondly, it's not right that Bermann, instead of replying in person,[5] always sends his élite authors out to do battle for him. It's undignified and vulgar. [. . .] He wheels out Thomas Mann with all his dignity for a rag where Heinrich Mann is pissed at in 4 offensive columns. He makes Thomas Mann into an ally of Korrodi's. Oh, it's all such a tangle of filth and craziness. Sense has moved out of our heads, without giving notice. We are mad and in hell, we are crazy shades, dead but still stupid. This world is in limbo. At the Rolland celebration,[6] they yelled out the "Internationale," 2,000 people, loathsome Comintern figures among them, today the papers are full of the execution of 5 disloyal Soviet officials in Petersburg, and what does the great man do: he protests against one lot of murders and uses his dignity to suppress the other. And is happy to be celebrated by people you could describe as principled murderers. Does it get any worse? I was happy you weren't there, I think it was the spirit of Erasmus that did it, it was his way of thanking you.

I'm drinking almost only wine, promise. I just want peace—3 months of it—and not these debts and worries! I won't be able to write anything after this novel. I'm physically drained from writing. If I'm to carry on, I need to stimulate myself—and that depletes me further. Do you think I don't know?

I see Ernst Weiss from time to time. He is both bitterer than I am and more contented. I am a little nonplussed by him. Often he is very, very sad. He likes you, one of the few honest likers. He has a lot of the virtue of justice, which is why I admire him. But it's not real affection.

Today it says in the paper that Laetitia[7] has been dead for 100 years. Her picture, which I've never seen before, is oddly close to my description of her. Nor did I know that she'd died blind, I made her weak-sighted in my book. Come along, come along.

Sincerely your   Joseph Roth

1. such enormous advances: one editor is quoted in Bronsen as saying, "I had a vision of whole generations of beggars when I saw Roth cadging an advance." In a letter dated 10 May 1935, René Schickele wrote, "Roth has left us. Gone to Amsterdam to sit beside the till. He was cross with [Valeriu] Marcu for giving him only half the travel money, instead of all of it. For us de Lange authors, Roth is a sort of vacuum cleaner. No speck of dust, no crumb from the master's table that doesn't get sucked into that bottomless hole. What's left for the rest of us?" It wasn't a good idea to turn up with a manuscript after Roth had been by.

2. the quarrel about Bermann: Samuel Fischer's son-in-law and publishing heir, Bermann Fischer, had just gone into exile, first to Vienna and then Stockholm, where he set up his own publishing company and continued to publish Thomas Mann and Stefan Zweig.

3. Korrodi: Eduard Korrodi, feuilleton editor of the *Neue Zürcher Zeitung*.

4. Bernhard: Georg Bernhard (1875 Berlin–1944 New York) was the editor and founder of the German exile newspaper *Pariser Tageblatt*.

5. instead of replying in person: but Bermann couldn't have replied from within Germany (where he was still based) to items in exile publications without making things hot for himself and the firm whose custodian he was, following the death of Samuel Fischer in 1934.

6. Rolland celebration: Romain Rolland's seventieth birthday was on 29 January 1936.

7. Laetitia: Marie-Laetitia Bonaparte, Napoleon's mother, a character in Roth's novel *The Hundred Days*.

370. To Stefan Zweig   *Hotel Foyot*
                                                Paris
                                                Wednesday [February 1936?]

Dear friend,

I am not at all offended, your wife must take my extreme despair for antagonism. It's most peculiar. You're tired out, I know, and I am inconsolable about the fact that I only tire you out more. I'm too shaky to be able to put it better and more delicately than that. I'm too confused at the moment, I'm not sure I shouldn't just go to bed, and wait for the end. But I do know this, that it's not possible for me to do anything else, as you suggested. For whom do I write articles? Or films? How do I make the time? Where's the money to tide me over? I'm running around with my tongue hanging out, a scrounger with drooling tongue and wagging tail. How do I avoid signing new contracts for new books? I don't even get offered those. What do I do, now, today, next week? All your perfectly correct thoughts have nothing to base themselves on. You just need to put yourself in my shoes, you can do that, in my typical day, I've told you what that's like. I have no more nights. I [sit?] around till 3 a.m., I lie

down fully dressed at 4, I wake up at 5, and I wander around the room. I
haven't been out of my clothes for two weeks. You know what time feels
like, an hour is a lake, a day is a sea, the night is an eternity, waking up
is a thunderclap of dread, getting up a struggle for clarity against fevered
nightmares. That's what it's all about, time, time, time, and I don't have
any. In two weeks I'll have a contract, in three weeks, I'm told, there'll
be a reply from America—and how much of my life do I lose in those
2 weeks! For nothing! For nothing! Humiliated, disgraced, indebted,
smiling, smiling through gritted teeth—an acrobatic stunt—so that the
hotel proprietor doesn't notice, my pen clamped, cramped in my hand,
desperately clinging to the idea I've just had, because it's galloping away
from me, sometimes starving, falling asleep in my chair after 3 sentences,
but what do you want, what do you want from a man who's half madman, half corpse? What else am I to do, if I don't write books? I'm old
and sick, I can't go back to the army, which is the only job I ever had.
Debts, ghosts, privation, and writing, talking, smiling, no suit, no shirt,
no boots, hungry open mouths, and scroungers to stuff them, and ghosts,
ghosts, wall-to-wall ghosts. And what a life behind me! What do you
want, my friend? How well you are able to describe it, and how alien it
sounds to me, your clever counsel. You know everything, don't you! You
know everything! You can sniff out the deepest secrets, and the things
that lie around on the surface, you see those too! Or do you miss them?
I can't sell film ideas, I can't compete on the English market with Lania,
etc., with [. . .] Frischauer—I'm not up to it. Please, my dear friend, take
me at my word. Either I'll be sick to death, or go crazy, or perhaps I am
already. Don't be angry, and remember I love you

    Your J.R.

371. To Stefan Zweig   *17 February 1936*

    Dear friend,
    it was kind of you to reply to me at once. I'll write you in more detail
as soon as the novel's finished.—I only want to tell you this, quickly, that

I am not bitter or embittered, not for a moment. You're mistaken there.
My respect for human beings is immense—and so every disappointment,
the least instance of harshness or obstinacy—not to me, but to others—
shakes me, enough to make me curse. I just don't understand the world,
I suppose. I demand too much—too much literature of myself, too much
humanity of others. I don't understand why so much evil happens on a
daily basis, and the fact that such a thing is possible makes me question
each individual. I sense squalor and betrayal. I think I can only understand the world when I'm writing, and the moment I put down my pen,
I'm lost. Alcohol isn't the cause, perhaps a consequence, though it makes
things worse. That's the truth. You give people too much credence, I too
little. Both are bad. What pains me with you is that you believe strangers sooner than you'd believe me. I have never broken my word. I'm too
loyal. It worries me. You worry me every bit as much as I you, no more,
no less. Your magnanimity worries me as much as my own pettiness.
My night porter[1] is a decent man, more honest than ten authors, and I
certainly prefer him to Kesten, say. That's just, that's not bitter. In the 60
years of his life, my night porter has committed fewer skulduggeries than
Marcu has in 10. Which in my eyes makes the porter Auguste noble,
and Marcu not. Quite apart from the fact that Auguste understands his
job better than ten mediocre writers. I cannot give up my respect for
Auguste, or his affection for me. *Vous êtes un bateau surchargé, vous coulez
à pic,* he said to me yesterday. *Mon pauvre vieux, venez chez moi.* Those
are *my* Nobel prizes.—In the whole of German literature, I don't know
of anyone, besides yourself, who understood *that*, precisely that. There is
only moral hierarchy, not intellectual, much less pseudo-intellectual. In
all literature, I love only you, only you are my friend, everyone else isn't
worth shit, in spite of my respect, which some of them deserve.—I'll
write you soon, after the novel's done. (And how badly will that turn out,
in such a time!)

Your Joseph Roth

1. my night porter: the night porter at the Hotel Foyot, invariably hailed by Roth
as "mon cher Auguste." He advised Roth on money and personal matters, publishing
questions, etc. A true friend of Roth's.

372. Stefan Zweig to Joseph Roth   *11 Portland Place*
                                                      London W 1
                                                      3 March 1936

Dear friend,

in haste, my congratulations! At last you'll be able to stop and draw
breath, a completed book is a happy boon—I hope to be where you are
now in another week, but for now I'm still in a state that makes a half-
decent letter a near-impossibility. You feel so vulnerable when you're
supposed to be concentrated on your work, people pressing and oppressing you on all sides. Sometimes I get quite desperate, and I see where
you're coming from. If only one could put one's entire strength in one's
work, and not fritter it away in a hundred trivialities—imagine what
that would be like! I am increasingly convinced that only purely selfish
people are able to use the full measure of their talent.

Tell me what your plans are. I take it you probably will be going to
Holland. I think it would do you a world of good to get out of Paris, if
only for a few days. You need to be able to lose yourself and those around
you every so often. I have very high hopes of your novel, and from what
you tell me of the contents, it will be of interest—and in terms of the
financial reward this is critical, nowadays—to the film industry. Your
final liberation can only come from that quarter, I believe. Zuckmayer[1]
and Bruno Frank[2] have been here for a week or two, and both came
away with gigantic sums. That's where I notice how clumsy you and I
are by comparison, and how you in particular struggle for tiny sums,
whereas canny authors earn as much at a stroke as for five or ten novels.

Don't worry about Manga Bell, it would be surprising, the way you live,
if her nerves *didn't* get frazzled. When you're better, she'll feel better too.

My exhaustion greets yours, my book greets yours, and once again,
with all my heart, my joy firstly at the fact that your book is finished, and
secondly that you've managed to keep your promise to yourself,

your faithful Stefan Zweig

1. Zuckmayer: Carl Zuckmayer (1896–1977), popular German playwright and novelist, friend of Brecht's. Went into exile in Switzerland, then the United States.

2. Bruno Frank (1887 Stuttgart—1945 Beverly Hills), playwright, novelist, screenwriter.

373. Stefan Zweig to Joseph Roth   *49 Hallam Street*
                                                        London W 1
                                                        16 March 1936

Dear friend,

your letter arrived just now. I'm hoping you just overreacted to a strain within your generally overstrained condition. Remember, you have a great book newly completed, and an indescribably difficult struggle with yourself every day. That will lead you to see things unduly pessimistically. You know I often urged you to take a month off. Two people living on top of each other, always sharing the same space, you can't work like that in the long run, and you will need an occasional break. I'm sure you will have completely recovered in two or three days alone in Amsterdam, and I'm sure you have friends in Paris who will keep you posted. Our work unfortunately keeps our imaginations exercised, and like all Jews, we have pessimistic imaginations. Just try and avoid delusions. Things will sort themselves out, and probably by the time you get this, you will have heard better news from your friends. But overall, you know my belief that you need to be away from Paris for a while, never mind where, and live by yourself with reduced commitments. Ideally, we should have been able to talk all this through face to face, only I can't break off now, or else I should have come over to see you. I have just moved apartments, and am settling into my new place. Note the new address and phone number,

sincerely your Stefan Zweig

I must beseech you, my dear friend, not to fall prey to gloomy delusions. You've finished a book, and it's bound to be a beautiful book, that has to be the important thing—what would a marriage be without crises, they're an essential part of things. Don't go running back to Paris now, you *need* to recuperate, nothing matters more than that you keep yourself going, seeing as you keep all those other people going!! More soon from your

St. Z.

374. To Stefan Zweig   *Thursday, 19 March 1936*
                                          Amsterdam
                                          Eden Hotel

Dear friend,

there is news, but wretched news. Mrs. Manga Bell [. . .] was unable to stay in the hotel. She had a temperature [. . .] I'm afraid I wasn't wrong. I'm a burned child.

On top of everything else, the new publisher, Mr. van Alfen,[1] has a flu. I won't know my fate till the middle of next week. So I'm wasting two weeks in Amsterdam. I couldn't stay with Landauer, he has his girl-friend[2] with him. I don't even have the strength, with all this uncertainty and panic, to dictate. Because I must patch my novel. It's all full of holes.

I made the lowest tender offer I could. Who knows whether it will be accepted. If it isn't—Mr. van Alfen is a completely unliterary type, he comes from the advertising world—then I don't know what will happen. If only I weren't so enfeebled. Even if he does give me money, that would mean I have to give him a novel by September. How will I do that? With whose head and what hand?

I'm leaving my wife at Gottfarstein's[3] for a time. It's a poor part of town, St. Martin, she'll see how Gottfarstein lives, and the almighty struggle he has every day to earn 10 francs. He is a good man. His girl-friend is Polish, and a good girl. My café life has spoiled the woman. [. . .]

I can only hope to make a plan once I know the fate of my novel and contract. But how am I supposed to write the next one so quickly? Nothing from Huebsch. I'll write to him again today. I implore you, *write to him please yourself*, please, now! He must know that I'm dependent on his sticking by me. He's silent as the grave. What can I do?

Please write me, at this address.

I enclose a letter to your wife. Show her this one as well, please.

I long to hear what she has to say, and I want her to be informed. Especially because Mrs. M.B. likes her.

Where shall I go? I won't go to London. I'm afraid of the language, and the people, and I have no connection to the cinema either.

Sincerely your old   Joseph Roth

1. Mr. van Alfen: Philip van Alfen (1894–1969), on the death of Gerard de Lange in 1935, took over the publishing firm of Allert de Lange; previously he had been in charge of an advertising agency.

2. his girlfriend: Thea Sternheim (who was furthermore addicted to drugs at the time—see no. 393).

3. at Gottfarstein's: Gottfarstein was a Talmudist, a Yiddish journalist in Paris, and a devoted friend to JR.

375. To Stefan Zweig   *Sunday*
                                          22 March 1936
                                          Amsterdam
                                          Eden Hotel

Dear friend,

thank you for your kindness and promptness. You are quite right, of course an elevator attendant here is better than a parliamentarian in Africa. But, to explain Mrs. Manga Bell's behavior, what was at stake for her was readying her son for a not inconsiderable inheritance. I can't say how great or small his expectations are, or what his repulsive father has already sold or hocked. But the mother has the duty, really, to prepare the son in class terms *in case* he one day comes into the inheritance. Negroes won't have the same respect for a servant. There's nothing to be done about that. No, the one thing I do hold against her is that never in

all those years did she think to enter him in a military academy, or in
the navy, or, as I tried once, in a monastery. [. . .] and she's more afraid of
discipline than he is. I understand her when I think of my own mother,
and the way she looked the first time she saw me in uniform. Outside
the barracks on the main street . . . I don't remember if I told you that
my wife, in those days when I was writing desperately around the clock,
came down with pleurisy, and was suddenly lucid, and asked after me.
I was so rattled. I sent my sister-in-law a little money. Now it's gotten
better—i.e., worse—again. I couldn't have borne it if my wife had died
sane, and me not with her.—That just by the by.—I don't know why I
am so tormented.—Why someone torments me further when he can see
that fate is already doing enough to finish me off.—I am so feeble, so
wretched, it's really true.

You're right, we do weigh others down, but when we leave them, they
are devastated.[1] I've seen it myself.

I'd like to be alone for three months, but how, and where? In Vienna
I'd run into all my wife's relations, all 60 of them, and I'd have to visit
her in the asylum, and so forth. I wouldn't mind Salzburg, except I'd be
reminded of you wherever I went. That wouldn't be relaxing. Maybe
Marseille—I tend to work quickly and well there.

Mr. van Alfen is a problem, the new publisher. He doesn't know what
a book is, or an author. Nor does he care about time, just money. (For
me they're the same thing.) He'll give me *at the most*—I'll learn finally
on Tuesday—money to see me through to September. Which means the
book must be done by September. And here I have at least another 2
weeks of patching the old one. I CAN'T send it to Huebsch as it stands.
I can only send something when it's properly finished! And if Huebsch
doesn't stand by his word, I'm done for. How do I get out of that?

Amsterdam is terribly expensive. I live terribly cheaply. (I cut the pages
you wrote on out of the notebook, and send them to you.) I've seen that,
for myself alone, I get through about 2,500 French francs a month. I've
also seen that my advance is only *1,000 gulden*. The accounts for the god-
damned *Hundred Days* aren't in yet, and I have the second novel, which

I'm just finishing now. I don't see why I am being continually tormented on all sides. Useless little writers get as big an advance as I do. People exaggerate my lack of responsibility. They exaggerate my strength.

I'm afraid of London. Maybe, without my fear, I might have had a chance of escaping from all my worries, with a film. I have lots of "ideas." But how, how, with my fear? You're right, I don't belong there. But how are you going to get here in time? How I need you, and how far away you are. And you go and put further miles between us, God knows, why do you do it.

You are unfair to me, you exaggerate my drinking and my foolishnesses. You have your own foolishnesses, you know. I am fairer to you than you are to me.—I'll write you on Wednesday, after the meeting with the publisher on Tuesday. But write to me in the meantime! *I need it urgently*.

Sincerely,   your Joseph Roth

Please give the enclosed letter to your wife.

Please write to me. I will need to be very strong on Tuesday, when I see Mr. van Alfen.

Also, please let your wife read what I write to you. I want her to see it—I want you both to see everything.

1. devastated: Friedl Roth, Andrea Manga Bell, but also the pending case of Friderike Zweig (see no. 388).

376. Stefan Zweig to Joseph Roth   *49 Hallam Street*
                                            London W 1
                                            24 March 1936

Dear friend,

I hope I'll hear good news from you tomorrow. My only fear is that you'll show the people too clearly how much you depend on them. Perhaps I'll get some word of you from Marcuse, who's supposed to be over here. Seriously, try not to think too much about domestic matters. You have every right just to be ill for a fortnight, and not to correspond. And be careful with the novel too. What you refer to as "patching"[1] seems not without its dangers to me. Your patching on the *Antichrist* didn't do that book much good, it seems to me. And when you told me the story of your novel, it was beautifully clear in outline, ornamentation would only weight it down.

Think hard about where you want to be. I wouldn't go for Salzburg, you would suffer in the atmosphere there, unless you were to go completely Catholic. Vienna wouldn't do either, if you have relations there. I personally felt very well in Czechoslovakia, with Marienbad as a workplace, and I'm sure Yugoslavia would be excellent, and perhaps even better for you. I always have the sense that a Slav environment stimulates you. Budapest is an extraordinarily charming city, unbelievably cheap and full of cafés. For the likes of us, not speaking the language, it's an ideal place to work. I thought about it once myself.

I need to read my proofs now, and am just feeling very dissatisfied. Well, I'll see how I get out of it. Warmly   St. Z.

Please read the enclosed.

---

1. "patching": Not that JR is a habitual "patcher," but SZ prided himself on his technique of reducing, cutting, sweating out words; his first drafts could be many hundreds of pages long. No wonder he reacts so allergically to JR's term. That remains the fundamental difference between the two writers: JR is fast and impulsive; in SZ one always hears the slowly ticking metronome.

377. To Stefan Zweig   *25 March 1936*
                                                          Amsterdam
                                                          Eden Hotel

Dear friend,

I have to tell you that I am absolutely washed up: de Lange won't give me a contract. The new publisher left me in the lurch for 14 days before telling me. All my work is for nothing, my life, my crazy industry, my diligence: every little shit gets a contract from de Lange, I don't. Alfred Neumann[1] gets 500 gulden a month, Gina Kaus[2] gets 300, but what can I say! Do you see now that I'm a beaten man, and don't need any more censure from you. Please be good to me at least, I'm so badly in need of a real friend. I'm lost. I beg you for a word.

Your Joseph Roth

After 3 weeks' work on the novel such a blow, such blows. I am being beaten. I'm finished, truly finished. It's all up with me, I have no more ideas. I've had a temperature of 38 since yesterday. All I can do is get me to a monastery, because I mayn't kill myself.

1. Alfred Neumann (1895–1952), novelist, playwright, and scenarist. Lived in Fiesole, near Florence, from 1933 to 1938, then Nice, then Los Angeles.
2. Gina Kaus (1894 Vienna–1985 Los Angeles), writer, biographer, went into exile in 1938 in Paris and London. Between 1933 and 1937, Allert de Lange published five of her books.

378. To Stefan Zweig   *26 March 1936*
                                          Amsterdam
                                          Eden Hotel

Dear friend,

forgive me for burdening you like this. I just got your letter with the extract. I think it's a report from the *Reichspost*[1] and therefore a distortion. Everyone knows that the *Reichspost* has been bought by Papen. But that's not to say that the Jesuits haven't been caught up in the general folly.

Here, it was exactly as I told you: Landauer is powerless, like a little employee. Mr. van Alfen, the new executive at the house is an advertising agent [. . .] He's never read a book in his life, he even boasts about it. Your letter to Landauer didn't do anything, even though he passed it on up. All Landauer's points about my silly life, and so forth, were unavailing.

I've been here for two weeks for nothing, though at 800 francs expenses. I've worked for nothing, to get the *Regular* into shape. On the contrary: since it is finished, and is due to appear in autumn, no other publisher can come and offer me a new contract. You can tell me advances are ruinous or immoral till you're blue in the face. It seems to me it would be more immoral to give up writing and living altogether. It's just a fact that I don't have any money. I can't live without advances. Fate is oppressing me in a terrible and tawdrily symbolic way, as if it were aping a stupid romantic novelist. I'm even ashamed of the blows it deals me. Such low blows.

I don't know what to do. (I know: it's my refrain.) For a long time I've had the feeling you can't stand to hear it any more. I have too much respect for your achievement not to understand that you don't care for unlucky friends like me; that we might even do you harm. But all I say to you is, *don't keep it from me*. That would be an unnecessary humiliation. Don't do it. It would really be a sin.

I can't go to Marienbad for the "season." Spas are sterile. I hate Budapest. And in Yugoslavia I'd be afraid of war breaking out. It's a barbarian country. I can only go to Austria. I know Belgrade, Zagreb, Dubrovnik very well. It's a police state. I'd have to get a residence permit, and suffer searches, etc. I was a reporter there once for the *FZ*,[2] they know all about me. In my condition police states are a non-starter.

But perhaps you'll let me tell you about that on some future occasion.
Sincerely,   your old Joseph Roth

1. the *Reichspost*: a reactionary Viennese newspaper.
2. the *FZ*: the *Frankfurter Zeitung*. Roth was in Albania and Yugoslavia in 1927.

379. Stefan Zweig to Joseph Roth   *49 Hallam Street*
                                                        London W 1
                                                        27 March 1936

Dear friend,

I can only hope what you wrote me was mistaken, perhaps based on some initial disappointment on your part. I can't imagine that de Lange and Landauer would drop you like that, and I'm sure things will be sorted out to your satisfaction. You must remember that in the last resort these are business people, who do sums, and buy and sell wares. It's the way of the world, and we can't change it. Probably it's just a sort of transition, and then they'll make you an offer that's more in keeping with their calculations. But don't let yourself be driven mad, there's only one thing that can save you, namely a good book, and I'm sure your new book will do the trick for you. And then you will have to switch over temporarily, and think film thoughts for a couple of weeks. That's the only way of getting at larger sums, since our old seventy million readership has deserted us.

Stay as calm as you can. Lamenting won't help, and you'll need all your strength for your work. I'm sure Landauer, who knows you and likes you, won't drop you. I wrote to him right away. I am more sanguine than you, and I'm sure it was just what theater people call a *fausse sortie*. Sincerely your

St. Z.

My dear friend, don't despair. I, as a professional pessimist, have known for years that you are bound to go from one crisis to the next. But on this occasion I feel optimistic. They won't drop you. But then, when it's all right again, you will need to get yourself properly in grip. Perhaps the only reason they're hesitating is to focus your mind properly.

380. To Stefan Zweig   *28 March 1936*
                                                    Amsterdam
                                                    Eden Hotel

Dear friend,

I've just gotten your nice letter. Unfortunately, you're wrong. I've already written to you that it pains me in my soul if you spend time, ingenuity, and energy writing letters to the helpless Landauer. The only reason he didn't write to say perfectly candidly that there was absolutely nothing he could do, was to save face. Perhaps he's too punctilious. But he's a mensch at least.

When will you finally believe that I have an incorruptible eye and an unerring nose for disaster! I can see Landauer being treated like a serf by the new boss. He's worried for his job and salary. I can see it! How can you still think people always approach me in a spirit of pedagogy, like so many trainers!—I don't understand you, you're always right about everything else.—You don't want to accept that, in spite of everything, I'm smart. I know Landauer! The janitor of the building he lived in for 20 years in Berlin always yelled at him when he forgot to wipe his boots in the corridor when it was raining—he stood for it. *He is gentle and decent and submissive.* He is a gentleman, but only among gentlemen. Otherwise he's a serf to serfs. Just by the by. I only mention it, so that you don't waste more of your time writing to a junior official. You demean yourself, and me with you. You don't even hear me when I say something true, because I say so much that's wrong.

But it's even worse than that. I went to Querido. But he and Dr. Landshoff won't give me a penny either. I won't be given a contract, not by anyone. Querido would pay 1,500 gulden, for a finished manuscript. Well, it's not finished, is it?—I can get a contract, if I want, from Querido, 1,500 gulden on delivery of a manuscript. What use is that to me? From the goodness of his condescension he bought one of my best stories[1] off me for 200 gulden, with all rights, including film. What else could I have done? At least I've now paid for my stay here. My room costs 2 gulden.

No less than 14 days de Lange's successor made me wait, only to tell me that he didn't want me. Landauer lent me 2 gulden a day on which to get by. Of course I'm grateful to him, but I also can't forgive him for playing the "publisher" in front of you and Dr. Wolff and Leites. Yes, he likes me. But he's a young dog, and a subordinate, and he likes to play at being something he's not.

What do I do now? Rattle a can outside a church? Go to a monastery? They won't have me there, you know, not until my affairs are in order. I'm so tired, and so clear-sighted at the same time. Crazy imaginings accompany my lucidity and my exhaustion.

You don't believe me. Then there's no point. If you're my friend, why don't you believe in my sense, the way you believe in my character and gift? We probably fritter away 50% of our friendship on that. Pity, eh?

I don't know why you take me for a fool. A madman isn't a donkey. You would know that best. I see clearer, straighter—personal things included.

But what's the point of rehearsing all this now! I see no way out, and if you want to think fast and true for me now, then tell me. It's a great sacrifice, I know that. I'm ashamed, too.

But, please, let's not go on at cross-purposes. Trust me at last, won't you. I beg you to, so that our precious friendship doesn't break over it. I have nothing more to say except my dying words. I love you and don't want to lose you, is what I'm saying. Just please stop not believing in my clarity of mind. Don't talk past me any more.

I am your sincere   Joseph Roth

1. one of my best stories: *The Leviathan*, first published by Querido in 1940, after Roth's death; the edition fell into the hands of the Germans, and was largely destroyed.

381. Stefan Zweig to Joseph Roth   *49 Hallam Street*
                                                      London W 1
                                                      31 March 1936

Dear friend,

I see you're subconsciously angry with me for not coming up with any sensible ideas. You have the feeling that I don't understand you, or appreciate the difficulties of your position. But, my dear friend, that's the awful thing about it, it's not that I don't understand the position *now*, but that, like all your friends, I've seen it coming for years. Everything you're experiencing now, we've experienced in advance for you, shared your worries, and more, we've anticipated the bad liver that drinking was bound to give you and the bitterness with which you *will* inevitably turn against us. You didn't have to be a prophet to see it all coming. Dear friend, if you really want to be clear-sighted, then you must concede there is no salvation for you unless you lead an utterly secluded life in some very cheap place somewhere. Not Paris, not the Foyot, no metropolis at all, *some voluntary cloister.* You saw how shocked we were when you failed to get by on two and three times what you're going to be reduced to now, and some secret sixth sense tells me you will begin to feel much better once you've left Paris, and are in some retreat somewhere, when you've performed the decisive adjustment you seemed not to want to undertake willingly. You must get it out of your head, the idea that we're somehow being rough with you, or hard on you. Don't forget we're living in a period of general doom, and we can count ourselves lucky if we get through it at all. Don't go accusing publishers, don't blame your friends, don't even beat your own breast, but finally have the courage to admit that however great you are as a writer, in material terms you're a poor little Jew, almost as poor as seven million others, and are going to have to live like nine-tenths of the human beings in the world, on a small footing and with a tightened belt. For me that would be the only proof of your cleverness: don't always "fight back," stop going on about the injustice of it all, don't compare your earnings to those of other writers who don't have a tenth of your talent. Now is your chance to show what you call modesty. And if you reproach me with not thinking you clever enough, then I just say to you: all right then, prove it! Be clever enough finally to give up all your false notions of "obligations." You have ONE obligation, which is to write decent books, and not to drink too much, so that you remain among us for as long as possible. I implore you not to waste your strength in futile rebellions, don't go accusing other people, decent business people who calmly and quite rightly do their sums, which is something you never learned to do. Now or never is the moment for you to change your life, and maybe it will have been a good thing that you were finally brought to a point where the old road didn't go on any more, and you were forced to turn back.

Warmly, your Stefan Zweig

382. To Stefan Zweig   *Amsterdam*
Eden Hotel
2 April 1936

Dear friend,

if you hadn't said in your last letter that I was "subconsciously (what's that supposed to mean, "subconscious"? It's pure Antichrist!) angry" with you, I wouldn't have written back to you at all.

It's only devils not human beings that are "subconsciously angry." That's a type of religious perspective; people are not, ever "subconscious," save in the sexual domain, and crime, and dream. And even that is a sin, or at least suspect. I'm not angry with you, I'm your friend! Why "angry"?

You know you've no need to tell *me* of all people what it is to be a poor little Jew. I've been that since 1894, and with pride. A believing Eastern Jew from Radziwillow. I would drop it if I were you. I've been small and poor for 30 years. Heck, *I am poor.*

But nowhere is it written that a poor Jew may not try to earn a living. That's the only advice I turned to you for. If you don't know, then say so. I thought you might be able to put me onto some film people, or something.

If it wasn't that I was convinced brotherly feeling dictated your letter, I would tell you I was "*consciously*" angry.

I'm not, as you know, because I'm always conscious.

I send you my warmest regards, your old friend   Joseph Roth
Please reply.

383. To Blanche Gidon   *Amsterdam*
                                                  Eden Hotel
                                                  4 April 1936

Dear, dear friend,

the only reason I haven't written you is because it's so cold and dark. De Lange's successor won't give me any money. I'm at the end of my rope, I can't think of anything at all. But don't think that I don't think of ·you with great gratitude and constant affection.—Maybe things will lift. If they do I'll write you a detailed letter, straightaway. I've been pursued by calamity for 2 years now. It surrounds me like a fortress. Forgive my German. I can't easily translate in this state.

I kiss your hand warmly and gratefully.

Your old   Joseph Roth

Mr. van de Meer seems to have lost a lot of money in one of the banks here. He hasn't written back to me either.

384. *Stefan Zweig to Joseph Roth*   *49 Hallam Street*
                                                      London W 1
                                                      6 April 1936

Dear friend,

you can write me as angry letters as you like, I won't be angry with you. Do you really think that if I had even the *ghost* of an idea, I would keep quiet about it, or not bring it up? Perhaps, though, you could work out a plan yourself, and lay it before us, how you could be helped in the straitened circumstances dictated by these times. Make it easier for us by coming up with some proposal. And you could also scribble out some film themes on a piece of paper, regardless of style and art, so we could have a basis for possible future negotiations. Berthold Viertel[1] has been struggling for the past two years for your *Radetzky March*, and still hopes to get it taken on somewhere, sooner or later.

Sincerely your S.

1. Berthold Viertel (1885–1953), poet, novelist, playwright, essayist, and director; lived in Vienna, Prague, Berlin, Hollywood, and Zurich.

385. *Stefan Zweig to Joseph Roth*   *[undated]*

Dear friend,

Huebsch sent me the letter for you under the same cover on purpose so that I should read it—he's really trying for you, and doesn't have any exploitative intentions. Please trust him.

I feel rather written out. I corrected the proofs, the book will be out soon.[1] The print run will be small, because it's a book for a male readership, and all the dictatorships of course are closed off (Italy, etc., Germany happened long ago) but I felt the need to speak my mind unambiguously. Now I'm working on a Jewish legend, I think it'll be good.[2]

I wrote to Landauer yesterday, concerning you. I would have come over in person, but the only planes are German, and frankly I'd sooner drown. But we must see one another soon. Please don't forget: draw up a plan for the next two months, so that we can help you together and have the certainty that it is helping you.

I am very down. My instinct for political calamity pains me like an inflamed nerve. I fear for Austria, and the loss of Austria would be the end of us, spiritually,

your St. Z.

1. out soon: *Castellio gegen Calvin*.
2. I think it'll be good: *Der begrabene Leuchter* (The Buried Candelabrum), 1937.

386. *To Stefan Zweig*

Eden Hotel
Amsterdam
30 April 1936

Dear friend,

my silence isn't truculence, but despair. Landauer's gone away. I'm all alone. You won't come either. It's not true that only German planes fly here. Only the 6 o'clock flight is Lufthansa. At 7:00, 11:00, 12:15, 2:10, and 7:45, there are *Dutch* ones. But you don't want to, and it would be better if you said so. But I can empathize with you, I can sense that you have no desire to see a man in utter distress. It's not pleasant, it's even harmful to see friends in a condition resembling mine. Do you remember, in your hotel room, when I was sitting on the prosecution suitcase,[1] that I told you I wouldn't be offered a contract, and that the next stop was either the Seine or the Salvation Army. That's where I'm at now. Your best and maybe your only friend is in the greatest physical and spiritual danger, and you don't come. I love you too much to be angry. You just make me bitter. I'm to pull myself together, you say, what with, by what means? Can't you see what a "pulling together" it already is if a 42-year-old man, having written 20 books by the sweat of his brow, and having experienced no end of suffering in his life, still continues to work. I write every day, simply so as to lose myself in fictional destinies. Don't you see, fellow human, friend, brother—brother, you called me once—that I am shortly to die. Please give the accompanying letter to your wife.—In old fervor,

Your Joseph Roth

Forgive me my bitterness, I would tone it down if I could.

I hear that Bruno Frank has good connections to the film business, I'll write to him, my novel is filmable.

1. the prosecution suitcase: a puzzling turn of phrase, but it sounds as though SZ (and maybe JR) had found a way of gaming through JR's predicament, involving one taking the best case, the other the worst, or one the prosecution, the other the defense, the respective points of view marked by something easily found in those days—a suitcase.

387. To Stefan Zweig

Eden Hotel
Amsterdam
4 May 1936

Dear friend,

thank you from the bottom of my heart for your friendly act. Unfortunately, Landauer's not back yet, and he may be some time still. The people don't pay up, even though they have the bearing of solid business-people. That terrible marriage of respectable and rapscallion. I've seen it now with my statement. At last I start doing my sums, and it turns out they've been cheating me the way a maître d' in a 5-star hotel cheats a drunk. I can hardly believe your publisher will want to pay. I had to fight for two weeks to get a statement out of de Lange. Then they told me it wasn't a final statement. Unfortunately Landauer isn't around. I'll be glad if I can save my hide till the autumn. Everyone else has relatives, a mother, a brother, a cousin, but I come from far away, I don't even remember the names of my relations in the East. Plus, if they're still alive, they're bound to be in dire straits. What shall I do? I have to view you as a brother, I beg you, please permit me to, I'm talking to you as to a brother. Mme Manga Bell is with her girlfriend in Jona near Rapperswil, but she can't stay there for longer than 4 weeks. What shall I do with her? She's probably madly in love with me. What shall I do about myself? However cheap this hotel is, as I have nothing, it's dear for me. What shall I do with myself question mark period?

It's too bad I hear only now that Bruno Frank has behaved disgracefully toward you. Dr. Landshoff from Querido has written to him on my account, and out of politeness I'm going to have to write to him myself. So I too have thrown myself at an unworthy person. Should I rescind my plea?

I am waiting with brotherly anticipation for your book,[1] and hope with all my heart that your novella[2] is successful, even though it keeps you from coming to see me. When are we to meet, anyway, and where? Everything seems tangled and hopeless to me. It's as hard to see a friend nowadays as it once was to defeat an enemy.

I am in despair anyway—not just for personal reasons, though that's reason enough. It's the confusion of the world! It looks as though Austria may be lost. Then the two Dutch publishers have decided to abandon their German lists. They say it quite openly now.—I congratulate you on your banning in Germany. What the hell are you and Hofmannsthal and Freud doing in Germany anyway?

I think my novel is very poor, I wrote it too quickly. Landauer didn't mention it at all to me. And even if it turned out to be good, what use would that be to me? The novel has to come out next month, and my name is finished. Through overproduction. What can I do?

I am physically sick as well. Every evening I run a temperature. The climate in Amsterdam is horrible. I hope I'm not seriously ill, but I'm working very hard, and that's the cause. I'm editing my first novel, and writing my second.[3] I'm chucking all the material into it that I wanted to save for my great book "Strawberries." It's a shame, but what else can I do? I'm living off the last of the money that Querido paid me for the stories: 5 weeks ago, 200 gulden, for all rights, it's extortionate. But what could I do? When Landauer's girlfriend turned up, he couldn't spare any more money for me.—I am so wretched, if I see you again, I'll frighten you. I'm sure of that, but I'm so utterly wretched. I want to know that there is someone in the little circle whom I can look down on.

Your Joseph Roth

I've just been forwarded an invitation for Freud's festschrift. I'm sending it on express. What else do I do with it? Copy it out again? What for?

1. your book: *Castellio gegen Calvin*.

2. your novella: *Angst* (Fear) was filmed in Paris in 1936.

3. and writing my second: probably *Confession of a Murderer* and *Weights and Measures*, respectively.

388. *To Stefan Zweig*   *Eden Hotel*
                                                   Amsterdam
                                                   7 May 1936

Dear friend,

thank you very much for your kind letter. It's a good thing that your wife has left. I don't think I'm being indiscreet if I say it's what I told her to do. I would have said it openly in front of you both. But you should never forget, my dear friend, that she is an extraordinarily loyal person, and deserves consideration, and that she's at an age when all women are afraid of being abandoned. It's the age of panic. Her sufferings over the last few years won't have been less than yours and mine. We too live in a state of continual panic. God knows who has the rights of it. She did write to me, never inflammatory letters, always perplexed and sad. Dear friend, it's important to love and love, these days. (We are all so tangled up.) Good luck with your story. I hope it comes out beautifully. God will assist.

I am in a dire situation. Landauer is ill, and is lying in the Hotel Siru in Brussels. Mr. Kroonenburg, the editorial manager of de Lange, told me today that your publisher won't have any money for another 6 months. On top of my hacking cough, I've had swollen legs and feet these last 3 days. I can hardly pull my shoes on, and at night I lie with my legs raised, which means I don't sleep. I'm afraid my heart will pack up.

But I go on working, and will soon be finished with my *new* novel. I can't go on. I really can't. Landauer and the publisher want to bring this new book out next. I think they have their reasons. It's all one to me, everything is busted, my head is only half working. I have dropsical feet. I couldn't send you my novel, because I had to deliver the only *handwritten* copy of the book to the publisher. It's being set on 1 June.

Listen, my friend, I'm in the depths of distress, listen to me, I'm dying, believe me, I'm dying. I have no idea what or where or how. I don't believe in the film. Even if, it'll be too late.—Please reply to me,

your old Joseph Roth

389. To Blanche Gidon   *Eden Hotel*
                                                      Amsterdam
                                                      8 May 1936

Dear friend,

don't be angry with me. I'm sick, and no one will give me an advance. You'll get my novel[1] when it's set. My feet are swollen to the knee, and I can't walk. Mrs. M.B. is very poorly, wretched, no money, staying with a Swiss girlfriend, but not able to stay there much longer. I am at my wits' end, and don't know what the rest of my life is for. Don't be angry with me, be kind. My heart is as empty as a desert and as black as an abyss. I am humiliating myself horribly, don't tell anyone, the help committee is paying this wretched red-light hotel for me, but the people here are kind to me. Sincerely, your grateful old

Joseph Roth

1. my novel: *Confession of a Murderer*

390. To Stefan Zweig

Dear friend,

what you write really doesn't make sense. How could I find you ungrateful, and what words are these: grateful, ungrateful, in this unfathomably bottomless thing called friendship. It seems to me you can't have had a friend before in your life. You were only ever a friend to others. Is there gratitude or ingratitude between brothers? How much less then between friends! If I can give my life for a friend a thousand times sooner than for a woman, will you then say I'm grateful or ungrateful? I would let myself be cut into tiny pieces for you, literally; within such a serious and tragic relationship as friendship, there is only the UNCONDITIONAL. THE UNCONDITIONAL. There are no criteria. Why do you tell me you give money to so many causes? I know you do. What concern is it of mine. You don't know—otherwise you wouldn't do it—how much you hurt me when you write: "Don't mistrust me!" There is no situation in which I would "mistrust" a friend. How is such a thing possible? There are moments sometimes when a friend may be mistaken, and then I will tell him. If I were to distrust you for a second, I wouldn't be your friend any more. But *within* this relationship called friendship, I am grateful for every kind word and action. If you save me from my doom—but I fear you may be overestimating your powers there, and my powerlessness— you will keep your friend for longer, and I will keep you longer. But how do you think it can go on? I can't live entirely off you, who are so overrun by needy people. One day your conscience won't be able to stand it any longer, and you will try and flee your own powerlessness, and rightly so. And then what will become of me? How many people do you have writing to tell you that you are their one source of support? I am ashamed, thinking about it, to say the same thing. But it's true. If there's nothing doing with the cinema, then I've gone under.

Landauer wants to publish the new novel in summer, he claims it's a good time, and then I could hope to get another contract in the autumn. There are supposed to be German Jews abroad then, buying books they won't find at home.[1] Perhaps he's right. In a fortnight you'll have galleys. It seems it is suitable for filming.—In response to your telling me the 3,000 francs were on their way, I went ahead and borrowed 50 gulden here in the hotel. That makes things a little easier for me.—What's terrible is my physical condition, the coughing and the swollen extremities. I'm going to see a doctor today. I'm drinking milk, to try and get the poison out of my system.

If you're finished in 14 days—perhaps you could come here? With your manuscript. Should I expect you?

The subject matter for my novel[2] isn't contemporary. But I have so many projects and themes. All it takes is for someone to tell me what they're looking for, and I'll supply something "appropriate."

Please, my dear friend, write back. I'm very ill, and I need kind words, and quickly.

Where is your wife, in Salzburg or Vienna?

WHAT IS YOUR STORY ABOUT?

Sincerely,　　　　　your old Joseph Roth

1. buying books they won't find at home: I don't know what's more striking here—to be so reduced, or still to be calculating.
2. my novel: *Weights and Measures*.

391. *Stefan Zweig to Joseph Roth*　　　　　　　*49 Hallam Street*
London W 1
20 May 1936

Dear friend,

Mr. Stols in Maastricht has suddenly bestirred himself, and ignoring my instructions, sent money directly to me, namely 24 pounds, 9 and a penny, without telling me how much that would be in Dutch, or how many copies it represents. Since I've just sent you other money, I'll save this for you for later. Please tell Landauer of this astonishing turnup.

My *Castellio* book is happily out. I hope it will go to you directly, not via Paris. On page 47 in the paragraph after the xxx in the first line, the word "before" has annoyingly been left out. Please write it into your copy.

I am working solidly. No news from Huebsch.

Sincerely, your Stefan Zweig

392. To Blanche Gidon

Eden Hotel
Amsterdam
26 May 1936

My dear friend,

please forgive me my silence. I'm ashamed when I think of your great kindness and noble friendship. I'm too ashamed even to thank you. The way I'm living here is humiliating. A committee had to lend me money, and then Stefan Zweig sent me funds that were owing to him from a Dutch publisher. When I'm a little better, I can perhaps give a lecture, for which I'll get 50–60 gulden. In the meantime, I'm working so as to desensitize myself. But I'm still not able to pay this hotel, which has only taken me on account of my name. If I hand in part of my new novel, I may be able to get 800 gulden. But I'm still exhausted from the last. I've finished correcting the manuscript amid indescribable agonies. It was the novel *The Regular.* Now it's to be called *Confession of a Murderer.* It's coming out in August, and you'll get the galleys in 10 days. I spent three days in bed, literally with my feet up. I drank a pint of milk a day to detoxify my system. The swelling has gone down. Today I am able to walk and sit down, without my legs swelling up again. I can't keep food down, it goes straight up again, I try to eat rice pudding. I drink red wine instead of schnapps. I'm afraid *my* mattress grave[1] will be in Holland. I had to send something to Mrs. Manga Bell. I don't know what's to become of her. She'll be pleased maybe if you write to her, so let me give you the address: Canton St., Gallen, Jona bei Rapperswil, Switzerland, Villa Grünfels. The schools haven't been paid. I don't know what will become of the children. That woman whose weakness is responsible for 50% of my grief is a poor soul herself, and I can't think of her without feeling very downcast.—I am unable to make plans—the best case, but really the very best, is that I have the wherewithal to live for another 3 months—but I have no strength with which to begin another book. Even a letter is a colossal effort. Don't be cross if I don't write. Frankly, even a stamp is a significant item for me. Give my warm regards please to Dr. Gidon. Forgive me for writing to you in German. I kiss your kind and friendly hand,

    your old Joseph Roth

    1. *my* mattress grave: the allusion is to Heinrich Heine.

393. To Stefan Zweig   *Eden Hotel*
                                                          Amsterdam
                                                          29 May 1936

My dear friend,

I've read your book[1] in the past three nights. I don't think I am deceived by personal feeling for you, or first impressions. I really believe you have said lasting and valid things about the present condition of mankind, and the latent good and evil in it. I believe you have found the decisive expression for the kindly, sincere skepticism that was always present in you, and that you persisted in stifling within yourself. For all your under-standing of the world there was a tendency for illusion in your books, for vague hope rather, a certain moral ballast. You've jettisoned that now, and as a result you've climbed higher. It's exactly what I like: clear, clean, pellucid writing, both in thought and form. No ponderous metaphors. Your style is more sinewy and "Latin." You will guess how happy that makes me, with my almost Calvinist fanaticism for pure language.—As I write this, I'm continually testing myself to see if my friend's and my literary conscience allow me to tell you this. I don't think I can reproach myself with anything. I remember your *Erasmus*. Compared to this book, it's like an idyll to a tragedy. Perhaps more than all your other qualities, what pleases me in this book is the emergence of your basically religious nature. The way you say: humanity, and conscience is with a different, a more sonorous undertone than before—humanity and conscience are almost grace. Yes, that's what especially delights me, the way I can hear the words at either end of your book: God help us, amen! An amen intones on every page. In that sense, and stylistically, it's surely the most mature and modest of your books. An old and good mirror that reflects the present day extraordinarily sadly and gruesomely. I think you've attained a sort of objectivity with this book. Yesterday afternoon I read some passages of it to a Dutch Catholic friend of mine, including the execution that C. avoids. So that you see the extent to which this stubborn fanaticism is still with us: my friend has employed a Calvinist butler, these past ten years. Ten days ago, he built a small pool in his garden so that his children could splash about in it. After the very first time, the butler gave notice, because he couldn't stand to see naked children in the garden. Before he left, my friend asked him to fetch the bicycle he had left at the station. The butler looked at the ticket, and gave it back and said, no he couldn't, because it was insured. It was wrong to intervene in God's councils and insure anything. (You should get your book sent to the local Catholic *Illustrated* magazine, Mr. W. van de Randen, Admiral de Ruyterweg 362 bis.) I'm trying to get attention for it, it's the right place. If possible, might I get another two paperbound copies.—I am so pleased for you, my dear friend. To me it's as if you'd found your way home, and I flatter myself you're a little closer to me. (Don't think I'm out to convert you—how easy it is for such a suspicion to take root.) I'm so glad you don't make the least concession, not stylistically, not intellectually. Quite apart from the fact that there's no one writing in German who is capable of combining clarity and truth, the way you do. (Usually the clear ones are shallow, and the deep ones skewed.) There is a fine quiet sheen over the book, in spite of its cruelties. (I have one single, minor complaint to make: you use "always" and "never" too frequently and emphatically.) What is the "legend"?[2] What is it about? (Freud?)

* * *

As far as I'm concerned: Landauer will send you the first—wretched— galleys of my book.[3] Read them with one eye shut. It's nothing close to final. I don't think you can get anywhere with your Hollywood man on my behalf. Even if you were successful, I'm tied up for another 3 months—if not more.

I can't get *anything* from Huebsch directly. De Lange won't make the Anglo-American rights available. I see no hope there.

I am very feeble, and barely able to walk. There's no particular illness. Every day brings with it different symptoms. If I don't vomit spleen and blood, then my eyes are inflamed, or my feet are swollen. Palpitations, heart pain, shocking migraines, teeth falling out. It sometimes seems to me that nature is kindly after all, because it makes life so rotten that you positively long for death. I still have a feeling for life, though, I want to write my "Strawberries," I don't want to die in wretchedness. I would so like to be able to stop and draw breath for 6 months. I can't, I just *can't*. I've been telling you this for a year. You have boundless optimism where I'm concerned, but you're mistaken, you see it yourself. You didn't believe me. I understand the laws that govern my life.

Now, what shall I do now? Do I go to the Salvation Army; to a monastery? I have only your support. And you're just a human being, overburdened yourself. You will leave sometime, you will forget the wretch. You've helped me, and I still have 20 gulden of yours, but I owe 8 of them already. I managed to get the price for the room down to 1 gulden today, but there's nothing more I can do. I have to drink wine now, no more schnapps for weeks now.—My room looks like a coffin; but a bottle of wine costs 2 gulden. I own 2 suits and 6 shirts. I wash my own handkerchiefs. I've never learned to iron shirts. I look completely dreadful.

Another 4 weeks and I'll be perfectly dead, but I need to remain alive for the next 4 months.

Brussels is cheaper, if they give me a visa here, I'd like to stay there for 2 months once the proofs are corrected. I have to give a lecture here still, there are lots of people here who read me and admire me, but I can't go telling them how I feel.—I don't know how much of the money from your Dutch publisher you're holding back for me, but please, send it to me next week, I hope it'll keep me for 3 weeks—4 lives and a little breathing space.

Please, won't you come here, if only just for one day!

Will I not see you again before you go?[4] I have no one, no one but you. I've wasted everything on others. Mrs. Manga Bell thinks only of her children, those children on whom, according to Landauer's calculations I spent 42,000 francs, and who call me *boche*. I've lent I think 8 writers sums up to 800–1,000 francs, none of them comes forward, and one has even savaged me in the press. The only one who is kind to me is Landauer. He looks after me like a brother. But he has a girlfriend, who unfortunately is addicted to morphine—and he has to give her almost all he earns.

How am I going to live? Tell me this, if you will: can I count on you, even after you're gone.

All I want is to take a deep, deep breath, and sleep for a week. Can you, will you help me?

I implore you, answer me right away, clearly, tell me clearly what I can expect and what not. I don't believe in my rescue by the film industry. Those things are always touch and go. There's no point, they're chimerical hopes. Maybe—maybe not.

Must I beg your pardon for writing you this? Who else do I say it to, if not you? Who else have I got? Even if I didn't love you, would I have to write you this just to survive?—I'm at the end of my rope.—Landauer tells me my situation is hopeless.

Will you write back? Will you not get all impatient, and in spite of your feeling for me, leave me hanging on, think it over, and finally say

to yourself: Oh, he'll find something!—He won't!—What is there? I
beg you, I beg you, please stifle your optimism in my regard. Now come,
come, I'm going to be here for another two weeks, longer if you come.
Answer me, please, right away. I'm half demented. Sincerely your

Joseph Roth

1. your book: *Castellio against Calvin*.
2. the legend: *The Buried Candelabrum*.
3. my book: *Confession of a Murderer*.
4. before you go: from August to October of 1936, Zweig was on his second tour of
South America.

394. Stefan Zweig to Joseph Roth   *49 Hallam Street*
                                                      London W 1
                                                      2 June 1936

Dear friend,

don't be cross if I don't write you a full letter. I'm tired, I have to go
soon, I have a lot to do, so just a sort of shorthand report.

Your novel[1] is excellent, and precisely because it's not overstretched.
The mistake of the last few years was simply that for purely practical
reasons you stretched out your material to more than its natural length
(*Tarabas, Antichrist*). This time the fit is *perfect*, and the Russian element
is not only in the characters, but also in the rhythm of the prose. Warm
congratulations—and more anon.

I've asked Landauer to *pay you the 200 gulden* due on signature, and I
hope that gives you a little breathing space.

I'm seeing Huebsch later today, and will take him the novel.

Castellio is making me quite ill. At a perfectly unimportant place
(the story of Bernardo Ochino) I've fallen prey to a wrong and romantic
source. It doesn't matter a great deal, but *imagine the delight* of the Calvinists to be able to denounce the whole book as a fable and window
dressing, I can't go to Geneva except to the pastor of Calvin's church, who

loves *Castellio*. But that too will be overlooked, once we've gotten over sundry other difficulties.

In haste, your Stefan Z.

1. your novel: *Confession of a Murderer* (Amsterdam: Allert de Lange, 1936).

395. Stefan Zweig to Joseph Roth
49 Hallam Street
London W 1
10 June 1936

Dear friend,

I just want to let you know that on the morning of the 15th I'm going to Austria, and will stay for about a fortnight. My address during this time will be c/o Herbert Reichner Verlag, Aegidienstrasse 6, Vienna vi, then I want to go somewhere quiet to work, and after that I'll probably go to South America. I'm looking forward to putting all sorts of things behind me, and to being away from Europe for a while.

Huebsch, who's attending a publishing convention here, will read your novel in the next few days. The film person hasn't arrived yet, but is expected daily.

Then this. I've spoken about your books to the owner of the Skoglund Verlag in Stockholm, and recommended them strongly. Perhaps, to remind him, you could ask your publisher to offer him *Job* and *The Radetzky March*. I'm pretty sure he'll do them, and that you'll have a lasting connection.

Perhaps you could drop me a line on a postcard to let me know where you'll be in July, maybe I can work it into my schedule, and Belgium might not be the worst, somewhere by the sea.

Sincerely, your rushed, tired, and somewhat exasperated
St. Z.

396. To Stefan Zweig   *Eden Hotel*
                                                          Amsterdam
                                                          15 June 1936

Dear, dear friend,

forgive me for leaving you without word for so long. I was working
very hard on a talk which I gave here on Thursday. It was a moral triumph, and even brought in a little money (50 gulden). Thank you very
much for making your royalty over to me.—On Sunday or Monday I'm
going to Brussels. Where shall I send you my Brussels address? I quoted
quite a bit from your book in my talk—I know it doesn't amount to a
hill of beans, but at least it won't have done you any harm.—In Brussels I'll probably be even lonelier than here, but I'll get by better and for
longer.—Don't be too irked by the misprint in your book! The way the
world is nowadays, hardly anyone will notice it. And the few who do
will be large-hearted or other writers, who'll know just how such things
come about. Please try not to worry about it.

I've heard nothing from Huebsch. Maybe he dislikes my novel.

I don't want to talk to you about my family life, it would probably spoil
your mood. Dear friend, why is it that the most banal things in this short
life obscure the serious ones, and create differences between friends?

Dear friend, will I see you before your big trip? Perhaps in Brussels?
Remember, one can never know which time will be the last. And letters are no substitute for the moment of seeing one another, exchanging
greetings, and then that other moment, of taking leave.

Will you reply here?

I am your old friend   Joseph Roth

397. Stefan Zweig to Joseph Roth   *Hotel Regina*
                                                      Vienna
                                                      [End of June? 1936]

My dear fellow,

I hope this letter gets to you in time. Either way, I'll be in Ostend for a month from 2 July to work, my friend Fuchs,[1] who helps me with the editing, will be there, and my secretary[2] is coming, I HAVE to have 110 typed pages ready by 1 August! Because that's when I'm going.

It would be wonderful to have you there as a sort of literary conscience for my legend. We could test one another in the evenings, and lecture each other, as in the good old days. You don't have to swim, I won't be swimming either—Ostend isn't a spa, but a CITY, prettier, and with more cafés than Brussels.

My address is *Ostend* poste restante Cursal. I hope to get a room on Monday night in the Hotel SIRU. They gave me my new passport[3] here, without any fuss,

warmly, Z.

1. Fuchs: Martin Fuchs.
2. my secretary: Lotte Altmann, later Zweig's second wife, dying with him in their suicide pact in Petropolis, Brazil, on 23 February 1942.
3. my new passport: Austrian, still. Zweig took British nationality later, in 1939.

398. To Blanche Gidon   *Eden Hotel*
                                                      Amsterdam
                                                      16 June 1936

Dear kind friend,

you must never reproach yourself for writing candidly to me. Of course I would do absolutely anything at all—if there was anything sensible I could do. But it's confusing cause and effect if you think my situation is the result of alcoholism. I haven't drunk any schnapps for 3 or 4 weeks now. (My situation hasn't improved thereby. My health not much either.) In the instant of standing over the abyss such considerations have little meaning. I'm drinking only wine, and still my feet are swollen, my heart is heavy as a stone, and in front of me is, quite literally, a black void. It's a terrible feeling not to know what you're going to live off in another week. Sixteen years ago I could bear it. Not any more.

I didn't write, because I had a talk to prepare here. It was a success, I made 150 gulden with it. With that—because it's cheaper there—I want to go to Brussels. Please write to me here first. I don't yet have an address in Brussels.

The galleys[1] you were sent aren't anything near final. I'm still making changes up to my departure.

Plon would be nice. But I don't know how Mr. Marcel feels about me at the moment. I have no very strong sense of the novel. Grasset or Michel or Plon: all that matters is that the publisher here sees some money come in. Maybe I can get another 6-month contract in September.

Thank you very much, to you and Mr. Gidon.

Please don't be cross about my writing in German.

I am so terribly tired.

In warm friendship   your Joseph Roth

1. galleys: of *Confession of a Murderer*.

399. *To Blanche Gidon*   *Eden Hotel*
                                           Amsterdam
                                           24 June 1936

Dear kind Madam and friend,

in case I do go to Belgium—I'm waiting for the visa to come—I want to say that this address is fine. My mail will be forwarded.—I'm working on some new thing[1] now. Please write to me, and forgive me for being so curt.

I'll write to you at greater length in a fortnight.—I'm very concentrated on my work.

Best wishes to Mr. Gidon.

I kiss your hand.

Please write me a few words, it's important to me, in this situation, which I can't describe to you just now,

your old and trusty Joseph Roth

1. some new thing: *Weights and Measures* (Amsterdam: Querido, 1937).

400. *To Stefan Zweig*

Eden Hotel
Amsterdam
Wednesday, 24 June 1936

Dear friend,

I've spent the past 6 days waiting for a Belgian visa, which for Austrian subjects has to be sent to their main domicile. I've been waiting for eight days. (I should have had to go to Paris to get it right away.)

(Will you give the accompanying note to your wife, please.)

I will probably be staying in the Hotel Siru in Brussels. It's supposed to be one of the cheapest and best [?] there.

Even so: a telegram from you to here will follow me there *by wire*. You can—it would be nice if you did—write here if you don't have my address in Brussels before your departure.

You're much too worked up about Calvin. How is it that you, who especially in your books shows the superior calm of great men, get so worked up as soon as the slightest mishap befalls you?—My dear friend, there's something not quite right there! You can't be agitated, not after you've depicted so much really tragic agitation so classically and perfectly. What do you care about the delight of the Calvinists and the Morgensterns? Don't you have to live, at least part way, like the characters you portray?—What is it that bothers you?—Please, keep your dignity.—In

Holland, from what I hear, your book has been picked up very favorably and respectfully, certainly among the Catholics.—I beg you, please come here, here or to Belgium, and don't leave me a *single* day without your address. *And reply to me here!* I am completely shattered again. Yet again.

I embrace you warmly,   your Joseph Roth

For Mme Friderike Maria Zweig:

My dear friend,

everything you write here will reach me. Mrs. M.B. hasn't replied to another two telegrams I literally had to squeeze out of myself. I don't even know where my—very important—correspondence and manuscripts—are. I don't know what's going on. So many years, and so much humanity in vain. I feel terribly sad that a person can drop me like unnecessary ballast. I feel terribly sad.

Sincerely,   your old J.R.

401. To Stefan Zweig   *Eden Hotel*
                                                          Amsterdam
                                                          2 July 1936

My dear good friend,

for certain reasons I couldn't write before today, and I couldn't go to Belgium before Monday. I got the visa yesterday (after appeals from the PEN Club in Brussels). As a result of the accompanying telegram, signed by Manga Bell's daughter, probably without the mother's knowing, I had to telephone my translator, and ask her to look and check, and then to call me back. This phoning back and forth cost me half my travel money, the money for my lecture doesn't come till Monday, and then I'll go straight to Brussels, Hotel Siru. The telegram was a crude shock tactic. It made me ill for 2 days. Awful. How bitterly one pays for any humanity and any human half-joy. Please write, so I'll have word at the Siru on Tuesday, and won't have to wire you too.

Sincerely,   your loyal old J.R.

P.S. It will be very embarrassing for me to run into Kesten and Kisch in Ostend—certainly not to be avoided. I can't stand any more jokers.

402. *Stefan Zweig to Joseph Roth*   *46 Promenade Albert 1er*
                                                  Maison Florial
Joseph Roth, Amsterdam, Eden Hotel   *[postmarked 4 July 1936]*

Dear friend,

I've just come from Brussels, where I spoke to Huebsch on his way through. Brussels is impossible to work in, you'll like Ostend better, there are hundreds of cheap hotels, and, as in the rest of Belgium, that for you very advantageous prohibition of spirits. We can help each other in our work, and I think could both use such help—let's bring back the old days of *Job*! And don't be upset about Ma. Be. It's lucky when things come undone quickly like that, it's better than a slow rending.[1] I'm looking forward very much to seeing you, come straight on, and forget dull old Brussels,

warmly your St. Z.

1. a slow rending: spoken with feeling, in view of Zweig's—on the face of it, mostly "amicable"—breakup with Friderike.

403. *To Stefan Zweig*   *Saturday [July 1936]*

My dear good friend,

I have to tell you in the manner of teenage girls[1] or schoolboys how nice you were to me today, with the hotel and everything, and so I'll say it to you the way I would have said it if I'd tried at age 18 to look you up in your apartment in Vienna. Thank you for a slice of youth and the sweet folly of saying it in writing, instead of speech,

your J.R.

1. JR's note seems to be strangely colored by Zweig's novella *Letter from an Unknown Woman*, which was often taken as being "about" Friderike, whose first approach took the form of an unsigned letter.

404. *To Blanche Gidon*   *Hotel Siru*
                                                           Brussels
                                                           8 July 1936

My dear kind friend,

forgive me for writing to you so late. Sorry too that I telephoned you on Sunday, and bothered you. I didn't know what else I could do, after the alarming telegram from Mrs. Manga Bell's daughter. It was signed by her, and she wrote: *prière venir immédiatement*. What else was I to think, other than that the very worst had befallen Mrs. M.B.? I spent the last 8 days lying down, unable to write. I had to have Zweig summoned on the telephone. He's coming here, and will whisk me away to Ostend for a fortnight. I'm going tomorrow, as soon as he gets here. I won't write any more now, but *all my post will be forwarded to Ostend, from the Eden Hotel, Amsterdam*; please write to me there. I'm very upset about Mrs. Manga Bell. Once I've said goodbye to Zweig—who's going to South America, and will leave me money for 2 months—I can *take her with me to Brussels*, because it's so cheap. I suggested it to her once. I'll write to her again. If you want to do me another kind turn, please help her *morally*. The woman is in pieces. I have the feeling the children are trampling all over her. Their trying to frighten me is senseless. I can't come. I spent half the travel money on telephone, telegram, and replies. The children still seem to think I can get by, even though I've been living off charity for the past 4 months. All I can do is work, and hope I'm offered a new contract in October. Hope!—And stay alive till then!—I'm feeling better, I've just arrived.—I'll talk to St. Z. about alcohol withdrawal. Excuse the bluntness.—I am so tired, and so fizzing. Give my best to Mr. Gidon.—Thank you for your grand kind friendship.—I have no other way to thank you but saying so. It hurts me really.

Sincerely your   Joseph Roth

405. *To Blanche Gidon*   *Ostend*
Hotel de la Couronne
15 July 1936

Dear friend,

thank you so much for everything! The story is unfortunately sold, along with the English rights. But if you are able to sell it, and send the royalty to Querido Verlag, Landshoff, then 60% of it will make its way back to me. Any interested party should apply to: Querido Verlag, Amsterdam, 333 Keizersgracht.

I sent Mrs. Manga Bell 200 francs. At the beginning of August, Stefan Zweig is going to South America. I could spend August in Brussels with Mrs. Manga Bell on the money he's leaving me. I put it to her, but she hasn't replied. The money's not enough for Paris. I have to work in peace and quiet, otherwise my life will be completely wrecked. I have endured a superhuman portion of work, of turbulence, of humiliation. Mrs. Manga Bell has steadily refused to adapt to the rules of my life. Her children were and are much more important to her than I am. I will not sacrifice myself to her children. The boy is old enough, and the girl could have the money that M.B.'s Swiss girlfriend unnecessarily sends the boy. They aren't children any more at all, but two adults who call me *boche*, and poison Mrs. Manga Bell against me. I myself am the lost, sick child. I can keep Mrs. Manga Bell on her own, but I've had it with the children. I'm standing on the brink of the abyss. I can no longer bear the least psychological pressure, it would kill me. And I don't want to die. And I don't want anything more to do with people who call me *boche*. That sort of thanks is unbearable.

I'm having my feet treated. I'm not drinking any alcohol, and for the last week I've eaten once a day. Zweig is so sweet to me, he's like a brother. Only I don't know how I'm going to finish in October, when I have money only through August. Zweig won't be back till November.

I haven't heard anything from Mr. Wasserbaeck. If you should happen to speak to him, please give him my address.

I hope you and Mr. Gidon have a good summer. Please drop me another line from Paris. No politics, afterward, from Austria! I'll be at this hotel—*vide supra*—till 1 August. I'm going to Steenockerzeel[1] for a couple of days. Keep quiet about this, but don't spend longer than 4 weeks in Austria. End of August is the deadline, it now appears. The friendship with Germany isn't real. Little Red Riding Hood is back to life as well.

I kiss your hand, and thank you for your friendship,

Your loyal   Joseph Roth

1. Steenockerzeel: where Archduke Otto von Habsburg and the loyalist court were based. See no. 454.

406. *To Stefan Zweig*   *[Ostend] 8 August 1936*

Dear friend,

thank you very much for the writing paper. I cadged a loan of this paper here,[1] I hope you like it. I wanted to write you something cheerful, but unfortunately it's going to be sad. Huebsch has dropped me. At a time when my reputation with the Amsterdam publisher could have been rescued only by interest from America. My book[2] wasn't that bad either. I'm sure Huebsch has been unjust to me, humanly, literarily, and in publishing terms.

I dog you with these things, you're already in a different world, but whom else am I to tell it to? Can you think of any consolation? It's set me back at least a fortnight in my writing. Landauer has written to tell me that even if I hand in the manuscript, I'm not getting any more money.

In sincere friendship,

All the best,   your Joseph Roth

1. this paper here: the letter paper is marked, "Bond Street Birch. A paper that is inexpensive but subdued in character. Smython of Bond Street." The noted collector

Zweig liked his paper, and JR—see no. 403—when not antagonizing his patron, went to considerable lengths to try and please him.

2. my book: presumably *Confession of a Murderer* (1936).

407. To Blanche Gidon (written in French)   [Ostend] 4 September 1936

Dear friend,

I was invited to Calais by my friend Wagner, who has left for London, which is why I didn't get your last letter. I am awaiting the return of Mr. Zweig to see it. I am hard at work, my novel[1] will be good, better than my life. I don't want to list any of the sorry details.

But it's important that you know I love you. Unhappy people have the right to remain silent. I am writing this in the tram. Excuse the shaky hand. My best wishes to Mr. Gidon.

Please continue to write to the Eden Hotel Amsterdam.

Your very true and old   Joseph Roth

1. my novel: *Weights and Measures*.

408. To Stefan Zweig   1 November 1936

Dear friend,

forgive me for not writing. I am in indescribable trouble. My health is shot. Please, if you would give me two weeks' time.

Thanks for the book.[1] Great delight to see again what in the "old," early years gave me such pleasure. It's still fresh. Your older things as much as the new ones.

Sincerest greetings,   your old Joseph Roth

1. the book: a second, expanded edition of Zweig's *Sternstunden der Menschheit*, originally translated as *Decisive Moments in History*.

409. To Blanche Gidon   *Vilnius, 28 February 1937*

Dear dear friend,

I owe you a detailed letter, but I feel so wretched. I can't say anything more than that I assure you of my loyalty. For months I've been eking out my paltry life with lectures in tiny places, an awful life. I have no idea how I'll ever get back to western Europe. My life is appalling.[1] I want to thank you for your first letter, and the second. You are more than kind: you are forgiving. Unless I die soon, I'll find an opportunity to thank you most sincerely. I go from place to place like a traveling circus, every other evening in penguin suit, it's terrible, every other evening the same talk. The PEN Club has fixed it for me,[2] otherwise I'd have been dead long ago.

If you can, try and *hold on to the first serial payment. Contractually*, it's *mine*. But I've quarreled with de Lange—I've taken an advance from him—and if it falls into his hands he will pocket it. If you can, try and prevent that happening—fast.

(My address till 15 March is: c/o Miss Paula Grübel, Lvov, Hofmana 7/1.)

Your letter about Mrs. Manga Bell and the children has followed me all the way here. Thank you for it. If she'd expended half her energy on the children while we were living together—and less on being malicious against me—we would never have gotten into that situation. If you see her still, please greet her from me. I'm sorry to say I have the feeling some mishap has befallen her, or threatens to. Those children will be the end of her.

I know that I owe you information about myself, and more than that. But please, stay friends with me, even if I say nothing.

I'm coming from Warsaw, and writing this in Vilnius.

I'm going to the border towns.

I have 4 more talks to give.

(You perhaps saw in the paper that the royalty for my novel was stolen from an Amsterdam hotel room.) It's the novel that the *Gemeenschap* is publishing.[3] Then I got the invitation from the PEN Club. Hotel Bristol should be a safe address—even if by then I'll be training elephants in Australia.

Give my best to Mr. Gidon. I'm sure he's laughing at me. He's right.

My only hope is Marlene Dietrich, who gave an entire interview[4] about me. Perhaps she'll buy one of my novels.

Write soon, but don't be surprised if I don't reply often.

I remain your old, true, and very grateful

Joseph Roth

1. My life is apalling: cf. Joseph Brodsky's distich "My life's grotesque / I sit at my desk."

2. The PEN Club has fixed it for me: a lecture tour of cities in Poland and the East. JR was accompanied by Irmgard Keun (1905–1982), who left a fictionalized record of her experiences—the locations, and some of the ambience—in the novel *Child of All Nations* (1938).

3. the novel that the *Gemeenschap* is publishing: *The Emperor's Tomb*, 1938.

4. an entire interview: not so, but as well as listing her favorite colors and prized attributes in men (sense of humor?), she did say that her favorite novel was Roth's *Job*.

410. *To Friderike Zweig*   *Lvov, 9 March 1937*

Dear dear friend,

I wrote to you by registered mail from Warsaw or Vilnius.

I hope you got the letter.

I don't dare write to Stefan.

I should be in Vienna on the 15th inst., please make life a little easier for me by asking Gabriel the porter at the Hotel Bristol whether I've gotten in yet.

Thank you very much for the invitation to Salzburg.

I don't think it would be good if you took on new staff in the wake of your servant's departure.

Of course I'll speak in the Urania,[1] if there's some money in it.

For example, I could give my Catholic-conservative talk about faith and progress.

Thank you again, and I hope you got my first letter.

Give my best to the girls,[2] always your   [Joseph Roth]

1. the Urania: a Viennese lecture club.
2. the girls: FZ's two daughters from her first marriage.

411. To Blanche Gidon   *Hotel Bristol*
                                                 Vienna, 2 April 1937

Dear dear friend,

I enclose the carbon of the letter I've just sent to Landauer, and also the letter to *Candide*,[1] which you should feel free to use in the event that de Lange doesn't pay me.

First serial rights are not covered in my contract with de Lange, so *Candide* had no right to send the royalty to the publisher.

I'd sooner the thing didn't appear at all, than that the publisher gets the sizable royalty.

If the royalty isn't paid to me, I can complain about the serialization, on the basis that the novel will appear in altered, abbreviated form.

Please write and tell me what you think, excuse typewriter, I promise I'll write you a personal letter by hand soon.

Best wishes to you and Dr. Gidon, from your always loyal friend
Joseph Roth

1. *Candide* was a conservative literary-political weekly in Paris. Roth is exercised about the fee for the French translation and serial rights for *Confession of a Murderer*.

412. To Blanche Gidon   *Salzburg, Hotel Stein*
                                                     20 April 1937

Dear dear friend,

please excuse typewriter (I'm now in Salzburg, at the Hotel Stein). This is important to me: de Lange has agreed that I should get a quarter of the fee that *Candide* is paying him. If you could manage to see that the money is sent immediately, and tell me (*because I don't trust the publisher*), I'd be very grateful for word at the *Hotel Stein in Salzburg*. I'll write you a detailed letter by hand, tomorrow or the day after.

In any case, my dear friend, you see I was right, and that the serialization rights belonged to me. It's a breach of contract to take them away from me (I didn't have money for a lawyer to contest this). At least by issuing a threat, I managed to secure a quarter of the money.

In old fondness, I remain your own and Dr. Gidon's old friend

Joseph Roth

413. To Stefan Zweig   *Hotel Stein, Salzburg*
                                                     [May? 1937]

Dear friend,

it's quite extraordinary what you're doing to me.

It's your DUTY to accept me as your friend, whether I don't write to you for ten or twenty or two hundred years; or whatever. You're on closer terms with shits than you are with me. (As I happen to know.) Your wife has NOTHING to do with it. If that were so, I would tell you (and above all, tell HER). *At once*!

The moment you begin to question my friendship is the moment you'd better end it. I will think the better of you for that, *and not* "take it amiss."

You don't know, you have no idea, how wretched I am; how I lose more and more of myself from day to day; you have NO CLUE. I remain, until you decide to terminate our friendship,

your old J.R.

414. *To Blanche Gidon*   *Vienna, 18 May 1937*

Dear dear friend,

by chance, I'm just reading the second installment of my novel in *Candide*.

Thank you ever so much for the wonderful translation. It shows your ability as much as your friendship with me.

I still haven't received any money from All. de Lange Verlag. He told me that an unbelievably small sum had been agreed upon. I don't believe him! I would be extremely grateful to you if you could find out what Grasset was paid for it. In my current destitution it would be of major importance. Stefan Zweig has confirmed that the sum reported by the publisher is far too small for *Candide*.

I kiss your hand, and thank you again, and send the professor my warm regards.

In old true friendship, your   [Joseph Roth]

415. *To Mr. and Mrs. Gidon (written in German and French)*

Hotel Cosmopolite
Brussels
20 June 1937

Dear friends,

you don't know what a pleasure you gave me. It was wonderfully generous of you to send me the photos, and at a moment when I was very ill, toxified, with swollen legs and bloodshot eyes, and my heart full of anguish. I'm a little better now. There is some hope from Holland.

You didn't understand me: I *know* that *Candide* paid 8,000 francs, and that of these, 4,000 are going to de Lange. But he WON'T pay me 2,000. He only wrote loosely to say he would give me "something" once the money has arrived. All I want to know is whether the 4,000 has already been paid to him. Even if he only gives me 500 francs, I'd be satisfied—though it's all flagrant breach of contract.

I got through the winter by giving talks, and in Austria by writing articles for Legitimists, on whose instructions and at whose expense I have come here. The books no longer bring in anything. A new one has just been set: *The Story of the 1002nd Night*, but not yet corrected and revised. I'll have to start a third, if I'm to stay alive. There's nothing else I can do. In Vienna my wife's sanatorium set the bailiffs on me. I do believe it is absolutely impossible to know or understand the folly in which I live my life.—But don't let me talk about those things! We'll speak in Paris. Are you going away this summer? Where to?

I'm looking at you both at the moment, your picture is on my desk. I have the feeling you can see me too.

Thank you for your friendship and LOYALTY.

Thanks to Mr. Matveev as well. He hasn't forgotten me. That's a further consolation.

Very warmly in old troth, to you and the dear doctor. His spectacles are glinting in the picture. His beard gleams, and his kindly skepticism shines forth

To your old   Joseph Roth

416. To Hermann Hesse   *Brussels*
                                                           5 July 1937

Esteemed Mr. Hermann Hesse,
today I got your sweet book of poetry. It had taken its time getting to me. It shames me as much as it honors and delights me. Because it seems that I am left owing the now sexagenarian poet of my youth respectful

and comradely congratulations. Please accept the word "comradely" as the expression of my happy feeling to have consecrated myself to the service of the language whose sweetness and strength I learned to love in your writings twenty years ago. Back then I was a soldier in the trenches, [. . . illegible] and resolved to remain in the army, and end my life as a major in Teplice or Brunn, if I should be spared. It was therefore as a layman twice over that I read your works then: not only was I not a writer, but I was a soldier. I will admit to you today in your festive year, that I reread your early works ten years later, then already an aspiring writer myself. They were as fresh as on the day they were printed, and they offered the "expert" the noble satisfaction of enjoying your "craft" and mastery with insightful admiration.—I beg you, to whom I owe so much, to forgive me for not having sent you a birthday telegram. For weeks I've been lying in bed with swollen feet, not so much unhappy as almost in despair and sometimes furious at my disobedient body. It's only in the past few days that I've recovered a little alertness. Alert enough to feel the doom doubly that threatens *our* world, our little islet of world where we will die, the last 10 of the Fourth Regiment.[1]

In continuing gratitude and admiration,   your Joseph Roth

1. the last 10 of the Fourth Regiment: from an Austrian soldiers' song. One imagines that the pacifist Hesse (then celebrating his sixtieth birthday) will have been bemused and alienated by the martial reference in particular and the letter altogether.

417. To Stefan Zweig   *Grand Hotel Cosmopolite*
                                          Brussels
                                          10 July 1937

Dear friend,

I received your grumpy letter. Why are you so afraid of words that won't come? They have less meaning than pebbles dropped into the sea. Haven't I written you worse things before? I'm a little concerned about you, and your letter added to my concern. Silly your suspicion I might have crossed your name off the list. I don't keep lists. With the number of friends I have, I don't need a list. But for a year now, since our melancholy goodbyes in Ostend, and more particularly since your return from South America, you've been in a state where either you don't respond at all to my communications, or you respond badly. You react a little egocentrically. You blame God for your aging, instead of thanking Him for it. You don't understand that people have gotten worse, because you were never willing to see them as good and bad and as human until Judgment Day, which you are so slow to believe in. How can I talk to you? Because you notice it getting darker, you stand there bewildered by the approach of night; and you think, furthermore, that it's something personal to do with you. Even currency devaluations you take as a personal affront, because you had thought you could save yourself by living in the isles of the blessed. Now, for the sake of money, you want to return to the Continent, and to its darkest part. (Mind you don't stay there too long!) You are independent of publishers and advances. You can afford to write nothing at all for two years. You truly are a "freelance." Who else can say that of himself? Rolland has disappointed you. My Lord! He always was a false prophet and in thrall to noble errors and idealistic self-deceptions. Just before the World War he idolized the Germans and put to sleep whatever alertness the Continent had. After the war he proclaimed the absolute goodness of humankind, and today he's a lackey of the Russian executioners. In the truest sense of the word, he has never known where God dwells, and he never will till his dying day. You already have a clear notion—being of the tribe of Asra, who have God, even if they never get him—of the inadequacy of all human idealisms that you bathed in from the time of your youth, and in which you have steeped yourself. You're bound to be disappointed. The nonviolence of Mahatma Gandhi is just as unhelpful to me, as Hitler's violence is detestable. Of course you shouldn't sign up for any party or group. I don't see why that should even occur to you. You are an unregistered member of a motley group as it is, with tumblers, men of the world, rascals and dilettantes and liars, all coexisting with a small handful of decent individuals. You think you have already withdrawn from it. Oh no, you haven't! Why for instance did you send a statement to be read out at the PEN Club? An organization where Communists and Fascists shoulder the yoke of politics and the state, and you come along and intone your: Down with politics! You're not serious. Don't you understand? That might be the way to speak in front of a republic of ghosts, but not to a lurid organization where assholes have seats and votes alongside brains. Do you think you'll tug at Feuchtwanger's conscience? Will you hell! Why do you do these things! You can't get over the loss of Germany! It's only if Germany exists that you can be a cosmopolitan.[1]

Show equanimity to the world and give what you have in the way of goodness to three or four individuals, not to "humankind,"

your old   Joseph Roth

I am going to Ostend again. It will remind me of you.

1. a cosmopolitan: these are all wounding and pertinent strictures to Stefan Zweig.

418. To Blanche Gidon   *Hotel Cosmopolite*
                                                 Brussels
                                                 13 July 1935
                                                 [postmarked: 13 July 1937]

Dear friend,

please excuse me for writing in German. I'm interrupting my work. It's difficult for me to make a sudden switch into French. Well, I thanked you from Salzburg for the sweet and lovely photos. I won't repeat my "witty" remarks. But I also asked you for *2 practical things*: 1. de Lange promised me of his charity to pay me "something" (my guess is 300–500 francs) of the *Candide* money, *as soon as Grasset has remitted it*. I ask you again please tell me if you can find out from Grasset when the money was dispatched to de Lange. The 2. question was: I've been asked for a couple of short stories by an American publication. I had a list of subjects written down somewhere, but I can't find the piece of paper. I now think Mrs. Manga Bell has it, and I think you see her from time to time. I've also forgotten the name of the lawyer in Nice to whom I gave all my papers. I'm sure Mrs. Manga Bell will remember it. In case she wants to keep hold of the original piece of paper (I know she likes her little memorials), she could copy it out for me. It would help me a lot.—If it's difficult for you to see Mrs. M.B., then just leave it. Querido does nothing for me in France. You could perhaps hawk the book[1] around, it might be more suitable for serialization than the *Confession*.—In any case, I'll write to Querido, even though we're *brouillés*. As the mail is so unreliable, as you see, I beg you for a speedy reply.—My best regards to Mr. Gidon. With all my heart, your old and grateful

Joseph Roth

1. the book: *Weights and Measures*.

419. To Blanche Gidon (written in French)   *Hotel Cosmopolite*
Brussels
[postmarked:
Ostend, 21 July 1937]

Thousand thanks, my dear friend, for your letter and your great kindness. Please excuse the pencil. I would like this postcard to reach you before your departure. I've sold just 1,100 copies of *Weights and Measures*. I don't think I will ever have a year in which I can take a rest from writing. I'm writing again now. I am battered and half demented at the same time.—Thank you for speaking to Mrs. Manga Bell, and thank her too—if you see her. The lawyer's name was Feblowicz, that's right. But Mr. Dohrn[1] must be away from Paris, just now. He doesn't reply to me. I don't think you'll have a moment to speak to him. But thank you in any case, from the bottom of my heart!

Drop me a LINE, please.

Happy holidays! to you and Mr. Gidon. I remain your very loyal and grateful, also very old

Joseph Roth

(Landauer is honest, but evil.) Will you be staying in the mountains for long?

I await your reply! Thank you for the translation! *Weights and Measures* is set in Bukovina, and not in the old Polish part of Austria.

1. Mr. Dohrn: Klaus Dohrn, who edited the Austrian monarchist publication (to which Roth contributed), *Der Christliche Ständestaat*.

420. To Stefan Zweig   [Ostend] 28 July 1937

Dear friend,

thank you for thinking of me with the obituary. Tschuppik[1] was much closer to me than you thought, and for many reasons, and the news of his death—conveyed to me by a telegram at 7 in the morning from the editorial office of a newspaper: "Please hurry obituary Tschuppik," robbed me of all strength. I am completely crazed. Angina pectoris in my heart. Everyone's dying, so far: Hermann Wendel, Walter Rode, von Gerlach, Stefan Grossmann, Wassermann, Werner Hegemann, and others besides.[2] Broken hearts: Hitler will have to pay for those at a dearer rate than for the simple murders. You've no need to call out to *me*: We must stick together. I don't think fucking Prussia is going to kill me off. I've always despised it. Ebert[3] or Hitler, I don't give a shit. For me that shitty country was what California is to the gold digger. If I survive my penury, then I'll outlive Germany.—But it won't be any help from Querido, de Lange, Huebsch—who, let me say, is my personal backstabber—that will see me through.—Ostend without you, the same bars, completely different. Very familiar, very remote, terrifyingly both at once. I stagger

from one week to the next. Please write and tell me where you'll be on 1
September.—And confirm receipt of this card, please, sincerely

Your old   J.R.

Grasset didn't remit any money for the serialization in *Candide*. Do
you know whom I can turn to?

1. Tschuppik: Karl Tschuppik (1877–1937), Austrian journalist and author of biographies of Maria Theresia and Ludendorff. A friend of Roth's, and another author in the Allert de Lange stable.

2. Wendel, Rode, von Gerlach, Grossmann, Wassermann, Hegemann: all German writers in exile.

3. Ebert: Friedrich Ebert (1871–1925), the first president of the Weimar Republic: an impressive if not altogether believable diatribe against Germany.

421. To Stefan Zweig   *2 August 1937*

Dear friend,

thank you so much! Your letter is a wonderfully comforting witness
to your recovery: style and atmosphere bespeak your health and clarity of
mind.—If you will, please read my second obituary to my dearly beloved
Tschuppik in the *Christl. Ständestaat*. But don't imagine for a moment
that I'll write you one, should I happen to outlive you. You are not just
intellectually close to me, but *physically. It's the umbilical cord of friendship,
there is such a thing.* With you I don't have the distance that is the prerequisite for an obituary.—You can't excuse Huebsch. He has destroyed me
materially, and wrecked my credit (all senses) with the Dutch boss. He
could have arranged a meeting between the three of us, but he doesn't
want to see me, and the fact that *you* wanted the meeting doesn't excuse
him. A man who embraces me and kisses me on the cheek has to take my
side, even if he doesn't have the financial clout. But he wrote to tell me
that my *Weights and Measures* was a *literary* disappointment! And, having
once had the authority to offer me 100 dollars a month—for a year—he

didn't have the right, purely legally, to suddenly withdraw it. That's what you should have held against him. In your place, that's what I would have done. It would be absurd to say: this isn't a reproach. It is—and it won't detract from our friendship.

I'll meet you wherever and whenever you want. I can't make plans. I am now writing my fifth book in 3 years. It was a long time ago that I wrote you to say I'm all washed up. The ending is a little protracted. I take more time dying than I ever had living.

I embrace you,   your J. R.

Greetings from Almondo,[1] Ostend

And Floréal[2] asks after you every day. I just ran into Almondo in the Café Flynt in the corner where I'm writing this. He gave me a bottle of Verveine!

1. Almondo: owner of the Café Almondo in Ostend.
2. Floréal: owner of the Café Floréal in Ostend.

422. To Stefan Zweig   *4 August 1937*

Dear friend,

an illustrated Yiddish paper in Riga asks me for 5 short stories of mine, at 1 pound apiece, and says they have discussed it with you. Is that— true? Please let me know. I can't imagine you gave the matter much attention—and why would you. But bear in mind that this Latvian Jew—surely no idealist—quoting your low price, also "depresses" the prices of the others. Imagine such an offer made to Ernst Weiss, or other noble souls who are befriended by you. You are by no means entitled to make yourself so available—*on behalf of other people*. You can give away their works *for nothing*, if you want to be generous. But remember that you know only extremes of liberality and expensiveness. You don't help the Riga Jews by being cheap. And to your friends (forgive me for using this rather loathsome but unambiguous business parlance in haste!) you "spoil the market," some obscure jobsworth who wants to make money out of photographs, and who lives better than you do, gets a staggering advance—from *you*. You don't need that one pound, thanks be to God, not yet. You are *obliged* to be either dear or free.

I can't bring myself to write to Mr. Brun. Unless Landauer's lying, Brun hasn't yet sent the 4,000 francs to Amsterdam, because the franc might fall further. Nor would it be *correct* on my part to chase him on behalf of my publisher. I know Mr. Brun too little, and Mr. Landauer too well. I have an offer from Niehans's *Mass und Wert*.[1] But the rates are absurd: 7 Swiss francs for "cultured prose." 8 days' work for 50 francs = 1 chapter of a novel that won't be bought.—I know you're inclined to see modesty as one of the primary attributes of the writer. But penury surely isn't. Your writing doesn't improve if you allow yourself to be suckered. Poverty is only a virtue if it's a grace. And that doesn't depend on us, alas. It's just as possible to go under through paltriness as through immoderation.

Sincerely, your old   Joseph Roth

1. Niehans's *Mass und Wert: Mass und Wert* was a bimonthly journal for free German culture, edited by Thomas Mann and Konrad Falke, in the Niehans Verlag, in Zurich, a somewhat more settled and conservative affair than Klaus Mann's *Sammlung*.

423. To Stefan Zweig   8 August 1937

Dear friend,

it will be difficult for you, perhaps even, God forbid, impossible, to pull me out of my worst situation thus far—and the one for which I am least to blame myself. It's hard for me to say it, as you know. See from the enclosed letter what's happening to me, only happens to me. I'm getting 125 gulden per month. Everything is adjusted to that, the hotel, all my personal needs. The publisher, the new one,[1] after Querido and de Lange, hasn't sent me this month's money and has gone away on vacation. I have nothing, except a couple of stamps bought in advance, and as if fearing the worst. The hotel, booked for 8 weeks, room payable every other week, is getting nasty. On the 15th I need to renew my Belgian visa in Brussels. I have 40 francs in my pocket. I don't know what to do. Should I not turn to you?[2] Perhaps it would have been right. There is so much unappetizing baggage, in terms of my poverty, my constantly varied little catastrophes which to me are earthquakes, in this rope that so long disdains to kill me once and for all, and just tightens spasmodically around my neck, it's soaked already in the sweat of my fear; nothing but the vacation of just one man who won't know any of this—I am his only German author—a puff of wind, some woman falling ill so that the managing editor can think of nothing else—takes me to the brink of Salvation Army and jail, unfortunately only in installments to the brink of the grave. I've finished my long novel *1002nd Night*, the other one is three-quarters done, I have to hand it in at the beginning of September. In Poland I was writing all winter—the lectures on the side—I was happy and cheerful to be getting 125 gulden till the end of '37. And for the past 4 weeks here I've been calm and industrious. Then yesterday the enclosed letter came. Whom can I send it to? Not to you, I know that. For almost a whole year I didn't bother you with my shitty little affairs. Excuse me! If you can excuse me. I hope at least you'll reply promptly. If you can somehow arrange for me to get the money through Belgium or Paris, then I can send 125 gulden back to your address (if it's still right?) on 1 September. What shall I do? Answer me, I beg you. Just now, two policemen are dragging a man across the street. I am so wound up that I can see myself there in their midst, with no visa, being schlepped to the German frontier, the directest way back to Austria. Almondo has asked me around, but if I take so much as one meal from someone like that I'd feel I was practically a con artist.—I have such huge fear of falling into the depth of those latrines. See how it pulls me in. Please see, it's not my fault. I've wrecked my reputation by industry, too many books in short succession. I've got this publisher to agree to publish my next book not at Christmas, but in 1938. But in order to live till the end of '37 I've

promised to deliver yet another novel by the beginning of September.[3]—
Oh, it's all shameful, pitiful, degrading. I'd seen the end so many times
already, please believe me it's not being delayed through any doing of
mine. I mustn't shoot myself—left to myself I would have done it, to
spare you the undignified spectacle of a lamenting friend. Please believe
me, I haven't done anything irresponsible, I came here for 3 months with
exactly 1,800 Belgian francs, to be in the cheapest country and in the
proximity of this strange publishing house, which doesn't understand the
least thing about packing, or printing or distribution, whose typesetters
don't even know German. I have to correct their exotic misprints myself,
there is no one else to do it. And Mr. Lion[4] turns up and says he would
never have thought someone who had put out so many books could be
any good. And there are many who think like that. You still believe in
my literary virtue. But you can see I can't work in a latrine.

I know that your mind, used to stability and to thinking in terms
of continual improvements, will view this catastrophe of mine—and
rightly—as a consequence of my overall situation, and that you will first
think how to improve the overall situation. Please bear in mind, though,
that this acute difficulty may make a subsequent overall situation impossible. Even a sort of reconciliation with Huebsch, which nothing suggests
he wants or is ready for, wouldn't help. He is certainly not the object
of my bitterness, you don't need to take him under your wing. He has
only followed the rules of *my* fate, he is a cat's-paw in the hand of the
destiny that has prepared all this for me.—But all this is not now. At
this moment I can see the policemen escorting the man back toward
the station. I feel a sudden desire to relieve him, to take his place and
say there has been an error, a mistaken identity—and so bring about
the final catastrophe. I can't go on. I see right away that there's such a
thing as literary honor. The reality is that I'll get another letter from the
hotel tomorrow, that the laundry bill hasn't been paid, and that I won't
be able to write anything any more, not even a letter. Today is Sunday.
On Tuesday you will have this disgusting letter, does that feel like a long
time! It's three years! Can you, will you send me a telegram?—And then

I'm afraid of the post. What if this doesn't find you? I'll send it express, and then a postcard as well. It's cheaper than registered. But believe me that, in this whole calamity, your saying that you forgive me remains the most important element. Please send me a wire. (I am not responsible for the nonsense that may appear here.) All I know is that these are the 8th, 9th, 10th, 11th, and that it's 24 days till I next get money from Holland.

I am so full of loathing for me, it's so awful, soon I won't care any more—and that frightens me.

I embrace you, send me a wire on Tuesday, I will go home late for fear of not finding one,

your J.R.

1. the publisher, the new one: the Catholic press De Gemeenschap, in Bilthoven, Holland.

2. should I not turn to you: Hermann Kesten remarks that, in addition to being one of the best-selling and most-translated authors in the world at that time, Stefan Zweig had substantial private means.

3. another novel by the beginning of September: this is *The Emperor's Tomb*, which ended up overtaking *The Tale of the 1002nd Night* in JR's choked production schedule.

4. Mr. Lion: Ferdinand Lion (1883–1965), essayist, critic, playwright. There is something in what he says. Thomas Mann, for instance, saw Roth primarily as a drunk, which Roth repaid by seeing Thomas Man(n) as primarily neuter (see no. 210).

424. To Blanche Gidon (written in French)   *Ostend*
                                                     Hotel de la Couronne
                                                     13 August 1937

Dear friend,

thank you, thank you for all the good you do me, I don't deserve it.

My life is constant trouble. I would like to see you in Paris again. But it's out of my hands.

The little I write to you—it comes from a good heart, and a silent heart. It's the first time I've experienced a deepening attachment. To this point all I've known of other people were either the stable ones or the others who slowly weaken and lose their way.

Excuse my French! Give the doctor my best wishes. Your devoted old Joseph Roth

I am just completing a book you will like very much. I know it—in the midst of my misfortunes I know it.

425. To Stefan Zweig   *18 August 1937*

Kind thanks from an oppressed heart,[1] my friend! Don't reproach me for railing at myself. It's the only thing I can do, I involve you in my catastrophes, which I probably deserve, though I do nothing to provoke them. Instead of the most exalted, I make merely the most putrid demands of you. I want to be near to you, and probably only succeed in being intrusive. Next follows a break-in to your restricted bank account, and the shameless imposition of further economies, all caused by me. I know you take far greater pleasure in sensual things than I do, a good express train, a decent meal, a spoonful of caviar, and I take the spoon away from you and I know what it feels like, to have one's wine glass taken away. No brother would do that to you. The counterweight is this: you have to imagine suddenly, with the help of one banknote, waking up from a coma, the women are once more walking down the avenues, the trees are green again, laughter and tears are back, the beloved pain returns that had been anesthetized by banal squalid worries. Your life returns to you, the hotel was a prison in which one was not allowed to be locked up, worse thereby than the others. Suddenly it becomes your airy bower again. These are actual sensations, my dear friend, if only I weren't so desperate to have them. It's too much, too often, I rack my brains for ways of breaking free of my publisher, but racking one's brains doesn't produce miracles. It'll be the death of me, this mixture of brain, hand, begging, advance, eager promises of works that my head isn't certain of being able to write—and all in vain, without readers, without the trust that comes from outside, an echo to the one within. I can feel myself having to violently regenerate morally and physically, in two months I have to be well, then abysmal feeling, panic and derangement, anguish, heart pain, darkness. Two or three proper catastrophes, the death of someone near to me, and I've had it.[2] Such loose talk as Lion's is very detrimental to me—in monetary terms too—believe me, it damages me with publishers, with Oprecht,[3] with Huebsch, with Querido, in Vienna, it builds up like an avalanche, and it crushes me. My productivity is taken amiss, my blocked colleagues take it for proof of lack of talent.

We will [see] each other whenever it suits you, God knows how I need to have you there, at hand, and how much I need you to need me. Even though the unhappy propensity to see each meeting as a farewell is becoming a real disease. I am half done in, and at the same time eerily taut. It doesn't go.

Please confirm receipt of this letter, and the date of your departure.

Your warm and trusty   Joseph Roth

1. an oppressed heart: JR's old friend on the *FZ* Friedrich Traugott Gubler used to say, half jokingly, that Roth should always be sad; the sadder he was, the better he wrote.

2. and I've had it: indeed, it was the news that Ernst Toller had hanged himself in New York that brought on JR's fatal collapse in May 1939.

3. Oprecht: Emil Oprecht, publisher and bookseller in Zurich.

426. To Stefan Zweig   *Ostend*
                                        Hotel de la Couronne
                                        26 August 1937

Dear friend,
I am VERY disquieted, because I have no reply.
Cordially,   your old J.R.

427. *To Stefan Zweig*

Ostend
Hotel de la Couronne
29 August [1937]

Dear friend,
where will you be going?
Perhaps we could meet anyway?
Loyally, to you both   Joseph Roth

428. *To Blanche Gidon*

Ostend
Hotel de la Couronne
[postmarked: Ostend, 3 September 1937]

My dear friend,
no good news. Au contraire! I force myself to write, purely so that you
know I am loyal, and that I'm resting. My worries are unending. I'd like
to talk. I can't write any more.
Wretched, and very sad
your old Joseph Roth

429. *To Stefan Zweig*

Ostend
Hotel de la Couronne
4 September 1937

Dear friend,
if you want to see me, it will be possible only in Brussels. I have to go
to Amsterdam on the 18th, *at the latest*. On the *15th* I have to have the
bulk of my novel finished. (My publisher still isn't back yet.) I should
have had it ready on 20 August (at last I got some ink)—I'm unable to
finish it, and then I won't have any money, not even through November,
wretchedly. My Belgian visa (extended) runs out on the 20th inst. I have

to write 10 pages a day, for the next 10 days here. I can *only* get to Brussels, and for one or two days. You can easily get a *transit visa* for 3 days. If you should need to extend it, it's inexpensive. All we need is a *4-hour block of time, intensive, undistracted*, for our most important things. Dear friend, wouldn't it feel absurd to be flying over my head, or rattling past me in a train.—You write, "above all, tell me what your plans are"—and you don't feel how that pains me. What plans could I possibly have? The man won't pay me anything, he's on vacation. What am I supposed to do? My freedom just about stretches as far as Brussels; and then only until my visa gives up the ghost. I'm expecting your answer to the effect that you'll expect me in Brussels BEFORE the 20th. Place? Hotel? Time and place?—If you *can't*, then please drop me a line to say so. I'm on tenterhooks.

Warmly and sincerely,   your J.R.

430. To Stefan Zweig   *Hotel de la Couronne*
                                          Ostend
                                          7 September 1937

Dear friend,

thank you for your card. You should have heard from me by now. I can't get to Paris, but you can very well go to Brussels. I need to go there on the 20th to renew my visa again. Which is absurd, seeing as I have to go to Amsterdam from here. I can only sketch things in, it's a waste of ink to go into detail. I hope very much that we do see each other. At least for a single day. But it mustn't be wasted either. So let me now talk about my essay in the *Christliche Ständestaat* that you were critical of, I don't quite know why. I didn't "adopt" the distinction between Christian and Jewish publishers; it was the Jewish publishers in Austria who were the first to adopt Hitler's distinction between Aryan and non-Aryan *authors*. It was the publishers who undertook that discrimination, not me. It's my duty to call to order those Jews who do Goebbels's bidding for him. Zsolnay, Horovitz, the silly idiot Tal, your jumped-up Reichner, who had the chutzpah to advertise you in Germany: they'll wreck the last few "Aryan" writers and publishers. Because these rightly make appeal to the fact that even the Jews follow the demands of the Reichsschrifttumskammer.[1] Quite the contrary: it's my duty to put a spoke in the wheel of those Jews who are making the calamity worse. And that's what I'll do.

You shouldn't attack me for doing it either. It wasn't Hitler or me who undertook this discrimination, but our old Jehovah. The Jews may not become anti-Semitic or anti-Christian, less than others. A Jewish publisher who won't publish a book because he can't sell it in Goebbels's Reich; who only publishes books that will do well with the anti-Semites: that publisher is the lowest worm, and I will inevitably always try to crush him. And for the rest: *tua et mea res agitur.*[2] We can't permit asskissers, true Jewboys, chutzpah-chappies, and weeping willows of Jewish origins not to publish me, because Goebbels doesn't like me. We have enough "Aryan" anti-Semites. We don't need Jewish ones. As long as it's possible for me to hurt them, I will do so: with delight. In order to hurt them, I wouldn't shrink from allying myself with "Aryan" anti-Semites. A non-Jew who does what Goebbels says is a poor son of a bitch. But a Jew, a publisher in Vienna, who turns me down, is vile scum. Mr. [. . .] a recent immigrant, anti-Semite from a safe distance, a Jewish spearcarrier for the Reichsschrifttumskammer; the widow Tal, who says: we must all start *over again, under pseudonyms*; that Horovitz, who delights in the name of "Phaidon"; the toilet manufacturer Zsolnay, whose Werfels have gone up; your chutzpah Reichner, whom you—bafflingly, for me—treat as if he were the Insel Verlag: those serfs of Pharaoh, those betrayers of Moses, that filthy shit is what you defend, you Jewish poet, against *me*? You, my friend, who have God in your heart. Whom you have long forgotten, and are now learning to love again? I would have thought my article should have given you pleasure.

But no: you're still on the side of "common sense." You've experienced repulsive things with me: but the terror is still ahead (believe me!).

In the *Ständestaat* there is only room for One. I am with Him. God asked for ten just men. I am a man: I am satisfied with *one*. This *Ständestaat* has at least kept going until today. Sufficient of a miracle. But if

Jewish publishers upset the miracle, if Werfel-Mahler[3] embraces the *Reichspost*,[4] I won't hesitate to hurt those desecraters. May lightning strike them, and I will try to get there before the lightning.

I hope that's all that needs to be said on that head, which might disturb our meeting.—

If I had a brother, I wouldn't wait for him any differently than I am waiting for you now. You know that—but that doesn't mean you have to come.

Sincerely your   Joseph Roth

1. Reichsschrifttumskammer: the organization, established by the Nazis in 1933, to which all writers had to belong in order to be able to publish in Germany.

2. *tua et mea res agitur*: ("it concerns us both") adapted from Horace's line "Nam tua res agitur, paries cum proximus ardet," "You yourself are in danger when the wall of your neighbor is on fire."

3. Werfel-Mahler: a scornful dubbing (and unmanning) of Franz Werfel, who was married to Alma Mahler.

4. the *Reichspost*: Viennese newspaper financed by Hitler's ambassador at the time, Franz von Papen.

431. To Stefan Zweig   *[Ostend] 8 September 1937*

Dear friend,

our letters will cross in the mail: I don't want you to be uncertain or—which is worse—ambivalent about me for a single day.

Do you know me so little as that? Don't you know that hatred is foreign to me, yes, since my devoutness, something sinful; and are you really so remote from me that you fail to see that the purest intentions animate my indignation, my rage, don't stoke my hatred?—Something in me rebels at the idea that a man who trades in books is just as capable of villainy as one who sells celluloid. And where does your forgiveness get you? Don't you see that you're doing exactly the same thing as all the politicians who left Hitler and Mussolini and Stalin to wreak their destruction? They say: "Get used to it, it's the way dictators are." And you say: "Get used to it, that's the way publishers are."—I say, one may be called to become a writer, but not a publisher. And someone who only wants to calculate, and to calculate with betrayal, who deals with Hitler, such a person should stick to celluloid. Apart from the fact that some publishers are swindlers—[. . .]—I don't even insist that they keep honest accounts; but that they don't shop *us* to the Reichsschrifttumskammer is the least I can ask for. If I had hatred in me, then I'd be sterile, and I'd know it. What it is is rage. I don't hate any man. I hate evil and its tools and weakness. Who's left to stand up for goodness, if even *you* want to make your peace with the wretchedness that permits a man who deals in our heart's blood to have the morals of a sock seller?—Have you so little respect for your own work, and in front of *them*?—My dear friend, it's too simple, the way you've made your peace with these terrible facts. I can't do it. I really feel no hatred, or, if you prefer, no more than Voltaire—no friend of mine—for the instigators of witchcraft trials. No more and no less. If you like: as much hate and as little as St. Boniface. You surely won't think I'm moved by personal spite? Me, just now undergoing my novitiate?

It would be serious if you couldn't come to Brussels. You are removing yourself from me before my very eyes, you are becoming too worldly, I love you and your cleverness, but I will cease to love you the moment you become a child of the world. For a long time, for some 8 months, I had that suspicion, and kept my distance from you. I'm embarrassed for you that you think you can tell me that publishers do sums—I know that, that's why I denounce them as sons of bitches—and the easy indulgence with which you accept a given set of circumstances strikes me as every bit as sterile as the hatred you warn me against. I have the feeling you don't seem to realize how much of your personal and professional dignity is sacrificed when you begin to show comprehension of the swine. *Tout comprendre c'est tout confondre.*[1]

I don't like it when you become complaisant, you least of all. And please forgive me if I'm being unfair, perhaps.

I'm writing you all this, purely so that we don't waste any of our precious time together, *if* we meet.

Be assured I know neither hatred nor resentment. They are mortal sins.

I hope we *do* meet up.

My situation is *desperate*. But I don't want to burden you with that, in this context.

Your loyal   Joseph Roth

1. *Tout comprendre c'est tout confondre*: (To understand everything is to mix everything up, or get everything wrong), JR's personal variant on the familiar *Tout comprendre, c'est tout pardonner.*

432. To Stefan Zweig   *Hotel de la Couronne*
                                          Ostend
                                          21 September 1937

Dear friend,

I am leaving today. I have hung on in vain, in the hope of seeing you.

Thanks to your secretary's mistake, your last letter (dated the 10th) only reached me on the 18th. But that was about a Zweig-Toscanini[1] meeting, not one between Zweig and Roth. The splendidly furious outburst of the old man against Furtwängler[2] reminded me somehow of you. Toscanini was certainly not "embittered." One has to oppose meanness, dilution, cowardice. In my place, Toscanini would have written exactly the same things against the Austrian publishers as I did. I am sure you didn't remonstrate with *him*.—When will you finally see what posture accords to your dignity and my love for you?

I am always your friend   Joseph Roth

1. Toscanini: Arturo Toscanini was opposed to Fascism and National Socialism.
2. Furtwängler: Wilhelm Furtwängler (1886–1954), who was often compared with Toscanini, was the most successful conductor in the Third Reich. His support for the Nazis and his decision not to leave Fascist Germany made him a deeply contentious figure after the war.

433. To Stefan Zweig [Amsterdam] 23 September 1937

Dear friend,

I've just received the address from your card sent to Querido. I have waited till now (7 in the evening, 23 September, Thursday). If I succeed in getting a contract in Amsterdam, I'll come to Brussels or Paris.— I'm faring very badly, dismally in fact. I don't understand why you preferred seeing Toscanini to me: or were prepared to miss seeing me for his sake. I've written to you in London, to tell you how much I admire and endorse his position.

Sincerely your   J.R.

434. Stefan Zweig to Joseph Roth 25 September 1937

Dear Roth,

why, oh why are you so easily offended—aren't we beaten about enough without baring our teeth at one another, even if . . . I am so consumed by my own fallibility that I have no more strength to defend myself against others. No, my friend, not articles now—for us it would be best to get ourselves wiped out by a gas bomb in Shanghai or Madrid, and maybe rescue someone with more joie de vivre. I was only in Paris for a day and a half, didn't see anyone except Masereel[1] and Ernst Weiss, saw some wonderful paintings, and am now back at work. This year '37 is a bad one for me, everything claws at me, I feel half flayed, my nerves are exposed, but I carry on working, and I would do better if it weren't for family and others' affairs that lame me, and demand twice the energy I have. Don't forget that I'm past 55, and since we seem to be living in wartime, I get tired some of the time—I positively *fled* back to my desk, the only support for the likes of us. You have no idea *how* much I needed to speak with you, I've just gotten another blow in the guts from a so-called friend, and I'm choking back gall with clenched teeth. It would be important to spend good time together, and if the conspiracy between dictators doesn't lead to the planned concentric assault on Russia (first the Bolshevists, then the Democrats, that's the way it was done in '33), if a frail sort of peace still endures, then I want to go to Paris in January for a month; I need my friends as never before and there are a few there, and you would come too, it would be lovely! From time to time I need to breathe in the air of conversation, and strengthen and intensify myself: we forfeit too much of ourselves in the current madhouse. Toscanini was forced to stay in Gastein at the last moment, I'm seeing him here; I am continually shaken at the way he, who celebrates the greatest "successes" on the planet, instead of egoistically enjoying them, suffers from all that happens around him—well, my novel[2] may have something to say about the suffering from pity. No, Roth, *don't* grow hard from the hardness of the times, that would mean assenting to it and strengthening it! Don't get pugnacious, implacable, just because the implacable ones are triumphing through their brutality—rather *refute* them by being different, permit yourself to be mocked for your weakness, instead of going against your nature. Roth, don't become bitter, we need you, for the times, however much blood they drink, remain anemic in terms of their intellectual force. Preserve yourself! And let's stay together, we few!

Your St. Z.

1. Masereel: Frans Masereel (1889–1972), Flemish illustrator and etcher, friend of Zweig's.
2. my novel: *Ungeduld des Herzens* (Beware of Pity).

435. *Stefan Zweig to Joseph Roth*   *[autumn 1937]*

My dear fellow,

got your letter a moment ago. It saddens me. I remember how we once wrote to each other; telling each other of our plans, celebrating our friends, and rejoicing in our mutual understanding. I know nothing now of what you are working on, what keeps you busy; in Italy people were telling me of a new novel of yours, and had read it, and I didn't know about it. Roth, friend, brother—what does all the shit going on have to do with us! I read the paper *once* a week, and that's enough for me of the lies of all countries, the only thing I do is try here and there to help an individual—not materially, but to try and get people out of Germany or Russia or out of some trouble: that seems to be the only way in which I can remain active. I won't deny it when you say I'm hiding. If you are unable to impose your own decisions, you should avoid them.—You forget, *you, my friend*, that I state my problem PUBLICLY in my *Erasmus*, and only stand by one thing, the integrity of individual freedom. I'm not hiding myself, there is *Erasmus*, where I portray the so-called cowardice of a conciliatory nature *without* celebrating it—as fact, and as DESTINY. And then *Castellio*—the image of a man I SHOULD LIKE TO BE.

No, Roth, I was never disloyal to a true friend for a second. If I wanted to see Tosc., then it's because I honor him, and because one should take every opportunity one gets of seeing a 72-year-old, and then *in the end I didn't even see him* (you must have missed that in my letter) because I had to go, Amsterdam wasn't anywhere on my route, and I had no idea if you were there or in Utrecht. Roth, there are so few of us and you know, however much you push me away, that there can be hardly anyone who is as devoted to you as I am, that I feel all your bitterness without opposing it with any bitterness of my own: it doesn't help you, you can do what you like against me, privately, publicly diminish me or antagonize me, you won't manage to free yourself of my unhappy love for you, a love that suffers when you suffer, that is hurt by your hatred. Push me away all you like, it won't help you! Roth, friend, I know how hard things are for you, and that's reason enough for me to love you all the more, and when you're angry and irritable and full of buried resentments against me, then all I feel is that life is torturing you, and that you're lashing out, out of some correct instinct, perhaps against the only person who wouldn't be offended thereby, who in spite of everything and everyone will remain true to you. It won't help you, Roth. You won't turn me against Joseph Roth. It won't help you!

Your St. Z.

436. Stefan Zweig to Joseph Roth   *17 October 1937*

Dear unfriend,

I just wanted to tell you that, finally, thanks to Berthold Fles,[1] whom I saw yesterday, I've managed to get some news of you, and I'm delighted to hear that you are so hard at work: *I know* you will manage to write those two books, and they will be a success. He told me you'd had an invitation to Mexico,[2] and I can't tell you how important it would be in my view for you to get a change of air, of scene, of place, to fill your lungs again, and how wonderfully you would depict such a new world—something like that, as I said to Fles, must be reasonably easy to finance as well. The smell of Europe's putrefaction is in all our nostrils: a little fresh air and you, my dear, my important friend, would feel refreshed in your soul. I am glad that at least you are in Paris—don't forget to take a look at the literary pavilion in the exhibition[3] ("ébauche d'un musée de littérature") the most impressive in the whole exhibition for me. Yesterday I completed the first draft of my novel, 400 pages, of course a completely inadequate rough sketch, the proper work will begin now, and how useful it would be for me to be able to consult you at such a moment! But you won't come to London (even though it would be important) and I will have to sit here till mid-December, when I will go to Vienna for a fortnight, and then maybe Paris for a month. *When* will we see one another? Now you know all my plans. In the next few days, you will get copies of two of my books, the essay collection and the *Magellan*.[4] I've really been hard at work these last few years, and done what I could in terms of quantity and energy; I hope the quality is acceptable! This is just a hello to the Foyot, and don't forget your unhappy lover, and discarded friend

St. Z.

1. Berthold Fles, a Dutch literary agent in New York, represented many of the exiled German writers.
2. Mexico: "pyre of Bierce and springboard of Hart Crane," where Malcolm Lowry (1909–1957) was currently at work on his epochal novel of alcoholic decline, *Under the*

Volcano (1947). It must be considered doubtful whether JR could have thrived there for any length of time.

3. exhibition: the World's Fair Exhibition in Paris in 1937. Here, as so often, one gets the impression that Zweig and Roth simply inhabited different planets, and couldn't open their mouths without wounding each other—Roth with acuteness, his intemperate malice and fury, Zweig with obtuseness, a kind of airy and spoiled imperviousness to everyone and everything. It is really hard to imagine the penurious Roth, whose orbit was down to one or two bars in what he called his *république Tournon* (the area around the café in whose upstairs he had a small bedroom), with swollen feet and in the last stages of alcoholism, doing something as otiose as taking himself to a literary exhibition.

4. the *Magellan*: *Magellan, der Mann und seine Tat* (Vienna, 1938).

437. To Rudolf Olden　　　　　　　　　　　　　　*Paris, October 1937*

Dear friend Olden,

thank you very much for the obituary of Karpeles. It's an obituary for us all: the last ten of the fourth regiment. Hail to you, the ninth, in sincere comradeship.[1]

Your old　　　　　Joseph Roth

1. This note, written on the letterhead of the *Neues Tagebuch* (New Diary), the Paris-based exiles' paper, suggests a group elegy. Benno Karpeles was the initiator and editor of the paper, to which Roth and Olden and others—Tschuppik, Kisch, Polgar, etc.—contributed. Almost twenty years before, they had all worked together on another paper, in Vienna, *Der Neue Tag*. Rudolf Olden died on the crossing to the United States, when the ship he was traveling on, *The City of Benares,* was torpedoed by the Germans on 17 September 1940.

438. To Stefan Zweig   *Hotel Paris-Dinard*
                                                          2 November 1937

To Mr. Stefan Zweig, London W 1, 49 Hallam Street
Dear friend,
this isn't a letter, just a notification of my new address.

The Hotel Foyot is being demolished on the instructions of the city magistrates, and yesterday I left it as the last of its guests. The symbolism is all too apparent.[1]

I am very much afraid that something of yours on its way to me may have gotten mislaid. I will be grateful for a prompt reply.

Your old   Joseph Roth

1. all too apparent: see Roth's piece "Rest While Watching the Demolition," first published in the *Neues Tagebuch* on 25 June 1938, included in *Report from a Parisian Paradise*.

439. To Stefan Zweig   *Hotel Paris-Dinard*
                                                          3 November 1937

To Mr. Stefan Zweig, London W 1, 49 Hallam Street
Dear friend,
in haste: the two manuscripts I sent you today are the only things I have found that might qualify as short stories.

Thank you very much. A proper letter will follow.

Your old   Joseph Roth

440. *To Stefan Zweig*   *Hotel Paris-Dinard*
                                           14 November 1937

To Mr. Stefan Zweig, Hallam Street, London W 1

Dear friend,

please excuse the hurried dictation. I hear from Mr. Fles that fourteen Jews were organized to help me, among them apparently yourself.

I find firstly the fact of it unbearable, and secondly the circumstance that you did not inform me of this yourself.

Sincerely, your old   J.R.

441. *To Stefan Zweig*   *Hotel Paris-Dinard*
                                           23 November 1937

To Mr. Stefan Zweig, 49 Hallam Street, London W 1

Dear friend,

I'm sorry, typewriter again. I was bedridden until yesterday, with a sleeping-pill poisoning. I am still barely able to eat anything. Work is out of the question.

Drop me a line if you would, to your old   [Joseph Roth]

442. *Stefan Zweig to Joseph Roth*   *[December 1937?]*

Dear friend,

I am shocked and alarmed at your letter—I had so hoped Paris would focus and stimulate you, instead of offering you endless irritations. I often think of you, always with love, and usually with concern. What will become of us? The plan that so upset you seems to have fizzled out, and I was sadly not at all sure I could participate fully in it—if Austria folds, then we are *all* done for. No more books of ours will appear in German and what I own there in stupid decency and honest patriotism will be *futsch*, and I have a dozen people's welfare depending on me. I too took sleeping pills tonight—the notion that the "democracies" would give us up just like that I simply can't get over, and Russia alone is unfortunately not strong enough to oppose that rapaciousness. I will probably go to Vienna this week[1]—I want to see it once more (and my old mother). Then back here, and in January a little place in the south. I don't want to see anyone, I don't want to read any newspapers, I'll probably go to Portugal, where my knowledge of the language is poorest. Dear friend, everything is at stake now, we are almost at the end! Gather up all your strength, don't waste yourself—the ultimate stands before us.

your St Z.

1. Vienna this week: The *Anschluss*, the annexation of Austria to the German Reich, occurred in February 1938.

443. *Stefan Zweig to Joseph Roth*   *[London, January 1938]*

Dear friend,

I feel a little calmer, because your latest letter (which I wish had been longer) once again was written in your clear firm hand; if everything goes well, we'll be seeing each other in just a fortnight, and then *I hope* (!!) all will be well with you. I have had problems with Reichner;[1] not only that he is ungrateful toward me and sometimes impossible, he does things that revolt me. It's a shame that being persecuted has brought out the worst in the Jews. I really don't know how I should assert myself in this relationship, not least as he has almost my entire opus in his hands— his continual truckling to Nazi Germany (which I don't profit from, I have my own number on the German index) turns me into someone who in his particular case is compelled to agree with Streicher. Ach, my friend, when I think of all the disappointments I have endured in these years, and you refuse to understand how painful your remoteness and silence are to me; that two friends each scrape open their own hearts without being brought closer doesn't make sense to me. Well, in a few weeks—I'll be going to Portugal, where there are no newspapers and no mail (everything a week old and more digestible in its staleness).

Sincerely   your loyal St. Z.

1. Reichner: but JR, by his own inspired methods, had reached the same conclusions 4 years earlier. See no. 321.

444. To Stefan Zweig   *Hotel Paris-Dinard*
                                 Monday [postmarked: 10 January 1938]

Dear friend,

it's good that you're going somewhere where you won't get letters. That way, you'll be spared possible news of me. Go with God! It's in His hands whether we see each other again or not.

Sincerely, always

Your old   Joseph Roth

445. Stefan Zweig to Joseph Roth   *49 Hallam Street*
                                 London W 1
                                 [January 1938?]

straight after getting your letter.

Dear friend,

I am terribly alarmed by your letter: the handwriting looked really sick to me, and I've sensed for a long time that you are desperate (perhaps still more than I, who is being driven *demented* by this time, in which EVERYTHING our arch-enemies attempt seems to come off). Can I do anything for you? It's so hard, because I know nothing of what you're going through. Couldn't kind Irmgard Keun[1] write to me about you— you have no idea (quite irrespective of *your* feelings for me) of how I cling to you, and am really permanently concerned about you. Perhaps I will come to Paris now, I had intended to go first to Lisbon, Estoril, and then work on the quiet Riviera there. The novel is basically done in outline, a first draft is also complete, but now it's at the second stage. But *I* am still unhappy about much of it, the dialog, the style. Tired as I am, it will take me longer than I thought, and I admire your penetration—though admittedly you're 15 years younger than me, and *what* years! My dear fellow, I'm blathering, but that should show you my deep need to sit with you again, to talk things over, and above all to hear about *you* and *your* work. I know *nothing* of you, and I don't want to lose you, it offends me when a new book comes out, that you, my friend, have struggled over for a year, and I don't know about it, I am the last to get to hear of it, when once I was proud to be the first and nearest and most involved.

Please look after yourself. Is Paris good for you? Mightn't the Midi be better? Ach, I'm asking you questions, and I know you won't answer me any more. But I go on asking, or rather my heart asks after you.

Warmest best wishes your old   St. Z.

As soon as I know when I'll be going, I'll write to you.

1. kind Irmgard Keun: German novelist who lived with Joseph Roth in Ostend and Paris from 1936 to 1938, and accompanied him on a PEN-funded lecture tour of Poland. Keun returned to Germany in 1940, where, aided by false reports of her death, she managed to stay concealed with her family.

446. To Pierre Bertaux   *Paris-Est*
                                            Buffet-Bar
                                            [24 February 1938]

Dear friend,
1. before my departure:
In Austria probably *a state of siege*,
to keep internal affairs in Skubl's[1] hands. 2. Jesuitical-typical: half the

Austrians Nazis who were set free, now locked up again. 3. For France MY advice:

a. WITH Russia;

b. WITH Czechoslovakia OPEN DECLARATION of a MILITARY ALLIANCE;

c. Intercede for Austria, openly

d. Pyrenees.[2]

Sincerely, my train's leaving

Your old   Joseph Roth

And please: Let *Ce Soir*[3] know that I'll be in touch from Vienna!

1. Skubl: Michael Skubl (1877–1964), from 1934 to 1938, Austrian chief of police. With the Anschluss looming, he resigned his post.
2. Pyrenees: remote southwest France, where Bertaux had a house
3. *Ce Soir*: pro-Communist evening paper in Paris.

447. To Blanche Gidon   *18 rue de Tournon*
                                           Paris
                                           [postmarked: 12 May 1938]

Dear friend,

please, if at all possible, try and do something for Dr. Broczyner. He is the model for my Dr. Demant[1] in the *Radetzky March*.

Also, I have a wonderful Austrian seamstress:

Elisabeth Streit,

23 rue de Liège

Very deserving and unhappy.

Also I have many suggestions to make to you. I myself am wretched.

Could you call me between 12 and 1? Danton 16-16.

Always your loyal   Joseph Roth

and Dr. Gidon's humble servant as well.

1. the model for my Dr. Demant: not so, apparently. Eduard Broczyner was a fellow pupil of JR's in Brody, and also knew him later in Vienna and during the emigration in Paris.

448. To Blanche Gidon   *rue de Tournon 18*
                                    [postmarked: Paris, 28 May 1938]

Dear friend,

Morgenstern[1] told me of your kindness. Of course I ask you, must unfortunately ask you again, to help me.

Can you call me today between 3 and 5? At 8 o'clock tonight the best German actor Ludwig Hardt will be reading from the best German writers at Rue de Rennes 44.

Can you make it? Please do call me!

Sincerely,   your old Joseph Roth

1. Morgenstern: Roth's friend and neighbor at the Hotel de la Poste, Soma Morgenstern.

449. Stefan Zweig to Joseph Roth   *[summer 1938?]*

Dear friend,

your silence is obdurate, but I think often and always kindly of you. My life of late is too crowded, I successfully went over the first draft of the novel (which with me is almost tantamount to rewriting the whole thing), then collected material for a novella (or a sort of symbolical novella)[1] that I am now already working on, though subject to many disturbances. I have to be alone for that sort of work (the creative, conceptual part), and for the past 10 days wanted to hole up in Boulogne, but the weather hasn't let up at all. In Germany, *Castellio* has cast a shadow, also the delivery of supplies to Hungary, Poland, etc.—Austria has no contract with those states—that hitherto went out to that noble land is now impossible, and there's no shortage of other minor irritants—I'm surprised still to be able to work at all. Here I'm living as in a cave, know about a tenth of the people I knew two years ago, and lots of leaves are blowing down from the old bands of affection. Well, the German ax has taken hefty swings at the tree!

And you! I am always filled with impatience when I think of you. Your first novel[2] must be finished by now, and I'm wondering how the work on the second is going. Where will you be? Where can I find you. I'm wary of Amsterdam, because I'd have to call on some 15 people there, and anyway only German Lufthansa flies there. How long are you staying there? Have you made any resolutions? Roth, I hope you keep it together, we *need* you. There are so few human beings, and so few real books in this overcrowded world!

Sincerely your Stefan Zweig

1. symbolical novella: this sounds like Zweig's *Chess Novella,* written between 1938 and 1941, published posthumously in 1942.

2. your first novel: *The Tale of the 1002nd Night,* with *The Emperor's Tomb* as the second.

450. *To Stefan Zweig*   *18 rue de Tournon*[1]
                                                Paris 6^e
                                                Paris, 19 September 1938

Dear friend,

this just provisionally, to let you know that I'm always thinking of you, and especially in these days. Please forgive the typewriter.

I am overloaded with Austrian matters, refugee committees, and the like.

Please don't be offended by the dictation, but won't you come here for a day. It's high time—and perhaps the last time—that we could see each other.

I heard your mother died. I would like to convey to you my really sincere commiseration.

I see your wife from time to time. Please, won't you come here for a day. It's easier for you than for me.

Sincerely,   your old Joseph Roth

1. 18 rue de Tournon: this is Roth's "last address," the Hotel de la Poste, around the corner from the now demolished Foyot. It was from there that he was taken on 23 May 1939 to the Hôpital Necker, where he died four days later. He told Soma Morgenstern, "I have finished my last book. I don't want a doctor, just a priest." It was not the easy death evoked in *The Legend of the Holy Drinker*. Friends reported seeing Roth strapped to his bed with delirium tremens, but he was denied alcohol by the hospital staff. That was a contributory cause of his death, whose official cause was given as pneumonia. He was buried on 30 May 1939 in the Cimetière Thiais, in the remote south of Paris.

451. To Leo Cenower   *18 rue de Tournon*
                                         Paris 6ᵉ
                                         Paris, 27 September 1938

To Mr. Leo Cenower, c/o Mandle, Zürich, Konradstrasse 51
Dear friend Cenower,[1]

ten days ago I might have been able to do something for your wife, but you didn't write me in time. Now there's mobilization, and there's nothing I can do. I myself am at risk. I might have to leave Paris any day now.

Try—this is my advice to you—to leave Switzerland yourself. It will be impossible for you there. Somewhere in the French provinces would be better. Do as follows. Perhaps you could cross over into France with the electrical tram, make inquiries about it . . . Unfortunately, that's all I can suggest.

Write to me straightaway, and if you come to Paris, let me know a day in advance.

Sincerely   Your [Joseph Roth]

1. Cenower was a war comrade of JR's.

452. *To Blanche Gidon*   *[Paris] 5 October 1938*
                                            Madame Blanche Gidon

Dear friend,

poor thanks to you for showing so much heart: I have another young
Austrian to commend to you, a Mr. Walter Ringhofer. He is one of the
best tailors. I have been trying vainly to help him for the past fortnight.
You will see for yourself how nice he is. Please, if you can, try and find
him a place somewhere. At the very least, I would beg you to listen to
him. He is unfortunately one of very many to have come to me from the
committees.

Please forgive me for taking advantage of your goodness, and till soon,
I hope,

Sincerely,   your old Joseph Roth

453. *To Stefan Zweig*   *[Paris] 10 October 1938*

Dear friend,

of course I'll talk to your wife. I have never—long before the
catastrophe—had any understanding of furniture and the like. I shit on
furniture. I hate houses. I will tell your wife.

I don't see, dear friend, why you describe our situation as "hopeless."
If it is, then only because you make it so: we have the duty, the absolute
duty, to show *not the least* pessimism.

The Mexican president of police wrote to me *spontaneously*. I can
befriend him right away. He is an old Austrian officer.

Our situation is by no means as hopeless as you would have it. You are
a defeatist.

In spite of which, I remain sincerely   your Joseph Roth

454. To Heinrich, Count Degenfeld   *18 rue de Tournon*
Paris 6ᵉ
Paris, 6 November 38[1]

His Grace,

Heinrich, Count Degenfeld[2]

Chateau Steenockerzeel near Brussels

Your Grace,

my friend Mr. Klaus Dohrn tells me that His Majesty, our Emperor, expresses the wish that I may recover my health, and accept medical advice.

I beg you, Your Grace, to give His Majesty my sincerest thanks, and assure him that I will of course obey any order[3] he cares to give me.

In particular I am delighted that His Majesty calls upon me to visit you in the course of the next week. I am moved in the extreme by the kindness of His Majesty in drawing your attention to me.

With thanks for your trouble, and your humble servant,

Your [Joseph Roth]

1. Paris, 6 November 38: one day later, Herschel Grynszpan, a young Polish Jew, shot a secretary of the German embassy in Paris. That provided the Nazis with the pretext for instigating pogroms against Jews in what became known as *Kristallnacht* (9–10 November).

2. Count Degenfeld: Count Degenfeld-Schonburg (born 1890) was first Otto von Habsburg's tutor (in 1922), then became his adjutant and private secretary.

3. any order: the "order" that Otto von Habsburg communicated to his loyal subject Joseph Roth, and which he was in no position to carry out, was that he should take better care of his health.

455. *To Blanche Gidon*   *Paris*
rue de Tournon 18
[postmarked: 15 November 1938]
Tuesday

Dear friend,

my eyes are in grave danger. May I count on you to find a moment to advise me in the course of the afternoon. I am very fearful. Please.

Your old   Joseph Roth

456. *Stefan Zweig to Joseph Roth*   *49 Hallam Street*
London W 1
[end of 1938]

Dear Josef Roth,

I have now written to you three or four times, always without reply, and think our old friendship gives me the right to ask you what you mean by this obstinate and hopefully not ill-intentioned silence. It is probable that I will pass through Paris on my way out or back, in January or March, and I would simply like to know which you prefer: that I try to visit you, or that I avoid you (as you so sedulously avoid me). I write without the least trace of chilliness, but purely and simply for information; your silence is too striking, too protracted and oppressive for me to be able to explain it away, say, by business on your part.

All best wishes and that the year ahead (in spite of everything) may be no worse than the one just gone.   Your Stefan Zweig

457. The American PEN Club to Joseph Roth[1]   *The P.E.N. Club*
(written in English)   *American Center*
    January 21, 1939

Mr. Joseph Roth, c/o Querido Verlag, Keizersgracht 333, Amsterdam, Holland

Dear Mr. Roth:

On behalf of the American P.E.N. Club, I have the honour to invite you to be a special guest at the World Congress of Writers to be held on invitation of the New York World's Fair on May 8, 9 and 10, 1939.

When the four basic freedoms—the right to speak, to publish, to worship, and to assemble—are being denied and threatened over an increasingly large part of the world, it seems to us particularly urgent that writers from all countries should gather to consider ways and means of defending free expression under difficult circumstances. We believe that this is the psychological time and the New York World's Fair—which is celebrating 150 years of democracy in America and emphasizing these four freedoms—is the logical place for such a meeting.

The P.E.N. Centers each have been invited to appoint a representative and we have compiled, in addition, a list of distinguished men and women of letters, such as yourself, to be invited as guests of honor.

We very much hope you will attend. Living expenses will be paid and entertainment provided for the three days of the Congress at the Fair and for three or four days more when we expect to entertain P.E.N. representatives and our guests of honor in New-York City and in country residences belonging to members of the American P.E.N. Club, their friends, and important patrons of literature.

We will also arrange a series of optional excursions of various lengths at reduced costs—including a trip to Washington where we expect the President of the United States to receive us—and hope to arrange for reduced steamship rates from Europe to New York. Details of all these arrangements will be sent later.

This Congress will provide an opportunity for the writers of the world to publicly and freely state their belief in the personal freedoms without which the creation of literature is impossible in a setting commanding international attention.

We would like you to be present and hope your plans will allow a visit at this time. May we have your early acceptance?

Sincerely,

Dorothy Thompson

President

1. This invitation, from Dorothy Thompson, who had translated *Job* and was an admirer of Roth's work, was found among Roth's papers at his death. It was marked in Roth's hand with the words "best thanks for the copy, dearest Friederike [Friderike Zweig?]. Your J.R." The sixth act of Roth's life begins here.

Bibliography

Bronsen, David. *Joseph Roth: Eine Biographie.* Cologne, 1974.

Cziffra, Geza von. *Der heilige Trinker: Erinnerungen an Joseph Roth.* Frankfurt and Berlin, 1989.

Kesten, Hermann. *Meine Freunde, die Poeten.* Frankfurt, Berlin, and Vienna, 1980.

Lunzer, Heinz, and Victoria Lunzer-Talos. *Joseph Roth: Leben und Werk in Bildern.* Cologne, 1994.

Morgenstern, Soma. *Joseph Roths Flucht und Ende: Erinnerungen.* Lüneburg, 1994.

Nürnberger, Helmut. *Joseph Roth.* Reinbek, 1981.

Roth, Joseph. *Aber das Leben marschiert weiter und nimmt uns mit: Der Briefwechsel zwischen Joseph Roth und dem Verlag De Gemeenschap, 1936–1939.* Edited by Theo Bijvoet and Madeleine Rietra. Cologne, 1991.

———. *Briefe, 1911–1939.* Edited by Hermann Kesten. Cologne, 1970.

———. *Gesammelte Werke in sechs Bänden.* Edited by Klaus Westermann and Fritz Hackert. Cologne, 1989–91.

———. *Geschäft ist Geschäft: Der Briefwechsel zwischen Joseph Roth und den Exilverlagen Allert de Lange und Querido, 1933–1939.* Edited by Madeleine Rietra with Rainer-Joachim Siegel. Cologne, 2005.

Sternburg, Wilhelm von. *Joseph Roth: Eine Biographie.* Cologne, 2009.

Index

Page numbers in *italics* refer to illustrations.

ABOUT THE JOSEPH ROTH ARCHIVES
AT THE LEO BAECK INSTITUTE

Since its founding in 1955, the Leo Baeck Institute (www.lbi.org) in New York has become the premier research library and archive devoted exclusively to documenting the history of German-speaking Jewry. Its role in preserving the literary legacy of Joseph Roth is particularly noteworthy and not surprising, since one of the first directors of LBI was Fred Grubel, a cousin of Joseph Roth. It was through this connection that LBI archives became the repository for a large number of his manuscripts and notes, including fragments of his novels from the 1920s and 1930s:

The manuscripts *Der blinde Spiegel* (The Blind Mirror), *Büste des Kaisers* (The Bust of the Emperor), the historical essay *Clemenceau* (Clemenceau), *Die Hundert Tage* (The Ballad of the Hundred Days), and an unfinished novel called *Trotzki Roman*, published after the Second World War as *Der stumme Prophet* (The Silent Prophet), are complete or close to completeness. The manuscript *Die Hundert Tage* (The Ballad of the Hundred Days) contains 220 pages in Joseph Roth's own handwriting and 898 pages of the typewritten manuscript with his own corrections. The manuscript under the title *Trotzki Roman*, alternatively known also as *Roman eines jungen Revolutionärs*, can also be found here.

In addition, there are substantial portions of other works, such as *Clemenceau, Legende von Trinker Andreas / Legende vom heiligen Trinker*, and *Kapuzinergruft*. These texts are partly in Joseph Roth's handwriting, partly carbon copies of his own handwriting, and partly typewritten with his own corrections.

Aside from the manuscripts of novels and longer works, there are articles, essays, and shorter pieces written between 1915 and the end of his life in 1939, newspaper articles published between 1926 and 1939, and a number of critical reviews of his works. The LBI Roth collections also contain correspondence and documents concerning his estate and rights to his works (compiled by his cousin Fred Grubel) as well as materials regarding scholarly works about Joseph Roth, academic conferences, and exhibits.

The photographs for *Joseph Roth* have all been provided from the Leo Baeck Institute archives.

Michael Hofmann, the son of the German novelist Gert Hofmann, was born in 1957 in Freiburg. At the age of four he moved to England, where he has lived off and on ever since. After studying English at Cambridge and comparative literature on his own, he moved to London in 1983. He has published poems and reviews widely in England and in the United States, where he now teaches at the University of Florida in Gainesville.

In addition to six books of poems (a *Selected Poems* appeared with Farrar, Straus and Giroux in 2009), he has edited the anthology *Twentieth-Century German Poetry*, translated a selection of the leading contemporary German poet Durs Grünbein called *Ashes for Breakfast*, and prepared a volume of Gottfried Benn's poems called *Impromptus* (all FSG and Faber & Faber); and brought out a selected poems of Günter Eich, called *Angina Days* (Princeton University Press). A selection of Hofmann's critical pieces was published by Faber as *Behind the Lines*. Another, with the provisional title *Critical Book*, is on the way, as is a new book of poems entitled *One Lark, One Horse*.

Michael Hofmann has translated over fifty works of German prose (from authors including Thomas Bernhard, Bertolt Brecht, Elias Canetti, Hans Fallada, Gert Hofmann, Franz Kafka, Irmgard Keun, Ernst Jünger, Herta Müller, Wolfgang Koeppen, and Wim Wenders). The present volume is his tenth translation from Joseph Roth, whom he first translated in 1988; he won the PEN/Book-of-the-Month Club Prize for *The Tale of the 1002nd Night* in 1998 and the Helen and Kurt Wolff Translator's Prize for *Rebellion* in 2000. For other translations he was awarded the International IMPAC Dublin Literary Award and the Oxford-Weidenfeld Translation Prize (twice). He is a Foreign Member of the American Academy of Arts and Sciences, and of the Deutsche Akademie für Sprache und Dichtung.

ABOUT THE AUTHOR

Joseph Roth was born Moses Joseph Roth to Jewish parents on 2 September 1894, in Brody in Galicia, in the extreme east of the then Habsburg Empire; he died on 27 May 1939, in Paris. He never saw his father—who disappeared before he was born and later died insane—but grew up with his mother and her relatives. After completing school in Brody, he matriculated at the University of Lemberg (variously Lvov or Lviv), before transferring to the University of Vienna in 1914. He served for a year or two with the Austro-Hungarian Army on the eastern front—though possibly only as an army journalist or censor. Later he was to write, "My strongest experience was the War and the destruction of my fatherland, the only one I ever had, the Dual Monarchy of Austria-Hungary."

In 1918 he returned to Vienna, where he began writing for left-wing papers, occasionally as "Red Roth," "*der rote Roth.*" In 1920 he moved to Berlin, and in 1923 he began his distinguished association with the *Frankfurter Zeitung*. In the following years he traveled throughout Europe, filing copy for the *Frankfurter* from the south of France, the USSR, Albania, Germany, Poland, and Italy. He was one of the most distinguished and best-paid journalists of the period—being paid at the dream rate of one deutsche mark per line. Some of his pieces were collected under the title of one of them, *The Panopticum on Sunday (1928)*, while some of his reportage from the Soviet Union went into *The Wandering Jews*. His gifts of style and perception could, on occasion, overwhelm his subjects, but he was a journalist of singular compassion. He observed and warned of the rising Nazi scene in Germany (Hitler actually appears by name in Roth's first novel, in 1923), and his 1926 visit to the USSR disabused him of most—but not quite all—of his sympathy for Communism.

When the Nazis took power in Germany in 1933, Roth immediately severed all his ties with the country. He lived in Paris—where he had been based for some years—but also in Amsterdam, Ostend, and the south of France, and wrote for émigré publications. His royalist politics were mainly a mask for his pessimism; his last article was called "Goethe's Oak at Buchenwald."

His final years were difficult; he moved from hotel to hotel, drinking heavily, worried about money and the future. What precipitated his final collapse was hearing the news that the playwright Ernst Toller had hanged himself in New York. An invitation from the American PEN Club (the organization that had brought Thomas Mann and many others to the States) was found among Roth's papers. It is tantalizing but ultimately impossible to imagine him taking a ship to the New World, and continuing to live and to write: His world was the old one, and he'd used it all up.

Roth's fiction came into being alongside his journalism, and in the same way: at café tables, at odd hours and all hours, peripatetically, chaotically, charmedly. His first novel, *The Spider's Web*, was published in installments in 1923. There followed *Hotel Savoy* and *Rebellion* (both 1924), hard-hitting books about contemporary society and politics; then *Flight Without End*, *Zipper and His Father*, and *Right and Left* (all *Heimkebrerromane*—novels about soldiers returning home after war). *Job* (1930) was his first book to draw considerably on his Jewish past in the East. *The Radetzky March* (1932) has the biggest scope of all his books and is commonly reckoned his masterpiece. There follows the books he wrote in exile, books with a stronger fabulist streak in them, full of melancholy beauty: *Tarabas*, *The Hundred Days*, *Confession of a Murderer*, *Weights and Measures*, *The Emperor's Tomb*, and *The Tale of the 1002nd Night*.